Government and the Economy

A Global Perspective

Jan-Erik Lane and Svante Ersson

continuum
LONDON • NEW YORK

Continuum
The Tower Building, 11 York Road, London SE1 7NX
370 Lexington Avenue, New York, NY 10017–6503

First published 2002

British Library Cataloguing-in-Publication Data
A catalogue record for this book is available from the British Library.

ISBN 0–8264–5491–7 (hardback)
    0–8264–5492–5 (paperback)

Library of Congress Cataloging-in-Publication Data
Lane, Jan-Erik.
   Government and the econmy: a global perspective/Jan-Erik Lane and Svante Ersson.
      p.cm
   Includes bibliographical references and index
   ISBN 0–8264–5491–7—ISBN 0–8264–5492–5
      1. Economic policy—Case studies. 2. Economic development—Case studies. 3. Mixed economy—Case studies. 4. Globalization—Case studies. I. Ersson, Svante O. II. Title.

   HD87 L374 2001
   338.9—dc21
                                                              2001037099

Typeset by YHT Ltd, London
Printed and bound in Great Britain by MPG Books Ltd, Bodmin, Cornwall

Contents

Figures

Tables

Preface

The stimulus to write this book was a concrete one. One of us was asked to go and teach a course at the University of Hong Kong. Visiting such a global place forces one to reflect upon the distinction between the state and the market, while acknowledging fully the consequences of globalization. The more we worked upon this question the more we became aware that new theoretical developments were necessary in order to grasp fully the implication of globalization for the distinction between state and market.

This book is a complete rewrite of our (1997) *Comparative Political Economy* (*CPE*) with the same publisher (then named Cassell Academic). Since it had already gone to a much revised second edition, we suggested to the publisher that the third edition of it would entail so many changes that it would be appropriate to use a new title. And so it was agreed. This book, although building upon *CPE*, has an entirely different core focus: globalization and its consequences for the state–market separation in a world with a global market economy and a set of 193 states searching for international co-ordination and co-operation.

We are certainly not going to argue that governments need to increase their operations or that markets always tend towards imperfections. But we wish to argue the case for the state by establishing reservations in relation to the jubilant market philosophy that comes out of the dominant economic school today, viz. the *Chicago School Economics*. Given the dominance of the teachings of scholars connected with this market philosophy, it seems that a positive statement for government can only be derived from a critique of the Chicago School positions. However, one also needs to emphasize not only that the state does have tasks that markets cannot handle but also that governments realistically can handle these tasks, which is what the *Public Choice School* questions.

Interestingly, the *grand maître* of the Chicago School – Milton Friedman – recently stated in an interview with *International Herald Tribune* that the world is witnessing a strong creep towards socialism (17 November 2000). By this he meant that government is still too big despite a decade of intense privatization and marketization. We believe to the contrary that the global market economy needs governmental intervention. And we wish to state why.

The presentation below employs some game theory. Thus, human interaction is described as a collection of various kinds of games between players, one of which is the government. Players can be individuals or organizations, private or public. The institutions of the economy are called the rules of the game. It is hoped that this elementary usage of modern game theory will not distract the reader.

Part I is devoted to giving the reader an overview of economic, social and political development around the world. Any theory about state and market must be based upon the macro differences between the countries of the world in terms of affluence, quality of life and democracy. At the end of this section, which is highly empirical, we examine the idea of a close association between affluence and democracy. In Part II, which is theoretical, we argue that the state comes before the market. Although market institutions have evolved over a considerable length of time expressing collective longtime experiences (spontaneous orders), it is still the case that it is the state that makes markets possible, at any time. The basic problem in a market economy is reneging, or the tendency towards defection from agreements. Markets cannot handle this problem on their own.

Part II evaluates empirically the outcomes of alternative politico-economic regimes. State and market can be mixed in various ways, institutionally speaking. Five major types of politico-economic regimes have been much discussed in the literature since Adam Smith. We present a global performance evaluation of these five political economies. Finally, in Part III we look at what governance is necessary in relation to the global market economy as well as discuss what structure of government exists or should exist to meet these governance needs, which basically spring from the same problem, namely reneging.

All this adds up to a total revision of *CPE*. Several new chapters have been added and all earlier chapters have been extensively revised, if not rewritten, with a complete update of all tables, including the addition of many new ones. Sylvia Dumons in the secretariat of the Political Science Department of the University of Geneva helped much along the way.

Jan-Erik Lane
Svante Ersson

Introduction: State and Markets

Consider the following puzzle. The market philosophy as expounded by numerous persons and organizations argues that the role of government must be diminished in relation to the economy. Markets being superior to states, governments must refrain from intervening in various ways in market operations. Yet, governments are still present in the economy, although the size of the public sector may have been diminished somewhat during the 1990s due to expenditure cuts or privatization. Why?

Whenever you scratch a little bit beneath the surface of markets, you discover the presence of governments. As soon as markets become volatile, the cry is for state intervention. It is argued Hong Kong is the market economy with the highest degree of economic freedom, where government is virtually absent. The factual situation is different. Using 23 per cent of its GDP, Hong Kong offers many public services – education, health care, housing – drawing upon the enormous state ownership of all land as a means of payment. Its public sector size is small, but it is not 15 per cent of GDP as Friedman has hinted at.

The economy is not only the market, as the state is active in many ways in economic affairs, directly or indirectly. How can we explain the many roles that governments play in the economy? The best approach is to examine the models, which claim that markets diminish the tasks of governments, which is the gist of the Chicago School of Economics message. It contains the most relevant and up-to-date exposition of the argument for markets. Perhaps the state is so much present in the economy, because the Chicago Message exaggerates the potential of markets and underestimates the importance of authority?

Now, this is the problem following from the puzzle above: When the economies of the world become linked into a global market place, then national governments will be challenged and the role of international organizations will increase. But is there not a need for a world government to match the global market? The answer to this problem depends on first how one theorizes the global market economy as well as the international regimes already in place. Second, it reflects whether one believes in state interference with markets or in public regulation.

We wish to argue for an optimistic view on globalization. It promises both wealth and peace. But it also holds dangers. Some kind of world government will be required but can it consist of a mere pattern of international organization? The process of regionalization promotes the process of globalization and helps governmental co-ordination at the world level.

Human interaction cannot take place without co-ordination. There are basically only two mechanisms of co-ordination available: markets and states. This is the classical way of framing the problem of making a demarcation between voluntary exchange and authority as the two fundamental tools for co-ordinating human beings. It is as relevant today as it was when Adam Smith first framed this manner of posing the key question of political economy in his *Wealth of Nations* in 1776.

It has been suggested that there are other mechanisms of co-ordination available for handling the problems in human interaction in the period of globalization. Thus, it has been suggested that people can take on major collective action endeavours without state authority. Or it has been suggested that once private property rights have become clarified or have been introduced, then individuals will find solutions merely through bargaining. These two arguments are not credible, given free riding and reneging as well as transaction costs. They state marginal possibilities, because only markets and states can operate on a large-scale basis, which is the typical predicament of the world at year 2000.

The market–state separation often phrased as the public–private sector divide, or the government–*laissez-faire* distinction comes up in any social question or public policy problem, whether a domestic or an international issue. What can be left to markets? What should governments take on? Answering such questions requires a theory about the market and a theory about the state. The prevailing theories of markets and states imply a strong preference for the former over the latter. Why is this so? Markets are analysed as accomplishing efficient solutions to human interaction whereas governments are modelled as enhancing state failure. This is the message from *Public Choice* or the so-called *Public Choice School*. Let us scrutinize the arguments one by one.

Markets operate on the basis of voluntary exchange whereas government employs the authority of the state. Thus, one asks: exchange or authority? The state is necessary to make voluntary exchange workable. Thus, the state is the ultimate guarantor of the market. The market starts from the Guardian State – no one denies this basic condition for the existence of markets. The Guardian State calls upon governments to take on various custodian roles, but is that all that the government can or should do? Well, this depends upon the advantages or disadvantages of contracting. The new classical pro-market argument claims that the limit of the market depends only upon property rights and transaction costs. The so-called Coase's theorem claims that voluntary exchange will always bring about efficient outcomes when transaction costs are zero, but that when transaction costs are high, then authority should replace exchange. It is not difficult to argue for a sizeable role of the state in the economy if one employs the transaction costs framework.

Transaction costs cover all the expenditures, real or non-measurable, that people make in order to arrive at implementable agreements. Governments may do many things to reduce transaction costs, thus making voluntary exchange possible – *the regulative state*. However, governments may also replace markets when transaction costs run high – *the allocative state*. The role of the state in the economy is intimately connected with collective action. When groups engage in common activities, then transaction costs tend to increase rapidly as a function of the size of the group. Thus, government will be responsible for many kinds of collective action.

Outside the transaction cost argument is the large role that governments play in correcting market outcomes for justice: *the redistributive state*. It is contested how much governments can accomplish by means of redistributive policies, but the position that distributive matters can be left entirely to the market or voluntary exchange (alms giving) have few adherents.

Adding together these three functions of a modern state, governments have to do much in the economy. *Chicago School Economics* underestimates what it takes for the state to accomplish guardianship, public allocation and redistribution. *Public Choice* overestimates the probability of state failure, pointing at the inefficient operations of governments and bureaucracies. Finally, the importance of the state to the economy presents an enormous challenge for the twenty-first century, as globalization promotes a global economy but there is no corresponding world state or global government.

We are not going to argue for the creation of strong state co-ordination at the international level. Nor will we argue for more state interference in the economy. What is needed now is to grasp the full significance of the state for the economy. The dominant frameworks in political economy today fail to recognize how central the state is in the economy and how governments contribute to economic performance. We certainly do not believe that the state should retreat even more – that would be a major mistake for reasons that will be spelled out below.

The distinction between the public sector and the private sector can be done in various ways. First there is the historical criterion, meaning that different countries have had different traditions for placing certain goods and services with the state and other goods and services with the market. Second, we have the ideological criterion, which may favour either government or the market, depending upon one's values, especially with regard to equality in relation to freedom. Finally, there is the economist search for systematic criteria, which would decide unambiguously which goods and services should be allocated by the state and which belong to the market. These systematic criteria focus basically upon the possibility of competition and the probability of the occurrence of free riding.

Human co-ordination can occur through authority (state) or by means of voluntary exchange (market). Political authority is today mainly exercised through legal or rational authority, of which democracy is one basic type. Voluntary exchange occurs in several forms, of which the competitive market is one basic type. The state is today either a democratic one or an authoritarian one. And the economic system of a country delivers everything from an extreme poverty to the affluent society. The key problem in political economy is to pin down how alternative mixes of state and market in the form of politico-economic regimes affect these outcomes.

Part I is devoted to the analysis of economic, social and political outcomes among the countries of the world. First, we draw a picture of the globalization drive. Then, we examine how things stand today with regard to macro-developmental differences in economic, social and political outcomes among the countries of the world.

Globalization, the Rules of the Economic Game and the Custodian State

We will discuss in this part why the state and the market are essential to the economy. This takes us right into theories explaining how markets and government relate to each other. The approach in these theories is basically normative, as the effort is to make a coherent separation between the market and the state that is valid generally. Thus, one asks questions like: What can markets do when they operate efficiently? What is left to the state, when markets do not work well? Questions like these have always been of central concern for political economy. Alternative answers can be found in the literature, either within public finance or within public choice. We will suggest a slightly different answer, which takes into account the recent evolution of a global market economy. States can make interventions for only two valid reasons: (i) markets simply do not work but there must be an allocation; (ii) markets do not operate efficiently or desirably. In the first case of market failure states replace markets whereas in the second case of market failure states correct markets by public regulation. Now, the key question today is: What does market failure imply in terms of state intervention in relation to the global market economy? Let us first pin down in Chapter 2 what the global market economy looks like. In Chapters 3 to 5 we will examine how countries differ in terms of economic, social and political outcomes. However, we begin with a preliminary discussion of the distinction between state and market and its present relevance in relation to globalization.

CHAPTER 1

The Rules of the Market Game

Introduction

The economy in the advanced countries is today most often referred to as 'the market economy'. It is also called 'capitalism', but perhaps not quite as often as in the past. Whereas 'capitalism' has a negative value bias, the word 'market economy' is more positive. Both these words, 'the market economy' and 'capitalism' denote the existing economic systems in the West, but their meaning is slightly different, as 'the market economy' has a sense that points more transparently to the rules of the game than the word 'capitalism' does.

The institutional aspects of economic life are analysed in a rapidly growing literature called 'law and economics' (see Cooter and Ulen, 1999). Rules are often mentioned as crucial when the advanced economies of Western countries are contrasted with the economies outside the occidental world, i.e. in the Third World or in Asia. Thus, these economic systems outside the so-called OECD world are described as having more of state interference, either as a legacy from the command economy or in the form of state-capitalist systems as with economic nationalism. The extent to which the economies in the Third World are market economies is a much debated topic, which can only be decided by detailed empirical studies.

We will not speak of 'capitalism' in general. Looking at economic history one finds numerous hypotheses about various kinds of capitalism (Schumpeter, 1989; Weber, 1995). Thus, there was ancient capitalism in the Greek and Roman period. The Medieval Ages saw its version of capitalism in the emerging commercial houses in the free cities, which flourished during the Renaissance. The industrialization process brought forward a new form of capitalism. Similarly, today global capitalism is said to be a new phenomenon.

This is not the place to enter into a debate about the nature of capitalism and all its different modes. When reading the works of Weber and Sombart, for instance, or Braudel and Bairoch, one becomes well aware of the fact that economic life has had a rich set of frameworks within which the drive for profit has worked itself out. One may distinguish between slave capitalism in the ancient period, agrarian capitalism in feudal times and industrial capitalism since the industrial revolution. In addition one may speak of Western capitalism and oriental capitalism, and so on (Braudel, 1993; Bairoch, 2000).

We prefer to speak of 'the market economy' in order to emphasize that we are looking at something that is different from the crime economy. The advanced economies of the world can only be understood if one includes institutions in the analysis of the normal incentives that drive any form of economic life. It then becomes an open question to be settled by research to what extent these rules are institutionalized in Third World countries or in the emerging global market economy.

The market economy is not just any economic system that produces wealth. The market economy appears to be highly efficient in producing affluence, but that is part of the outcomes of a market economy, and not part of the definition of the concept. The meaning of the word 'market economy' concentrates upon certain rules that must work at an acceptable level of compliance and fairness. These institutions include: (i) private property on a large scale; (ii) contractual relationships; (iii) limited liability companies; (iv) stock exchanges or bourses; (v) the rights of labour (association, strike). The conclusion with regard to the implementation of the rules (i)–(v) is that government is chiefly the umpire for the economy and not a player in the economy.

Although each of these five institutions developed separately and according to its own logic, one can still maintain that they create a coherent whole. People who have full property rights would want to use these in order to enter into contractual relationships, thereby reaping the full benefits of their property rights. On the other hand, when people can fully contract, then they can also be the residual claimer of any benefits from economic activity. The Limited Liability Company limits the property implications of firm activities, but at the same time makes risk manageable for private individuals. When there are many limited liability companies, then bourses would have to be used to control them. Individuals contracting about stocks and bonds, issued by limited liability companies, face staggering information costs, which bourses can handle. The rights of labour correspond to the rights of property, as private property rights protect the owners of capital whereas the rights of labour protect the wage earners.

One may decide to call the set of institutions (i)–(v) 'capitalism', but what purpose would that serve? Capitalism is said to have existed in all the known ages of human civilization, at least from the Roman period and during the medieval period to modern capitalism starting with industrialization (Weber, 1978). However, these five institutions were clearly not in place during ancient, medieval or early modern capitalism. Distinctive of the market economy is the institutionalization of capitalism by the creation and implementation of transparent rules for economic activity, which channels it towards the peaceful pursuit of reciprocal gain to the players. The market economy is different from wild capitalism or the crime economy.

Whatever definition one chooses for the word 'capitalism', it is important to underline that a market economy is not just another capitalist system.

The market economy is characterized by a highly developed set of institutions that are policed by special organizations. At end of the day it is the state that guarantees the market economy by offering mechanisms for the implementation of the basic rules (i)–(v). Thus, states come before markets. It is the machinery of the state that supplies the mechanisms for the implementation of the market rules, where the big problem is that of *reneging*.

Today 'capitalism' could equally well stand for the crime economy that has taken on such huge proportions both globally and especially in certain countries where economic institutions can successfully be reneged. However, the market economy is different from the crime economy, not only in ideal terms but also in reality. One could look upon the whole paraphernalia of judges, police, prisons and lawyers as having one single function, namely that of making reneging a very costly strategy for persons who balance the pros and cons of illegal economic activities.

In traditional economics the basic institutions of the market economy were taken for granted, i.e. they were assumed to exist and to operate without major problems. In new economic theories called 'institutional economics' this is no longer the case. One attempts to explain the smooth functioning of market rules stating the institutional conditions that enhance market performance, and including also the difficult question of how market institutions develop over time (Eggertson, 1990). Our argument is that the role of the state has been underestimated.

Role of the state

Suppose that we accept the proposed definition of the market economy above. This acceptance has no implications for the deliberation over how to mix markets and state. We still have not shown that markets work well if these five institutions are implemented fully. Nor have we raised the even more fundamental question of when these five conditions can or cannot be met without grave difficulties. Putting these conditions (i)–(v) on the table is just to start the debate about the role of governments in the economy. And this debate must take into account globalization and its consequences. Now, the state has a role to play in the economy besides implementing the conditions (i)–(v) when:

1　The conditions (i)–(v) do not apply: i.e. property rights cannot be introduced, contracting is deficient, the limited liability form is not appropriate or bourses cannot be used.
2　The conditions (i)–(v) do not produce outcomes which are desirable according to either criteria of efficiency or equity.

There are several standard theories that deal with these two situations, but they all assume a closed economy. What needs to be researched is how globalization resulting in open economies affects both situations.

Just making the market economy work gives governments much to do. To make sure that the five conditions above are met governments have to operate a large number of programmes. Each one of these conditions poses numerous challenges to government. They concern basic issues in the running of states. To accomplish these conditions above, governments have to put in place what one may call a *custodian state*. The crux of the matter is that this will have to be done in a world today characterized by globalization. The custodian state is the machinery that implements the rule of law in a society, based upon the sovereign will of the state. However, the globalization process is conducive to the reduction of state sovereignty. How, then, is a global market place to be protected against reneging?

The market economy is not merely business as usual. The increasing emphasis placed upon the contribution of the market economy to affluence, employment and economic development goes hand in hand with a realization of the full institutional requirement of the successful operation of a market economy. At the same time as the market economy has spread around the world as globalization increases its momentum, it has become more transparent how the market economy differs from what is called 'modern or post-modern capitalism'. The market economy is not the same as economic nationalism, economic exploitation or the crime economy.

The market economy institutionalizes economic activity in terms of five rules that the state puts in place in a transparent manner. Many countries do not fully respect these rules of the game and thus have deficient market economies. In a market economy, governments cannot be first and foremost players, as they should focus primarily upon being umpires. In a market economy land, capital and labour are protected as property rights and the rights of labour strengthen the view that the owners of the factors of production also constitute the persons with the residual claim on the gains from economic activity. The rights of association belong not only to capital but also to the wage earners.

However, in many parts of the world economic activity takes place through the laws of the jungle, as many forms of exploitation of children, women and labour are allowed by governments in countries with a weak economy. Trade unions are not permitted to operate freely and property rights are not policed, inviting economic crime. Typical of the advanced economies of the world is that they score high on the institutionalization of the market economy. In the long run, the complete adherence of capitalist economy to the rules of the market economy benefits economic activity and increases output and income. Governments play many and different crucial roles in accomplishing a market economy, reducing the risk of a crime economy and the space for manoeuvring of '*capitalisme sauvage*'.

The global economy and global politics: the big mismatch

One hears the phrase 'the global market place' so often that one forgets to ask what it stands for and why it is something new. The global market place is one aspect of the global economy, which refers to the way in which the stock markets or the financial markets of the world have become connected lately. Although this is an important change, it is a reflection of the global economy rather than being a cause of it.

The global economy is both a real and a financial economy. It is often emphasized that the financial flows are today larger than the trade flows in goods and services. As a matter of fact, the flows in financial transactions are so large that they now bypass the total value of all goods and services produced. The financial economy or the financial markets are now firmly in the driving seat, although the financial economy should merely reflect the real economy.

The global economy implies the existence of many open economies. An open economy is an economy where imports and exports have become so huge that together they constitute about 50 per cent of the GDP of a country. When the economies become open, then trade takes on a size that makes the country extremely vulnerable to changes in the economies of other countries. Increasing trade sets off other kinds of exchange between countries, including currencies, investments, production and capital. The global economy is the outcome of increasing trade, multinational corporations and financial integration. What are the implications of globalization for the market economy and its governance?

In the global economy the multinational corporations (MNCs) play a major role and they propagate themselves by means of foreign direct investments (FDIs). A crucial question is how they are to be regulated, since governments are restricted to national legislation. The MNCs also constitute a challenge for the trade unions, as they also operate on a country basis. Thus far, economic regulation of the world economy has not kept pace with the evolution of either the real or the financial economy. Consequently, the regulatory schemes are patchy on the global level but more consistent at the regional level, i.e. within the so-called TRIAD of the European Union, the North American Free Trade Agreement and the Association of South East Asian Nations (the EU, NAFTA and ASEAN).

The standard index on the degree of openness of an economy says something about the degree of economic integration around the globe but leaves out the enormous flows of financial capital. The average score on impex has increased for almost all countries of the world, but the expansion of trade has taken place in a continuous manner, world trade expanding each year by a few percentages. Although some countries have such giant internal markets that their impex score is close to 20 per cent (USA, China), they are still highly vulnerable to changes in international trade.

When countries in one region of the world suffer from economic difficulties, then the critical question is whether this will reduce world trade. During the Asian crisis between 1997 and 1998 there was a widespread fear that world trade would be reduced for the first time since the 1960s. However, this did not occur, to the relief of countries in other regions of the world. International trade makes countries interdependent in relation to the business cycle, as short-run disturbances are propagated through the world economy.

The financial flows of capital are much larger than the trade flows. With the deregulation of capital markets around the world financial capital can move much freely from one country to another overnight. The flow of financial capital chasing its highest return possible has taken on such proportions that the national autonomy in setting exchange rates and interest rates is a thing of the past. Countries may decide to peg their currencies to the value of another leading currency, but to defend such a pegged rate requires either that capital flows cannot be free or that monetary policy must be abandoned.

The financial flows in the world economy have made countries so interdependent that national economic policy-making is very much restricted, especially monetary policy. When there are massive movements of financial capital in one direction, either in or out of a country, then all the economic parameters in the country are affected without government being able to do much about it. Typically governments react by taking drastic measures, which even when workable can only be applied for a short period of time. When a central bank tries to defend a currency against the outflow of capital, it usually runs out of reserves after a couple of days. It has become increasingly difficult for central banks to control the interest rates in their own country, when capital flows are not controlled. Interest rates tend to be determined at the international stock exchanges, where interest rates reflect both the level of inflation and the riskiness of the country in question.

The question of currency stability and instability has been a central one in all forms of world-level regulation. The two alternatives: fixed exchange rates versus floating exchange rates, have been long discussed, including such matters as the gold standard, one currency leader, and monetary unions of various kinds. The problem of exchange rates is connected with two other problems, namely capital flow controls or not, as well as government discretion in fiscal and monetary policy-making. The 'irreconcilable trinity' covers: (i) fixed exchange rates; (ii) national independence in macroeconomic policy; (iii) capital mobility. Only two of these three can be had at any one time.

Whereas most people favour more of international trade, many people are hesitant about the integration of financial capital. Thus, calls for state interventions have been made in order to limit the flux of money, including a so-called Tobin tax but also strict quotas handled by a currency board of the Malaysian type. However, free capital flows are essential in order to enhance the efficiency of capital, for instance through direct foreign investments (FDIs).

There is the inevitable trade-off among fixed exchange rates, independence in macro-economic policy and capital mobility: the 'irreconcilable trinity'. Governments endorse stable exchange rates and discretionary monetary policy to promote economic growth and steer their economies in the business cycle. Governments want free capital movements to facilitate foreign investment. However, all these three means cannot be used at the same time.

Economic integration between countries takes more and more the form of foreign investment either by setting up new factories for production or by buying into already existing production facilities by means of company acquisitions or acquiring equity in a firm. To a much larger extent than merely 20 years ago, companies and production facilities are owned by foreigners. Multinational companies have expanded rapidly to create production links all over the world in order to accomplish economies of scale. Multinationals engage in brand competition in order to increase their market power, producing their products at one place but selling them all over the world. Often production involves the assembly of the final product at one place using other production plants in other countries for the production of the parts that enter the final product. This makes world trade intra-firm trade to a large extent.

Given these developments involving a sharp increase in FDIs, it is small wonder that much of the world trade is intra-industry trade and not inter-industry trade. Firms wish to accomplish economies of scale in their production, meaning that it becomes vital to produce huge quantities that can only be sold to the world market. Industrial nations trade more and more with each other in order to arrive at economies of scale (Krugman and Obstfeld, 2000).

The overall development concerning trade has been a steady reduction in tariffs and quotas. But there are still a large number of technical hindrances. International trade and international financial flows call for state regulation, as there is always the possibility of reneging. Individual countries can try to direct trade into terms that are favourable for home firms. International capital flows may be used for money laundering.

Global institutional integration

The institutional consequence of globalization is to force countries to harmonize their legal systems so that the rules concerning the foundations of the market economy (i)–(v) are roughly the same in all countries with an open economy. This entails the construction of a global market economy along the following regulatory lines. In relation to the global economy in search of institutions there must be a resolution of the following problems:

1   Universal respect for private property; rules against arbitrary socializa-
    tion; nationalization must be based upon strict criteria and compensa-
    tion must be based upon market prices; the use of all forms of property
    must be compensated, including intellectual property rights; innova-
    tions must be protected in all countries.
2   Similar contract law; rules against economic nationalism; right of
    establishment, non-discrimination. This implies that FDIs must be
    accepted without many strings attached to them. Labour regulations
    according to the International Labour Organization Standards. Level
    the playing field; rules against trade barriers; lowering of tariffs and
    quotas; the World Trade Organization framework.
3   Rules about multinational companies against hindrances such as anti-
    dumping clauses, performance requirements and local content require-
    ments.
4   Free capital flows, including currencies; rules in favour of currency
    convertibility, and against barriers to capital movements; the Interna-
    tional Monetary Fund and World Bank framework.

Typical of the world economy is that there is no one single Hobbesian
authority that implements the above institutions. The institutional conclusion from the above problems has been institutional regionalization (e.g. the
EU) but no world government. Instead regulation is spread out over various
international organizations and regional co-operation mechanisms. The
nation-states used to provide the guardian state for the economies of the
countries of the world. But with economic integration taking place on an
international scale, the question naturally arises: Where are the guardians of
the global market economy? This question is a real one, as the alternative to
an effective guardian mechanism is the crime economy. How fast the
underground economy can spread and take over huge parts of the official
economy has become apparent lately, as events in countries such as
Colombia, Sierra Leone, Afghanistan and Russia have shown.

The basic problem is again: reneging. The likelihood of reneging being
successful increases when national economies open their borders and
become integrated in a world economy. Organized crime can move around
more easily in the global market place than it did before. Globalization
without guardianship poses a problem to economic life not only because of
reneging. There are also transaction cost reasons involved in relation to
normal economic activities. Without international rules and effective
implementation economic life will not reach output maximum.

Supporters of Adam Smith maximize their self-interest. They search for
the best deal when exchanging with other individuals. People have two kinds
of interests, as we have known since the ancient Greeks, namely self-interest
and collective interest. Some interests we pursue in confrontation with
others, meaning that what we gain they lose – this is narrow self-interest.
Other interests we pursue together, meaning that we share in the partition of

this interest – this is group interest. Altruism, or the pursuit of the best for other people without any self-consideration, does not exist in the Adam Smith approach.

One of the most crucial group interests is to arrange for collective action, in which everyone may share without reducing other people's potential to enjoy common goods. Thus, people work together in collective action to provide common goods, because they tend to be lumpy. If people share in the provision of such goods, then they cost less. Since anyone can enjoy them, there is no rationale in providing them privately. This sets up a prisoners' dilemma game of collective action where free riding makes collective solutions difficult. The classical argument for the state is to make collective action possible or to itself supply common goods in the form of so-called public goods. In Part II we will analyse the implications of the most general form of free riding, namely reneging, and we will argue that reneging is a real threat to the use of markets to solve problems of human co-operation and co-ordination. The necessity of a state is to be found in the difficulty of markets to handle reneging as well as in the benefits to groups from collective action of various kinds.

Conclusion

The arrival of a global economy means that one must rethink the relations between the state and the market. The micro theory of the role of government in the economy originating in microeconomics has focused upon domestic market failures but has had little to say about the consequences of economic interactions across borders. The macro theory about state intervention based upon macroeconomics started from the model of a closed economy but developed more and more towards a model of an open economy. Yet, the true dimensions of the task of governance in a global market economy have yet to be spelled out.

We have taken the position above that state governance of the market economy is a *sine qua non*. This is not an argument for state intervention of the traditional kind, as with either the command economy or the state-capitalist model. To us government is the guarantor of the market economy so that the market economy does not slip into wild capitalism or even worse the crime economy. The guarantor role involves all branches of government – executive, legislative and judicial. Its decisive importance for the market economy derives from the problem of reneging, which voluntary exchange mechanisms like the market have such great problems in handling.

In many but not all countries governments have been able to provide these guarantor roles in relation to the domestic economy. In some countries – stateless societies – this guardianship of the economy has not taken place and there have been disastrous consequences. Governments do more things in the economy than providing the guarantees of the market economy. However, the guarantor roles are the essential ones. But when globalization has become a reality, where is the government that will take on the tasks of guaranteeing the global market economy?

Globalization creates the need for new forms of co-ordination. Global market integration is not enough although it has proceeded a long way already. State co-ordination must take place in one form or another to handle the collective action problems that arise with a global market economy. However, there are almost 200 sovereign states, meaning that mechanisms for regional and international governance must be created. First, we will analyse the country variation in political economy aspects. Then we will discuss how co-ordination between countries could be accomplished.

CHAPTER 2

Globalization

Introduction

It is often said that the world is becoming more and more one market place and that one arena for many things other than economics exists. The globalization argument must be confronted in any analysis of market and state. Before we research what are the main consequences for the political economy of the world as globalization increases, we need to clarify what 'globalization' stands for. This is the main problem we address in this chapter.

In a most general sense, the concept of globalization stands for more of international contacts, more of exchanges between people, organizations and nations on a global level. Let us first quote some attempts to define globalization in this general and necessarily vague manner:

> Globalization as a concept refers both to the compression of the world and the intensification of consciousness of the world as a whole. (Robertson, 1992: 8)

> We can therefore define globalization as: A social process in which the constraints of geography on social and cultural arrangements recede and in which people become increasingly aware that they are receding. (Waters, 1995: 3)

> Globalization is 'the intensification of economic, political, social and cultural relations across borders'. (Holm and Sorensen, 1995: 1)

> a process (or set of processes) which embodies a transformation in the spatial organization of social relations and transactions – assessed in terms of their extensity, intensity, velocity and impact – generating transcontinental or interregional flows and networks of activity, interaction, and the exercise of power. (Held *et al.*, 1999: 16)

> globalization as referring to tendencies to a worldwide reach, impact, or connectedness of social phenomena or to a world-encompassing awareness among social actors. (Therborn, 2000: 154)

Allowing for the rather imprecise nature of these definitions of 'globalization', we wish to underline that the process of globalization has stimulated an intensive debate about its nature, strength and consequences recently (Beynon and Dunkerley, 2000, Bartelson, 2000). It presents a set of fundamentally contested issues, which are in no way resolved (Krugman, 2000). Below we will identify a number of contentious aspects of globalization.

What is globalization?

As a phenomenon globalization tends to constitute a paradox. The manifestations of globalizations are at the same time extremely visible and yet very hard to pin down and measure. We will use a number of indicators to tap the globalization process. One must conclude that 'globalization' stands for a very broad concept, referring to the processes by which events, decisions and activities in one part of the world come to have significant consequences for individuals and communities in quite distant parts of the globe. How can these processes be identified and measured? This is the key task today for the social sciences. At least the following questions are involved:

1   *Its measurement*: It is easy to be impressed by all the journalism that speaks of globalization, but can one really measure strictly how it has grown in the past decades? The world trade has expanded continuously since the end of the Second World War, but globalization has only been spoken of since the 1980s. What has happened in particular during these last decades before the year 2000? Is globalization mainly a financial phenomenon, to be measured by means of the size and the spread of the global financial economy? But, surely, globalization is something more than merely the coupling of the financial markets around the world in terms of one single encompassing global market place for money, bonds and equity where information flows at an ever-increasing pace, partly through the Internet.

2   *Its geographical spread*: The concept of globalization implies that the whole world is affected by the integration of countries and states. But it is often emphasized that world integration is a very uneven phenomenon. Sometimes huge areas are portrayed as marginalized, remaining outside world economic or technological integration. Certain regions are singled out as especially integrated, quite naturally the three regions of NAFTA, EU and ASEAN. Perhaps then globalization is better described as regionalization?

3   *Its impact*: Globalization has been described simultaneously as having enormous consequences but also as having little if any real impact upon the lives of ordinary people in the sense of involving the common man in increasing individual responsibility (Kiely and Marfleet, 1998; Prakash and Hark, 1999). It has been described as the final stage of capitalist integration of all peoples and cultures into one huge economy dominated by multinational corporations being preoccupied chiefly by financial transactions in order to create a complex web of ownership across borders. But is has also been described as the advent of true universal brotherhood, where wars could be abolished and famines are able to be counteracted by international action.

4   *Its nature*: Globalization is either analysed as an economic phenomenon or as an intergovernmental phenomenon. Thus, globalization impacts

upon economic integration either in the real economy or in the financial economy. It is just as well expressed in the growth of international organizations, their number as well as their competencies. The most typical expressions of *financial economy globalization* include the immense interdependencies between the world major stock exchanges on the one hand and the immediate and immense flow of currency exchanges on the other hand. The typical features of *real economy globalization* meaning production include the emergence of regional economics governed with some intergovernmental or supra-state competencies. Integration in law – *institutional integration* – seems to be the characteristic effect of globalization, as expressed in the growth of both public and private international law (Wiener, 1999).

5   *Its sources*: If it is difficult to identify the consequences of globalization, its sources appear to be more readily discerned. What basically drive the international integration phenomena are first and foremost technological breakthroughs which make communication quick, reliable and voluminous. One could add economic forces to technological innovations, although this has been contested, as some claim that the extent of economic integration has been exaggerated (Krugman, 2000). Or one may point to the growth in understanding among countries and cultures as to what international co-operation and co-ordination require in terms of common institutions. One could well argue that the globalization process once started reinforces itself, its sources being its effects, as it were.

Measuring aspects of globalization

In order to give a picture of how the large-scale process of globalization is manifested in various real events, we analyse a few aspects below using a variety of indicators. Recognizing the complexity of globalization, we argue that it would be illuminating to try to map globalization aspects with respect to at least four different kinds of things: (i) the states; (ii) population movements; (iii) communication channels; and (iv) the internationalization of the economy. The whole world will be used as the unit of analysis, thus trying to identify worldwide trends over time.

Important sources are data released by international organizations such as the World Bank (WB), the International Monetary Fund (IMF) and the United Nations Development Programme (UNDP). Other important publications are *Vital Signs* edited by Brown *et al.* (2000), the German series *Globale Trends* published by Stiftung Entwicklung und Frieden (1995–1999) and the study by M. Beisheim *et al.*, asking whether we are *Im Zeitalter der Globalisierung?* (1999).

The states

'Globalization' refers to a number of different things, one of which relates to the state and its position in a globalized world. Thus, globalization means the 'increased political and military interdependence of a set of sovereign nation-states' (Meyer, 2000: 233). Or globalization implies 'the forging of a multiplicity of linkages and interconnections between the states and societies which make up the modern world system' (McGrew, 1992: 56).

Globalization entails that states lose their sovereignty and become players in so-called multilevel games. Globalization as a political phenomenon basically means that the 'shaping of the playing field of politics itself is increasingly determined not within insulated units'; instead we have a set of 'complex congeries of multilevel games played on multilayered institutional playing fields, above and across, as well as within, state boundaries' (Cerny, 1997: 253). It appears that states have relinquished a great deal of power to either higher-level governments or lower-level governments during the post-war period.

We are here confronted with a few key arguments concerning the impact of globalization upon the state. On the one hand, we have the prediction of the end of the state as a consequence of the globalization process (Ohmae, 1995). On the other hand, there is a rejection of such notions as the withering away of the state (Mann, 1997; Weiss, 1998; Østerud, 1999). In any case the concept of the state needs to be reconsidered in the light of globalization.

Let us attempt to map some developmental trends worldwide for the state. There is no doubt that the number of independent states has increased substantially over the post-world war period. In 1950 the number of member-states of the United Nations was 60, while in 1999 it had increased to 188 with the admission of a few new states: Kiribati, Nauru and Tonga. Counting independent states as they may be defined in a conventional way, we find that the number had increased from 85 in 1950 to 191 in 1999. This trend is detailed in Figure 2.1, and there are no signs of a decrease in the number of independent states.

The increase in the number of states in the 1990s is connected in large part to the break-up of the Soviet Union. But new states may be introduced in both the First and the Third Worlds, as the birth of East Timor shows.

The global state system, as identified in public international law, recognizes a huge set of actors, who are formally on an equal basis. However, globalization is said to increase the inequalities among states. At the same time, we may note that there is an increase in the number of actors on the international arena who are not based in the state. Here we may include so-called NGOs (non-governmental organizations) but also so-called IGOs (intergovernmental organizations). Further, it is possible to distinguish between conventional international organizations and all other international organizations.

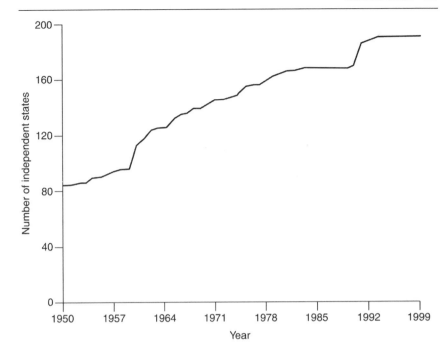

Figure 2.1 Number of independent states of the world 1950–99
Sources: *Encyclopaedia Britannica*; *Fischer Weltalmanach*

Looking at data for the period 1981 to 1999 – see Figure 2.2 – we may establish that there is an overall increase in the number of conventional international organizations. In particular, this is true for the NGOs, as this form of internationalization may be seen as a most visible aspect of globalization. We may, however, note that the number of conventional IGOs (i.e. UN-related) has been rather stable over time, and if there has been any change they have declined in numbers during the 1990s.

Thus, we find that complexity has increased in the state system since 1945, as the number of actors is sharply up at the same time as the international polity has included more and more international regimes. Yet, the international polity is based upon the states and provided by international regimes which act through international co-ordination channels.

Another aspect of the state is its size. Is the size of the state changing due to the globalization process? Let us take a look at how the public sector in general has developed over time, but also at how the military sector is changing, since the provision of defence by the military may still be seen as the core function of the state. In Figure 2.3 and Table 2.1 we display some estimates of the public sector on a world scale. Figure 2.3 contains data on central government expenditures in relation to world GNP as estimated by ACDA, i.e. the US Arms Control and Disarmament Agency (ACDA) and its successor the US Bureau of Arms Control (BAC).

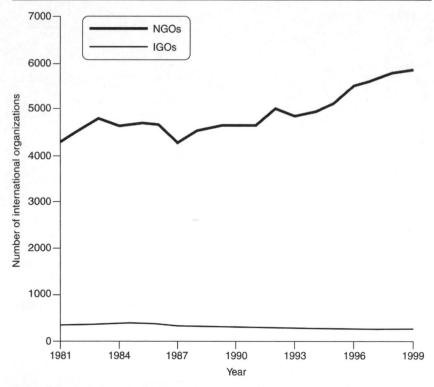

Figure 2.2   Number of conventional international organizations 1981–99
Sources: Union of International Associations (various years) *Yearbook of International Organizations*

The national government – the central or federal government – has shrunk during the last two decades of the twentieth century. This trend confirms the theory that national governments tend to off-load tasks to civil society or lower levels of government, partly as a response to market forces, where there is a valid claim that markets work better than state bureaucracy. Let us, however, take a longer time perspective. Table 2.1 has data on general government expenditures from *c*. 1870 up to the 1990s. This measure covers all levels of government, but it only includes a sample of the industrialized countries.

We may conclude from Table 2.1 that the expansion of the public sector has been a true trend occurring with the coming of the industrial urban society. The size of the state has increased sharply in the long run. But if we look at a shorter time period from the late 1970s to the late 1990s, then there is no such seminal increase. Is this halt to public sector expansion an outcome of globalization? One aspect of the globalization process is the philosophy of the global market economy, according to which the public sector should not be allowed to expand further. Instead it was argued in the 1980s that the public sector ought to be decreased as a response to government overload.

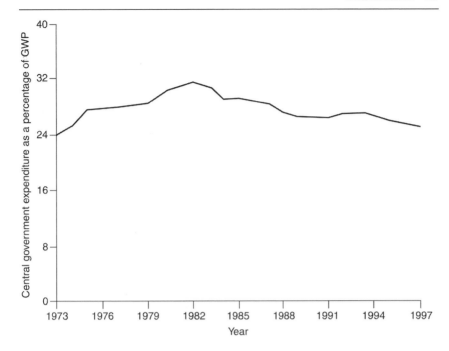

Figure 2.3 Estimates of world public sector size: central government expenditures/ GNP (%) 1973–97
Sources: ACDA (1985, 1997), BAC (1999) *World Military Expenditures and Arms Transfers*

Let us look finally at the military sector. Figure 2.4 has data on military expenditures and also the size of the armed forces worldwide for the period 1973 to 1997. It is evident from this figure that these two indicators change over time in a similar way. Military spending and the size of the armed forces have decreased since peaking in the early 1980s. No doubt the decline and fall of the Soviet Union has been important for this developmental

Table 2.1 Estimates of general government expenditure for 14 industrialized countries 1870–1996

Year	General government expenditures as percentage of GDP
c. 1870	10.8
1913	13.1
1920	19.6
1937	23.8
1960	28.0
1980	41.9
1990	43.0
1996	45.0

Source: Tanzi and Schuknecht, 2000: 6–7

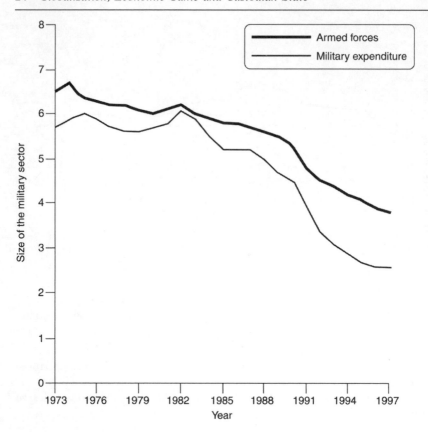

Figure 2.4 Estimates of the size of the military sector: expenditures and armed forces worldwide; military expenditure/GNP (%) and armed forces/capita 1973–97 *Sources*: ACDA (1985, 1997), BAC (1999) *World Military Expenditures and Arms Transfers*

trend, but it may also be due to the decline in the occurrence of armed conflicts over time. Does globalization promote peace?

The sharp decline in Figure 2.4 reflects first and foremost the disappearance of the arms race between the USA and the USSR. Yet, globalization may also add to the reduction, as it favours international negotiation instead of armed struggle.

Figure 2.5 and Table 2.2 have data on conflicts around the world during the post-world war period. Looking at the number of conflicts starting in a particular year, we may find a long-run increase from 1945/46 to the mid-1980s when it peaked in 1987 to be followed by a decrease in the number of conflicts started. These are the estimates presented from the *Correlates of War Project* at the University of Michigan, where they measure militarized interstate disputes being classified as wars. The Figure captures for each year the number of wars started.

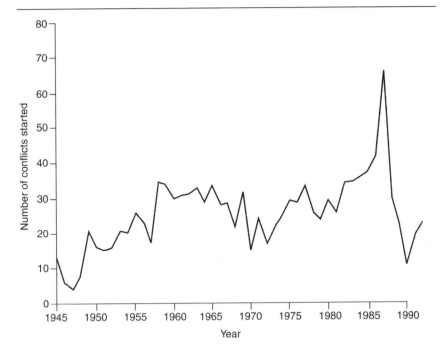

Figure 2.5 Number of conflicts started 1945–92
Source: Data from the *Correlates of War Project* made available by Peace Science Society (International) (1999)

Table 2.2 Armed conflicts in the world 1989–99

Year	Number of armed conflicts[a]	Number of locations[a]	Number of armed conflicts[b]
1989	47	37	42
1990	49	39	48
1991	51	38	50
1992	55	41	51
1993	46	33	45
1994	42	32	41
1995	35	30	36
1996	36	29	31
1997	34	27	29
1998	37	32	32
1999	37	28	35

[a] Wallensten and Sollenberg
[b] AKUF
Sources: Wallensten and Sollenberg, 2000: 636; AKUF as reported by Brown *et al.* 1992–2000: 111

A decline has occurred in warfare, in the 1990s when measured by the number of armed conflicts. At the same time, this decade witnessed large-scale war not only in the Third World (Iraq) but also in the First World (Serbia).

To get a picture of the developments after the end of the cold war we rely on estimates from two research groups, one in Sweden (Wallensten and Sollenberg) and one in Germany (AKUF). Their estimates are presented in Table 2.2 and to a large extent show the same picture. There is a decrease in the number of conflicts during the 1990s as the number of armed conflicts is distinctly lower in 1998 than was the case in 1989 or 1990. Thus, we may conclude that the 1990s constituted a period of a decreasing number of conflicts. Despite that we must note a slight increase in the number of armed conflicts at the very end of this decade. Still the conclusion remains that globalization enhances peace and promotes peaceful mechanisms of conflict resolution by reducing state autonomy and increasing reciprocity between governments. Globalization makes states more and more interdependent, with the consequences that war becomes more and more costly. State clashes immediately become an affair for the international community. However, states keep spending huge sums of money on arms.

Although the number of armed conflicts has gone down, there are still many wars that mankind must face in the world around 2000, like, for instance, the anarchy in Congo. One could search for a cultural basis for the occurrence of many armed conflicts. The violent conflicts between states sometimes run alongside ethnic or religious lines, but there remain numerous other causes or reasons for armament and war (Payne, 1989).

To conclude this overview of the state in the era of globalization, let us take a look at the process of democratization that is taking place in its so-called third wave since 1789 (Huntington, 1991). One indicator is to look at the number of free countries in the world as identified by the Freedom House during the period 1980 to 1999. In Figure 2.6 we display the number of free countries as a percentage of all the countries in the world. There is no doubt that in relative numbers the trend displayed is an upward trend, especially after 1989. While the number was 53 in 1980, it had increased to 88 in 1999, i.e. 46 per cent of all countries. It is still too early to tell whether the world has become safer, or more precisely safer for democracy. The process of democratic consolidation is still evolving, with uncertain outcomes in, for example, Colombia, Venezuela and Ecuador as well as in the Khanates or in South East Asia. In any case, the number of non-democracies remains larger than the number of democracies. Democracy has stabilized in several Latin American countries, although Africa has seen reversals. Dictatorships are numerous in Asia, despite democratic advances in South Korea and Taiwan.

The upward trend in the number of democratic regimes is unmistakable in Figure 2.6. However, there are two tendencies that counteract the democratization around 2000. First, several governments proclaim that

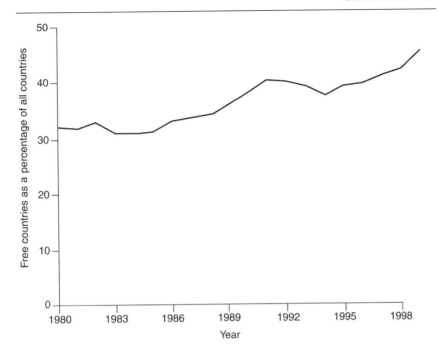

Figure 2.6 Free countries as a percentage of all countries in the world 1980–2000
Source: Freedom House (1999, 2000), Gastil (1986, 1987)

they have a democratic regime, while at the same time they have mounting problems with maintaining order and avoiding anarchy. Second, several countries in the Arab world continue to adhere to monarchy, be it traditional or disguised. Thus, the king's or the president's son is predestined to be the successor whether in a legitimate fashion or not.

To sum up: Over time we find a number of distinctive developmental trends in the global system of states that we may link with the ongoing process of globalization. The number of independent states has increased at the same time as the number of actors on the international arena – IGOs and NGOs – has increased sharply. The system of states has been reinforced by numerous more rules at the same time as power has increased for IGOs to implement the institutions of the global polity, with the states losing sovereignty. Over the long run we can establish that government is on the rise but not as a function of globalization. Actually, globalization seems to reduce the size of the state. Military spending and the number of armed conflicts show a decrease for the last decade of the twentieth century at the same time as the number of free – or democratic – countries is on the rise. Globalization promotes international intermediation and underlines the respect for human rights.

Population changes: migration

Globalization very much stands for increased movements of population across national borders. Thus, globalization may be defined as 'an expanded flow of individual persons among societies through socio-economic migration, travel and political expulsion' (Meyer, 2000: 233). When enquiring into the population aspects of the globalization process, we will take a look at the size and structure of the world population as well as the patterns of migration worldwide.

Estimates of total mid-year population of the world suggest that the overall size in 1950 was 2556 millions which had risen to 5925 millions in 1998. As we may see from Figure 2.7, this involves a steady rising trend, as the average growth rate in 1950 was estimated to be 1.47 per cent, whereas it was estimated to be 1.32 per cent in 1998. During 1999 the 6000 million threshold were passed. India has today over 1000 million people. The sharp upward curve in Figure 2.7 poses an enormous challenge to the states participating in the globalization process as it involves finding work, food and safety for immense numbers of people. What is the role of governments and markets, globalization forces us to ask.

Accompanying a steady rise in the size of world population, there is the changing sex ratio and a change in the proportion of various age groups. We

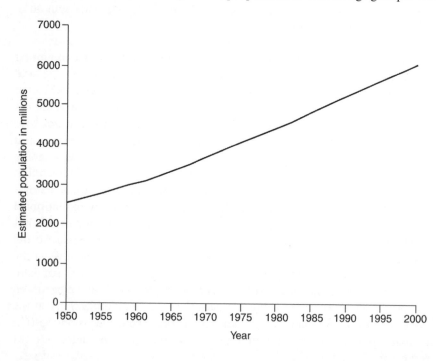

Figure 2.7 Population of the world 1950–2000
Source: US Bureau of Census (2000)

Table 2.3 World population structure: sex ratio and age structure 1950–95

Year	Sex ratio	Percentage 65 years or older
1950	99.6	5.2
1955	99.6	5.3
1960	99.8	5.3
1965	100.1	5.3
1970	100.4	5.5
1975	100.8	5.6
1980	101.0	5.9
1985	101.3	5.9
1990	101.5	6.2
1995	101.5	6.5

Source: United Nations (1998)

find an increase in the proportion of men from 1950 to 1995. The lower rate of 1950 was partly due to the impact of the Second World War, while the higher value for 1995 probably has to do with the decrease of the female populations in both India and China, which has become evident from the 1980s (Sen, 1990). The percentage of the old-age population is increasing, but it is only in the 1990s that there has been a more noticeable increase. Considering the immense cohorts of youth in the Third World, the trend in Table 2.3 is all the more noticeable.

One aspect of population changes that is highly relevant from a globalization perspective is international migration, i.e. the movements of populations over borders by free will or not. It is obvious that the size of the migrant stock is increasing in numbers over time, but if it is related to the size of the world population there is no longer any upward trend. The migrant stock of 1950 may be estimated to be around 2.3 per cent of world population, and the relation is the same in 1990. This has been noted by one expert who writes: 'Those focusing on the process of globalization note that although there has been a tendency to free the flows of goods and capital, there has been no parallel trend at the global level to free the flows of people' (Zlotink, 1998: 430). Yet, in absolute numbers migration has doubled between 1950 and 1990. And in real life it is real numbers that count, not percentages. This has implications for not only air traffic but also for the concept of citizenship.

A special group in the flow of people is the set of refugees (see Figure 2.8). Looking at the developmental trend for world refugee populations during the post-world war period, we may establish that up to 1993 there was a distinctive increase in refugee population – from 2.4 millions in 1970 to 18.2 millions in 1993 – but after that there has been a slight decline to an estimated 11.5 millions in 1998. One must, of course, be aware that estimates of the number of refugees are very rough (see Crisp, 1999). Still, the figures do indicate that the refugee groups have reached a size that must be

Table 2.4   Estimates of migrant stock on a world scale 1950–90

Year	Stock in 1000s	Stock as % of world population
1950	*c.* 60000	2.3
1965	75214	2.3
1975	84494	2.1
1985	105194	2.2
1990	119761	2.3

Sources: 1950: Segal, 1993: 119; 1965–90: Zlotink, 1998: 431

politically relevant in many countries. They both enhance cultural variety and trigger nationalistic responses.

The refugee population is rather evenly distributed around the world. Looking at the continents, the African continent has the largest proportion of refugees, followed by Europe. But considering the variation within the continents in the late 1990s, Western Europe probably had a larger refugee population than Eastern Africa. In Western Europe, Germany was the country having the largest number of refugees in absolute numbers.

To sum up: We observe the steady increase in the world population. The migrant stock remains more or less the same, relatively speaking, whereas the world refugee population declined somewhat in the late 1990s, also in

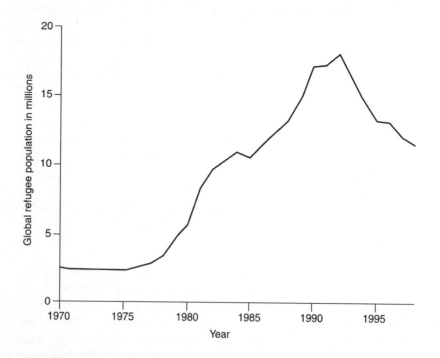

Figure 2.8   World refugee population in millions 1970–98
Source: UNHCR (various years)

relative terms. However, considering the tripling of the absolute size of the world population, the waves of migration and refugees have grown strongly, which changes to a considerable extent the composition of entire societies, especially the rich ones towards which immigration is almost exclusively directed. Here we have one of the mighty sources of multiculturalism.

Communication

Globalization understood as a tremendous increase in communications across the world implies more and more of exchanges of ideas and information between individuals and organizations from different parts of the world. This means that globalization may also be defined in terms of 'the expanded interdependence of expressive culture through intensified global communication' (Meyer, 2000: 233). For instance, themes from music to ethnic revival tend to spread like fads throughout the world society. Organizational structures arise to spread these fashions involving all types of actors from individuals to the governments who sometimes see such 'happenings' as a way to boost popularity.

More specifically, new information technologies have played a decisive role in facilitating the emergence of a rejuvenated and more flexile market economy, by providing networking, distant communication, the storing and processing of information as well as the co-ordination of individual work

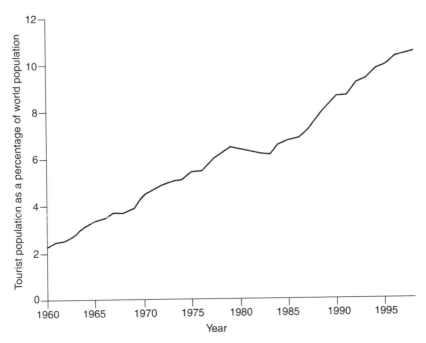

Figure 2.9 World tourism as a percentage of world population 1960–98
Source: WTO (1999)

(Castells, 1998: 337). The global communication system is to a considerable extent dominated by the huge American companies targeting the Internet.

We will look at the globalization process of world communications with respect to three very different aspects: tourism, aviation and Internet use. World tourism – measured as arrivals of tourists from abroad according to the World Tourism Organization (WTO) – displays a steady increase over time, also when related to the size of the world population (see Figure 2.9). In 1950 it was estimated to include some 25 million people, and it increased to 69 millions in 1960, but world travelling encompassed a staggering 625 millions in 1998.

Closely related to the development in tourism is the development of the number of civil aviation passengers. In addition to tourist passengers we have business passengers. Estimates suggest that in 1970 the total number of civil aviation passengers was 312 millions, while it had increased to a staggering 1294 millions in 1995. This upward trend over time is displayed in Figure 2.10. Can the world of non-renewable resources in combustibles sustain for a long period such an increase in world travelling, especially when the use of the automobile has continued to increase?

As our final indicator on communication development it seems highly relevant to choose Internet use. This is measured by relating the number of Internet hosts worldwide to world population. The first counts of Internet hosts goes back to 1981 and at that time they numbered 213; in 1984 the

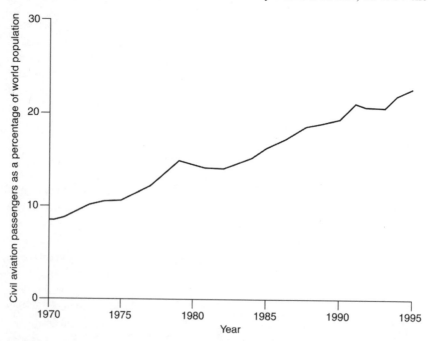

Figure 2.10   World aviation passengers as percentage of world population 1970–95
Source: United Nations (various years) *Statistical Yearbook*

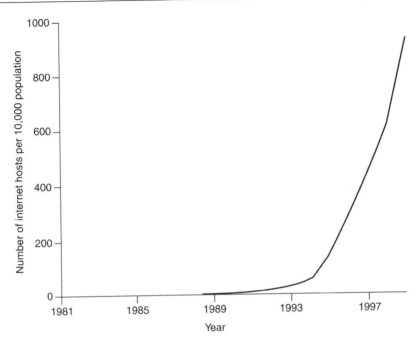

Figure 2.11 Internet hosts worldwide per 10,000 population 1981–2000
Source: Internet Software Consortium (2000)

number had increased to 1024. In 1992 more than 1 million hosts were counted and the count reporting for January 2000 shows more than 7243 million hosts (Internet Software Consortium, 2000). This very sharp increase in the use of the Internet is displayed in Figure 2.11. One can also count the number of people who use the Internet. Here there only exist a few crude estimates, but they do all point in the same direction. In 1995 the number of people being 'online' was suggested to be 26 millions, constituting 0.63 per cent of the total world population. In mid-year of 1999 the size was estimated to be 185 million people (4.41 per cent) and in mid-2000 the number had increased to 333 millions or 5.4 per cent of world population. Although we here have a most impressive increase in the use of the Internet, it still is the case that 95 per cent of the world population is not yet 'online' (Nua Internet Surveys, 2000).

To sum up: Within the communication sphere we find a number of developments that may be associated with a worldwide globalization process. Tourism, civil aviation and Internet use display (albeit in various degrees) developmental trends which suggest something very new developing over the last three decades. Maybe this sphere could be the core within the globalization process, as the changes are rapid, stunning and immense. What has been characterized as the coming of a whole new economy is very closely linked with the communication revolution.

The economy

It must be admitted that the concept of globalization has most often been looked upon from an economic dimension. Whereas there has been much talk about the internationalization of the national economies, globalization not only stands for increased economic interdependencies across borders but also for interaction among actors that are based globally.

Globalization consequently means the 'increased economic interdependencies of a set of national or subnational economies', where multilateral and international public and private organizations are involved, states and firms being the main actors (Meyer, 2000: 233). According to IMF, globalization refers to the growing economic interdependence of countries worldwide through the increasing volume and variety of cross-border transactions in goods and services and of international capital flows, and also through the more rapid and widespread diffusion of technology (IMF, 1997: 45). National economies are undoubtedly becoming steadily more integrated as cross-border flows of trade, investment and financial capital increase. Consumers are buying more foreign goods, a growing number of firms now operate across national borders, and savers are investing more than ever before in far-flung places (*The Economist*, 1997: 103). One particular dimension of the economic globalization is the role played by transnational companies (TNCs) in this process.

One may construct the economic globalization thesis as implying that a truly global economy has emerged, in which distinct national economies have merged into one global market place. Domestic strategies of national economic management are becoming more and more irrelevant. The world economy has 'internationalised in its basic dynamics'. Moreover, 'it is dominated by uncontrollable market forces, and it has as its principal economic actors and major agents of change truly transnational corporations', and these multinationals do not 'owe allegiance to any state, locating wherever in the globe market advantage dictates' (Hirst and Thompson, 1996: 1). Globalization couples the *real economies* into one giant web of production and trade. It also links the *financial economies* instantaneously in a system of bourses (New York, Tokyo, London, Frankfurt) that is in operation all the time.

In Marxist analyses it is often stressed that globalization is a new stage in the historically determined development of capitalism. Thus, it is argued that: (i) There is the spatial extension of capitalism directly associated with the collapse of the USSR and the Communist regimes of Eastern Europe, as well as the turn to capitalism in China and Vietnam, where the Communist Party élites are laying the ground for transforming themselves into new bourgeoisies. Moreover, we have (ii) the ideological and cultural sweep of capitalist ideas and values that defines our neoliberal era, whereby the bourgeoisie 'makes the world in its own image' with an impunity almost unparalleled since Marx wrote the words 150 years ago.

Moreover, Marxists argue that globalization is (iii) the process of international class formation of recent years, especially transnational integration among the capitalist classes. However, this is a process which is, by no means yet very far advanced as is evidenced by the national locus of several of the owners and boards of directors of the leading multinational corporations. Finally, we have (iv) 'the new stage of capital accumulation on a world scale, developing out of the contradictions of the post-war Keynesian/Bretton Woods order, which is characterised by a vast increase in the size, flow and speed of foreign direct investment and trade, and accompanied by an even more vast creation of international credit, currency flows, speculation, future markets, and private and public debt' (Panitch, 1998: 12–13). Most generally speaking, globalization may be characterized by increasing core economic activities and more of organizational flexibility leading to greater power for management in its relation to labour. Thus, competitive pressures, flexibility of work, and the weakening of organized labour have led to the retrenchment of the welfare state, which used to be the cornerstone of the social contract in the industrial era in advanced countries.

In discussing the economic aspects of globalization, we will focus on developments over time in trade, foreign investments, transnational

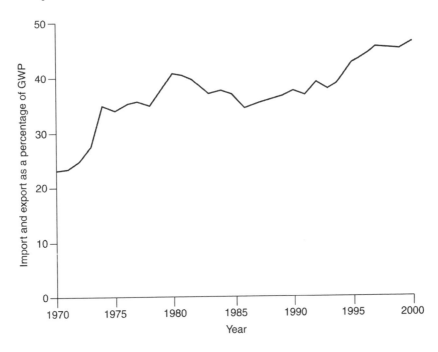

Figure 2.12   World import and export as a percentage of Gross World Product 1970–2000
Source: IMF (2000) 'World Economic Outlook'

companies, world debts and world income distributions. The institutional developments that go along with economic globalization pertain to the emergence of regional co-ordination mechanisms and the growth in world regulation by IMF, the World Bank and the WTO.

Trade is the exchange of goods and services over national borders, where increases in trade entail increases in transactions. Let us first take a look at the growth of world import and export as a percentage of Gross World Product (Figure 2.12). It is obvious that the trend from 1970 to 2000 was a rising one, going up from 1970 when it was 23.1 per cent to almost double in 2000 with 46.3 per cent. Still, it is important to note that the percentage reached in 1980 (40.8 per cent) was passed only in 1995 (42.6 per cent).

While examining the size of the world trade is one thing, then it is also interesting to look at the direction of world trade which has a clear bias. As we can see from Figure 2.13, the major share of the world trade takes place between the industrialized countries, although a slight decrease of this share may be noticed: in 1978 the share was 68.7 per cent and in 1997 64.0 per cent. This decrease involves, to a certain extent, a redirection of trade towards the Asian countries. While these countries had a share of 7.8 per cent in 1978, it had more than doubled in 1997 to 18.1 per cent.

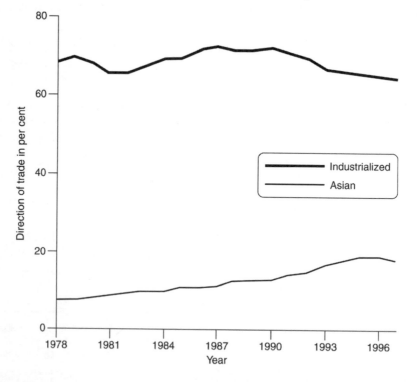

Figure 2.13   Direction of world trade: export to industrialized countries and to Asia 1978–97

Sources: IMF (various years) *Direction of Trade Statistics*

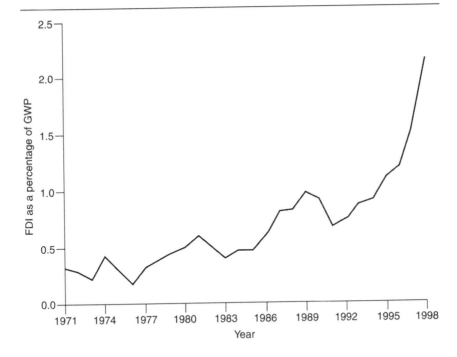

Figure 2.14 Foreign direct investment inflows as a percentage of Gross World Product (UNCTAD estimates) 1971–98
Sources: UNCTAD (1997, 1998) *World Investment Reports*

The size of the Asian exports was so large as to provoke a global economic crisis when the Asian miracle came to an end in 1996. As the three major regions of the global economy are not in the same stage all the time with regard to the business cycle, a depression in one region has serious consequences for the other two regions.

Another important aspect of the economic globalization is made up of the actions of business in directing its investments inwards or outwards. Data about foreign direct investments (FDIs) in relation to the Gross World Product may be employed to tap the role of foreign investments in the world economy. As is displayed in Figure 2.14, we observe a distinct upward trend over time, although there are both ups and downs. While it amounted to some 12 billion of dollars in the early 1970s, it is estimated to be worth around 400 billions in 1997 – an almost phenomenal increase, creating global dependencies over huge distances.

It is apparent that the 1990s is the decade when the pace of globalization accelerates. Foreign investment more than doubled since 1990 – this is a true global market place with lots of new production by foreign investments. To some this increase in foreign investments has enhanced economic domination and made governments weak against international capitalism.

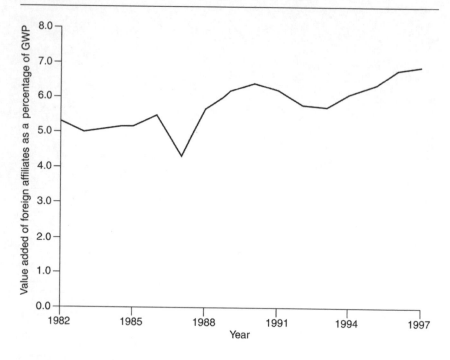

Figure 2.15   Foreign affiliates: value added as a percentage of the estimated Gross World Product 1982–97
Source: UNCTAD (1998) *World Investment Reports*

Closely related to this trend is the rise in the value added by these foreign investments as they appear in the foreign affiliates of world business. Estimates suggest that this value added constituted some 5.3 per cent of Gross World Product in 1982, then decreased in the late 1980s, to rise again in the late 1990s. It reached 6.9 per cent in 1997. Thus, there is no doubt that over time foreign investments and foreign affiliates have come to play an increasing role in the world economy, although one must remember that the absolute figures are still comparatively low (Figure 2.15).

Globalization in the world economy is increasing rapidly but it has not reached staggering levels. FDI inflows are estimated to amount to some 2 per cent of the Gross World Product, and the value added by foreign affiliates is only slightly higher in 1997 when compared with 1982. In the new global economy, the key actors constitute a set of transnational players who cross borders in relation to production, ownership and the financial interactions. Important actors in the economic globalization process are the transnational corporations (TNCs). Let us here present an overview over the 100 largest TNCs in the 1990s. First we are interested in identifying the domestic bases of these corporations, and second we wish to shed some light on the importance of their foreign, or non-domestic, interests.

Table 2.5 displays the home countries of these major TNCs. The figures

Table 2.5 Distribution of the 100 largest transnational corporations 1992–96 by domestic country

Domestic country	1992	1993	1994	1995	1996
USA	29	32	32	30	28
Japan	16	21	19	18	18
France	12	9	11	11	11
UK	11	9	9	11	10
Germany	9	11	11	9	9
Switzerland	6	5	5	5	5
Canada	3	3	3	4	4
Netherlands	4	3	4	3	4
Sweden	4	3	2	3	4
Australia	1	1	2	3	3
Italy	2	3	2	2	3
Belgium	2	1	1	2	2
South Korea	0	0	0	1	1
Venezuela	0	0	0	1	1
Norway	1	0	1	0	1
New Zealand	1	1	0	0	0
Finland	1	0	0	0	0

Sources: UNCTAD (1994–98) *World Investment Reports*

Table 2.6 Foreign parts in the 100 largest TNCs 1992 and 1996

Year	Foreign assets as % of assets	Foreign sales as % of sales	Foreign employment as % of employment	Transnationality ind.
1992	37.9	44.4	47.3	50.0
1996	43.0	52.3	50.4	54.8

Sources: UNCTAD (1994, 1998) *World Investment Reports*

vary slightly from one year to another, but it is obvious that the USA and Japan constitute the main bases for these corporations. Together they account for almost 50 per cent of the largest TNCs of the world. With a few exceptions they all belong to the industrialized First World. The exceptions are TNCs from South Korea and Venezuela.

Most interestingly, from Table 2.6 we also learn that among the TNCs the trend is towards increasing importance for the foreign part of the TNCs. This is true for foreign assets, sales and employment. When it comes to sales and employment, the foreign part played the major role in 1996.

However, this economic globalization process that makes country borders obsolete is to a large extent a process that is taking place among the industrialized countries, whereas the Third World countries are less and less involved. Globalization and distribution constitute a set of highly contested issues. It is still the case that the Third World countries are most heavily

Table 2.7   Estimates of debts in developing countries 1980–99

Year	Total debt stock as percentage of GDP	Interest payments on debts as percentage of GDP
1980	20.3	1.6
1990	34.2	1.7
1991	37.8	1.8
1992	38.1	1.6
1993	40.1	1.6
1994	40.3	1.6
1995	38.9	1.8
1996	36.0	1.7
1997	34.9	1.6
1998	42.1	2.0
1999	41.5	2.2

Source: WB (1998–2000) *Global Development Finance*

indebted. As is indicated in Table 2.7, however, the debt burden is less hard in the mid-1990s than was the case in the early 1990s, which may be due to the stricter economic policies imposed by the IMF and the World Bank. One must, however, note that these indicators are again on the rise towards the end of the 1990s. There has been some debt forgiveness towards the very poor countries that have no capacity to repay but the problem of the debt burden of the poor countries of the Third World is far from any solution. When debt payments become so large that they cause a lot of harm to economic recovery, then a policy of debt forgiveness may be the optimal policy.

A major attendant outcome of globalization is that the distribution of the world income is less and less to the advantage of the poor countries. Estimating the global income distribution between countries is sensitive to the kind of data used. It makes a difference whether one measures the total income of a country in terms of foreign exchange rates (FX) or in terms of purchasing power parities (PPP). Using estimates of the global income distribution based upon FX, a widening gap appears between the countries of the world, although this is not quite so dramatic if measures based on PPP are used. This is illustrated in the data presented in Table 2.8. The measure of the world income distribution for the period 1965 to 1990 is the Gini index, where higher scores indicate a less equal income distribution and lower scores, more equal distributions.

The two non-adjusted estimates based on FX are very close and they both indicate a sharp rise in global inequalities. The deviating estimate – the one based on PPP, which is probably the more accurate estimate – indicates little change in the global income distribution for the period between 1965 and 1990. Thus, we may not yet draw any definite conclusion that globalization is conducive to a growing inequality in the distribution of incomes between the countries of the world, although some evidence indicates exactly this.

Table 2.8 Estimates of world income distributions 1965–90: Gini coefficients

| Year | FX-based estimates | | | PPP-based estimates |
	Gini: FX[a]	Gini: FX	Gini FX, adjusted[b]	Gini: PPP[b]
1965	0.658	0.661	0.643	0.560
1970	0.662	0.666	0.647	0.558
1975	0.677	0.674	0.650	0.555
1980	0.682	0.681	0.650	0.550
1985	0.703	0.706	0.663	0.539
1990	0.740	0.733	0.683	0.543

Sources: [a]Korzeniewicz and Moran, 1997: 1021; [b]Firebaugh, 1999: 1611

To sum up: We may identify a number of aspects of economic globalization indicating much more in the way of cross-border exchanges as well as more of importance for non-domestic actors and structures. At the same time these data suggests that this process of globalization to a considerable extent is a process only embracing the industrialized world. Economic globalization is a real phenomenon, or strictly speaking, a set of real phenomena, changing mainly the affluent countries through its immense effects on production, trade and financial assets. There is a real danger for a marginalization of many Third World countries, burdened as they are by their huge debts and debt payments. Globalization in the world economy extends the benefits of rising affluence to new people but at the same time concentrates it to fewer.

Conclusion

The evidence in this chapter shows that globalization is a real phenomenon or a set of real phenomena. It denotes the many changes in the world system of states and economies, which have occurred after the Second World War and have one common feature, namely the development towards further integration and connectedness since the Second World War. With so many changes taking place, as indicated in the many Figures and Tables in this chapter, globalization is not only a quantitatively important phenomenon but also tends to change the world qualitatively. Since 1945 the macro-social system of the planet has moved from a rather small set of autonomous countries with certain links between each other to a complex order where a large set of countries are highly interlinked, politically, economically and technologically.

It should be pointed out that the globalization process displays a multiplicative impulse. When the different developmental trends described above combine, the outcome is not additive but multiplicative. Each of the trends stated above – in connection with the states, the economy, the population, and communication – constitute important paths in and of themselves. But when they share one basic communality – world integration

– the resulting outcome of all of these kinds of trends is an immense leap in the direction of reciprocity, mutuality, interdependency and connectedness. The links in the global market place and the global state system are becoming as critical as the entities constituting the globe, whether people or organizations.

Let us now analyse the major elements in the global economy and polity, namely the countries of the world. How do they vary in terms of a few key dimensions from the perspective of political economy?

CHAPTER 3

Developmental Differences around the Globe

Introduction

Development has been a key word when comparing countries, as some countries are said to be highly developed whereas other countries are labelled underdeveloped. Even when these words are not used, similar distinctions are made by means of other more diplomatic phrases. In the official statistics we find the following categories: low-income economies, middle-income economies and high-income economies, industrial market economies and non-market economies (World Bank (WB)). Alternatively, developed market economies are distinguished from developing countries and centrally planned economies (*World Economic Survey*, 1999).

At the same time the notion of development is an essentially contested conception (Sen, 1988, 1999). It has been argued that the concept of development is a value-loaded notion, expressing Western preconceptions about basic values in social life. It presupposes or requires that the non-Western world adheres to a similar culture to that of the advanced economies, giving priority to economic growth and its derivatives. Moreover, it has also been claimed that there could be no general concept of development as the country-specific patterns of evolution are simply too diverse (Meier, 1984).

The concept of development occurs in several disciplines. Thus one talks about individual, attitudinal, cultural, group, organizational, social, community, urban, global and model development. It must by no means to be taken for granted that 'development' in these contexts has the same meaning (Riggs, 1984: 132–3). Sometimes the word is employed in relation to improvements (land, capital), sometimes to activities (plans, projects), sometimes to agents (persons, organizations) or parameters (resources), sometimes to Third World countries (developing countries) or industrialized areas (developed areas), or sometimes in relation to studies (development studies) (Riggs, 131–2). Moreover, the word 'development' may denote a process or a state of affairs – a condition. It is important to keep this distinction in mind when one proceeds to the phenomenon of development in the context that interests us, i.e. the seminal trends of Third World countries. A picture of this distinction between process and condition is reproduced in Figure 3.1.

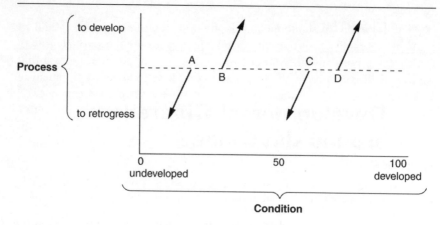

Figure 3.1   Aspects of the concept of development

In social science contexts a number of treatises on development may be found. The purpose of chapters 3–5 is to discuss the major connotations of this word when it is used by economists, sociologists and political scientists in order to research the realities of development. Here we start with economic development.

Economic development

'Economic development' used to be synonymous with 'economic growth' or even 'economic progress' in general (Sen, 1988, 1999). It was measured by the rate of expansion in gross domestic product (GDP) per capita. The difficulty was not the meaning of the term nor how it was to be measured in aggregate national statistics, but how to account for economic development, i.e. to identify the forces that were conducive to a rapid expansion of income per capita. There was sharp disagreement between alternative theories or approaches to economic development – neo-classical, Keyensian, institutionalist, dualist, dependence, neo-liberal schools (Thirlwall, 1983; Todaro, 1985; Bardhan, 1988; Balassa, 1991).

During recent years this solid foundation for the concept of economic development has been eroded, as the development notion has come to be more and more an essentially contested one *per se* (*Handbook of Development Economics I–II*, 1988–89). It has been argued against a simple notion of economic development that 'economic development' refers to more than simply growth in national income per capita. One has to consider broad welfare indicators – the so-called social indicator approach. Moreover, the handy equation, economic development = economic growth, bypasses the distributional problem of how national income is divided among social groups or, in general, how the resources are allocated to various collective or individual purposes. Finally, it is argued that the implicit value bias in economic development as economic growth should be brought out explicitly as one cannot take for granted that economic growth is something positive under all circumstances. It may even be the case that what is labelled economic development is conducive to underdevelopment of a country within the confines of a world capitalist system (Streeten, 1972; Toye, 1987; Chenery and Srinivasan, 1988, 1989; Sen, 1988; Syrquin, 1988).

It is easy to find references to economic development where this is regarded as the key to human progress. Look at the following statements about development:

> (1) [it] ... implies more than just a rise in real national income; that it must be a sustained, secular rise in real income accompanied by changes in social attitudes and customs which have in the past impeded economic advance. But at this point agreement on what constitutes development would probably end. (Thirlwall, 1983: 22)

> (2) [it is] ... a multidimensional process involving major changes in social structures, popular attitudes, and national institutions, as well as the acceleration of economic growth, the reduction of inequality, and the eradication of absolute poverty. (Todaro, 1985: 85)

What can be done here is to make a few distinctions that are relevant to measuring economic development. It seems important to separate the following: (i) level or rate of growth in GDP total or per capita; (ii) level or rate of change in a set of social indicators measuring individual well-being on an average; (iii) the distribution of income or wealth and measures of skewedness in relation to these. We then approach economic development as two hypotheses, namely whether higher levels of national income per capita mean greater welfare as well as a more equal distribution of incomes. The traditional approach to economic development bypasses the simple fact that a larger GDP may be spent on purposes other than the reduction of poverty – such as defence, national symbols or conspicuous consumption. Such an approach to the development concept implies a broadening of the perspective from economic indicators to social indices. However, it seems to be a good strategy to associate the analysis of economic development with established growth theory. As Thirlwall emphasizes, it is possible to conceive of economic growth without economic development taking place at the same time, but it is hardly conceivable that there may be a process of economic development without a basis in sustained economic growth. Let us begin by discussing the country differences in affluence and economic growth.

The 'gap' model: country differences in affluence

Below we present an overview of the differences in economic output between major countries in the world by taking up one well-known development theory (Lal, 1983; Jones and Kenen, 1984; Chenery and Srinivasan, 1988). The so-called gap theory figures prominently in the interpretation of development data (Thirlwall, 1983, 4th edition, 1986). The hypothesis states that the income differences between a set of rich countries and a set of poor countries are tremendous and tend to increase over time. The hypothesis is pessimistic about development as it predicts that the between-country differences in affluence will increase. We will question whether the gap theory is confirmed when a large number of countries, rich as well as poor, are included in the analysis of development data.

It is often stated that the income gap between rich and poor countries is increasing and that there is a north–south divide hidden behind these sets of countries (Brandt Report, 1980). This trend, if true, is certainly a cause of concern since it would counteract important ambitions behind the development ideology as interpreted by the United Nations. The quest for development has no doubt dominated much of the politics in several Third World countries and it has inspired the United Nations to initiate its programmes for developmental decades and its call for a new international economic order.

We will look into how valid these statements are to the effect that the so-called developing countries are not only not catching up but are also lagging behind even more than before – the *gap theory*. The set of developing countries is not a homogeneous one, which implies that we need to look at the variation in levels and rates of development not only between rich and poor countries but also within different sets of so-called less developed countries or LDCs (Syrquin, 1988). There may also exist a variation within the set of rich countries that needs to be pinpointed as this set covers not only the rich market economies but also what may be called the then communist systems in the northern hemisphere (now CEE and CIS), i.e. excluding mainland China. The use of the concept of newly industrializing countries – the NICs – seems to imply that the identification of rich and poor countries may change over time. In order to pinpoint the issue it is necessary to consider how the concept of development is to be measured.

We make a broad enquiry into the country differences in economic output after the Second World War in order to test whether the gap theory is true or not. The gap theory needs to be tested in a close examination of data because it is often reiterated in several contexts, both academic and practical. The gap theory corresponds probably to the standard image of the economic gulf between the occidental countries and the rest of the world. However, we wish to show that it is not based upon a correct assessment of how the country differences in affluence have developed over the years. It fails to realize how heterogeneous the Third World is.

First, the gap theory implies that there was a sharp gulf in economic affluence between a set of rich countries and another set of poor countries at the end of the Second World War. Second, the gap theory suggests that this gap has increased during the entire post-war period, not only during the 1950s and the 1960s but also during the 1970s and the 1980s through the 1990s. Third, the gap theory claims that this unbridgeable gulf coincides roughly with a major geographical separation between the northern and southern parts of the hemisphere. Fourth, the gap theory predicts that the income differences within the sets of rich countries and the sets of poor countries are less than the differences between these sets.

The Summers and Heston data series allow us to evaluate these implications of the gap theory by taking a close look at the variation in levels of overall economic well-being between and within sets of countries from 1950 to 1998. An analysis of the growth differentials in real GDP per capita complements the study of levels of average GDP per capita. The differences between sets of countries may be as important as the variation in real GDP per capita income within these sets of countries – see the eta-squared statistics. The coefficient of variation (CV) may be employed to indicate the within-group differences where a CV score of more than roughly 0.50 may be said to indicate a substantial variation.

Indicators and data

GDP measures the total final output of goods and services produced by an economy by residents and non-residents regardless of the allocation to domestic and foreign claims. It is calculated without making deductions for depreciation. Let us start from this rather simple but helpful indicator, turning to more complex measures of well-being later on. This statistic – GDP per capita – may be employed to measure the level of economic affluence. It is an open question whether other indicators on social welfare co-vary considerably with the GDP per capita indicator. The GDP per capita indicator displays problems concerning both validity and reliability. In terms of indicator validity, GDP per capita measures are sensitive to the size of the money economy, the price level and the currency exchange rate. With regard to reliability, the national income accounts of various countries have been estimated with different procedures, which affects the comparability of the information (Kuznets, 1965, 1966, 1968; Streeten, 1972; Little, 1982).

The raw data about GDP rendered by various countries have to be examined and recalculated in order to remove a number of errors and make the data series comparable between nations. When a GDP per capita index is constructed from such a cautious procedure, it is possible for the GDP per capita indicator to be used to arrive at a crude but informative picture of economic differences between various countries.

First we have employed one standardized series – real GDP per capita in international prices relative to the US dollar – compiled by Summers and Heston (1994). The data series give annually, in addition to population and exchange rates, real product and price level estimates for four different national income concepts estimated for some 130 countries from 1950 to 1992. A second data set that we will employ covers similar data and basically the twentieth century and has been compiled by Maddison (1995).

Another data set covers the most recent years and employs data from the WB (entitled *World Development Indicators* – CD-ROM) (WB, 2000a), covering at most some 150 countries, and also containing some slightly different income concepts, namely purchasing power parities (PPP). It would strengthen the argument put forward below if the overall tendency was the same in any two data series that measure affluence in different ways.

When mapping the cross-country variation we will employ a set of seven macro regions of the world, which takes account of geographical as well as developmental aspects. The seven macro regions that we have identified are: the occidental countries, the former communist countries in Central and Eastern Europe as well as in the Commonwealth of States, i.e. CEE and CIS, countries in Central and Latin America, countries being part of Sub-Saharan Africa, countries forming the Arab World, countries in South Asia as well as those in South East Asia.

Economic development since 1900

Let us start with economic development from the early stages of the twentieth century. Maddison (1995) presents a longtime series for a sample of countries. Table 3.1 maps the rise in the level of GDP/capita from 1900 up to the 1990s. On an average we may note that the GDP/capita has increased almost 4.5 times from 1900 to 1992, according to the estimates made by Maddison.

Although the average income in the rich occidental countries increased considerably during the roughly 20 years from 1970 to 1990 covered in Table 3.1, one also observes the sharp rise in affluence among Asian countries, amounting to almost a tripling. The data indicates a decline in the former communist countries (CEE and CIS) after the system transition as well as a serious stagnation for Latin America and Africa.

Table 3.1   Real GDP per capita 1900–92 (international US dollar)

Region	1900		1913		1970		1980		1992	
	Value	*N*	*Value*	*N*	*Value*	*N*	*Value*	*N*	*Value*	*N*
Occidental	2957	19	3497	20	10544	20	13407	20	16226	20
CEE and CIS	1543	3	1641	5	4681	7	6070	7	4626	7
Central and Latin America	133	7	1733	7	5299	7	6128	7	5949	7
Sub-Saharan Africa	462	1	1049	2	1271	8	1360	8	1131	8
Arab World	509	1	743	2	1714	3	2269	3	2892	3
South Asia	634	4	661	4	772	4	851	4	1114	4
South East Asia	855	7	992	7	2863	7	4438	7	7682	7
Average/total	1892	42	2201	47	5699	56	7244	56	8473	56
Eta-squared	0.668		0.624		0.760		0.816		0.816	
Significance	0.000		0.000		0.000		0.000		0.000	

Source: Maddison (1995)

Table 3.2 GDP/capita in 1950 and 1960 (international US dollar)

Region	1950		1960	
	Value	*N*	*Value*	*N*
Occidental	4516	22	5861	23
CEE and CIS	–	0	1588	4
Central and Latin America	1922	19	2318	21
Sub-Saharan Africa	1054	7	877	36
Arab World	879	3	1906	10
South Asia	619	4	759	6
South East Asia	1021	3	1359	11
Average/total	2611	58	2342	111
Eta-squared	0.549		0.688	
Significance	0.000		0.000	

Source: Summers and Heston (1994)

Around 1900–13, we find the following among the richest countries of the world: the UK, Australia and New Zealand as well as Argentina, but these countries have not been able to maintain this position, as the 1992 data shows, especially the decline of Argentina. Rich countries do not necessarily maintain their edge and poor countries can close the gap.

Allowing for all the objections to the use of a GDP per capita indicator on the average economic affluence in a country, we may establish that this measure really indicates profound between- and within-country set differences. Here we will rely on the estimates made by Summers and Heston (1994) in order to make a detailed analysis of post-war developments. We will start with the year 1950 and look at national averages between the different sets of countries as well as the variation within these sets themselves (see Table 3.2).

The average income per capita in the set of occidental countries amounted to $4516 which was double that of the average income in Latin America. No figure is available for the average income in the then communist systems, but one may estimate it at a lower level than that of Latin America, given the devastating effects of the Second World War. The average economic affluence would, according to these data, be higher in Africa than Asia, which partly reflects the small number of countries covered around 1950. However, we must note the substantial variation within the occidental set. In the USA which fought in the war mainly outside its borders, the average income was about seven times (8772) higher than that of Portugal (1208).

Around 1950 the level of affluence in the occidental countries was clearly higher than in the Third World. This is true in relation to the average income scores for Sub-Saharan African countries (1054) and South Asian countries (619) as well as South East Asian countries (1021). But the set of Latin American countries that also did not have to fight a war within their borders constitute an exception, as the average for the occidental countries is only double that of Latin America whereas it is four times that of Africa and seven times that of South Asia.

Not only is the Latin American mean real GDP per capita of $1922 substantially higher than most other Third World countries, but the maximum score in Venezuela (4799) surpasses the country scores for several occidental countries. Had one looked only at the data for 1950, it is far from obvious that the gap interpretation had been proposed at all. Considering the GDP per capita income in Argentina (4032) and Uruguay (3451), it remains a fact that Latin America does not fit the simple classification: rich versus poor or north versus south.

Thus, in 1950 the average income of the occidental countries was about five times higher than that of African and Asian countries but only roughly twice as high as that of Latin American countries. In order to indicate somewhat more extensively the country differences at the beginning of a long period of overall economic growth and of staggering expansion in world trade, we will look at the variation within these six sets of countries (see Table 3.3).

The gap theory is based on a hypothesis about a north–south divide in the separation between rich and poor countries. Yet we see from Table 3.3 that geographical situation does not coincide with the division into rich and poor countries. Australia (6678) and New Zealand (6667) were among the most well-off countries in 1950, second only to the USA and Switzerland (6813). In addition, there was a rather sharp north–south division within rich Western Europe, as Italy, Greece and Spain scored lower than Venezuela, Uruguay and Trinidad. In fact, both Greece and Portugal were more close to the average values for the Third World than for the occidental set.

As we turn to country data for the developing nations a lot of variation is to be expected since we know that the countries in the Third World have walked along different paths of economic development since 1850 (Reynolds, 1985). Table 3.3 indicates that the country variation within the five subsets of developing nations was larger than within the subset of rich countries. Although not very many countries in Asia, Africa and Latin America can be compared at this time due to problems with reliable data, what is most striking is not the general poverty in the Third World but the substantial variation. There was in the 1950s a clear and large gulf between Latin America and the other parts of the Third World, which hardly fits in with the gap theory. Clearly, it must be misleading to designate Mexico (2198), India (590) and Ethiopia (221) all as underdeveloped countries, as if they were of one kind or on a similar level.

The country differences between the set of African and Asian countries were not pronounced in 1950. Burma-Myanmar (228), Pakistan (602) and the Philippines (778) had a low GDP per capita as had Nigeria (456), Kenya (590) and Egypt (751). There were extremely poor countries in Africa: Congo-Kinshasa (332) and Uganda (543). Mauritius (3295) and Sri Lanka (1058) did better. Had information about more countries been available this

Table 3.3 GDP/capita in 1950 (international US dollar)

Occidental		Central and Latin America		Africa	
USA	8772	Venezuela	4799	Mauritius	3295
Switzerland	6813	Argentina	4032	South Africa	1941
Australia	6678	Uruguay	3451	Kenya	590
New Zealand	6667	Trinidad and Tobago	3046	Uganda	543
Luxembourg	6534	Chile	2431	Nigeria	456
Canada	6380	Mexico	2198	Congo-Kinshasa	332
Sweden	5807	Guatemala	1532	Ethiopia	221
UK	5395	Peru	1504		
Denmark	5263	Colombia	1503	*Arab World*	
The Netherlands	4532	Costa Rica	1457	Turkey	1065
Belgium	4433	Panama	1309	Morocco	821
Norway	4358	Bolivia	1274	Egypt	751
France	4045	Brazil	1265		
Iceland	3808	Paraguay	1253	*South Asia*	
Finland	3506	El Salvador	1206	Sri Lanka	1058
Germany	3421	Ecuador	1194	Pakistan	602
Austria	2930	Nicaragua	1152	India	590
Italy	2743	Honduras	981	Burma-Myanmar	228
Ireland	2730	Dominican Republic	949		
Spain	1913			*South East Asia*	
Greece	1409			Japan	1430
Portugal	1208			Thailand	857
				Philippines	778

Source: Summers and Heston (1994)

gloomy picture of Africa may well have been more pronounced. In order to find out whether these country differences are stable or change as the gap theory predicts, we compare the 1950 data with similar information for 1960.

The overall developments of the 1950s corroborate the gap theory in so far as the distance between the occidental countries and the sets of Third World countries increased. The gap model is only true of how average per capita income developed in the Occidental on the one hand and in Latin America and Africa on the other hand. As the world economy entered a long period of staggering growth in output and trade, the mean average income in African countries actually did not increase between 1950 and 1960 whereas that of the set of Latin American countries increased slowly. The beginnings of the economic expansion in Asia are already apparent in the 1960 figures.

The differences between the 1950 and 1960 data may partly reflect the simple fact that we cover more countries in 1960. Thus, when the then communist countries (CEE and CIS) are included, then we see that the difference between them and the occidental amounts to a factor of roughly 3.5. Although we find in the data for 1960 (taken from Summers and Heston

(1994) again) signs that indicate the gap theory, not all the facts confirm the gap theory. During the 1950s all the so-called rich countries benefited from high levels of economic activity. The increase in GDP per capita in Japan was a high 100 per cent in this decade, but other rich countries also expanded their national income rapidly: the FRG, Spain, Portugal and Italy. Several countries in Asia hardly increased their average income per capita at all during the 1950s, mainly as a result of sharp increases in population. Some Asian countries faced a severe poverty problem around 1960, although it is somewhat arbitrary to identify a poverty line: China (567), Indonesia (638) and Pakistan (638) per capita – all nations with tremendous populations. However, in the set of Asian countries there were also some examples of an average GDP per capita higher than the minimum value in the occidental set: Iran (2946), Iraq (3427), Saudi Arabia (3884) and Hong Kong (2247).

Already in 1960 Africa was different from Asia and Latin America as dismal poverty was much more prevalent. The set of African countries really constituted a special Third World set of countries where the average income tended to be always below that of the mean income in the other two sets of Third World countries. The standard predicament in Africa was one of extreme poverty: take for example Malawi (380), Rwanda (537), Mali (535), Congo-Kinshasa (489) and Niger (532). Only in the Northern countries and in the Portuguese colonies was there a more decent level of income: Algeria (1723), Tunisia (1101) as well as Angola (931) and Mozambique (1153). Gabon (1789), South Africa (2191) and Madagascar (1191) scored much higher than Tanzania (319) and Togo (367).

In relation to the 1950 and 1960 data the gap theory fails to recognize the large difference between Africa and Latin America. Some countries in Latin America did fairly well around 1960 even when compared not only with communist systems but also with some occidental nations. High average income scores were to found in Venezuela (6338) and in Uruguay (3968) as well as in Argentina (4462), Chile (2885) and Mexico (2836) – far above the minimum value for the occidental set.

The 1960s were again a decade with strong expansion in the world economy and several countries achieved high yearly growth rates in their economies. Yearly growth rates of about 3–4 per cent were not uncommon and some countries accomplished even more. What was the impact of a decade of high levels of economic activity on the global income distribution between countries? Does the gap theory prediction of larger differentials between the rich countries and the Third World hold true? What can we see from examining Table 3.4?

The gap theory prediction of a widening gap between the rich and the poor countries only partly fits the data from around 1970. The decade of strong economic growth around the world benefited some countries more than others. The occidental nations and the communist systems except China considerably increased the income gap to Latin America as well as

Table 3.4   GDP/capita in 1970 and 1980 (international US dollar)

Region	1970		1980	
	Value	*N*	*Value*	*N*
Occidental	8412	23	10735	23
CEE and CIS	2835	6	4310	7
Central and Latin America	2951	21	3757	21
Sub-Saharan Africa	1075	37	1220	37
Arab World	2851	13	6980	15
South Asia	907	6	1018	6
South East Asia	2462	11	4116	11
Average/total	3263	117	4643	120
Eta-squared	0.716		0.500	
Significance	0.000		0.000	

Source: Summers and Heston (1994)

Africa. The already dismal development in Africa continued, especially Sub-Saharan Africa, whereas several countries did well in Northern Africa or in the Arab World. The economic advances in South East Asia in particular are clearly apparent in the data (see Table 3.5).

As we see, the gap theory is not validated due to the developments in a few Asian countries, the so-called baby tigers of Singapore (3017), South Korea (1680) and Taiwan (2188). These countries entered what Rustow referred to as the take-off stage in the 1950s which resulted in growth rates that bridged the gap to the affluent world (Rustow, 1991). Perhaps also Japan should be included among these aggressive new industrializing countries as the average income per capita in Japan grew from 2954 US dollars in 1960 to a staggering 7307 US dollars in 1970. A number of the then communist countries had incomes far above the minimum value of the occidental set: Russia (4088), the GDR (4825) and Hungary (3358).

How does the mixed picture of 1970 compare with data for 1980 which indicate how the gap theory fared when the world economy went into a sustained period of recession? The recession in the world economy in connection with the oil crises did not break the pattern that emerges when data about levels of average income per capita are compared since 1950. The increase in the mean value for the Occidental, the communist systems and the Asian countries continued during the 1970s whereas the average scores for Latin America and Africa changed little.

The trends of the early 1980s implied a break with the seminal tendencies from 1950 to 1980. Several countries suffered real setbacks in their average GDP per capita income, in particular Latin America and Africa but also the communist systems. And the variation within all the five sets of countries increased, suggesting that the setback in the world economy hit countries differently. The development pace among the Asian countries was far higher than that of the Latin American countries and that of African countries.

Table 3.5   GDP per capita in 1970 (international US dollar)

Occidental		Central and Latin America		Sub-Saharan Africa	
USA	12963	Venezuela	7753	Gabon	3704
Switzerland	12942	Trinidad and Tobago	6795	South Africa	3254
Sweden	10766	Argentina	5637	Namibia	2642
Australia	10756	Uruguay	4121	Mauritius	2398
Canada	10124	Mexico	3987	Congo, Brazzaville	1670
Luxembourg	9782	Chile	3605	Côte d'Ivoire	1615
Denmark	9670	Costa Rica	2904	Mozambique	1497
Germany	9425	Peru	2736	Sierra Leone	1435
New Zealand	9392	Jamaica	2645	Angola	1165
France	9200	Panama	2584	Madagascar	1146
The Netherlands	9199	Brazil	2434	Senegal	1146
UK	8537	Nicaragua	2359	Benin	1118
Belgium	8331	Colombia	2140	Zambia	1117
Finland	8108	Guatemala	2028	Zimbabwe	1082
Norway	8034	El Salvador	1810	Ghana	1059
Italy	7568	Ecuador	1789	Liberia	982
Austria	7510	Bolivia	1661	Somalia	921
Iceland	6772	Dominican Republic	1536	Mauritania	872
Israel	6004	Paraguay	1394	Botswana	823
Spain	5861	Honduras	1237	Niger	805
Ireland	5015	Haiti	834	Cameroon	804
Greece	4224			Nigeria	767
Portugal	3306	*Arab World*		Central African Republic	747
		Saudi Arabia	7838	Congo-Kinshasa	686
CEE and CIS		Oman	6633	Chad	660
Russia	4088	Iran	4796	Rwanda	647
Hungary	3358	Iraq	4409	Uganda	647
Yugoslavia	3297	Syria	2294	Togo	618
Poland	2941	Turkey	2202	Kenya	586
Czech Republic	2520	Algeria	1826	Guinea	467
Romania	809	Tunisia	1442	Malawi	440
		Jordan	1422	Tanzania	424
		Morocco	1342	Mali	419
		Egypt	1163	Lesotho	419
		Yemen	879	Burkina Faso	374
		Sudan	817	Burundi	341
				Ethiopia	296
		South Asia			
		Bangladesh	1280	*South East Asia*	
		Sri Lanka	1243	Japan	7307
		Pakistan	1029	Hong Kong	4502
		India	802	Singapore	3017
		Nepal	670	Taiwan	2188
		Burma-Myanmar	418	Malaysia	2154
				Papua New Guinea	1896
				South Korea	1680
				Thailand	1526
				Philippines	1403
				Indonesia	715
				China	696

Source: Summers and Heston (1994)

The gulf between the rich world and the world of LDCs increased with regard to Africa and Latin America but not in relation to Asia.

One can see that the 1980s were a lost decade for both the communist countries and many Third World countries, especially in Latin America and Africa. The basic implication is a widening gulf between the rich sets of countries or the north and the sets of Third World countries or the south holds only with regard to the comparison between the occidental countries on the one hand and countries in Africa and Latin America on the other. Up until 1980 the occidental countries did not outdistance the planned economies. When later data has become available, then the decline of the command economies has become apparent. Poland's decline from 4419 US dollars per capita in 1980 to 3826 US dollars in 1992 was not a single phenomenon among the East European economies during the 1980s, the setbacks were showing up in a striking manner by 1990. It is not, however, generally true in relation to all parts of the Third World.

Among the occidental countries there is a sort of north–south division as the northern parts had a higher level of economic affluence than the southern parts with the exception of the UK and Ireland. Japan (15105) had by 1992 passed Australia (14458) and New Zealand (11363) in spite of the fact that in 1950 the gap was quite large as Australia and New Zealand had a per capita income four times higher than that of Japan (1430). Had Japan been classified as a Third World country, then there would have been one major exception to the gap theory. The economic development among African countries has been negative since 1970. The average income among the African countries included in this analysis stood almost still between 1980 and 1992. The variation is immense on the African continent from Mauritius (6167) to Central Africa (514) and Burkina Faso (514), the northern and southern parts doing better than the central parts. The trend was the same among the Latin American countries where an average income per capita hardly changed between 1980 and 1992. The shift to a lower level of economic activity in the world economy in the 1980s hit some parts of the Third World more harshly than other parts however.

What invalidates the gap theory is the continued strong increase in real GDP per capita in several Asian countries. Even when the world economy went into slump the average income per capita among the set of Asian countries grew, from 2479 US dollars in 1970 to 4690 US dollars in 1992. Whereas in 1950 the average income per capita was six times larger in the set of occidental countries than among the set of Asian countries, the same gap had narrowed down to a 3:1 ratio in 1990. The sharp advance of this part of the Third World was not, however, evenly distributed within that set.

In the set of Asian countries we note the so-called NICs and NECs: Singapore (12653), Taiwan (3942), Malaysia (5746) and Hong Kong (16471). How precarious it is to generalize about a development pattern in the Third World appears evident from a comparison with these aggressive growth nations and the more populous countries. Thirty years of

Table 3.6   GNP/capita 1998

Region	PPPW 1998		GNPC 1998	
	Value	N	Value	N
Occidental	21791	23	24106	23
CEE and CIS	5508	24	2309	24
Central and Latin America	5079	21	2813	21
Sub-Saharan Africa	1869	34	755	35
Arab World	5272	13	3233	13
South Asia	1780	6	458	6
South East Asia	8116	14	7517	14
Average/total	7381	135	6216	143
Eta-squared	0.721		0.704	
Significance	0.000		0.000	

Sources: PPPW 1998 and GNPC 1998 (*World Bank Atlas*, 2000)

development in India (1282), Pakistan (1432) and the Philippines (1689) have enabled these countries to increase their living standards only marginally in excess of the income implication of the strong population growth. The gap theory fails to take into account the tremendous income differences within the Asian part of the Third World.

The same objection to the gap theory may be made with regard to the set of Latin American countries and the set of African countries. It is true that there was little progress between 1960 and 1992 in countries like Zaire, Zambia and Nigeria as well as in Argentina, Venezuela and Uruguay. But on the other hand there are countries with exceptional economic progress in the same sets of countries: Tunisia and Botswana in Africa as well as Brazil and Chile in Latin America. The country differences in development pace are most substantial in the Third World. As a matter of fact, they are so large that the general notion of a set of rich countries becoming richer than a set of poor countries is more confusing than clarifying. This is especially true as long as it has the connotation of the north versus the south or the Occidental and the then communist countries versus the Third World generally.

Table 3.6 contains data for the late 1990s. The data comes from the *World Bank Atlas* of 2000 and measures GNP/capita in two ways. One measure (PPPW 1998) takes into account differences in purchasing power parities, while the other one (GNPC 1998) measures GNP/capita in current US$, according to what is called the Atlas method.

Although the numbers differ for the two measures the cross-country variation is very much the same, as is indicated by the fact that the correlation coefficient for the 135 countries where data is available is r = 0.97. At the same time there is a huge difference for the ratio between the richest set (the occidental one) and the poorest one (South Asia) going from 12.2 for PPPW 1998 to 52.6 for GNPC 1998. Let us therefore take a closer look at the variation within the seven sets of countries using the PPPW 1998 measure as displayed in Table 3.7.

Table 3.7 presents a picture of today's differences between the countries of the world in terms of affluence. First, there is an immense difference between the very rich countries and the extremely poor ones. Second, some Third World countries have managed well to close the gap to the First World. Third, most of the countries of the world are placed in between the very rich and the very poor. However, within this intermediate set the variation is quite substantial.

Let us finally enquire into how the variation in the level of GNP/GDP/ capita within these sets of countries has developed during the post-world war era. To capture this variation we employ the CV measure, which indicates the amount of variation within a certain data set. The higher the value of the CV measure the more of variation within the set. Table 3.8 has the relevant information.

Looking first at the total set of countries we may note that the CV measure is slightly higher during the later period than during the earlier period, although the changes are quite small. We may also note that the within set variation is lowest in the richest and the poorest sets of countries, the occidental one and the South Asian one, while the highest within set variation is to be found in Sub-Saharan Africa (poor set) and in South East Asia (going rich set).

Economic growth

An analysis of average growth rates in the economy may complement the focus above on country differences in levels of affluence. Various indicators may measure the pace of economic development. We will employ the real GDP per capita measures collected by Summers and Heston and calculate average growth rates for the sets of countries specified above for various time periods. It should be pointed out that using GDP per capita data for measuring economic growth means that we take the population change directly into account. A country may have a strong increase in total production, yet show little economic growth due to strong population increase.

The gap theory implies a definitive country pattern with regard to average growth rates. The yearly growth rates of the economy of a country may hover due to short-term factors. However, here we focus on seminal growth trends over long time periods. If it were true that the overall income differences between the sets of rich countries on the one hand and the sets of Third World countries on the other were increasing over time, then there would be higher average growth rates in the economies of the rich countries than in the economies of the Third World countries. Is this true? Let us look at Table 3.9 with GNP/capita growth data. GNP measures the total domestic and foreign output claimed by residents. It comprises GDP plus

Table 3.7   GNP/capita 1998: PPPW 1998

Occidental		CEE and CIS		Africa	
Luxembourg	36703	Slovenia	14400	South Africa	8296
USA	29240	Czech Republic	12197	Mauritius	8236
Switzerland	26876	Hungary	9832	Botswana	5796
Norway	26196	Slovakia	9624	Gabon	5615
Iceland	24774	Estonia	7563	Namibia	5280
Denmark	23855	Poland	7543	Zimbabwe	2489
Belgium	23622	Croatia	6698	Lesotho	2194
Austria	23145	Belarus	6314	Ghana	1735
Canada	22814	Lithuania	6283	Guinea	1722
The Netherlands	22325	Russia	6180	Mauritania	1500
Germany	22026	Latvia	5777	Côte d'Ivoire	1484
Australia	21795	Romania	5572	Cameroon	1395
France	21214	Bulgaria	4683	Togo	1352
Finland	20641	Kazakhstan	4317	Senegal	1297
Italy	20365	Macedonia	4224	Central African Republic	1098
UK	20314	Georgia	3429	Uganda	1072
Sweden	19848	Ukraine	3130	Angola	999
Ireland	17991	Albania	2864	Kenya	964
Israel	16861	Kyrgyzstan	2247	Burkina Faso	866
New Zealand	16084	Azerbaijan	2168	Benin	857
Spain	15960	Armenia	2074	Congo, Brazzaville	846
Portugal	14569	Uzbekistan	2044	Chad	843
Greece	13994	Moldova	1995	Madagascar	741
		Tajikistan	1041	Nigeria	740
Central and Latin America				Mozambique	740
Argentina	11728	*Arab World*		Congo-Kinshasa	733
Uruguay	8541	United Arab Emirates	18870	Niger	729
Chile	8507	Saudi Arabia	10498	Zambia	678
Mexico	7450	Turkey	6594	Mali	673
Trinidad and Tobago	7208	Tunisia	5169	Ethiopia	566
Brazil	6460	Iran	5121	Burundi	561
Colombia	5861	Algeria	4595	Malawi	551
Costa Rica	5812	Lebanon	4144	Tanzania	483
Venezuela	5706	Morocco	3188	Sierra Leone	445
Panama	4925	Egypt	3146		
Dominican Republic	4337	Syria	2702	*South East Asia*	
Paraguay	4312	Jordan	2615	Singapore	25295
Peru	4180	Sudan	1240	Japan	23592
El Salvador	4008	Yemen	658	Hong Kong	20763
Guatemala	3474			South Korea	13286
Jamaica	3344	*South Asia*		Malaysia	7699
Ecuador	3003	Sri Lanka	2945	Thailand	5524
Honduras	2338	India	2060	Philippines	3725
Bolivia	2205	Pakistan	1652	China	3051
Nicaragua	1896	Bhutan	1438	Indonesia	2407
Haiti	1379	Bangladesh	1407	Papua New Guinea	2205
		Nepal	1181	Vietnam	1689
				Laos	1683
				Mongolia	1463
				Cambodia	1246

Source: See Table 3.6 for source

Table 3.8 Variation within and between the regions: CV measures

Regions	Summer and Heston data					World Bank data: PPP					
	1950	1960	1970	1980	1990	1975	1980	1985	1990	1995	1998
Occidental	0.439	0.367	0.293	0.243	0.226	0.234	0.240	0.264	0.258	0.241	0.233
CEE and CIS	–	0.527	0.395	0.356	0.203	0.191	0.324	0.353	0.382	0.612	0.621
Central and Latin America	0.582	0.659	0.618	0.639	0.521	0.431	0.460	0.433	0.430	0.473	0.509
Sub-Saharan Africa	1.085	0.627	0.729	0.831	0.957	1.143	1.034	1.000	1.050	1.134	1.140
Arab World	0.187	0.583	0.812	1.240	0.363	1.487	1.501	1.193	1.166	1.006	0.909
South Asia	0.548	0.423	0.373	0.364	0.246	0.258	0.348	0.357	0.311	0.338	0.361
South East Asia	0.348	0.522	0.784	0.763	0.887	0.886	0.880	1.008	1.110	1.073	1.088
Average	0.805	0.971	0.971	1.069	0.986	1.039	1.044	1.022	1.037	1.090	1.090

Sources: Summers and Heston (1994), World Bank (WB) (2000a)

net factor income from abroad, and it also takes population growth into account.

Economic growth from one year to another reflects a number of temporary factors, which increase or decrease the pace of economic development. Of interest here is the average growth rates over longer periods of time, i.e. the speed of economic expansion when the yearly economic fluctuations have been taken into account. Countries differ considerably in terms of average growth rates, but are the variations in accordance with the prediction of the gap theory?

The mean average growth rates between 1961 and 1973 differ among the seven sets of countries. It is true that the mean average growth rates in the sets of occidental countries and the then communist countries are higher than that of the set of Latin American countries or that of the African countries – as the gap theory implies. However, the mean average growth

Table 3.9 Average yearly growth rates in GNP/capita

Region	1961–73		1973–90		1990–98	
	Value	N	Value	N	Value	N
Occidental	4.1	22	2.1	22	1.8	22
CEE and CIS	6.4	1	2.7	3	−4.2	17
Central and Latin America	2.6	18	0.5	20	1.9	21
Sub-Saharan Africa	2.0	24	0.4	28	−0.2	35
Arab World	2.8	5	1.4	10	1.8	12
South Asia	1.0	4	2.4	5	2.9	7
South East Asia	4.9	10	4.3	10	3.3	14
Average/total	3.1	84	1.5	98	0.7	128
Eta-squared	0.244		0.300		0.460	
Significance	0.001		0.000		0.000	

Source: WB (2000a)

rate among the South East Asian countries is higher than that of the occidental countries, which is exactly where the gap theory falters.

Developing countries are not of one kind as there was one single average growth rate for all Third World countries. On the contrary, there are considerable differences in economic growth over time within all seven sets of countries. Let us look at the country variation within the so-called set of poor countries with regard to 1973 and 1990 when the world economy in general did not develop as it did in the 1960s (Table 3.10).

Table 3.10   Percentage increase in GNP/capita 1973–90

Occidental		Central and Latin America		Sub-Saharan Africa	
Luxembourg	3.91	Trinidad and Tobago	3.59	Botswana	9.23
Norway	2.89	Paraguay	2.98	Mauritius	4.75
Portugal	2.83	Ecuador	1.99	Lesotho	4.11
Iceland	2.75	Colombia	1.81	Cameroon	2.83
Italy	2.65	Brazil	1.75	Burundi	1.84
Finland	2.63	Mexico	1.51	Congo, Brazzaville	1.78
Austria	2.53	Dominican Republic	1.39	Gabon	1.17
Ireland	2.52	Chile	1.21	Rwanda	0.96
Spain	2.24	Uruguay	1.11	Burkina Faso	0.93
Belgium	2.18	Costa Rica	0.87	Kenya	0.85
France	2.07	Honduras	0.40	Malawi	0.16
UK	2.02	Guatemala	0.38	South Africa	0.11
Greece	1.90	Panama	0.02	Mali	−0.05
Canada	1.88	Haiti	−0.12	Zimbabwe	−0.13
Netherlands	1.76	Venezuela Republic	−0.97	Togo	−0.17
Denmark	1.61	Argentina	−1.00	Nigeria	−0.24
United States	1.60	El Salvador	−1.05	Chad	−0.24
Israel	1.58	Peru	−1.47	Benin	−0.25
Sweden	1.56	Jamaica	−1.74	Senegal	−0.46
Australia	1.35	Nicaragua	−3.51	Mauritania	−0.58
Switzerland	1.25			Central African Republic	−1.06
New Zealand	0.43	*South East Asia*		Sierra Leone	−1.09
		Korea, Republic	7.05	Ghana	−1.36
CEE and CIS		China	6.46	Côte d'Ivoire	−1.52
Latvia	3.33	Hong Kong, China	5.89	Madagascar	−1.95
Hungary	2.52	Singapore	5.73	Zambia	−2.07
Georgia	2.23	Thailand	5.34	Niger	−2.28
		Indonesia	4.74	Congo-Kinshasa	−2.93
South Asia		Malaysia	4.03		
Sri Lanka	3.24	Japan	3.22	*Arab World*	
Pakistan	2.94	Philippines	1.15	Oman	4.95
India	2.59	Papua New Guinea	−0.72	Egypt, Arab Republic	4.19
Bangladesh	2.24			Morocco	2.19
Nepal	1.14			Tunisia	2.11
				Turkey	1.96
				Syrian Arab Republic	1.45
				Algeria	0.89
				Sudan	0.04
				Saudi Arabia	−0.56
				Kuwait	−3.57

Source: WB (2000a)

Table 3.11 Percentage increase in GNP/capita 1990–98

Occidental		Central and Latin America		Sub-Saharan Africa	
Ireland	6.46	Chile	6.32	Mauritius	4.24
Norway	3.2	Argentina	4.07	Uganda	3.72
Portugal	2.71	Uruguay	3.44	Mozambique	3.59
Denmark	2.34	Panama	3.3	Botswana	2.31
Netherlands	2.25	El Salvador	3.06	Guinea	2.05
Israel	2.21	Peru	2.84	Benin	1.65
Australia	2.15	Costa Rica	2.41	Malawi	1.6
Luxembourg	2.02	Trinidad and Tobago	2.32	Namibia	1.46
Spain	2.00	Dominican Republic	2.16	Ghana	1.44
Austria	1.81	Nicaragua	2.02	Burkina Faso	1.17
Belgium	1.77	Colombia	1.6	Ethiopia	1.07
USA	1.60	Mexico	1.57	Lesotho	0.98
Iceland	1.53	Guatemala	1.56	Nigeria	0.79
UK	1.37	Bolivia	1.55	Tanzania	0.78
Greece	1.32	Venezuela, Republic	1.38	Côte d'Ivoire	0.78
France	1.25	Ecuador	1.15	Senegal	0.76
Finland	1.10	Jamaica	0.81	Mauritania	0.7
Italy	1.06	Honduras	0.72	Mali	0.25
New Zealand	0.80	Brazil	−0.08	Gabon	0.13
Canada	0.63	Paraguay	−0.28	Zimbabwe	0.01
Sweden	0.45	Haiti	−2.86	Kenya	−0.28
Switzerland	0.09			Chad	−0.39
		South Asia		South Africa	−0.61
CEE and CIS		Sri Lanka	3.83	Madagascar	−0.9
Poland	2.86	India	3.76	Central African Republic	−1.05
Slovak Republic	−0.01	Bangladesh	3.38	Togo	−1.14
Hungary	−0.01	Nepal	2.3	Zambia	−1.35
Czech Republic	−1.41	Bhutan	2.2	Congo, Brazza	−1.47
Belarus	−1.86	Pakistan	1.81	Rwanda	−1.55
Estonia	−1.89			Niger	−1.61
Romania	−2.7	*South East Asia*		Cameroon	−2.91
Lithuania	−2.89	China	8.52	Burundi	−3.48
Bulgaria	−3.03	Singapore	6.09	Angola	−5.2
Latvia	−4.06	Vietnam	5.67	Sierra Leone	−6.28
Kyrgyz Republic	−5.14	Korea, Republic	4.66	Congo-Kinshasa	−8.31
Kazakhstan	−5.7	Malaysia	4.33		
Russian Federation	−6.52	Thailand	4.17	*Arab World*	
Ukraine	−9.24	Laos People's Democratic		Lebanon	7.02
Azerbaijan	−9.85	Republic	3.57	Turkey	3.37
Georgia	−9.98	Indonesia	3.21	Tunisia	3.22
Tajikistan	−10.02	Hong Kong, China	2.02	Iran, Islamic Republic	3.06
		Japan	1.56	Sudan	2.83
		Papua New Guinea	1.51	Egypt, Arab Republic	2.55
		Cambodia	1.4	Syrian Arab Republic	1.53
		Philippines	1.04	Morocco	1.19
		Mongolia	−2.07	Jordan	1.04
				Algeria	−1.15
				Saudi Arabia	−1.3
				United Arab Emirates	−1.32

Source: WB (2000a)

The average mean country growth rate among the occidental countries was 2.1 per cent between 1973 and 1990. The finding is again that there are several Third World countries that have been successful in bridging the gulf between themselves and the rich countries. There are also several countries that have fallen behind even more, but that does not change the fact that the gap theory implication is not confirmed. Besides the gap theory we need a theory about the so-called NICs that develop in a manner different from the pattern of the gap theory. How about economic development after 1990?

This evidence points to that affluence is growing faster outside the rich set of countries with the exception of the former communist countries where the data clearly indicate decline. The increase in average affluence in South East Asia is staggering, considering such a short time period. But also Latin America and South Asia have started to pick up at the same time as economic growth in Africa and the CIS has been dismal (Table 3.11).

Is the gap model true?

We can now make a final assessment of the gap model. Let us quote from Nobel Prize winner Kuznets who stated in a classical analysis some 30 years ago:

> It follows that the current international difference in per capita product, which is roughly between fifteen and twenty to one (based on the average for the developed countries and that for the populous Asian countries with per capita GDP in the early 1960's of below $100), results partly from differences in growth rates over the nineteenth and twentieth centuries, and partly from disparities in initial per capita product (Kuznets, 1966: 304)

This was at the time a factually correct assessment about historical developments. But Kuznets also made a prediction about the trends that would evolve after the Second World War. He went on to claim:

> Furthermore, since most countries that have enjoyed modern economic growth had initially high per capita product, international differences have grown wider and have continued to do so even in the post-World War II year. (Kuznets, 1966: 305)

This is hardly generally true any longer. Since 1960 the traditionally sharp distinction between poor and rich countries has lost its discriminating power. The well-known gap theory about development implies a pessimistic view of what future economic development may bring about. The gap theory argues that there was a sharp gulf between a set of rich countries and a set of poor countries at the end of the Second World War and that this gap has tended to increase during the post-war period.

It is believed that this separation between rich and poor countries coincides with the distinction between occidental countries and communist countries, with the exception of China on the one hand and the Third World countries on the other, or with a divide between the north and the south. Looking at the real GDP data, we cannot confirm the gap theory as it is not

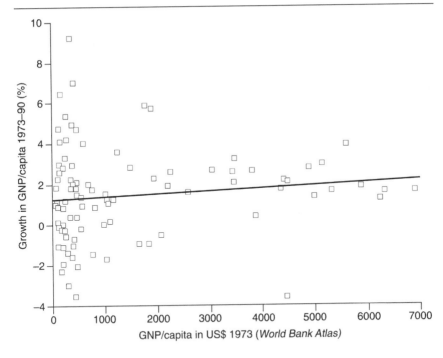

Figure 3.2   Affluence in 1973 and economic growth 1973–90
Source: WB (1996, 2000a, 2000b)

true that this sharp gulf already existed in 1950 or that the gap between the occidental countries or the communist countries and all sets of Third World countries continue to grow over time. Figure 3.2 shows the relation between the level of affluence in 1973 and the average rate of economic growth between 1973 and 1990 ($r = 0.10$, $N = 95$).

There is not the kind of relationship between level of economic affluence and average economic growth that the gap theory implies. There are important sets of Third World countries that have been able to close the gap to the occidental countries during the post-war period. Some countries have moved out of poverty. It is not the case that the level of affluence in a country determines the average rate of economic growth, which suggests that the development alternative is a real one. Let us look at a similar figure for the last decade. Figure 3.3 contains a scatterplot of economic affluence around 1990 and economic growth between 1990 and 1998 ($r = 0.13$, $N = 120$). Again there is no connection between level of affluence and average growth rates.

Conclusion

It is a widely held belief that the distance between the rich occidental nations and the poor Third World countries is increasing: in spite of several decades

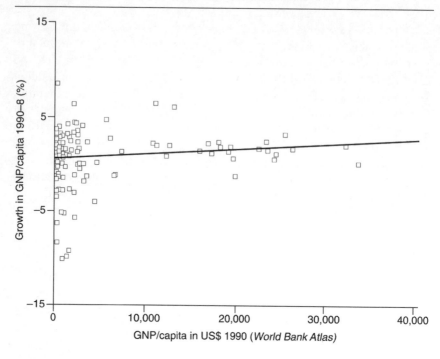

Figure 3.3 Affluence in 1990 and economic growth 1990–98
Source: WB (1996, 2000a, 2000b)

of various kinds of efforts at development the gap has not been closed nor is it narrowing. It is true that there were substantial country differences in income per capita around 1960 reflecting a distinction between a rich Occident and a poor South, but it is not true that the same country differences are simply maintained or even increase. To emphasize the major finding: There is no relation between level of affluence and rate of change in affluence on a per capita basis. This means that the development alternative is a real one. Some countries have moved out of poverty during the post-war period. The developmental process displays such considerable variation among the countries of the world that the traditional separation between rich and poor countries in terms of the distinction between industrialized occidental nations and non-industrialized Third World countries is inadequate.

One may give a most concrete example of the tremendous increase in affluence in some Asian countries by looking at Hong Kong, although it is not a state. The rise in GDP per capita in this British crown colony starts from 2247 international US dollars in 1960 and stood at 16,471 international US dollars in 1992, which latter figure ranks Hong Kong higher than Sweden (in contrast to the time when Sweden (in 1960) was four times more affluent than Hong Kong).

The development process among various sets of countries displays so much variation both between and within these sets – Occidental, CEE and CIS, Central and Latin America, Sub-Saharan Africa, Arab World, South Asia and South East Asia – that the traditional separation between rich and poor countries, the northern versus the southern hemisphere, or affluent countries and Third World countries is more confusing than illuminating

Now, development may mean several things. If the concept of development refers to economic change in particular and social welfare in general, then one would want to know if and to what extent the developmental process may bring about considerable social change as a result of economic growth. But how close is the connection between economic development and social development? The next chapter deals with this problem. Thus, we will next look at social development by focusing on the concepts of quality of life and of equality in income distribution.

CHAPTER 4

Macro Differences in Social Development

Introduction

The concept of development has been much debated in the social sciences. Recently, however, it has been stated that the development approach is flawed, since Third World countries cannot really become similar or 'develop' into First World countries. Perhaps the time has come to abandon this concept entirely, which is both multidimensional and value-loaded. 'Development' stands for a set of properties that refer to economic or social aspects of life (Bardhan, 1988; Lewis, 1988). Myrdal presented a broad focus upon development, including the social and economic aspects of the phenomenon which reinforce each other:

> What is actually meant in characterising a country as 'underdeveloped' is that there is in that country a constellation of numerous undesirable conditions for work and life: outputs, incomes and levels of living are low; many modes of production, attitudes, and behavioural patterns are disadvantageous; and there are unfavourable institutions, ranging from those at the state level to those governing social and economic relations in the family and the neighbourhood. (Myrdal, 1968: 1840)

In fact, one of the most debated problems in development theory is the extent to which social and economic indicators on the level of development of a country tend to co-vary. Thus it has been argued that a simple economic indicator on development like GDP per capita does not tap the social aspects of development (Adelman and Morris, 1967, revised 1973; Morris, 1979). The level of social development involves more than just an average income measure like the extent of inequality in the distribution of income and wealth or the real life access to basic necessities like food, physicians and shelter. We will look at the hypothesis that social and economic aspects of development are related, Myrdal, for instance, argued that there exists a vicious circle between the various aspects of development: '[there is a] general causal relationship among all these conditions, so that they form a social system. It is the task of the study of underdevelopment and development to determine this relationship within the social system' (Myrdal, 1968: 1840).

We will ask in chapter 5 whether there is not also a political aspect of development – i.e. political development? Thus, within the field of comparative politics in political science there has been a search for a counterpart to the notion of socio-economic development, namely political development. With the aid of such a concept one would understand the transition from a so-called primitive political system to one that is called a 'modern' one, not only in terms of economic change but also as political change.

Social development and social change

One much-debated problem in development theory concerns the value-loaded character of the concept. Again, Myrdal raised this issue, when talking in the following manner about the constellation of development attributes: 'They are evaluated undesirable – or low or disadvantageous or unfavourable – from the standpoint of the desirability of "development" – a characterisation afflicted with vagueness but definite enough to permit its use.'

When the implicit (Western) values hidden in the development notion are made explicit, then one enters the general theories of social change or the grand sociological theories of the coming of a Western society (Higgott, 1983). The emergence of the occidental type of society and polity is described with pairs of polar concepts: community versus society (Tönnies), mechanical versus organic solidarity (Durkheim), modernism versus traditionalism (Weber), primary versus secondary social attachment (Cooley), status versus contract (Maine), folk versus urban culture (Redfield) and sacred versus secular social orders (Becker). When applied to the Third World, grand social theory presents two difficulties.

The first difficulty involves the fact that one faces a severe problem of how to model the relationship between economic and social development on the one hand and political development on the other. One may distinguish between different aspects of development (Portes, 1976). But then we need to clarify how they interact:

1   Does economic development enhance social development?
2   Does socio-economic development produce one kind of political development, e.g. democracy?

One should sort out theories of political development from general theories of social and economic transformation. In chapter 5 we focus primarily upon what theories of development amount to with regard to politics, government, the state or the political system, whichever concept one may prefer.

One principal difficulty concerns the direction of change involved in the notion of development. Sometimes it is admitted that we may talk about both positive and negative development, but the overall impression is that development is something inherently valuable, i.e. the opposite of development is decline or decay. If this is correct, then a theory of change would have to be far more encompassing than a theory about development.

It has been argued that the value component in theories of development reflects a Western bias, as only certain kinds of change would qualify as 'development' (Wiarda, 1983).

It must be emphasized that there is no single unanimously accepted definition of development in the literature (Todaro, 1985; Thirlwall, 1986; Sen, 1988). When some national income statistic is mentioned in relation to development it is clearly understood that it is only one among several possible indicators. Myrdal approached the concept of development as multidimensional referring to: production output and incomes, conditions of production, levels of living, attitudes towards life and work, institutions and policies (Myrdal, 1968: 1860). Although Myrdal treated these aspects of development as separate from each other, he also claimed that they co-vary, each reinforcing the others in a process of circular causation (ibid.: 1859–66). No doubt income measures are given priority in the development literature, in particular GDP per capita (Gersovitz *et al.*, 1982).

Economic or socio-economic development typically relates to a positive change – a real increase – in total output or in the well-being or material welfare of the citizens of a country. The value component of the concept of development is here quite explicit and straightforward: a developing nation is a country that is becoming better off and a developed country is one that is well off. But here the agreement between scholars also ends. What is contested is how to measure the extent of welfare of a nation as well as how to explain which factors are conducive to development as increased well-being. We will deal with the two counter-arguments one at a time.

Often a simple economic indicator such as level or rate of growth in GDP is considered a tool for analysing welfare in a society. There are basically two counter-arguments. On the one hand, it has been claimed that an indicator like GDP per capita does not adequately map individual welfare which includes other things like health, employment, housing and so forth, meaning that we have to pay attention to broad social indicators. On the other hand, we have the argument that what matters is not the overall size or growth rate in GDP but its distribution among various social groups. Attempts have been made to construct more complex indices measuring more generally social welfare like, for example, the Physical Quality of Life Index and the Disparity Reduction Rate which taps the change in physical quality of life over time (Morris, 1979; Pourgerami, 1989). A rising national income may be used for many purposes except raising the level of affluence among the poor. Thus we have to look at the extent of inequality in the distribution of income.

It is not necessary, however, to commit oneself to any of these positions as one may approach socio-economic development in an open fashion. To what extent do various measures – economic or social – co-vary in a data set covering some 75 nations in various parts of the world? What is the main relationship between affluence on the aggregate level and the distribution of income?

Quality of life

The problems encountered when comparing countries in relation to the general notion of affluence or rate of change in affluence are well known (Kuznets, 1966). First, there are the difficulties in getting access to data; for some countries this has been difficult except for the last ten years. Generally, longitudinal data series are more problematic than cross-sectional data. Second, there are severe problems of interpretation and comparability (Meier, 1984; Thirlwall, 1983, 4th edn., 1986). How can we know that the indicators measure the same phenomenon? Problems of indicator validity and reliability are confounded by culture barriers. Indicators that tap one dimension in one context cannot be transferred to another context with a similar interpretation. These data problems impose limits on what can be achieved in terms of country comparison, but they do not exclude an analysis of levels or rates of development.

It may be worthwhile to penetrate the extent to which the above picture about differences in affluence is generally true when alternative indicators of affluence are resorted to. Are we to conclude that the per capita differences in income as measured by GDP co-vary with similar country differences in standards of living? Material well-being or social welfare is a difficult notion to pin down in measurement indices. A number of social indicators are relevant for consideration in the measurement of welfare. We include indicators measuring the following for roughly three periods of time, i.e. the mid-1970s, the mid-1980s, and the mid-1990s: energy production, GNP/capita, illiteracy rates, infant mortality rates, estimates of life expectancy at birth, number of physicians in the population, radios per capita, secondary and tertiary school enrolment, telelines per capita as well as television sets per capita.

The claim that underdevelopment is a general predicament that distinguishes between countries implies that these social indicators co-vary to a high extent. Moreover, development theory also implies that the per capita income indicator co-varies strongly with each of the social indicators. Table 4.1 comprises a factor analysis with findings that are relevant for these beliefs.

The findings of the factor analysis offer substantial weight to the argument that there is a general predicament of underdevelopment because there is strong co-variation between the indicators. Countries that have a low level of affluence as measured by the GDP per capita indicator tend consistently to score low on the most basic indicators of material well-being, but there seems also to be a more luxurious aspect to welfare that these basic indicators do not co-vary with. The fact that underdevelopment is a general social predicament does not imply, however, that there are two homogeneous sets of countries, developed and underdeveloped. Yet we may note that over time the explained variance of the first factor declines, suggesting that some of these indicators do not capture human welfare as well in the mid-1990s as they did in the mid-1970s.

Table 4.1 Factor analysis of welfare indicators around 1975, 1985 and 1995: loadings of the unrotated first factor

Indicators	c. 1975	c. 1985	c. 1995
Energy production	0.857	0.767	0.731
GNP/capita US$	0.789	0.829	0.818
Illiteracy in %	−0.860	−0.841	−0.787
Infant mortality	−0.895	−0.876	−0.862
Life expectancy	0.905	0.880	0.860
Physicians in population	0.881	0.855	0.717
Radio per capita	0.821	0.853	0.573
Secondary school enrolment	0.932	0.900	0.899
Tertiary school enrolment	0.839	0.841	0.840
Telelines per capita	0.904	0.908	0.927
Television sets per capita	0.954	0.894	0.931
Explained variance in %	77.0	73.8	67.1

Source: WB (2000a)

The Human Development Index, created by the United Nations Development Programme for their publication *Human Development Report*, may be used to map the average country variations in quality of life. It is based upon a composite index with indicators used in the factor analysis displayed in Table 4.1, namely: life expectancy at birth, adult literacy rate, combined school enrolment ratio and an adjusted per capita income in PPP US dollars. The variation in the HDI is shown in Table 4.2 with regard to the late twentieth-century situation.

The connection between quality and life and affluence as measured by economic output is not linear, as quality of life first rises proportionately with affluence but then levels off. Thus, the country differences in quality of life are not that pronounced except with regard to Africa, where the human condition is in many places dismal. Quality of life has gone down in the post-communist countries but advances in many Asian countries.

One major developmental trend affecting quality of life is the rapid urbanization process in Third World countries. In 1975, 66 per cent of the world population lived in the countryside with the remaining 34 per cent in urban areas – 18 per cent in industrialized countries and 16 per cent in the developing countries. Today about 50 per cent live in rural areas and 50 per cent in urban, with 15 per cent in industrialized countries and 33 per cent in the developing world. However, around 2025 only 39 per cent will live in rural areas, as 48 per cent will live in urban areas in the developing world and 13 per cent in the industrialized world. Actually, the majority of the world's population will live in cities for the first time in history, and many in so-called mega-cities. There are now many such mega-cities all having more than 10 million inhabitants: Mexico City, Los Angeles, New York, Buenos Aires, São Paulo, Bombay, Calcutta, Beijing, Shanghai, Seoul, Osaka, Tokyo, Rio de Janeiro, Paris, Moscow, Manila, London, Lagos, Karachi,

Table 4.2 Human development index (HDI) for 1999–2000 in macro regions

Region	HDI 2000		HDI 1999	
	Index	*N*	*Index*	*N*
Occidental	0.912	23	0.908	23
CEE and CIS	0.762	25	0.748	25
Central and Latin America	0.729	22	0.730	22
Sub-Saharan Africa	0.450	35	0.456	35
Arab World	0.679	17	0.677	17
South Asia	0.546	7	0.531	7
South East Asia	0.715	14	0.717	14
Average/total	0.680	143	0.677	143
Eta-squared	0.744		0.733	
Significance	0.000		0.000	

Sources: HDI 2000: UNDP, 2000; HDI 1999: UNDP, 1999

Johannesburg, Jakarta, Dhaka, Delhi, Cairo and Bangkok. The political implications of massive urbanization have not been sufficiently researched.

Gender equality

The importance for development of gender empowerment has been recognized rather late. The status of women matters positively for social development. Donor organizations and the WB have increasingly begun to target the quality of life of women and girls, as women empowerment plays a role for strategic development objectives such as birth control, literacy and political participation. Economic activity may also be stimulated by women emancipation. Table 4.3 presents a gender index, measured over the subsets of countries of the world.

The status of women in relation to men only approaches something like equality in the occidental world. Gender empowerment is a big future task in South Asia, the Arab World and Sub-Saharan Africa, where it has to struggle with different kinds of difficulties stemming from prejudice, religion and tradition. Although the relevance of gender equality is more and more stressed, it remains that equality tends to be approached as a question of the distribution of national income.

Income distribution

A fundamental objection to the use of the standard GNP or GDP per capita indicator on economic affluence is that it says nothing about the distribution of affluence in a country. This is a real limitation of this indicator as a growth in total output or overall national income over and above the population increase does not necessarily imply that poverty has been reduced for all social groups. Economic growth in poor countries implies

Table 4.3   Gender empowerment measures (GEM)

Region	GEM 2000		GEM 1999	
	Index	*N*	*Index*	*N*
Occidental	0.648	23	0.690	21
CEE and CIS	0.472	11	0.497	12
Central and Latin America	0.481	17	0.492	15
Sub-Saharan Africa	0.336	15	0.353	3
Arab World	0.280	11	0.306	5
South Asia	0.260	4	0.307	2
South East Asia	0.421	9	0.453	5
Average/total	0.458	90	0.529	63
Eta-squared	0.712		0.728	
Significance	0.000		0.000	

Sources: GEM 2000; UNDP 2000; GEM 1999: UNDP, 1999

that there are more resources to be distributed among various social strata, but which groups benefit is an open question.

The GDP per capita indicator needs to be complemented with an index that measures the extent of inequality of the income distribution. The literature contains a few indices measuring the variation in income between households or regions: the Gini index or some kind of Lorenz curve as well as various measures of the share of either the top 10 or 20 per cent or the bottom 10 per cent. It should be pointed out that there is a reliability problem when handling income distribution data for a large set of countries. In some countries the statistical information is not quite accurate and the definitions of income or economic affluence vary from one country to another, which reduces the comparability of such data. It is of course interesting to observe whether income differences increase or decrease as the world economy expands. Table 4.4 presents the situation around 1990. The data employed here stems from different World Bank publications.

Although these data series are not strictly comparable, one may observe the same country pattern in the 1970 data as in the 1990 information. Communist countries score lower on income inequality than the other country sets, where especially Latin America displays huge income differences. In Africa, South Africa has shown the most pronounced income differences reflecting its racist past. It may be interesting to examine closely the country variation in income inequality. Table 4.5 lists the country scores on one such measure: Gini (WB, 2000a) for roughly the 1990s.

The country differences in income inequality are huge, and one must remember the problem of the reliability of the data. But there is a consistent overall pattern, namely: Latin American countries are characterized by extreme income differences. Some African countries also display such huge differentials. Former communist countries and Arab countries display more of income equality, but income equality is mainly to be found within certain

Table 4.4 Income inequality around 1990

Region	Gini[a]		Gini 1970[b]		Gini 1980[b]		Gini 1990[b]	
	Value	N	Value	N	Value	N	Value	N
Occidental	31.5	22	33.3	20	32.3	20	33.0	13
CEE and CIS	31.9	19	25.1	5	26.9	8	28.1	10
Central and Latin America	49.8	19	48.6	14	49.3	13	48.0	10
Sub-Saharan Africa	45.4	23	52.5	4	41.4	11	47.7	17
Arab World	37.3	7	44.2	4	39.8	7	40.0	3
South Asia	34.7	5	37.7	5	35.2	5	30.9	3
South East Asia	38.4	12	39.8	9	38.7	10	37.9	7
Average/total	39.1	107	39.4	61	37.8	74	39.3	63
Eta-squared	0.515		0.684		0.589		0.624	
Significance	0.000		0.000		0.000		0.000	

Sources: [a] WB (2000b-printed version); [b] Deininger and Squire (1997)

occidental countries such as the Nordic countries. Why this pattern of country differences? The basic model linking income distribution to affluence is the Kuznets curve.

A higher average GDP per capita does not imply a higher standard of living for the entire population. The standard indicator on levels of economic affluence says nothing about the distribution of economic affluence. The Kuznets theory proposed in 1955 suggested that a rise in economic affluence had a somewhat contradictory impact on the pattern of distribution (Kuznets, 1955). At first, the income differences would increase but later on these differentials would decrease. Thus, there would be something like an inverted U-shaped curve linking levels of affluence with some measure on the extent of inequality in the distributions of incomes. A similar hypothesis was suggested by Myrdal (1957) and Hirschman (1958).

There has been much research on the Kuznets theory but so far no conclusive answer (McCormick, 1988). Part of the difficulties in testing theories about income distribution arises from the lack of reliable data for a large number of countries. Various indicators may be employed, but there are not enough cross-sectional or longitudinal data for more refined tests. Part of the confusion also stems from the interaction between the two entities. A low or high level of economic affluence may have one kind of impact on the income distribution whereas the income distribution may have another kind of impact on levels of economic affluence. Moreover, other factors like public policy may change the impact of the two variables on each other. It is also an open question as to whether the Kuznets theory should be tested by means of cross-sectional or longitudinal data (Bigsten, 1987).

The data set employed allow us to examine the Kuznets curve at different points of time as the relationship between income distribution and levels of economic affluence need not be stable. Even if Kuznets was correct in

Table 4.5   Income inequality around 1990: country scores

Occidental		Central and Latin America		Sub-Saharan Africa	
Austria	23.1	Jamaica	36.4	Rwanda	28.9
Denmark	24.7	Trinidad and Tobago	40.3	Ghana	32.7
Belgium	25	Bolivia	42	Burundi	33.3
Sweden	25	Uruguay	42.3	Côte d'Ivoire	36.7
Finland	25.6	Ecuador	43.7	Tanzania	38.2
Norway	25.8	Peru	46.2	Mauritania	38.9
Luxembourg	26.9	Costa Rica	47	Uganda	39.2
Italy	27.3	Panama	48.5	Mozambique	39.6
Germany	30	Dominican Republic	48.7	Ethiopia	40
Canada	31.5	Venezuela	48.8	Guinea	40.3
Spain	32.5	Nicaragua	50.3	Senegal	41.3
Netherlands	32.6	El Salvador	52.3	Kenya	44.5
France	32.7	Honduras	53.7	Madagascar	46
Greece	32.7	Mexico	53.7	Burkina Faso	48.2
Switzerland	33.1	Chile	56.5	Zambia	49.8
Australia	35.2	Colombia	57.1	Mali	50.5
Portugal	35.6	Paraguay	59.1	Niger	50.5
Ireland	35.9	Guatemala	59.6	Nigeria	50.6
UK	36.1	Brazil	60	Lesotho	56
Israel	36.6			Zimbabwe	56.8
USA	40.8	*South Asia*		South Africa	59.3
New Zealand	43.9	Pakistan	31.2	Central African Republic	61.3
		Bangladesh	33.6	Sierra Leone	62.9
CEE and CIS		Sri Lanka	34.4		
Slovakia	19.5	Nepal	36.7	*Arab World*	
Belarus	21.7	India	37.8	Egypt	28.9
Czech Republic	25.4			Algeria	35.3
Croatia	26.8	*South East Asia*		Jordan	36.4
Slovenia	26.8	Japan	24.9	Morocco	39.5
Romania	28.2	Laos	30.4	Yemen	39.5
Bulgaria	28.3	South Korea	31.9	Tunisia	40.2
Hungary	30.8	Mongolia	33.2	Turkey	41.5
Latvia	32.4	Vietnam	36.1		
Lithuania	32.4	Indonesia	36.5		
Ukraine	32.5	China	40.3		
Poland	32.9	Cambodia	40.4		
Uzbekistan	33.3	Thailand	41.4		
Moldova	34.4	Philippines	46.2		
Estonia	35.4	Malaysia	48.5		
Kazakhstan	35.4	Papua New Guinea	50.9		
Kyrgyzstan	40.5				
Turkmenistan	40.8				
Russia	48.7				

Source: See Table 4.4 for the source of this table

linking a reduction in income differences with growing affluence, the magnitude of the impact of affluence upon income equality may differ at various points of time, reflecting for instance how the division of the income between labour and capital hovers.

Looking at the relationship between average real GDP per capita in a country around 1970 and the degree of inequality in its income distribution between households, we find a negative relationship between level of affluence and income inequality ($r = -0.62$) (see Ahluwalia, 1976; Weede, 1980). The empirical finding that income inequality is reduced the larger the national income per capita of a country is in accordance with Kuznets' inverted U-curve. Let us do more tests.

Even if it is true that income inequality may vary considerably between Third World countries like Brazil and Pakistan, it is still the case that income inequality decreases the larger the average GDP per capita in a country. It is true that income inequality rises somewhat as we move from very poor countries to countries with a higher level of affluence, but, in general, the richer a country the larger the probability that its income distribution is more equal. The Kuznets curve suggested in the 1950s may be partly traced in the data from the 1970s (Figure 4.1) where the correlation coefficient indicates a negative relationship ($r = -0.54$).

The cross-sectional test of the Kuznets hypothesis may be complemented

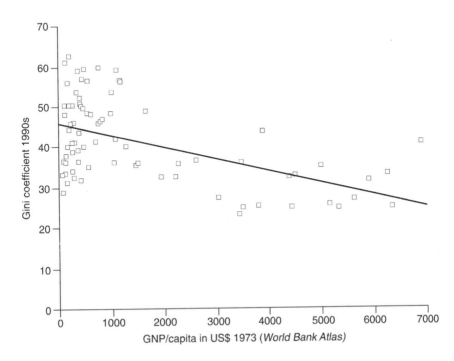

Figure 4.1   Affluence in 1973 and income distribution in the 1990s

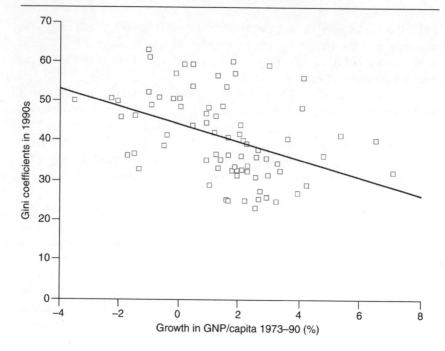

Figure 4.2   Economic growth 1973–90 and income distributions in the 1990s

by a longitudinal test. It is often argued that the extent of income inequalities in a country like India or Brazil has increased over time (de Carvalho and Wood, 1980; Mathur, 1983). Since there has also been some economic development during the same time period, it may be argued that the Kuznets curve fits longitudinal data about an association between economic growth and income inequality. Figure 4.2 relates the degree of income inequality to average rates of economic growth between 1973 and 1990, achieving a coefficient of $r = -0.42$.

Even if the hypothesis of a Kuznets curve is not strictly validated, the amount of income inequality varies independently of the rate of growth in the economy. It is not possible to predict the variation in income inequality knowing the average country growth rates in the economy between 1960 and 1980. There are cases of all conceivable extremes: a low growth rate and much inequality (Zambia) or more equality (Peru) versus a high rate of growth and much inequalities (Brazil) or more equality (Japan). But it is possible to trace out something like a Kuznets curve around an inverted U-shaped curve linking income inequality with level of affluence.

Let us look at more recent data. Figures 4.3 and 4.4 may be consulted, the first showing the interaction between income inequality and real GDP per capita 1990 and the other income inequality and economic growth in the period 1990–98.

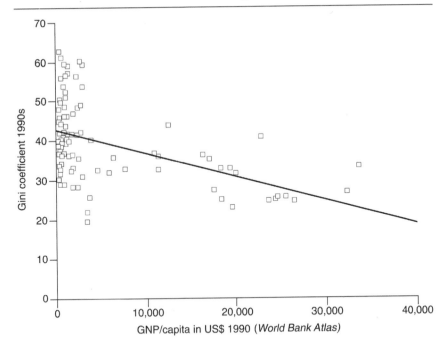

Figure 4.3   Affluence in 1990 and income distributions in the 1990s

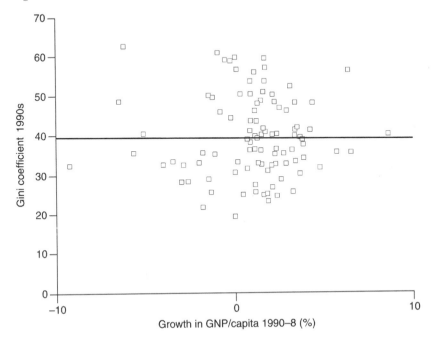

Figure 4.4   Economic growth 1990–98 and income distributions in the 1990s

It appears from Figures 4.3 and 4.4 that the Kuznets effect is slightly weaker in the 1990s than it was earlier. The correlation (r) between the Gini coefficients and GNP per capita in 1990 equals -0.48 and with economic growth 1990–98 amounts to -0.01. Could it reflect the triumph of a market ideology since 1989? Among the factors that impact upon the shape of the Kuznets curve, one must mention not only affluence but also public policies (Nordic countries, Japan) as well as religion (Islam).

A cautious interpretation of more recent data suggests that there is a probability that at first the extent of income inequality increases as the level of affluence rises, but that the overall relationship between income inequality and level of affluence remains negative. Thus, there is some cause for optimism with regard to the impact of economic development upon economic equality. Whether a rise in affluence will bring about a higher standard of living depends upon how the developmental process evolves.

The developmental process: output and population growth

Developmental theory designates some countries as developed and others as underdeveloped or the former as highly developed and the latter as less developed. The advanced industrial nations have passed through the process of social change, taking them out of agrarian poverty and into industrial affluence and the welfare state. Such a pattern of social change is considered the main objective for the poor countries according to the theory and practice of the modernization theme. The basic policy problem is to identify the strategy of modernization: planning- or market-induced change? The historical experiences of the market economies and the lessons from the Soviet Union and China suggest two ideal types which may be combined in practice in various ways. The Japanese development is often referred to as state-led capitalism whereas China appears to be moving towards so-called market socialism, at least in its free zones and in Southern China.

Although there is considerable disagreement about the means and goals of development, it can be stated that the zest for modernization may meet with success. Developing countries are not of one kind. Some have developed very quickly, accomplishing vast social change, whereas others have hardly modernized at all. Even if it is true that generally the gap between rich and poor countries has not been reduced it is also not the case that it is impossible for countries in the Third World to close that distance.

Development has a dynamic connotation. It singles out a set of countries that try to find the path from poverty to affluence. Developmental countries are those countries that are moving at varying rates of speed from a low level of social welfare to a higher level. Sometimes the ambition is high as the rich countries are depicted as models of what the developmental process should result in. Sometimes the modernization zeal is more realistic as the goal of the developmental process is only to move the countries out of poverty.

Table 4.6 Average yearly growth rates in GNP

Region	1961–73		1973–90		1990–98	
	Value	*N*	*Value*	*N*	*Value*	*N*
Occidental	5.2	22	2.8	22	2.6	22
CEE and CIS	6.8	1	3.1	3	−4.2	17
Central and Latin America	5.2	18	2.7	20	3.8	21
Sub-Saharan Africa	4.6	24	3.3	28	2.5	35
Arab World	5.4	5	4.7	10	4.5	12
South Asia	3.4	5	4.5	6	4.7	7
South East Asia	7.4	10	6.3	10	5.2	14
Average/total	5.2	85	3.6	99	2.4	12.8
Eta-squared	0.162		0.265		0.589	
Significance	0.028		0.000		0.000	

Source: WB (2000a)

Let us consider an economic indicator, GNP growth as measured by data collected by the World Bank (2000a) (Table 4.6).

Growth in the economy varies from one year to another and reflects a number of factors that are not related to development. What is of interest here is the average growth rates in different countries, i.e. the speed of the developmental process after accounting for economic fluctuations from one year to another. Countries differ substantially in so far as the long-term growth rates between 1961 and 1999 are concerned.

Growth rates have been lower in Third World countries than in the rich countries. The exception is to be found among the Asian countries where the mean growth rate – around 5 per cent or more – exceeds that of the occidental countries – less than 3 per cent. The growth in the economies in Africa has been particularly weak – or a mean of less than 2–3 per cent – whereas the average growth rate in Central and Latin America is not that low – or roughly 3–4 per cent. The mean growth rate of the communist systems studied here was quite high, at 5 per cent, a figure which seems to be an exaggeration; data for the 1990s suggest a negative growth rate. The severe pollution problems in Eastern Europe are not captured by this measure which reveals that it is not a perfect indicator on well-being.

There are two explanations of the pattern in growth/capita: output or population. Either the rate of increase in production in the Third World has been weak or the rate of population growth has been very strong. It is not primarily the dynamism in the economies of the Third World that is at fault. Actually, the average increase in output in Third World countries is as good as that of the rich countries. With regard to the Asian world it may even be stated that the rate of economic growth is higher. What accounts for the low increase in income per capita in LDCs is the rapid rise in the population (Bairoch, P. and Levy-Leboyer, 1981; Bairoch, P., 2000). Table 4.7 reveals that the expansion of the population is almost as large as the increase in

Table 4.7 Average yearly population growth rates

Region	1961–73		1973–90		1990–98	
	Value	*N*	*Value*	*N*	*Value*	*N*
Occidental	1.0	23	0.6	23	0.7	23
CEE and CIS	1.5	25	1.0	27	0.1	27
Central and Latin America	2.5	22	2.1	22	1.8	22
Sub-Saharan Africa	2.5	37	2.8	37	2.6	37
Arab World	3.7	17	3.6	17	2.6	17
South Asia	2.2	8	2.2	8	2.2	8
South East Asia	2.4	15	1.9	15	1.8	15
Average/Total	2.2	147	1.9	149	1.8	149
Eta-squared	0.361		0.555		0.575	
Significance	0.000		0.000		0.000	

Source: World Bank (2000a)

output. This indicates that the overall change in level of affluence per capita will not be enough to bridge the gap between the rich countries and the poor, except in a few rapidly developing countries.

The economic development in Japan, South Korea, Singapore and Malaysia with persistently high rates of economic growth each year has meant a strong expansion in the level of affluence between 1960 and 1996. At the same time population growth has been low. The figures for GNP growth in these countries are comparable to those of the occidental countries. However, in Sub-Saharan Africa population growth has been stronger than output growth with the attending macro consequences for quality of life. One notices also the problematic developments in the former Soviet Union area involving negative economic growth and very low population increases.

Trade pattern and globalization

A seminal hypothesis in development theory argues that foreign trade is characteristic of advanced or developing countries. The theory of international trade implies that the more a country engages in trade with other countries, the more likely it is that it will benefit from the consequences of an open economy in a way which improves the prospects for rapid socio-economic expansion at home. The basic Ricardian theory of comparative advantages claims high gains for all the interacting countries from productive specialization and trade (Yarbrough and Yarbrough, 1988). Although the debate on the potential benefits and costs of extensive international trade between countries has developed far beyond the Ricardian model (Lal, 1983; WB, 1987), there is still the fundamental notion that trade or openness of the economy is typical of countries with a high level of affluence or with a high level of average economic growth (Bhagwati and Ruggie, 1984; Caves and Jones, 1985; Choksi and Papageorgiou, 1986; Chacholiades, 1985).

Table 4.8 Openness of the economy

Region	Impex 1980		Impex 1990		Impex 1997	
	Index	N	Index	N	Index	N
Occidental	70.5	22	70.5	22	76.4	23
CEE and CIS	65.4	5	72.0	17	92.2	23
Central and Latin America	53.5	21	54.8	21	63.7	21
Sub-Saharan Africa	71.2	33	59.7	36	67.8	35
Arab World	74.8	14	75.5	14	70.5	12
South Asia	37.2	7	34.8	7	45.1	7
South East Asia	110.8	10	98.1	14	117.1	14
Average/total	69.4	112	66.8	131	77.0	135
Eta-square	0.115		0.101		0.163	
Significance	0.042		0.038		0.001	

Source: WB (2000a)

Is it true that extensive international trade always characterizes rich countries and that a heavy concentration on the home market is typical of poor countries? Let us test this idea in relation to an indicator on the scope of trade in an economy: the *impex index* or the sum of exports and imports in relation to GDP. Table 4.8 has the variation for the country sets for the period from 1980 to 1997.

Interestingly, when almost all the countries of the world with a population larger than 1 million are included in the analysis, then we do observe that some countries are much more open than others. An open economy where imports and exports constitute more than 60 per cent of GDP is to be found in the occidental countries as well as in South East Asia. The area of the globe where openness of the economy is high is the so-called TRIAD, or the three main economic regions of the world: NAFTA, the EU and the ASEAN plus Japan. Globalization benefits the trade between these three regions involving rising inequalities between the countries in the world, because trade tends to increase affluence for both trading parties, all other things being equal.

Let us take a closer look at how impex varies between countries within these macro regions, using most recently available information, that is from 1997 (see Table 4.9).

There is a quite substantial variation in the extent to which the economy of a so-called rich country is an open one. The small affluent countries in Western Europe have considerably more open economies than the USA and Japan where the domestic market is very large. A very high degree of openness is characteristic of the Dutch, Belgian and Irish economies.

Again we find that small countries tend to have a more open economy than large countries, all other things being equal (Katzenstein, 1985). The very high scores of Singapore and Hong Kong must be pointed out, as it exemplifies the nature of these city-states as locations for *entrepôt* trade,

Table 4.9   Impex within macro regions in 1997

Occidental		Central and Latin America		Sub-Saharan Africa	
Luxembourg	186.4	Nicaragua	118.6	Lesotho	160.4
Ireland	141.5	Jamaica	115	Congo, Brazza	144.7
Belgium	141.3	Trinidad and Tobago	110.2	Mauritius	130.7
Netherlands	104.9	Honduras	98	Angola	121.2
Austria	85.26	Paraguay	95.14	Namibia	110.8
Sweden	80.56	Costa Rica	93.48	Gabon	106
Canada	79.67	Panama	82.87	Mauritania	88.46
Norway	75.46	Dominican Republic	67.62	Côte d'Ivoire	86.45
Switzerland	75.34	Mexico	60.79	Zimbabwe	82.21
Israel	75.02	Ecuador	59	Botswana	78.66
Iceland	72.21	El Salvador	58.64	Togo	75.97
Portugal	71.55	Chile	56.12	Nigeria	75.18
Finland	70.78	Bolivia	51.18	Senegal	73.48
Denmark	68.59	Venezuela, Republic	49.11	Zambia	68.72
UK	57.84	Uruguay	45.43	Kenya	63.68
New Zealand	57.13	Guatemala	41.55	Ghana	62.4
Spain	55.56	Colombia	33.33	Mali	61.32
Germany	52.12	Haiti	31.37	Malawi	59.04
Italy	50.32	Peru	29.48	Benin	58.44
France	49.36	Argentina	23.28	Chad	52.26
Australia	42.18	Brazil	17.74	Madagascar	51.82
Greece	39.68			South Africa	48.4
USA	25.59	*South Asia*		Cameroon	47.69
		Sri Lanka	80.14	Tanzania	46.36
CEE and CIS		Bhutan	75.29	Congo-Kinshasa	46.11
Estonia	167.7	Nepal	64.04	Central African Republic	44.39
Belarus	130.3	Pakistan	38.39	Mozambique	42.92
Slovak Republic	127.6	Bangladesh	31.04	Ethiopia	42.21
Moldova	127.2	India	24.81	Guinea	41.7
Lithuania	119.6	Burma-Myanmar	2.15	Niger	39.97
Czech Republic	119			Burkina Faso	38.9
Bulgaria	118.3	*South East Asia*		Uganda	34.32
Slovenia	115.4	Singapore	315.6	Rwanda	33.22
Latvia	110.4	Hong Kong, China	264.2	Sierra Leone	31.15
Croatia	97.41	Malaysia	185.5	Burundi	24.18
Hungary	91.45	Mongolia	137.6		
Macedonia, FYR	85.94	Papua New Guinea	111.2	*Arab World*	
Kyrgyz Republic	84.48	Philippines	108.5	Jordan	125.6
Ukraine	84.24	Vietnam	95.26	Yemen, Republic	96.45
Azerbaijan	82.05	Thailand	94.75	Kuwait	92.88
Armenia	78.55	Cambodia	71.94	Tunisia	90.34
Kazakhstan	72.37	Korea, Republic	70.47	Saudi Arabia	76.5
Romania	66.47	Laos, People's Democratic		Syrian Arab Republic	70.02
Uzbekistan	57.78	Republic	65.98	Lebanon	64.25
Poland	55.65	Indonesia	55.99	Turkey	54.97
Albania	46	China	41.64	Algeria	52.85
Russian Federation	44.44	Japan	21	Egypt, Arab Republic	45.06
Georgia	38.72			Morocco	44.72
				Iran, Islamic Republic	32.28

Source: See Table 4.8 for source

meaning that they import many things for direct export. Not all countries have augmented the openness of their economies, although the overall trend is a development towards increased openness in the economies of a dynamic world trade. One may note that the openness of the economy reflects more the size of the country, large countries having more closed economies. Thus, we have the following correlation between the degree of openness of the economy and LNpopulation 1990 = −0.44 (*N* = 131).

Is there a clear relationship between the openness of the economy and basic indicators on economic growth and average level of affluence? On the one hand, Balassa argued strongly for the existence of a causal connection between foreign trade and economic growth (Balassa, 1989). One may speak of a so-called trade theory of economic growth, which argues that the trade patterns of a country are of decisive importance for its dynamism (Nurkse, 1961; Little *et al.*, 1970; Kreuger, 1978). On the other hand, there is the opposite argument that economic growth influences the trade pattern (Johnson, H., 1958, 1975). Figures 4.5 and 4.6 present scattergrams displaying the relationship between economic development and trade.

Examining correlations we find that trade is conducive to affluence, although it is far from explaining all the variation in national income. Trade theory offers two competing explanations of why countries engage heavily in trade, namely the theory of comparative advantage and factor endowments (Heckscher-Ohlin) and the theory of economies of scale (Krugman).

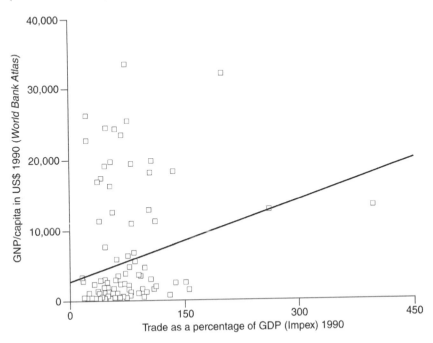

Figure 4.5   Impex 1990 and affluence in 1990 (r = 0.23; *N* = 119)

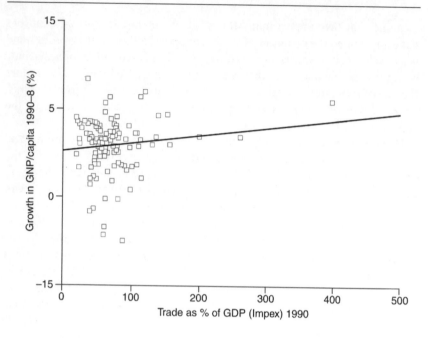

Figure 4.6   Impex 1990 and economic growth 1990–98 (r = 0.14; N = 122)

Both theories mean that more of trade is a positive for economic growth. Figure 4.6 confirms this conclusion, but only weakly.

Trade links up a country with the global market economy. It does not reduce its level of affluence, but neither does it by itself bring a high level of economic growth. The openness of a country may matter for political outcomes, as it makes autarchy impossible. And autarchy tends to be linked with dictatorship and dismal social inequalities.

Conclusion

When economic development benefits the broad masses of the population, then economic growth translates into an improvement in the living standards of ordinary men and women – i.e. quality of life. The human development index (HDI) may be employed to probe the social consequences of economic development. It takes aspects of living conditions into account and not simply economic output. Above the world average we have the occidental countries, Latin America and Eastern Europe as well as South East Asia. Below this average, which does not take population size into account, we find Sub-Saharan Africa, South Asia and the Arab World. What we wish to emphasize here is that the level of human development is more important for development than a high level of affluence is. There is a clear connection between economic wealth and social development, but it is not a linear relationship. Figure 4.7 shows the relationship between affluence and the HDI for 1998 where r = 0.67 and N = 136.

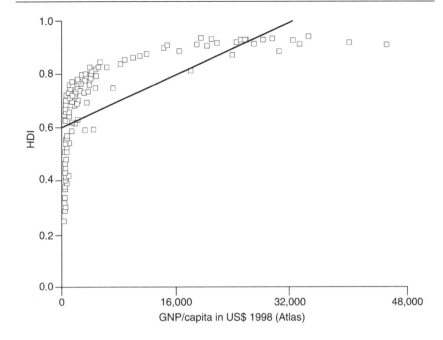

Figure 4.7   Affluence and HDI
Source: UNDP (2000) and *World Bank Atlas*, 2000

One may establish that as it is absolutely essential to raise the living standards from very low levels to moderate levels, one needs only rather modest increases in affluence. After a certain level, a higher level of affluence does not translate into a proportional increase in quality of life, as high levels of affluence may be expressed in conspicuous consumption. Countries may move out of the poverty trap, as the first move to a higher level of affluence implies a substantial rise in quality of life. The correlation between PPP1990 and economic growth 1990–98 is r = 0.13 (as shown in Figure 3.3 in chapter 3), which is in line with the argument launched here that affluence and economic growth are independent of each other, suggesting a bias in favour of a hope that poverty can be reduced.

Income equality is another vital objective when one moves from economic development to social development. There is evidence to the effect that higher levels of affluence are conducive to a greater degree of income equality. But the so-called Kuznets effect is not as pronounced today as it used to be. Generally speaking, richer countries have more equal distributions of income, but there exist several poor countries where the income distribution is also rather equal, simply because almost all are poor. A few poor or middle-income countries in Latin America and in Africa display extreme income differentials.

We may conclude that economic development and social change are closely connected. Economic affluence promotes strongly quality of life and it drives down income inequality as well as enhancing gender equality. Let us look now at political developments.

CHAPTER 5

First World and Third World States

Introduction

Chapters 3 and 4 looked at the economic and social characteristics of the countries of the world focusing upon the macro variation. The time has come to enquire into the political organization of the countries of the world from the perspective of political economy. A modern state – what is that? To analyse this question we will combine Weberian theory about the bureaucratic state with Marxist ideas about the relative autonomy of the state in relation to society.

The key difference to be found is that between First World states and Third World states, but the variation within the Third World must also be recognized. How do we develop indicators that will tap these pertinent differences? The states in Third World countries are often described in terms of properties that deviate from the Weberian ideal type: the 'neo-patrimonial', 'prebendal', 'bureaucratic-authoritarian' and 'the post-colonial' state (Leftwich, 1994). How much do Third World states deviate from the Weberian ideal type of a formally bureaucratic government? This is the first major question.

The second major question is whether this difference between modern bureaucratic governments in the First World and the 'underdeveloped state' in the Third World is a function of the socio-economic differences between the societies in these countries. The hypothesis that the state reflects the socio-economic development of its society would hold that the state in the Third World can only reflect its weak societies, but this would deny the well-known argument of the relative autonomy of the state. The idea of 'soft states' or 'weak states' goes in the direction of denying state autonomy, but the argument about 'developmental states' supports the relative autonomy thesis.

The literature on macro-political change has employed the concept of political development as if it was the counterpart in political science to socio-economic development in economics. The basic problem, however, is whether there exists an identifiable entity to be denoted by such a concept. It seems that democracy is often considered as the most important dimension of political development (Lipset, 1959). But there are other connotations of 'political development' that need to be taken into account.

One basic problem in the study of modern state organization is how it relates to general processes of social and economic development – *modernization*. Some look upon political development as a function of social change, whereas others regard political change as conducive to economic development and social transformation. Let us look at this problem from different angles emphasizing the variation in state characteristics around the world. In this chapter we enquire first into how the state varies around the globe, using a set of indicators measuring certain key state features derived from state theory in general. Second, we examine how democracy as a political regime interacts with economic and social development. If democracy is the core meaning of the concept of political development, then how is democracy related to economic development?

The modern state: bureaucracy

The states in the world today can be described by several attributes. Starting from the definition of the state within public international law, we arrive at a few characteristics which are present in different forms in the states of the world. A country has a state when an organization has effective control of the use of physical violence among a population within a specific territory by means of the employment of a legal order (Weber, 1978).

Different states may be identified in relation to these key characteristics which any and all states have: (i) legal order; (ii) effectiveness; (iii) territory and population. As these state properties may vary from one country to another, one may raise the question of whether political development entails a process of change towards a so-called modern or developed state. A state may be considered to be modern or fully developed when it has one or more of the following features: (i) the institutionalization of valid legal order for a territory completely accepted by a people; (ii) resources: the capacity to maintain itself and protect its people within its borders; (iii) democratic legal order.

This definition of political development of a modern state draws upon the extensive literature on state development in First World and Third World countries. It is not a very precise one, but it reflects the ambiguity of this concept. One may regard political development towards a modern state as a three-stage evolutionary phase. First, a government manages to establish a legal order that is accepted as legitimate by a people – nation-building. Second, this state raises enough resources to maintain itself within its territory. Finally, the government of this state is elected through some democratic mechanism. Phase 1 may be seen as a precondition to phase 2, which is a precondition to phase 3. But not all states of the world have reached or successfully established these stages. In some countries not even stage 1 is accomplished.

The fundamental difficulty is to nail down what political development amounts to more specifically when it comes to the nature of the state. One may underline the basic objective of states – the safety of citizens, or one may emphasize the organization structure of the modern state – the bureaucratic machinery of impartial civil servants. As long as governments pursue this objective and employ a bureaucracy, they are to be considered as modern states, although they may not be democratic. From this perspective it is certainly very alarming that scholars have started to talk about a systematic link between the African state and crime (Bayart, *et al.*, 1997).

When governments start to do business in crime activities or when government cannot undo or control war lords, as is often the case in West Africa, the Great Lakes Area, Angola and Somalia, then one would definitely doubt the existence of a modern state. The lack of a state is obvious when countries plunge into anarchy and civil war, as in Afghanistan. However, countries may still have a government but it does not operate as a modern state. To some scholars only governments which respect and implement human rights constitute developed political systems. Other scholars would search for the characteristics of a modern government in its adherence to a system of institutions.

The neutrality and objectivity of the state would in such a Weberian approach qualify it as 'modern'. When government operates under a legal order in a predictable fashion avoiding arbitrariness, then it would satisfy the requirement of being 'modern'. One would also wish to demand that such a government respects the classical objective of the state, namely to enhance the protection of its citizens. To tap the existence of a modern state in this approach one may measure the spread of corruption in government. An index measuring the lack of corruption in a country has been developed recently – see Table 5.1. If lack of arbitrariness and absence of corruption is at the core of the occidental state, then Table 5.1 may be consulted for a first impression of the difference between First World states and Third World states.

Table 5.1 Perceived lack of corruption 1980–2000

Region	Index 1980	Index 1990	Index 2000
Occidental	7.6	7.7	7.9
CEE and CIS	3.9	4.7	3.3
Central and Latin America	3.7	3.4	3.9
Sub-Saharan Africa	3.4	3.2	3.2
Arab World	3.5	3.8	4.3
South Asia	2.0	1.6	2.8
South East Asia	4.8	4.6	4.6
Average	5.3	5.3	4.8
N	54	54	90
Eta-squared	0.517	0.575	0.631
Significance	0.000	0.000	0.000

Source: Transparency International (2000)

There are immense differences in perceived corruption between the states in various regions. The basic difference is between the occidental world and the other regions, but the South East Asian numbers are in between the high ones in the occidental world and the low ones in the Third World. Corruption is to be found mainly in South Asia, Sub-Saharan Africa, Latin America and the former Soviet Union. The corruption index is not identical with democracy, as a state may score high on perceived lack of corruption and yet be non-democratic. Similarly, a democratic government could find itself in difficulties over trying to stem corruption. According to modernization theory it is not enough for a modern government to be institutionalized in order for it to qualify as a modern state. It is only a necessary condition and not a sufficient one.

Modernization

The approach that political development would result in a democratic regime was first suggested in a succinct form by Lipset in 1959. Criticizing the Lipset approach for its lack of measurement quality Bollen (1980) suggested an index of democracy which could be used in quantitative analyses of political development. And Bollen was successful in confirming the Lipset hypothesis about a close association between the introduction of democracy and high levels of socio-economic development. The Cutright analysis of 1963 is a version of the same theme as is found in the work of Russett (1964) and Dahl (1971). The study of Adelman and Morris (1967) pointed in the same direction, but it was soon recognized that the problem of the economic and social conditions for democracy is a complex one (Rustow, 1970).

The theory about an almost direct link between economic development and the strengthening of democratic regimes was severely questioned by O'Donnell in *Modernization and Bureaucratic-Authoritarianism: Studies in South American Politics* (1973). O'Donnell argued that high levels of modernization in Latin America coincided with various types of authoritarian rule. This stimulated an enquiry into any relationship between capitalism and right-wing authoritarianism (Collier, 1978). The democracy approach looks upon the political system as the dependent variable whereas socio-economic development is considered as the independent variable. However, it is possible to reverse the relationship and consider in particular economic development as the dependent variable.

Political development may be seen as a reflection of more general processes of social development. The classical theory of modernization stated that political development is an offspring of more general developmental trends – industrialization, urbanization and mass literacy – moving a society from a traditional state to a modern one (Binder, 1986). Often modernization theory was more orientated towards a static comparison of two kinds of society or polity – traditional or modern – than towards the process of change from one to the other.

Lerner presented a model distinguishing between three ideal types of orientations – modern, transitional and traditional – on the basis of the following criteria: literacy, urbanism, media participation and empathy (Lerner, D., 1958: 71). The process of modernization is the movement away from traditional society which involves three basic phases: urbanization, literacy and media participation. The special contribution of Lerner to the modernization theme is the emphasis on communication mechanisms which mould the transition process. Political development refers to mass participation involving the use of modern media systems which have replaced the old, oral systems. Lerner identified four dimensions in modernization which are correlated to a considerable extent: urbanization, literacy, media participation and political participation. These findings refer to the 1950s and it may be questioned whether these phenomena really are interrelated today.

Deutsch made an attempt to quantify the often diffuse concepts in the modernization theme. Frequently, modernization theory simply employed a pure distinction between two ideal types to portray the meaning of modernization. However, some authors adopting this approach attempted to model the modernization process by means of quantitative equations. Two different models were employed: one describing the general process of modernization or the coming of a Western-type society – industrialization, urbanization and mass mobilization. The other model placed the modern polity in a context where it was preceded by the process of social modernization.

Typically, political development was looked upon as a reflection of more basic socio-economic transformations. Social mobilization denotes, as Deutsch writes:

> a concept which brackets together a number of more specific processes of change, such as changes of residence, of occupation, of social setting, of face-to-face associates, of institutions, roles, and ways of acting, of experiences and expectations, and finally of personal memories, habits and needs, including the need for new patterns of group affiliation and new images of personal identity. (Deutsch, 1961: 493)

Deutsch conceived of these changes as interacting resulting in a 'cumulative impact', which tend to transform political behaviour.

Whereas functionalism focused on the static differences between two types of society or two kinds of polity, the modernization approach emphasized the dynamic processes of change from one type of society to another. Apter (1965) elaborated modernization theory by focusing on political system responses to the problems of the transformation from traditional to modern society characterizing Third World events. These polity-type responses include: a neo-mercantilist state, a mobilization state and a reconciliation state (Apter, 1965: 420).

Some authors really tried to specify more definitely what modernization was all about, i.e. a statement of the major differences between the industrialized world – the OECD countries as well as the communist world – and the Third World LDC countries. The following characteristics of a traditional society versus a modern society were suggested:

> *Agricultural society*: 1. Predominance of ascriptive, particularistic, diffuse patterns. 2. Stable local groups and limited spatial mobility. 3. Relatively simple and 'occupational' differentiation. 4. A 'deferential' stratification system of diffuse impact.
>
> *Modern industrial society*: 1. Predominance of universalistic, specific, achievement norms. 2. High degree of social mobility. 3. Well-developed occupational system, insulated from other social systems. 4. Egalitarian class system based on generalized patterns of achievement. 5. Prevalence of associations, i.e. functionally specific non-ascriptive structures.
> *Source*: Sutton (1963).

Modernization theorists argued that the transition from one kind of society to another kind implies a radically different polity. Rustow and Ward identified a list of properties of the so-called modern polity or state: (i) a highly differentiated and functionally specific system of governmental organization; (ii) high degree of integration within this governmental structure; (iii) the prevalence of rational and secular procedures for the making of political decisions; (iv) the large volume, wide range and high efficacy of its political and administrative decisions; (v) a widespread and effective sense of popular identification with the history, territory and national identity of the state; (vi) widespread popular interest and involvement in the political system, though not necessarily in the decision-making aspects thereof; (vii) the allocation of political roles by achievement rather than ascription; (viii) judicial and regulatory techniques based upon a predominantly secular and impersonal system of law (Rustow and Ward, 1964: 6–7).

The question is whether a state that complies with the criteria (i)–(viii) is a democratic state? Or could that modern state also be an authoritarian regime? Here is one of the great puzzles in the theory of political development. On the one hand, all agree that traditional authority or even charismatic authority is not in agreement with a modern state, because these two types of authority lack the institutionalization of power that is typical of legal or rational authority in Weberian theory. On the other hand, some tend to equate legal authority as the characteristic of the modern state with Rule of Law in general or human rights in particular. However, some modern states are authoritarian without being traditional or charismatic regimes.

Let us make an overview of relevant state characteristics in order to analyse the variation globally. Distinguishing between modern and non-modern states as well as between First World states or Third World states involves the consideration of a number of state properties such as institutionalization, democracy and capacity.

Identification of state characteristics

Based upon this review of the classical state and modernization literature it is possible to identify a number of characteristics that may be associated with the modern state. In particular we recognize institutionalization, state capacity, democracy and political stability. Now the question is: what may be understood by identifying these properties? In order to give these properties a concrete content, we will go into some more detail about what they may stand for, and employ factor analysis to sort out some possible indicators that will allow us to measure these theoretical properties, but also make it possible to map the variation of state characteristics across the countries of the world.

Institutionalization

Since it is difficult to identify what change really represents development that is conducive to modernity, then perhaps political development is the capacity to cope with processes of development? Huntington equated political development with the growth of political institutions in general (O'Brien, 1972). He stated that it is useful to distinguish political development from modernization and 'to identify political development with the institutionalisation of political organisations and procedures' (Huntington, S. P., 1965: 386). Huntington writes:

> Institutionalisation is the process by which organisations and processes acquire value and stability. The level of institutionalisation of any political system can be defined by the adaptability, complexity, autonomy and coherence of its organisations and procedures. (ibid.: 394)

These defining concepts – adaptability, complexity, autonomy and coherence – are very abstract and we need more information about how they are measured and then how these measures may be added together into a single index of institutionalization as political development.

The concept of institutionalization may appear to be abstract, but the truth is that it is generally agreed that the measurement of the concept refers to state consolidation and nation-building (Rokkan, 1970; Tilly, 1975). First we have the general index of institutional sclerosis which is a recent attempt to measure the period of time of uninterrupted organizational growth in a society suggested in order to tap the strength of so-called distributional coalitions or special interest organizations (Olson, 1982; Choi, 1983). Second, there is the introduction of modernized leadership – political as well as economic – at a crucial point of time in the history of a country – *modernized political leadership* and *modernized economic leadership* (based

Table 5.2 Factor analysis of institutionalization indicators (N = 44); varimax rotated factor loadings

Indicators	Factor 1	Factor 2
Institutional sclerosis	0.936	0.273
Modernized political leadership	0.942	0.290
Modernized economic leadership	0.897	0.236
Age of constitution in 1978	0.386	0.828
Age of constitution in 1985	0.254	0.862
Age of constitution in 1996	0.152	0.825
Explained variance in %	46.7	38.7

Sources: Institutional sclerosis: Choi (1983); modernized political and economic leadership: Black (1966); age of constitution: *Encyclopaedia Britannica* (various years)

on Black, 1966). Third, we identify the age of the current constitution during different periods of time at the end of the twentieth century – *age of constitution*. The outcome of a factor analysis employing these three kinds of indicators is displayed in Table 5.2.

The finding is that these indicators on institutionalization identify two phenomena, the age of modernized leadership and the age of constitutions, that may be associated with 'state-building'. They may be tapped by the employment of the indicators for institutional sclerosis, modernized political leadership and the age of the constitution.

State capacity

One may certainly question whether democratization is the only existing or the only valuable form of political change. Perhaps a modern state is first and foremost a state with a considerable capacity to maintain itself in an uncertain and changing environment? State stability would be as relevant as democracy, at least the so-called functionalist approach to the state has argued so.

The functionalists approached the political system as fulfilling functions in terms of structures. On the one hand, we have the input functions: political socialization and recruitment, interest articulation, interest aggregation and political communication. On the other hand, there is the set of output functions: rule-making, rule application and rule adjudication (Almond and Coleman, 1960: 17). And political development is specified as the degree of specificity with which structures fulfil functions as well as the extent to which political structures are separated out of each other.

Functionalists looking at the state emphasized the increase in system capabilities, in conversion processes and adaptation functions. Influenced by Easton (1965), the functionalists speak of inputs and outputs as well as demand and support. Political systems have a varied capacity for handling inputs and outputs as conceptualized in the idea of system capacity: regulative, extractive, distributive and responsive capability (Almond and Powell, 1966: 1–33). The functionalist theory of political development refers to three aspects of state structure: differentiation, autonomy and secularization. The basic proposition claims that the more modern or developed a state is, the more it is characterized by differentiation, autonomy and secularization (Almond and Powell, 1966: 323).

Almond's approach to political development was much influenced by the general theory of structural-functionalism as interpreted, for example, by Sutton (1963), building on Talcott Parsons and his associates in the late 1940s and the 1950s (Parsons and Shils, 1951; Parsons, 1951; Levy, 1952; Parsons and Smelser, 1956). The general rebuttal of sociological functionalism contributed to a severe reaction against the Almond framework. Thus, the functional approach to political development focused on state attributes such as system capacity and structural differentiation. Modern states in the First World tend to be more developed than states in the Third World, because they have more differentiated structures. But how is this concept of state capacity to be measured?

Pye surveyed the literature on political development and found no less than nine properties: (i) the political prerequisites of economic development; (ii) the politics typical of industrial societies; (iii) political modernization; (iv) the operation of a nation-state; (v) administrative and legal development; (vi) mass mobilization and participation; (vii) the building of democracy; (viii) stability and orderly change; (ix) mobilization and power. Pye states that '*capacity* of a political system' is a function of a modern state. 'Running through much of the discussion of political development is that of *differentiation* and specialisation', he says, implying that 'offices and agencies tend to have their distinct and limited functions, and there is an equivalent of a division of labour within the realm of government' (Pye, 1966: 46–47).

Coleman stated that the modern state required: '(1) new patterns of integration regulating and containing the tensions and conflicts produced by increased differentiation, and (2) new patterns of participation and resource distribution adequately responsive to the demands generated by the imperatives of equality' (Coleman, 1965: 15). Perhaps there was a contradiction in the functionalist approach. To identify political development with system capacity and system differentiation implies that political development is somehow a function of an increase in state involvement: the stronger the state, the greater political development. However, when political development is identified with autonomy and system differentiation it seems as if it implies less state involvement. The less encompassing the nature of the state and the more subsystem autonomy there is, the more political development we have.

If political development does mean both state involvement and autonomy, this simply reflects that both processes of change may be considered valuable. If this is so, then perhaps what matters is modernization in general? We must take up the general approach to political development in the form of modernization, as a transformation towards the type of 'social, economic and political systems that have developed in Western Europe and North America from the seventeenth century to the nineteenth' spreading later to the South American, Asian and African continents (Eisenstadt, 1966: 1).

Political development may not be interpreted as deterministic change towards some desirable end state, but as the successful path to some temporary predicament. This novel theory of political development was elaborated by Binder, who said:

> If we re-examine these five areas of critical change, or these five crises of political development, the crisis of identity, the crisis of legitimacy, the crisis of participation, the crisis of distribution, and the crisis of penetration, we will find that all five types of change may occur without any concomitant strengthening of the political institutions of the country affected. (Binder, L., 1971: 65)

Thus political development may not be order or institutionalization *per se*, but is related to a successful institutional response where élites cope with challenges maintaining the valuable entity of order, whether rightist or leftist. Brunner and Brewer (1971) explained processes of change in modern Turkey and the Philippines, including factors which the political élite could manipulate, again emphasizing choice and response to political system crisis. Almond and Rostow also suggested this new approach to political development, emphasizing choice and response by actors, identifying various kinds of processes of change involving political unrest and the conscious response to political instability by leaders and institutions (Almond *et al.*, 1973; Rustow, 1970).

Political system capacity is expressed in various ways or it may constitute a potential that may be drawn upon in times of exceptional events. Different factors in a society may be conducive to polity strength or state capacity. The indicators on political capacity range from the size of the population – a source of great power ambitions – over actual involvement in war activities – one traditional expression of political ambitions to display strength – to ordinary measures of the size of the state or the public sector. Since small states and peaceful societies that are welfare states have big governments we should expect to find that the capacity indicators do not co-vary. In the factor analysis presented in Table 5.3 we employ indicators measuring military spending and military personnel as well as those measuring different aspects of the public sector size: spending and incomes. We report the findings from analyses covering the mid-1980s as well as the mid-1990s. As expected, capacity in a political context may mean two very different things:

Table 5.3 Factor analysis of capacity indicators (1985: $N = 78$; 1995: $N = 82$); varimax rotated factor loadings

Indicators	1985		1995	
	Factor 1	*Factor 2*	*Factor 1*	*Factor 2*
Military exp. as % of central gov. exp.	−0.222	0.896	−0.377	0.854
Military exp. as % of GNP	0.265	0.925	0.033	0.971
Military empl. as % of lab. force	0.276	0.860	0.199	0.802
Central gov. consump. as % of GDP	0.612	0.444	0.750	0.294
Central gov. exp. as % of GDP	0.934	0.255	0.960	0.041
Central gov. curr. rev. as % of GDP	0.925	0.070	0.963	0.007
Taxes as % of GDP	0.904	−0.092	0.941	−0.079
Explained variance	44.5	38.2	49.3	34.4

Sources: Military personnel and military expenditures: WB (2000a); central government consumption, expenditure, revenue and tax: also WB (2000a)

welfare spending (central government expenditure as a percentage of GDP), or military effort (military expenditure as a percentage of GNP).

Democracy

The final property of the state that we will deal with is the kind of regime the state tends to adhere to. One crucial distinction in this context is between democracies and non-democracies. The term 'democracy' may be defined in various ways. One may stress political democracy, economic democracy or social democracy. In our context we focus on what is most commonly labelled as 'political democracy', which implies the existence of extensive political rights and civil liberties, as suggested by Dahl in his discussion of polyarchy (Dahl, 1971; see also Bollen, 1990). Although there is some consensus on what this interpretation implies with regard to the referents of the concept, i.e. the countries that are to be designated as 'democracies', there remain issues where opinions differ, e.g. what the concept implies outside the political sphere.

There are now a number of measures available on democracy, human rights or similar concepts (Bollen, 1986). The first systematic attempt is to decide whether it is possible to characterize democracy in terms of properties that are categorical or continuous. One line of argument is that democracy is an inherently categorical variable: it is only meaningful to distinguish between democracies and non-democracies. Democracy in this sense is indivisible; either a state is democratic or it is non-democratic. There may also be something called 'semi-democracies' (Huntington, 1991: 11).

The other line of argument states that it is meaningful to distinguish between states that are more or less democratic, meaning in this way that democracy is a measurable property (Bollen, 1980; Bollen and Jackman, 1989; Bollen, 1990). Following this idea a series of indicators on democracy or proxies for democracy have been constructed, from Lerner (1958) and Lipset (1959) down to Bollen (1980) and Humana (1992).

We adhere to the latter standpoint arguing for the utility of constructing continuous measures of democracy, which make it possible to map the variation in democracy between nations, in space as well as time. This does not mean that it is an easy task; some may even argue that this is more or less impossible, since such indicators tend to be inherently culturally biased towards the Western political culture (Barsh, 1993). Even though it is problematic to use such measures, we find that these measures allow for a much more systematic analysis of problems related to democracy that are highly relevant today.

We explicitly focus on indicators of political democracy that try to capture the extent of political rights and civil liberties available to the citizens of a given polity. This means that we reject the inclusion of measures referring to economic democracy or economic freedom (Spindler, 1991). At a conceptual level, political democracy must be distinguished from economic democracy or economic freedom, although there may exist interrelations between the indicators of these concepts, especially political democracy and economic freedom. Measures of these concepts are to be found in Bollen (1979, 1980), who constructed widely used empirical scores for the years 1960 and 1965. He was preceded by others: Cutright (1963), Neubauer (1967), Adelman and Morris (1967), Smith (1969) and Jackman (1975). Gastil (1986, 1987) and Freedom House (1999, 2000) have worked on such measures from 1973 and other attempts in this direction have been reported by Perry (1980), Humana (1983, 1986, 1992), Pourgerami (1988), Coppedge and Reinecke (1990), Vanhanen (1990, 1992) Gurr (1990), Arat (1991) and Hadenius (1992).

Among the many indexes available, we have chosen three sets of index: Bollen, Humana and Freedom House. Together they cover a large part of the latter part of the twentieth century, and they also conceptualize democracy and measure it in a slightly different way. What we want to know, therefore is whether they still capture one dimension. This is what we test in the factor analysis reported in Table 5.4.

What we find from the factor analysis is that the different indexes, although they are constructed in different ways and measure different time periods, still capture a single factor explaining more than three-fourths of the variation in the data. Thus we may conclude that these indicators tend to measure an important regime property among the states of the world, the property of democracy versus non-democracy.

Whether each and any of these dimensions constitute political development in a real sense is an open question. Perhaps at the end of the day it can only be resolved by normative argument, as it has been claimed that the concept of political development can only arrive at a conception of the modern state through the employment of values. Thus, political development contains a value bias.

Table 5.4 Democracy indicators ($N = 59$); non-rotated factor loadings

Indicators	Factor loadings
Bollen, 1960	0.829
Bollen, 1965	0.825
Bollen, 1980	0.886
Humana, 1983	0.934
Humana, 1986	0.943
Humana, 1991	0.803
Freedom House, 1981–85	0.958
Freedom House, 1991–95	0.825
Explained variance	77.0

Note: The Freedom House index has been reconstructed so that it is a linearly transformation by adding the scores for political rights and civil liberties into an index going from 10 = democracy to 1 = non-democracy
Sources: Bollen here refers to Bollen's index for 1960, 1965 and 1980; Humana refers to Humana's index for 1983, 1986 and 1991; Freedom House refers to the Freedom House's index for 1981–85 and 1991–95

Political development: a value biased notion?

Political development is differently conceived of depending upon how one perceives the institutional response to crisis. One may separate between: (i) the liberal theory of development: democracy and equality as systems response; (ii) the state theory: increased control, planning and technology; (iii) the revolutionary theory: mobilization of the masses and socialist transformation; (iv) the dependence theory: increased centre–periphery dependency (Binder, L., 1986). Some identify the concept of political development with democracy, others with étatism, and still others with revolution or socialism.

There are two main implications arising from the consequences of socio-economic changes such as modernization of the society for the stability of the polity. One popular theme implies that political development leads to more stability as political systems adapt to the new exigencies. Thus we find attempts to measure political development by various indicators of political stability (Sigelman, 1971: 36–7): government stability, political participation by the military, interest articulation by anomic groups, political leadership, interest articulation by associational groups, and the character of bureaucracy.

Alternatively, another major theme implies that instability is typical of political development. There is a search for indicators of political development in phenomena of political instability, such as *coups d'état*, major constitutional changes, cabinet changes, and changes in the effective executive (Banks, 1972). No doubt the state of the concept of political development is bewildering. No less conspicuous is the 180° reversal of development as being conducive to underdevelopment. If political development is the outcome of processes of change that present real challenges to political élites, then could it be that these social and economic change processes result in undesirable outcomes? Perhaps the overall movement is one towards political underdevelopment?

Frank introduced a quite novel paradigm for interpreting broad processes of social, economic and political change – partly inspired by earlier Marxist interpretations by Baran and Sweezy, among others (Frank, 1967). The crucial distinctions in the Frank framework are the ones between undeveloped and underdeveloped and between centre and periphery. The transition from traditionalism to modernism is one of movement from an undeveloped stage towards underdevelopment – the opposite theme to that of the modernization theorists. The process of underdevelopment is governed by the logic of the interaction between a world capitalist centre and Third World periphery in terms of which the predicament of the so-called developing nations become worse. How do we test this new radical theory of development as underdevelopment? Does it imply something more specific about political change?

According to the theory of world system analysis proposed by Wallerstein (1974, 1979), processes of change in various parts of the world are interdependent in terms of a more or less zero-sum game. The centre of the capitalist world, including the East European countries, are the winners in this world system interaction whereas the poor Third World countries are the losers. The basic criterion of change is the increase in inequality between these nations and within the peripheral countries. Wallerstein looks upon development as being determined by commodity production for profit in a world market which is characterized by various forms of labour exploitation based on asymmetrical power relations between powerful states and peripheral areas.

Thus development results in inequality, inflation and unemployment in the Third World. What are the implications for political development? Although the radical approach to development has resulted in an abundant literature about capitalism and the Third World (e.g. Chilcote and Johnson, 1983), there is perhaps not a distinct radical theory about political development. In it we still find the same hope for some kind of desirable political change process.

Political development would necessarily imply political change, but the opposite is not true. And where there is polity change there may also be the typical expressions of political instability: protest or violent protest as well as the occurrence of violence in state and society in general. Of course, the first type of phenomenon may be accompanied by the second kind and vice versa. Here our choice is to equate political development with political or social stability as it may be tapped by indicators measuring the occurrence of protest and violence phenomena. In the factor analysis portrayed in Table 5.5 we employ data reported by Banks (1996) on these kinds of phenomena for the early 1970s, 1980s and the 1990s. The data employed here simply reports the number of occurrences.

Table 5.5   Factor analysis of stability indicators (1971–75: N = 127; 1981–85: N = 130; 1991–95: N = 149)

Indicators	1975		1985		1995	
	Factor 1	*Factor 2*	*Factor 1*	*Factor 2*	*Factor 1*	*Factor 2*
General strikes	0.863	0.099	0.727	0.084	0.709	−0.167
Riots	0.916	0.189	0.861	0.065	0.785	0.150
Anti-government demonstrations	0.809	0.202	0.828	0.020	−0.062	0.894
Assassinations	0.405	0.485	0.432	0.627	0.376	0.462
Guerilla warfare	0.362	0.734	0.101	0.908	0.028	0.876
Revolutions	−0.052	0.891	−0.127	0.873	−0.062	0.894
Explained variance	42.3	27.6	36.1	33.2	32.9	30.8

Note: The data employed in the factor analysis are the mean values for each variable for the respective five-year periods: 1971–75, 1981–85 and 1991–95
Source: Stability indicators: Banks (1996)

The various indicators on protest and violence are both interrelated and independent to some extent. We may distinguish between two rather distinct factors: non-violent protest, on the one hand, and the occurrence of political violence on the other.

Thus far, the radical theory of development as the underdevelopment of an undeveloped area has offered little in terms of suggestions about the political implications of this process of underdevelopment. The Frank–Wallerstein theme is mainly a socio-economic theory. When political development is discussed along the lines of this theme the approach is exclusively normative. Ocampo and Johnson, on the other hand, define political development in the following way without tying it to ideas about how to reverse the trend towards development: 'Development involves the liberation of man from condition of exploitation and oppression. Politics is the means of human liberation' (Ocampo and Johnson, 1972: 424). However, underdevelopment theory has been criticized as being too deterministic and general in describing everything with the centre–periphery concepts as well as being too little action-oriented (Phillips, 1978; Taylor, 1987).

Comparative analysis of state properties

So far we have been able to identify a number of basic state properties, or state characteristics: institutionalization, state capacity, political stability and democracy. For each of these properties it is also possible to identify indicators capturing various aspects of these state properties. The next step in the analysis will therefore deal with how these state properties vary between the countries of the world in a cross-sectional fashion. To do this mapping we employ the same macro regions of the world as we have used in the two previous chapters. We thus construct a set of regions distinguishing between an occidental, Central and East European, Central and Latin American, Sub-Saharan African, Arab World, South Asia and South East Asian set of regions. Let us start with the basic regime type, namely the variation in democracy worldwide.

Democracy

The variation in democracy scores as measured by the three different indicators is presented in Table 5.6. The three indicators are scaled in a roughly similar way, meaning that the more democracy the higher the value. Full-scale democracy comes close to 10 while non-democracy comes close to 0 or 1 depending upon how the indicators are scaled.

Politically developed countries in the sense of democratic regimes are not unsurprisingly to be found in the set of occidental countries. The experience of democracy is particularly low in the sets of African and Asian countries whereas some Central and Latin American countries go back and forth in between authoritarianism and democracy in a circular time frame. The high eta-coefficient indicates that the differences between these categories of countries are larger than the differences within the same categories. Let us take a closer look at the occurrence of democratic regime characteristics in the world around 1991.

Countries that score low on the democracy index within the occidental set of nations are the ones that have recently experienced the dismantling of an authoritarian regime: Spain in 1975, Portugal in 1974 and Greece in 1974. The status of democratic institutions in Turkey is still precarious. In Asia there are a few countries which have a strong democratic tradition although not a long one: India. There is hardly any country in Africa except

Table 5.6   Democracy scores 1960–95

Region	Bollen 60	Bollen 65	Bollen 80	Hum. 83	Hum. 86	Hum. 91	Freedom 81/85	Freedom 91/95
Occidental	9.0	9.0	9.8	9.0	9.3	9.3	9.7	9.7
CEE and CIS	2.6	2.6	1.5	4.2	3.8	8.3	2.1	5.9
Central and Latin America	6.8	6.2	4.4	6.5	6.7	7.1	6.2	6.7
Sub-Saharan Africa	5.9	4.5	2.6	5.3	4.6	5.5	3.0	4.3
Arab World	4.1	3.9	2.3	4.8	4.3	4.1	3.4	2.8
South Asia	5.8	5.8	3.7	6.3	4.7	4.5	4.3	4.2
South East Asia	5.0	4.4	3.7	5.5	5.0	5.0	4.2	4.8
Average	6.2	5.5	4.2	6.4	6.1	6.4	4.9	5.7
Eta-squared	0.379	0.400	0.531	0.551	0.599	0.623	0.647	0.524
Significance	0.000	0.000	0.000	0.000	0.000	0.000	0.000	0.000

Source: See Table 5.4 for source

Mauritius and Botswana that could qualify as a democracy and only a few cases in Central and Latin America: Costa Rica, Venezuela and Colombia. Major changes of regime in a direction towards more of a democracy have taken place among the countries in Central and Eastern Europe since the fall of communism in Europe around 1989 and 1990.

Political capacity

Political capacity is understood to be captured by public sector size as well as military spending. While we may formulate a hypothesis that political development as political system capacity implies that countries with large public sectors are to be found among the developed nations this is not necessarily so when it comes to military spending – the other political capacity indicator. Table 5.7 displays the variation cross-country wise for two periods of time, namely the mid-1980s and the mid-1990s.

Let us first look at the public sector indicator. Extensive public expenditure patterns are to be found in either welfare states providing citizens with the public provision of several services including social security or in those Leviathan states where for one reason or another military expenditures are the reason for comprehensive public budgets.

Not surprisingly Sweden scores highest in the occidental set, and is sometimes considered the model for a future welfare state. The Scandinavian countries score high generally whereas Southern European nations score lower. The countries on the other side of the Atlantic also come out high on this dimension but for different reasons. The high score of the USA reflects its military commitment whereas the high scores of the other nations indicate high welfare spending. As we move on to consider political system

Table 5.7 Average polity capacity scores 1985 and 1995: public sector size and military spending

Regions	Public sector (1985)	Public sector (1995)	Military spend as a percentage of GNP (1985)	Military spend as a percentage of GNP (1995)
Occidental	40.4	38.5	3.6	2.4
CEE and CIS	46.7	34.4	7.9	3.0
Central and Latin America	23.4	21.8	3.3	1.7
Sub-Saharan Africa	23.7	27.0	2.9	2.8
Arab World	33.7	32.4	13.3	6.7
South Asia	22.5	21.7	2.6	3.7
South East Asia	21.8	17.7	5.5	4.5
Average	29.4	29.7	4.9	3.3
Eta-squared	0.384	0.443	0.307	0.150
Significance	0.000	0.000	0.000	0.001

Source: See Table 5.2

Table 5.8   Exports and imports of arms as a percentage of total exports/imports 1985 and 1995

Region	Arms export (1985)	Arms export (1995)	Arms import (1985)	Arms import (1995)
Occidental	1.8	0.6	1.4	0.7
CEE and CIS	4.4	1.1	2.2	2.0
Central and Latin America	0.2	0.4	4.9	1.2
Sub-Saharan Africa	0.0	0.0	9.1	0.7
Arab World	0.5	0.1	17.9	6.9
South Asia	0.2	0.0	11.9	7.7
South East Asia	2.4	0.6	11.7	1.5
Average	0.9	0.4	8.0	2.2
Eta-squared	0.160	0.088	0.099	0.181
Significance	0.003	0.039	0.071	0.000

Source: WB (2000a)

capacity in the Third World it must be recognized that the cause of big budgets as a percentage of overall national resources is almost without exception military spending: take, for example, Egypt, Iran, Iraq, Jordan, Morocco, Tunisia, Algeria, Zambia and Congo-Kinshasa.

Among the occidental nations the USA is really the only country with a high score on this political capacity dimension. Iceland, Luxembourg and Switzerland have very low scores. Outside the occidental framework the situation is very different: take for example, Asia in particular but, also, Africa.

Two areas in the world stand out when it comes to the imports of arms on a huge scale: the Arab World and South Asia (see Table 5.8). Also several countries in South East Asia import arms for considerable sums of money, measured in a percentage of total country imports. The major exporters of arms are to be found among a few occidental countries and in the former USSR. The import of arms is related to the occurrence of conflict between states or within states – see Table 5.9.

Although the numbers given in Table 5.9 are crude, they indicate that Asia, Africa and the Middle East are the areas of the world where armed conflicts occur regularly. In Europe armed conflict has taken place mainly in the Balkans. A detailed listing of armed conflicts is given in Appendices 5.1 and 5.2.

Institutionalization

The institutionalization index is scored in such a way that high scores mean a lengthy time period of institutionalization and low scores stand for recent institutionalization. Politically developed in this interpretation of the concept are those countries where a modernized leadership or a process of

Table 5.9 Armed conflicts worldwide 1989–99

Year	Intrastate	Interstate	Total	Europe	Middle East	Asia	Africa	America
1989	44	3	47	2	4	19	14	8
1990	46	3	49	3	6	18	17	5
1991	50	1	51	6	7	16	17	5
1992	54	1	55	9	7	20	15	4
1993	46	0	46	10	7	15	11	3
1994	42	0	42	5	5	15	13	4
1995	34	1	35	5	4	13	9	4
1996	34	2	36	1	5	14	14	2
1997	33	1	34	0	3	15	14	2
1998	35	2	37	2	3	15	15	2
1999	35	2	37	3	2	14	16	2

Source: Wallensteen and Sollenberg, 2000: 638

nation-building was introduced in the late nineteenth or early twentieth century. Let us look more closely at the country variation within the seven categories of countries (Table 5.10).

The developed nations in this interpretation are to be found in the rich world, in Central and Latin America. Very high scores are to be found for the UK, the USA, Switzerland, France, Belgium and Denmark, as well as for Uruguay, Mexico and Brazil. Less institutionalized are the countries in Asia and Africa. Several of these nations date their birth to the post-Second World War period: Zambia, Malawi, Congo-Kinshasa, Kenya and Madagascar in Africa, as well as Singapore and Malaysia in Asia.

The institutionalization scores basically measure state longevity, where a state is dated to the introduction of modernized leadership which in some cases may come before the actual declaration of formal independence. They

Table 5.10 Indexes on institutionalization

Region	Instit. sclerosis	Modernized political leadership	Constit. age (1978)	Constit. age (1985)	Constit. age (1996)
Occidental	65.0	186.1	71.2	71.1	67.1
CEE and CIS	–	134.1	14.1	21.1	6.6
Central and Latin America	44.9	116.0	24.9	27.1	20.2
Sub-Saharan Africa	11.1	42.7	14.1	17.4	9.3
Arab World	26.4	68.7	16.9	29.6	19.7
South Asia	24.8	59.4	9.4	15.6	23.2
South East Asia	22.6	72.0	15.4	19.5	21.5
Average	40.2	98.8	26.4	30.5	22.2
Eta-squared	0.744	0.735	0.323	0.233	0.383
Significance	0.000	0.000	0.000	0.000	0.000

Source: See Table 5.2

reflect to some extent political stability, since statehood often requires time in order to function in a predictable fashion. Yet, institutionalization does not entail state performance as some democracies are young states like Botswana and Mauritius whereas there are some authoritarian states which score high on the index of state institutionalization, such as, for instance, Jordan.

Political stability

Similarly, early state institutionalization does not entail social order or the absence of political protest and the occurrence of political violence. Let us first look at the protest phenomenon. Table 5.11 maps the occurrence of political protest phenomena.

It appears that political protest occurred more often in the 1990s and the 1970s than in the 1980s. Protest phenomena like strikes and popular demonstrations are very country-specific phenomena, reflecting political instability. When one talks about protest as a country characteristic, then one refers to a few countries that are highly politically unstable: Central America, West Africa, the Middle East and the Khanates. One cannot, however, draw the conclusion that the occurrence of political violence is the same thing as protest phenomena. Table 5.12 has the country scores on the second political stability indicator – occurrence of political violence.

One notes the same trend in these data, i.e. the level of political violence is up in the early 1990s compared with the 1980s, but at a lower level than was the case in the 1970s. Countries characterized by civil war or the collapse of civil society score high on this indicator: Rwanda, Burundi, Somalia, Togo, Sri Lanka, Central America, Lebanon, Papua New Guinea, Tajikistan and Georgia.

Table 5.11   Protest scores 1970s ($N = 127$), 1980s ($N = 130$) and 1990s ($N = 149$)

Region	Protest index 1971–75	Protest index 1981–85	Protest index 1991–95
Occidental	2.55	1.35	2.19
CEE and CIS	1.33	1.27	2.03
Central and Latin America	1.87	1.42	3.71
Sub-Saharan Africa	1.25	0.70	2.07
Arab World	1.24	0.77	1.68
South Asia	2.47	2.29	4.30
South East Asia	1.93	0.93	1.85
Average	1.74	1.11	2.38
Eta-squared	0.138	0.130	0.134
Significance	0.006	0.008	0.002

Source: See Table 5.3

Table 5.12   Violence scores 1970s (N = 127), 1980s (N = 130) and 1990s (N = 149)

Region	Violence index 1971–75	Violence index 1981–85	Violence index 1991–95
Occidental	1.73	1.15	1.41
CEE and CIS	1.46	0.66	1.94
Central and Latin America	2.82	2.19	2.64
Sub-Saharan Africa	2.38	2.14	2.16
Arab World	2.98	2.02	2.77
South Asia	3.20	2.76	4.22
South East Asia	3.19	1.76	2.12
Average	2.49	1.86	2.25
Eta-squared	0.103	0.076	0.097
Significance	0.039	0.132	0.023

Source: See Table 5.3

The hypothesis that political instability is a typical concomitant event to political change follows from the interpretation of development as crisis-conducive processes. However, the overall finding is that the variation in the two main expressions of political instability do not follow the variation in the other aspects of political development.

Complexity of political development

The theme of political development aroused the interest of political scientists in the late 1950s as they were moving away from a particularistic concern with occidental political systems on the basis of a mainly legalistic approach. The new theme soon generated a vast literature. So numerous were the attempts at interpreting desirable political change stemming from the grand socio-economic transition from agraria to industria (Riggs, 1964), and so shifting the variety of theoretical models, that there had to come a final statement fitting all the hypotheses into the theory of political development (Pye, 1987). It would give to political science what economic growth theory gave to economics. We all know that this was not what happened. The theme fell apart, rejected as methodologically flawed due to its unrecognized Western value biases (Leftwich, 1990).

However, whatever the scientific value of the set of theories of political development may be, it is impossible to disregard vital phenomena of political change. A fresh start may be found where the elusive concept of political development was left off. Recognizing the crucial part played by so-called value premises (Weber, 1949; Myrdal, 1970), the political development concept may be unpacked into manageable dimensions. Explicit multidimensionality is substituted for implicit ambiguity. And the derivation of different aspects of political development may be substantiated in the interpretation of data for a selection of countries of the world, thus validating the theoretical distinctions derived.

Is it the case that the various aspects of political development hang together? The use of clear-cut indices for five dimensions of political development does discriminate between categories of countries as well as between countries within the sets of the occidental set, Central and South American, African and Asian countries as well as post-communist countries (CEE and CIS) at the present.

These state properties only go together to a certain extent and this seems to be the case with the way in which regime type, or democracy, co-varies with the other state properties. We will display this pattern of co-variation for a few of these relationships for the 1990s through the employment of scattergrams. Figures 5.1 to 5.4 contain these scattergrams. The first one captures the strong co-variation (r = 0.80; sig. = 0.000, N = 62) between democracy and institutionalization. The stronger the institutionalization of the state, the higher the score for democracy tends to be.

The next relationship covers democracy and public sector spending. Making use of a worldwide data set we find that high scores of democracy go together with a larger public sector (r = 0.53, sig. = 0.000; N = 71). This correlation is quite stable, although it may decrease somewhat whenever the sample size increases. Still, we may note that there is a positive relationship between these two properties.

So far we have identified a few relationships where democracy co-varies positively with other state properties. The two remaining relationships to be displayed will deal with negative relationships. The first one of these

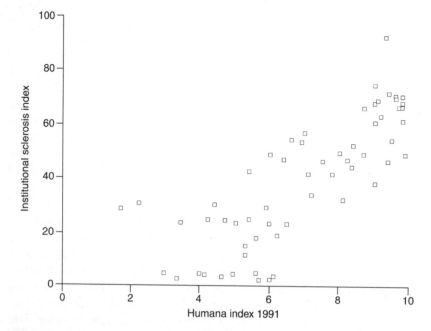

Figure 5.1   Democracy in the 1990s and institutionalization
Sources: See Tables 5.1 and 5.4

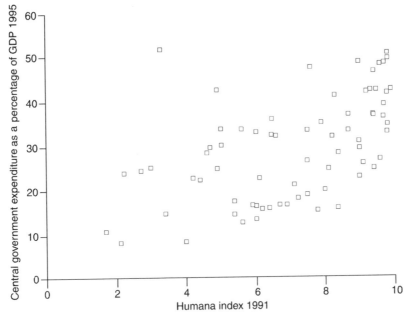

Figure 5.2.   Democracy and public sector size in the 1990s
Sources: See Tables 5.2 and 5.4

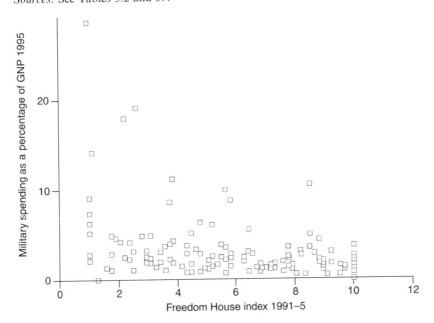

Figure 5.3   Democracy and military spending in the 1990s
Sources: See Tables 5.2 and 5.4

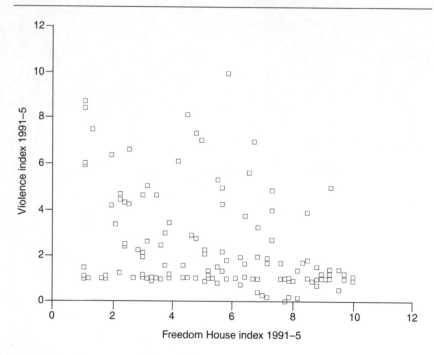

Figure 5.4   Democracy and instability: occurrence of violence in the 1990s
Sources: See Tables 5.3 and 5.4

negative co-variations captures democracy and military spending. Although we cannot say that there is a strong negative relation, it is obvious that we find increased military spending in non-democratic countries ($r = -0.36$, sig. $= 0.000$, $N = 141$) – see Figure 5.3.

The final scattergram (Figure 5.4) displays the relationship between democracy and political instability as it is captured by the occurrence of violence phenomena. Again we find a negative relationship, but not strongly so ($r = -0.34$; sig $= 0.000$, $N = 142$). The occurrence of violence phenomena seems to be more frequent in non-democracies than in democracies.

What these scattergrams suggest is that democracy tends to go together with other state properties, either positively or negatively. Democracy is thus important for other state characteristics that may be developed in a country. Having recourse to a few measurable aspects of political development is a necessary condition for moving ahead to analyse the causes and effects of political development. Let us proceed to an analysis of the social and economic sources of one prominent phase of political development: democratization. Now we ask: How valid is the hypothesis that there is a close connection between human and economic development and democracy as a political regime? This is the question that will be addressed in the next section of this chapter.

Democracy and development

In the literature on political development democracy has been one of the key connotations. A democratic regime has an intrinsic value in itself, because its political norms cherish the active participation of the people in government. Moreover, democratic states meet certain criteria of political decency, such as the institutionalization of human rights, which are considered to be intrinsically valuable in international law as well as in several constitutions.

In the early 1990s democracy was widely recognized as the best political regime yet invented, because its citizens were both treated with respect or dignity and had a say somehow in political decision-making. But we must also consider the extrinsic value of democratic rule. Do democracies in the long run tend to deliver other favourable outcomes, i.e. presenting their citizens with a high level of social and economic development? If this was not the case, then people could start searching for other types of regime which could lead to a higher level of affluence or sustained economic growth over a longer time period.

Here we wish to enter the discussion of the second part of the argument favouring democratic regimes, the extrinsic merits of democracy. Is it true that democracies generally deliver better outcomes than other kinds of political systems? Is social or economic development more favourable in democracies than in non-democracies?

It is not enough merely to look at the overall performance of democratic states. One must also try to pin down the causal link between democracy and development, if indeed there is such a connection. The occurrence of a democratic regime in an affluent society could be accidental or it could result from the impact of socio-economic development upon democracy. Is income equality higher in democratic countries than in authoritarian regimes and, if so, why?

One may identify different approaches focusing on the relation between democracy and development. One tradition starts with the concept of democracy, asking first how to measure democracy and then ranking regimes as more or less democratic, in order to proceed finally to look at what consequences democracy may have for development. This position has been taken up by political scientists or sociologists (Bollen, 1980; Bollen and Jackman, 1985, 1989; Muller, 1988). Another tradition looks at a variety of factors which may have an impact on development, among which institutional factors in politics are included. Here we mostly find economists or political economists (Scully, 1988, 1992; Pourgerami, 1988; Grier and Tullock, 1989).

Starting from the recognition of a factual association between levels of affluence and degrees of democracy, the problem was defined as to how to interpret such an empirically given relationship. Development as conducive to democracy was the classical argument put forward by Seymour Martin

Lipset (1959) (see also Diamond, 1992; Rueschemeyer *et al.*, 1992; Lipset *et al.*, 1993; Lipset, 1994). 'Development' here means the level of affluence as measured, for instance, in terms of GNP per capita. A high level of affluence would enhance democratic institutions by creating a broad middle class with cross-cutting cleavages, thus tempering conflicts and enhancing the practical politics of bargaining. However, nothing excluded the contrary hypothesis that democracy could foster economic development. Still another possible interpretation was that democracy and affluence could accompany each other or interact, reinforcing each other reciprocally.

What is at stake here is the precise question about politico-economic causality, that is whether democracy is conducive or not to social and economic development (Sirowy and Inkeles, 1990; Pourgerami, 1988). We will test a number of models that somehow claim that democracy has direct consequences for socio-economic development. 'Development' is a general concept that stands for various things such as economic growth and level of affluence or even social development as measured by a complex set of indicators. We are particularly interested in any evidence that supports the hypothesis that the direction of causality is from democracy to development, and not the other way around.

We will evaluate the evidence for such models in this chapter. A conflict model argues that democracy and development tend to clash, whereas a compatibility model states that democracy may enhance social and economic development. Finally, a sceptical model hints that democracy and development may accompany each other, but it is hardly the case that democracy is a major cause of socio-economic development, at least not in the short run.

Does democracy matter?

Thus far, we have presented a few apparently reliable measures of democracy and different aspects of development such as economic growth, human development and income distribution (in chapters 3 and 4). In order to be able to say something about which effect, if any, democracy has on development, we adopt the following path of analysis – the regression analysis. In order to test for the impact of democracy on development we try to model this interaction taking into account some of the factors generally suggested in the literature as relevant for explaining the variation in socio-economic development.

The democracy indicators to be employed in the correlation analysis will the ones we have made use of earlier in this chapter (Tables 5.4 and 5.5); in the regression analysis only three of them will be employed for two periods of time, the 1980s and the 1990s. When employing regression analysis it is important to specify models that satisfy reasonable demands for theoretical relevance. When the sources of socio-economic development have been researched within a cross-sectional framework a set of important factors having clear impact has been identified (Levine and Renelt 1992; Mankiew *et al.*, 1992; Barro, 1991; Kormendi and Meguire, 1985). The so-called convergence theme emphasizes the starting point or the initial per capita income as countries with a low output at an early stage tend to catch up with rich countries, given the same growth potential as determined by access to human capital (enrolment in secondary schools), physical capital and technology. Other relevant factors include the openness of the economy (trade as a percentage of GDP) or the economic system. Non-economic factors considered are cultural factors like religion, age of political regimes but also the character of the political regime such as the degree of democracy.

Democracy and human development

Let us first enquire into the impact of democracy on human development. The general model attempted is roughly the same as the one suggested above, i.e. in addition to democracy measures the independent variables contain information on level of economic development, economic system, openness of the economy and non-economic factors like strength of protestantism and time of political modernization. The dependent variable, human development, is the human development index (HDI) developed by the UNDP, and it is measured for on the one hand the mid-1980s, and on the other hand for the late 1990s. Three indicators of democracy are used – Bollen, Humana and Freedom House – for two periods of time, the early 1980s and the early 1990s. The findings of these estimations with respect to the democracy measures are reported on in Table 5.13.

When taking into account the effect of the level of initial economic development we find there is no longer any stable positive relationship between democracy and human development. The strength of the relationship seems to vary with which democracy measure that is used, the time period chosen and the sample size employed. Democracies are at times to be found in societies where the human development scores are high and vice versa. But this relationship is not stable, and it is also difficult to say what is cause and what is effect.

Democracy and income distribution

Our second indicator of socio-economic development is income distribution. One may expect a negative relationship between democracy and our measures of income distribution: the more democracy, the more equal the distribution of income, the lower the scores on our measures, i.e. the Gini coefficients. The form of presentation of the analysis follows the same pattern as in the preceding analyses, i.e. besides the estimates for the democracy indicators we only report variables that in any of the five models have a significant impact on the dependent variable – income distribution; the estimates are reported on in Table 5.14.

Table 5.13   Democracy and human development: regression analyses

Indep. variables	Coeffs	HDI 1985			HDI 1998	
LN GNP/capita	coeff	0.358	0.078	0.349	0.276	0.275
	t-stat	5.207	5.02	5.24	5.77	6.34
LN GNP/capita sq	coeff	−0.021	−	−0.021	−0.014	−0.014
	t-stat	−4.07		−4.14	−4.54	−5.06
Investment	coeff	0.003	0.004	0.003	0.003	0.004
	t-stat	2.36	2.21	2.41	3.63	4.49
Trade	coeff	−	−	−	−	−
	t-stat					
Economic freedom	coeff	−	0.019	−	0.032	0.031
	t-stat		2.17		5.26	5.33
Mod leader	coeff	0.000	0.001	0.001	0.001	0.001
	t-stat	3.750	2.75	3.23	5.05	5.31
LN Protestant	coeff	−	−0.017	−	−	−
	t-stat		−2.85			
Demo ind 1	coeff	0.008	−	−	−	−
(Bollen)	t-stat	3.09				
Demo ind 2	coeff	−	−0.006	−	−0.002	−
(Humana)	t-stat		−1.08		−0.52	
Demo ind 3	coeff	−	−	0.014	−	0.005
(Freedom House)	t-stat			3.85		1.52
Constant	coeff	−0.939	−0.006	−0.927	−0.919	−0.949
	t-stat	−4.23	−0.107	−4.30	−5.12	−5.87
Adj r square		0.88	0.87	0.88	0.90	0.91
N		85	54	85	84	101

Note: Criteria of statistical significance at a reasonable level, i.e. the t-statistics should roughly be $+/-$ 2 or larger
Sources: HDI (Table 4.2); GNP/capita (Table 3.8); Investment, Trade (World Bank 2000a); Economic Freedom (Gwartney and Lawson, 2000); Modernized Leadership (Ruston, 1966); Protestantism (Encyclopaedia Britannica); Democracy indices (Table 5.6)

In most cases the democracy variables shows the expected negative sign. But still, none of these estimates is significant. Therefore it is not possible to say that democracy is conducive to a more equal income distribution. Neither can one say that inequality is a consequence of democracy. The relations estimated simply say that democracy is more or less irrelevant for the kind of income distribution found in a society. Other factors have more impact, and it is obvious that the more equal distributions are to be found in the set of rich countries having a tradition of protestantism.

Democracy and economic growth

The preceding analysis will now be applied to economic growth in the 1970s up to the 1990s. Similar models will be tested, but somewhat modified due to availability of relevant data. The purpose of the analysis is once again to

Table 5.14 Democracy and income distribution: regression analyses

Indep. variables	Coeffs	Gini index 1980s			Gini index 1990s	
Model		(1)	(2)	(3)	(4)	(5)
LN GNP/capita	coeff	50.604	51.106	51.421	22.786	15.235
	t-stat	6.03	4.59	6.88	3.21	2.45
LN GNP/capita sq	coeff	−3.978	−3.860	−4.08	−1.659	−1.261
	t-stat	−6.215	−4.58	−7.09	−3.71	−3.16
Economic freedom	coeff	1.717	–	1.66	–	–
	t-stat	2.023		2.20		
LN Protestant	coeff	2.037	1.99	1.951	1.510	1.470
	t-stat	2.99	2.11	2.98	2.33	2.45
Demo ind 1	coeff	−0.571	–	–	–	–
(Bollen)	t-stat	−1.72				
Demo ind 2	coeff		−1.13	–	−0.212	–
(Humana)	t-stat		−1.29		−0.26	
Demo ind 3	coeff			−0.248		0.683
(Freedom House)	t-stat			−0.54		1.19
Constant	coeff	−123.323	−118.59	−125.84	−34.254	−7.253
	t-stat	−4.35	−3.21	−5.02	−1.28	−0.310
Adj r square		0.49	0.40	0.49	0.31	0.29
N		56	43	59	77	95

Note: Criteria of statistical significance at a reasonable level, i.e. the t-statistics should roughly be $+/-2$ or larger
Sources: Gin (Table 4.4); GNP/capita (Table 3.8); Economic freedom (Gwartney and Lawson, 2000); Protestantism (Encyclopaedia Britannica); Dermocracy indices (Table 5.6)

enquire into the robustness of the impact of the democracy variable within various model specifications. In Table 5.15 we report the estimations of the impact of the independent variables on the two dependent variables, namely economic growth from 1973 to 1990 and economic growth from 1990 to 1998.

It is striking that economic factors like investment in physical capital have a positive impact on economic development. This is more evident for the first period. For the second period we may note that economic freedom strongly goes together with economic growth. Economic growth is also negatively related to the initial per capita income as predicted by the convergence or maturity hypothesis – this is at least true for the first period 1973–90. This is more or less the general pattern, but our interest is primarily focused on the impact of democracy. What is the finding with regard to this factor?

The finding is that democracy has no stable impact upon economic development, it is neither negative nor positive for economic growth. During the first period democracy shows a positive sign in two of the models, while the sign is significantly negative in one of the models for the second period. Other factors are of much greater importance: investment in physical capital and

Table 5.15   Regression models for economic growth 1973–98

Indep. variables	Coeffs	Econ. gro. 1973–90			Econ. gro. 1990–98	
Model		(1)	(2)	(3)	(4)	(5)
LN GNP/capita	coeff	−0.874	−9.460	−1.225	–	–
	t-stat	−3.71	−3.84	−4.03		
LN GNP/capita sq	coeff	–	0.672	–	–	–
	t-stat		3.72			
Investment	coeff	0.135	0.121	0.155	–	0.065
	t-stat	3.84	3.13	4.36		2.38
Trade	coeff	0.009	0.009	–	–	−0.010
	t-stat	2.26	2.45			−2.29
Economic freedom	coeff	–	–	0.476	1.335	1.312
	t-stat			2.47	8.16	6.96
Mod leader	coeff	–	–	–	–	−0.016
	t-stat					−3.83
LN Protestant	coeff	−0.415	−0.665	−0.368	−0.437	−0.315
	t-stat	−2.96	−4.30	−2.55	−3.44	−2.62
Demo ind 1	coeff	0.287	–	–	–	–
(Bollen)	t-stat	4.09				
Demo ind 2	coeff	–	0.045	–	−0.523	–
(Humana)	t-stat		0.343		−4.38	
Demo ind 3	coeff	–	–	0.294	–	−0.023
(Freedom House)	t-stat			2.86		−0.22
Constant	coeff	3.071	31.590	2.782	−3.205	−5.817
	t-stat	2.69	3.80	2.24	−3.42	−6.36
Adj r square		0.33	0.37	0.32	0.45	0.44
N		90	56	86	84	101

Note: Criteria of statistical significance at a reasonable level, i.e. the t-statistics should roughly be +/− 2 or larger

Sources: Economic growth (Table 3.9); GNP/capita (Table 3.8); Investment, Trade (World Bank, 2000a); Economic freedom (Gwartney and Lawson, 2000); Modernized leadership (Rustow, 1966); Protestantism (Encyclopaedia Britannica); Democracy indices (Table 5.6)

the starting point of economic development. We may, however, also conclude that it is not the case that democracy is an obstacle to economic development.

Conclusion

Basic state properties vary considerably among the states of the world. Perhaps it is more difficult to employ the concept of political development to distinguish between First World states and Third World states than is recognized in the developmental approach. A so-called modern state may be identified in various ways – democracy, lack of corruption, state capacity institutionalization – and there is hardly available a method by which one may designate one definition as being more correct than another.

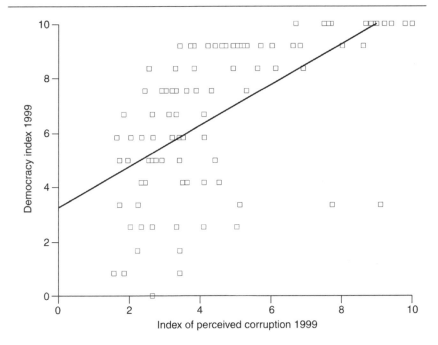

Figure 5.5 Democracy and lack of corruption

One may follow the modernization approach and link the modern state with the establishment and implementation of human rights. Or one may choose to tie the modern state to predictability of procedures and the lack of arbitrariness. These two dimensions may of course coexist, but this is not necessary. Figure 5.5 shows a scatterplot where the index of democracy is displayed against the index of lack of corruption.

The correlation is r = 0.63 (s = 0.000 for N = 98), indicating that state modernity may actually refer to two different things, which only go together moderately. On the one hand, we have the modern state as a machinery that operates in a neutral and predictable manner, based upon a perception of absence of corruption (x–axis). On the other hand, there is the conception of the modern state as a democratic state, which respects human rights, displayed as a high measure on DEMO (y–axis).

When enquiring into the relationship between democracy and development we have tried to use reliable measures on democracy and on development that are available for different periods of time after the Second World War. We have also identified three dimensions of development, namely economic development, human development and income distribution. The purpose of the enquiry is to evaluate whether democracy is conducive or not conducive to development. We are looking for a robust relationship, meaning a relationship that is stable over time, and valid irrespective of reliable measures that are used.

The findings tend to be negative. There is not one single robust relationship between democracy and development that we have been able to identify. This means that it has not been possible to establish a stable relation between democracy and economic growth or between democracy and degree of income equality or democracy and human development. There are for certain measures and for certain periods evidence for the existence of a positive relation between democracy and economic growth, and democracy and human development – but it is not stable. The same applies even more to the evidence of an impact of democracy upon income distribution. The positive conclusion is that democracy is not an obstacle to human development, economic growth or a fair income distribution.

Now, let us ask the following question: Given that the countries of the world greatly differ in economics and politics, is there some common core of principles in political economy that appears in all these countries? One may search for an answer in the theory of an optimal division between state and market in any society. Part II is devoted to questions related to the best mix of market and state.

Appendix 5.1: Armed conflicts 1945–90

Countries	Dates	Type
India v. Pakistan	1947	Interstate
Israel v. Egypt and others	1948	Interstate
Berlin	1948–49	Interstate
Korea North v. South Korea	1950–53	Interstate
Israel v. Egypt	1956	Interstate
USSR v. Hungary	1956	Interstate
India v. Pakistan	1957–59	Interstate
India v. Goa	1961	Interstate
India v. China	1962	Interstate
USA v. Cuba	1962	Interstate
Indonesia v. Malaysia	1962–66	Interstate
India v. Pakistan	1965	Interstate
USA v. Dominican Republic	1965	Interstate
South Vietnam v. North Vietnam	1965–73	Interstate
Israel v. Egypt and others	1967	Interstate
USSR v. Czechoslovakia	1968	Interstate
El Salvador v. Honduras	1968–69	Interstate
China v. USSR	1969	Interstate
Bangladesh v. Pakistan	1971	Interstate
India v. Pakistan	1971	Interstate
North Yemen v. South Yemen	1972	Interstate
Israel v. Egypt and others	1973	Interstate
Libya v. Chad	1973	Interstate
Ethiopia v. Somalia	1977–78	Interstate
North Vietnam v. Cambodia	1978	Interstate

Tanzania v. Uganda	1978–79	Interstate
North Vietnam v. China	1979	Interstate
Iran v. Iraq	1980–88	Interstate
Argentina v. UK	1982	Interstate
Israel v. Lebanon	1982	Interstate
USA v. Grenada	1983	Interstate
India v. Sri Lanka	1987–90	Interstate
USA v. Panama	1989	Interstate
Iraq v. Kuwait	1990	Interstate
Indonesia	1945–48	Intrastate
Greece	1945–49	Intrastate
Bolivia	1946	Intrastate
China	1946–49	Intrastate
Indochina	1946–54	Intrastate
Paraguay	1947	Intrastate
Taiwan	1947	Intrastate
India	1947–48	Intrastate
Madagascar	1947–48	Intrastate
Costa Rica	1948	Intrastate
North Yemen	1948	Intrastate
Myanmar	1948–51	Intrastate
Colombia	1948–58	Intrastate
Indonesia	1950	Intrastate
China	1950–51	Intrastate
China–Tibet	1950–51	Intrastate
Philippines	1950–52	Intrastate
Yemen N	1950–52	Intrastate
Malaysia	1950–60	Intrastate
Bolivia	1952	Intrastate
Kenya	1952–53	Intrastate
Tunisia	1952–54	Intrastate
Morocco	1953–56	Intrastate
Guatemala	1954	Intrastate
Oman	1954–59	Intrastate
Algeria	1954–62	Intrastate
Argentina	1955	Intrastate
Cameroon	1955–60	Intrastate
Sudan	1955–72	Intrastate
Indonesia	1956–61	Intrastate
Rwanda	1956–65	Intrastate
China	1957–62	Intrastate
Lebanon	1958	Intrastate
China–Tibet	1958–59	Intrastate
Cuba	1958–59	Intrastate
Iraq	1958–59	Intrastate
Guatemala	1958–90	Intrastate
South Vietnam	1959–65	Intrastate
Laos	1960–62	Intrastate
Zaire	1960–65	Intrastate
Iraq	1961–	Intrastate
Angola	1961–75	Intrastate

Algeria	1962–63	Intrastate
North Yemen	1962–69	Intrastate
Guinea Bissau	1962–74	Intrastate
Tanzania	1963	Intrastate
Uruguay	1963–72	Intrastate
Laos	1963–73	Intrastate
Peru	1965	Intrastate
Chad	1965–	Intrastate
Indonesia	1965–66	Intrastate
Mozambique	1965–75	Intrastate
Uganda	1966	Intrastate
China	1966–68	Intrastate
Nigeria	1967–70	Intrastate
Namibia	1968–88	Intrastate
Philippines	1969–	Intrastate
Jordan	1969–73	Intrastate
Cambodia	1970–75	Intrastate
Sri Lanka	1971	Intrastate
Burundi	1972	Intrastate
Philippines	1972–76	Intrastate
Pakistan	1972–77	Intrastate
Zimbabwe	1972–79	Intrastate
Chile	1973–74	Intrastate
Vietnam	1973–75	Intrastate
Cyprus	1974	Intrastate
Argentina	1974–76	Intrastate
Angola	1975–	Intrastate
Western Sahara	1975–	Intrastate
East Timor	1975–76	Intrastate
Cambodia	1975–78	Intrastate
Nicaragua	1975–79	Intrastate
Laos	1975–87	Intrastate
Lebanon	1975–88	Intrastate
Ethiopia	1976–78	Intrastate
Turkey	1976–80	Intrastate
Argentina	1976–82	Intrastate
Zaire	1977–78	Intrastate
Afghanistan	1978–	Intrastate
Colombia	1978–	Intrastate
Iran	1978–79	Intrastate
Mozambique	1978–90	Intrastate
North Yemen	1979	Intrastate
Cambodia	1979–	Intrastate
El Salvador	1979–89	Intrastate
Turkey	1980–	Intrastate
Peru	1980–90	Intrastate
Uganda	1981–86	Intrastate
Nicaragua	1981–88	Intrastate
Zimbabwe	1983	Intrastate
Sri Lanka	1983–	Intrastate
Sudan	1983–	Intrastate

South Africa	1983–86	Intrastate
Bangladesh	1985	Intrastate
Suriname	1985–87	Intrastate
South Yemen	1986	Intrastate
Uganda	1987–88	Intrastate
Sri Lanka	1987–89	Intrastate
Somalia	1988	Intrastate
Iran	1989	Intrastate
Romania	1989	Intrastate
Liberia	1990	Intrastate

Source: Sullivan, 1991: 34–8

Appendix 5.2: Armed conflicts 1989–99

Countries	*Dates*	*Type*
Panama v. USA	1989	Interstate
India v. Pakistan	1989–90	Interstate
Mauritania v. Senegal	1989–90	Interstate
Iraq v. Kuwait	1990–91	Interstate
India v. Pakistan	1992	Interstate
Ecuador v. Peru	1995	Interstate
India v. Pakistan	1996–99	Interstate
Eritrea v. Ethiopia	1998–99	Interstate
Comoros	1989	Intrastate
Morocco	1989	Intrastate
Nicaragua	1989	Intrastate
Panama	1989	Intrastate
Paraguay	1989	Intrastate
Romania	1989	Intrastate
Indonesia	1989–90	Intrastate
Laos	1989–90	Intrastate
Lebanon	1989–90	Intrastate
El Salvador	1989–91	Intrastate
Ethiopia	1989–91	Intrastate
Uganda	1989–91	Intrastate
Bangladesh	1989–93	Intrastate
Mozambique	1989–93	Intrastate
South Africa	1989–93	Intrastate
UK	1989–93	Intrastate
Chad	1989–94	Intrastate
Philippines	1989–94	Intrastate
Angola	1989–95	Intrastate
Guatemala	1989–95	Intrastate
Iraq	1989–96	Intrastate
Liberia	1989–96	Intrastate
Papua New Guinea	1989–96	Intrastate
Somalia	1989–96	Intrastate
Cambodia	1989–98	Intrastate
Afghanistan	1989–99	Intrastate

Colombia	1989–99	Intrastate
India	1989–99	Intrastate
Israel	1989–99	Intrastate
Myanmar	1989–99	Intrastate
Peru	1989–99	Intrastate
Sri Lanka	1989–99	Intrastate
Sudan	1989–99	Intrastate
Turkey	1989–99	Intrastate
Mali	1990	Intrastate
Trinidad and Tobago	1990	Intrastate
USSR	1990–91	Intrastate
Niger	1990–92	Intrastate
Rwanda	1990–94	Intrastate
Haiti	1991	Intrastate
Togo	1991	Intrastate
Yugoslavia	1991	Intrastate
Spain	1991–92	Intrastate
Georgia	1991–93	Intrastate
Iran	1991–93	Intrastate
Djibouti	1991–95	Intrastate
Sierra Leone	1991–99	Intrastate
Venezuela	1992	Intrastate
Croatia	1992–93	Intrastate
Azerbaijan	1992–94	Intrastate
Bosnia and Herzegovina	1992–95	Intrastate
Tajikistan	1992–96	Intrastate
Egypt	1992–98	Intrastate
Algeria	1992–99	Intrastate
Moldova	1993	Intrastate
Russia	1993–96	Intrastate
Mexico	1994	Intrastate
Yemen	1994	Intrastate
Uganda	1994–99	Intrastate
Pakistan	1995–96	Intrastate
Burundi	1995–99	Intrastate
Congo-Kinshasa	1996–99	Intrastate
Congo-Brazzaville	1997–99	Intrastate
Nepal	1997–99	Intrastate
Senegal	1997–99	Intrastate
Lesotho	1998	Intrastate
Angola	1998–99	Intrastate
Guinea Bissau	1998–99	Intrastate
Rwanda	1998–99	Intrastate
Yugoslavia	1998–99	Intrastate
Indonesia	1999	Intrastate
Russia	1999	Intrastate

Source: Wallensteen and Sollenberg (2000)

PART II

State or Market? Beyond the Great Debate

In the so-called Great Debate in the early twentieth century, it was much discussed whether a planned economy could be as efficient as a market economy, which included the attack of Hayek on the Barone solution. However, today Barone is really dead, not only physically but also mentally. No one says today that government can achieve what markets can do in terms of allocative efficiency. Walrasian markets operate perfectly – this is admitted. But, and this is the new argument, no real markets come ever close to the Walrasian market ideal. The markets that exist are full of market imperfections. This is an entirely different approach from the Barone one. And it has to be met on its own playground, i.e. with an argument that real-life markets tend towards Walrasian markets, if left alone by governments. Should the real world be far away from the Walrasian market model, then there could be several reasons for government intervention. The theory of the roles of the government in a market economy focuses upon the occurrence of market failures and their policy implications. In chapter 8 we will discuss the problem of rent dissipation which is one form of market failure, as well as the implications of market power for state intervention. Chapter 9 examines theories of state failure.

The pro-market argument may appear to be sound as long as one assumes that the institutions of the market economy have been clarified and are being implemented by an outsider, the state. However, the anti-market argument does not have to question the theoretical perfection of the market model or launch a claim that government could be as efficient as the competitive market. The anti-market argument moves the battle to another playground, namely the real-life attributes of markets, which – it is claimed – tend to be quite apart from the Walrasian ideal type. Let us first discuss the model concepts of the market and the state in chapter 6 and then in chapter 7 look at real-life politico-economic regimes.

The Simple Dichotomy: State or Market?

In political economy the basic question is: market or state, the private sector or the public sector, or exchange against government authority. Since these two modes of co-ordination are the two fundamental ones, each and every society has to decide whether to co-ordinate human interaction with markets or to rule with command. One may apply this question to each sector of the economy in order to arrive at an aggregated division for the whole society: What is to be public and what is to be private?

The two criteria used in deciding and discussing about political economy are efficiency and equity. The argument in favour of markets is usually stated in terms of efficiency, whereas the argument favouring politics typically makes reference to justice. Market theory is based upon the Pareto approach to efficiency meaning that any form of social change is acceptable as long as no one loses but at least one player gains. Equity, on the other hand, appears to be eminently difficult to define in terms of a robust set of criteria. Justice tends to define as the outcome of a decision process where all concerned have been given a voice. Since people who decide upon what is just may end up casting votes in order to resolve disagreement, politics is close to equity.

However, the equation that markets deliver efficiency and politics justice comes from a recently suggested argument. At the turn of the nineteenth century when capitalism confronted socialism, the big issue was exactly whether markets or state deliver the most efficient economy. One may regard the events in the twentieth century as a real experiment testing whether capitalism or socialism scored best on efficiency criteria. Basically, efficiency means that output is maximized, *ceteris paribus*. Which mechanism, the invisible hand of the market or the visible hand of state planning, produces the highest amount of goods and services that people are willingly going to purchase?

Among the classical economists the market was evaluated very differently. Few shared the enthusiasm of Adam Smith and his claim that markets result in the highest amount of efficiency. There were reservations stated in different ways. On the other hand, few went as far as Karl Marx in the search for an alternative mechanism. One could argue that markets reveal the value of things, as with Ricardo, but one could also blame the market with various misfortunes. It was not until Leon Walras delivered the first proof of the properties of market equilibria that one could really claim that markets achieve efficiency. However, that required the marginalist revolution in economic thinking, linking value with the marginal willingness to pay and not with the amount of labour put into the production of something, i.e. one kind of cost.

Competitive prices in markets have several advantages over administrative prices in a planned economy. They are conducive to efficiency in resource allocation. They enhance flexibility and rapid adjustment. They reveal the value of goods and services momentarily and serve as an optimum medium of communicating preferences. Their weakness is lack of stability and predictability (Stigler, 1966).

Competitive prices presuppose the operation of markets with numerous suppliers and demanders. Producer and consumer differences are to be reflected in the market by means of price and quantity. This model may operate well in a society with capitalist institutions including private ownership and a variety of incentive mechanisms where individuals may express preferences in the form of possessions as long as the problems in relation to externalities, economies of scale and distributional equity have been resolved somehow. If, however, the emphasis is on control and predictability then market allocation may be questioned as the appropriate medium of communication.

Theoretically speaking, in any society resources have to be allocated between alternative uses. There are, basically, two institutional mechanisms for the allocation of resources: markets and budgets (Borcherding, 1977). They complement each other only to a limited extent, as stated in the theory of public goods (Baumol, 1965; Arrow, 1983; Samuelson, 1983). Resources may be owned in two basic ways, publicly or privately. The structure of ownership sets limits on the employment of the two mechanisms of allocation. It may be derived from political economy theory that there is a definite limit on the tendency of publicly dominated ownership structures to move towards the use of markets. Similarly, the continued existence of private ownership means that there is a boundary for the growth of government or the expansion of the scope of budget allocation. The so-called mixed economy is a hybrid of market and budget allocation.

The Lausanne School

The Lausanne School delivered what several economists had faintly imagined but not been able to prove, namely that competitive markets result in a unique equilibrium between demand and supply which is an efficient allocation. Uniqueness and efficiency are two different properties of market outcomes, and it was up to Leon Walras to produce the general equilibrium proof and for Wilfredo Pareto to demonstrate the efficiency of market equilibria.

Competitive market equilibria are called Walrasian after Walras, who proved not only that there exists a unique solution to market interaction but also that markets coupled together produce one unique equilibrium. Thus, the price clears all markets involved in the allocation of a good or service: the goods market, the labour market and the capital market. The clearing price emerges from a process of bidding, arranged by the auctioneer, who tenders the allocation of the good in question.

Walras employed a system of equations modelling demand and supply in a series of markets where the output of one market is the input of another. The market-clearing price allows for an instantaneous determination of price and quantity allocated in all markets, which will be a stationary outcome as long as nothing changes. This was a major achievement, proving the unique outcome of a market game, where players are led by their own incentives towards one and only one solution.

Uniqueness is a highly valued property in the analysis of human interaction, i.e. in game theory. This allows one to predict outcomes and explain them as well. Uniqueness is not the general result in game theory, as many games have more than one equilibrium. The famous Nash proof from 1951 that all games have at least one equilibrium in pure or mixed strategies does not entail uniqueness. On the contrary, games may have several equilibria making it very difficult to predict the outcome of human interaction and thus explain the occurrence of events.

However, besides the question of uniqueness there is the equally vital problem of desirability, meaning whether social equilibria also are to be recommended for some reason or another. Here, we come to the great contribution by Pareto, demonstrating that the Walras equilibrium is an efficient allocation. An outcome is Pareto efficient if it cannot be improved upon by increasing the amount allocated. The Walrasian equilibrium is such a Pareto-efficient outcome. Thus, at the market-clearing price it is impossible to make Pareto superior moves. No competitive market outcome is a Pareto-inferior outcome.

General equilibrium theory is the branch of economics that has perfected the insights of the Lausanne School. The basic result, proved by several scholars within welfare economics, is that a competitive market has outcomes, which are both Nash equilibria and Pareto optimal. To speak with another voice, market outcomes tend to be in the interests of the players both individually and collectively. In welfare economics it is always emphasized that the proof of market perfection rests upon four critical preconditions, namely:

1   no economies of scale
2   no external effects
3   full information
4   no consideration of distributive matters.

We would wish to add a fifth condition that the Lausanne School did not pay attention to, although Walras and Pareto were extremely conscious about the special nature of the competitive market. We are referring to the probability of reneging, which can occur from the initiation of a market deal to its fulfilment. It must of course be close to zero, if players are to be confident about market outcomes. We will return to these four conditions later, but we will now bring out the natural question in relation to the Pareto result, namely: Could the state also provide allocative solutions that fulfil the efficiency criteria?

One may wish to portray the achievements of the Lausanne School with a simple figure, showing the logic of allocative outcomes, which satisfy the Nash–Pareto criteria. One could argue that when a few of the four conditions above are not satisfied, then allocative outcomes would only be Nash but not Pareto. Thus, externalities and economies of scale just as information asymmetries do not rule out Nash equilibria, but Pareto optimality will not be forthcoming. The fourth condition is really outside the framework of the market economy, as it introduces justice into the picture. Figure 6.1 shows how income can be divided between two groups x and y in various utility combinations. If the economy is at point Y, then economic growth can well bring it to point W or to point V which is a Pareto improvement. However, the choice between W and V can only be done by contributional criteria handed down in a so-called social welfare function.

In the framework of welfare economics, all solutions along the utility possibility frontier constitute Pareto optimal points. To choose one of them one needs a criterion other than economic efficiency, namely social justice. A theory of social justice could deliver a criterion by means of which the utility

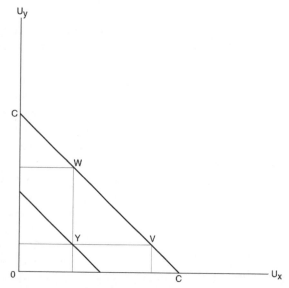

Figure 6.1   Welfare economics: efficient outcomes and equity

of one group x could be compared with the utility of another group y. One may suggest the difference principle of Rawls or rely upon a strict egalitarian criterion. In welfare economics such criteria are to be handed down by means of a so-called social welfare function which clarifies how the utility of two groups is to be compared. The social welfare function is a political principle or political decision-making process that delivers a solution like Y, W or V (Mueller, 1989).

Barone: right but yet wrong

A pupil of Pareto, Barone, stunned the world of economics at the turn of the century when he delivered a theory about the optimal Ministry of Production. Since the conditions for economic efficiency were known in the Pareto framework, the Ministry of Production or the Ministry of Finance could design a plan that accomplished these conditions. Such a plan would cover the entire economy and contain an input-output scheme for the way in which resources and factors would be employed to provide outputs that the economy needed. The visible hand of planning and command would do exactly what the invisible hand of the market achieves, namely an efficient allocation.

The Barone set of input-output plans for the economy, a vast system of tables transforming inputs into outputs at the intermediary and final stages, would accomplish Pareto optimality as long as the equations guiding state actions were correct. But how about the Nash condition, or that the government would also find it to its interest to find and implement Pareto optimality?

Government acting as the agent of the people may have its own goals – re-election, salary, prestige – that are not necessarily connected with its capacity to accomplish economic efficiency. One may wish to emphasize this gulf between the principal and the agent in the state to an extremely high degree, as with the public choice school. Yet, whatever the nature of the principal–agent interaction in the state, government must make use of effort to find and implement efficient solutions to allocative problems. Thus, we arrive at the critical and practical question: Will government and its bureaucracies be capable or willing to devote enough effort in order to move the economy from Pareto-inferior solutions within Figure 6.1 to some point on the production possibility curve?

The first scholar to argue that a socialist economy was impracticable was Ludwig van Mises. Coming from the Austrian School, von Mises emphasized the limitations on knowledge. Within a socialist economy information will not flow freely. Thus, the cognitive capacities of government will be highly limited, as innovations and entrepreneurs are not naturally forthcoming. If information is a non-tangible asset for a society, like social capital, then it will spread with the invisible hand of the market but be mishandled by the visible hand of government. This is basically the position of Hayek, who looks upon information as the collective wisdom, which compensates for the irrationality of individuals.

As long as the question concerned socialism or capitalism, one could say that the fall of the Berlin Wall had once and for all decided the issue: Hayek was right, and had all the time since 1935 been on the right side. Socialism was impracticable and not feasible as an economic system, whatever its merits as a political system. However, the fall of communism has changed little when it comes to the debate about the proper role of government in a market economy. How come?

The Hayek position, stated in 1935 and repeated several times afterwards, is in reality a very narrow one, bypassing a great number of questions about the functions of government in a modern economy. As a solution to the problem of how to mix state and market, the public and the private, or the problem of the governance of the economy by the government or by the market Hayek's position that markets can accomplish everything and government nothing was always too exaggerated, too simplistic.

It is true that Hayek received a renewed relevance when the market revolution set in the 1970s against the welfare state and economic nationalism, calling for privatization, deregulation and more competition in both markets and state. His Nobel Prize in 1974 confirmed that his time had come, given that the economics of planning and state control had seen its best days. However, Hayek's theory offers little guidance today when we approach the problem of how to combine state and market without using the categories of socialism versus capitalism. In the empirical analysis of economic regimes one allows for the existence of more than just two basic models. Thus, at least four types of politico-economic regimes are identified, if not five – see chapter 8.

Beyond Hayek

Bypassing the Great Debate, a number of arguments can be presented as to why government must be present in the economy in addition to markets. Looking into the reasons for a public sector, the distinction between socialism and capitalism is not very helpful. Instead one needs new tools for conceptualizing how the public and the private may mix, in terms of functions as well as organization. Let us look at the main arguments in favour of a public sector. Actually, they come up in the form of a number of debates between people who believe in them and people who reject them, as in the socialism–capitalism controversy.

The Great Debate was conducted within a setting that is radically different from that of today's discussion about governments and markets, because at that time the economies of the countries were basically closed economies with international trade taking place but on a limited scale. Today the country economies are closely connected by trade, production ¬d finance to such an extent that most of them are open economies participating in the global market place. However, the implications of globalization remain to be stated in terms of the distinction between the public and the private.

Hayek correctly argued that the Barone equations would be deficient because they cannot draw upon the maximum available knowledge in a society. Information when stored by government becomes rapidly deficient. When prices carry information, then it tends to be both fuller and more accurate. Information handles both the knowledge available and future innovations. When prices are competitive no one can manipulate the information they carry. Hayek went on to interpret the crucial importance of information by means of a theory about collective rationality compensating for individual irrationality. Since human beings have a limited cognitive capacity, institutional orders emerge that compensate for this limitation. When institutional mechanisms develop over time, then they result in spontaneous orders, which are more rational than individual men and women. The market is one such order, which is always superior to the planning of governments.

The preference of the Austrian School for markets against state may be said to have been confirmed by the débâcle of the common economy during the twentieth century. However, in political economy there was never merely a choice between only a system based upon *laissez-faire* or *laissez-aller* on the one hand and the totally planned economy on the other hand. On the contrary, much economic and political thinking has been devoted to finding a mix of the market and the state, based upon systematic criteria of efficiency and equity.

The recent developments in China must be taken into account when one examines the outcomes of the command economy. Since 1980 economic growth has been by all measures quite astonishing in direct opposition to the failure of the COMECON economies in Eastern Europe. Mainland China has managed an economic transformation unprecedented in history. Within a very short time, China had doubled its national income, as modern enterprises have increased economic output tremendously, often in joint ventures with foreign firms. China has thus narrowed the gap that divided it from Hong Kong and Taiwan, although the latter have different economic regimes than does mainland China. Can a command economy really perform in such a manner that it actually outperforms both a *laissez-faire* economy like Hong Kong and a South East Asian model development country like Taiwan?

The explanation of the Chinese miracle is basically an institutional one. The economic regime in mainland China is no longer the command economy, as markets are employed for the allocation of many goods and services, as well as labour and capital. However, ownership of most Chinese firms remain in the hands of the state. The economic system in China is thus labelled 'market socialism' or 'market communism'. The question of how markets operate in China is a matter of dispute. Some claim that there are efficient markets for many goods and services, whereas others argue that capital markets are still severely underdeveloped, especially the banking sector. The state remains a key player in the economy despite all the transformation of the state-owned public enterprises. The agricultural sector is in the process of rapid change from a socialized system towards one with more private ownership, as millions of Chinese families take to the cities to find work (Chow, 1999; Harvie, 2000).

The Chinese government foresees another decade of high rates of economic growth, which it tries to underpin by accepting more of private ownership and initiative while at the same time making huge efforts to keep the currency of the county, the yuan, stable against other major currencies. The obvious question is: Can China go on benefiting from the positive side of market socialism without facing some of its drawbacks? In the short run market socialism may well continue to work miracles in China, but in the long run the problem of sustainability becomes a major one for both the economic and the political system.

The enterprise system in the mainland Chinese economy has step by step moved away from a strong reliance upon the state-owned enterprises (SOEs), that were created in the old planned economy. Thus, there is now a heterogeneity of firms: SOEs, township and village enterprises (TVEs), private firms or entrepreneurs and joint ventures. However, the hand of government is still highly visible in the main sectors of the economy and the banking sector can hardly be said to have reached the stage of an autonomous part of a market economy. As long as the profits are kept within the enterprises and not handed down in the form of private property, there is a clear risk for inefficient allocation of capital, investments and savings.

The concerns of political economy today are different from the traditional ones, dealing with the contest between capitalism or socialism. What has emerged out of the Great Debate between the adherents of capitalism and socialism respectively is the realization that economic activity benefits critically from the market economy. The market economy delivers a higher output, which entails more income for people. There is no reason why a country would refuse itself the benefits of the market economy.

The triumph of the market economy over socialist schemes of production is not the end point of the debate within political economy, but the starting point of a discussion of other themes that are equally essential.

On the one hand, there is a set of difficult questions about the nature of the market economy, as it is not just one form of capitalism. The institutional foundations of the market economy have begun to be better researched, but there remain some topics pertaining to the limits of the market economy yet to be dealt with. Resolving these has large consequences for how we understand the contribution of the state to the economy. Despite the appearance that the market defeated the state in the Great Debate, it is still the case that market operations depend upon the activities of governments in several ways, especially the legal arm of the state.

On the other hand, the process of globalization posits a number of questions about the functioning of the market economy. What is at stake is the stability of the global market place, where shocks to economic activity tend to become global waves. The interconnectedness of the economies of the countries of the world has increased to such an extent that it is questionable whether they can be described at all as national systems. The mechanisms of the global market economy link all forms of economic activity, from trade to production to financial markets.

When these two remarks are combined, we arrive at the crux of the matter: How to regulate the global market economy? Without the state, the market economy degenerates rapidly into the crime economy. The global market economy needs a state to balance it, but there no world government exists. However, there has emerged a system of intergovernmental organizations as well as regional co-ordination mechanisms, that stabilizes markets. The great question for the future of mankind is how this system is to be improved upon. Whether markets are efficient or not, they depend upon the implementation of certain institutions. The rules of the market games have been much researched recently in a literature called 'Law and Economics', which attempts to arrive at the rules that make markets work smoothly. The rules of the market are a set of legal institutions that are closely connected with the state.

Existing politico-economic regimes

In political economy the distinction between the public and the private sectors and its implications for the polity and the economy is one principal focus. It deals with how the state is involved in the economy of a society and what the economic consequences of the size and structure of the public sector are in both the short and the long run (Palgrave, *Dictionary of Political Economy*, 1899: Vol. III; Palgrave, 1987: Vol. 3).

In this chapter we will introduce some basic concepts pertaining to the public/private sector distinction, by means of which one may identify the types of politico-economic regimes evaluated in chapter 7. These terms refer to mechanisms for the allocation of resources, to the size and orientation of the public redistribution of income and wealth, and to structures of ownership of the means of production (Margolis and Guitton, 1969; Stiglitz, 1988).

The political economies of the countries of the world differ along these three dimensions: mechanism of allocation, extent of redistribution and ownership structure. One of the chief questions in political economy, old or new, is whether economic development is related to how the basic politico-economic system is built up around the allocative, distributive and ownership structures (Pryor, 1968; Eckstein, 1971; Kornai, 1986). We have here a whole set of problems for comparative research into how development is affected by the public/private sector distinction, which we will look at in the ensuing empirical chapters. In this chapter we examine this question from a theoretical point of view.

Four ideal types

One basic problem in any society is how to allocate the resources in an efficient manner. A second fundamental problem is the ownership question or how the means of production are to be owned. The efficiency question is how to devise a system whereby the resources are allocated to various uses in such a way that it would not be possible to achieve a better result had the resources been allocated differently. The ownership problem relates to basic questions about equity and power in society.

In any society resources or different factors of production have to be allocated among various usages and income as well as wealth to be distributed to the households (Musgrave and Musgrave, 1980). Overlooking such phenomena as gift exchange and heritage there are in principle only two mechanisms for deciding about allocative and distributive matters: markets or politics (Arrow, 1963; Akerloff, 1970). The use of politics as the mechanism of allocation implies budget-making and planning as well as the resort to hierarchies to implement the budget document or plan. When markets are trusted with allocating resources, the basic mechanism of choice is individual agreement or voluntary exchange (Buchanan, 1967, 1986).

Allocative questions may be handled to a considerable extent by markets, but the results of or the preconditions for voluntary exchange may be the target of public policy-making, the state attempting redistribution of income and wealth by means of the budget (Stiglitz,1999 *et al.*, 1974; Rosen, 1988). It is not always easy to distinguish between allocative and redistributive programmes in the public sector, as redistribution does not have to be in money but may involve goods and services – redistribution in kind. The welfare state with its huge public budget mixes allocative and redistributive programmes to such an extent that it is difficult to tell which programme is which (Atkinson and Stiglitz, 1980; Musgrave and Musgrave, 1980).

In any society the means of production may be owned by the state or the society. The questions about the ownership of the means of production used to be framed as capitalism versus socialism. The ownership problem remains central in the political economy approach. But this distinction between two polar types of ownership of the means of production, either exclusively private or public, is too simple in relation to present-day realities, given high state intervention in the market economy in terms of either ownership, taxation or regulation.

One fundamental type of resource allocation system employs competitive prices as the tool for allocating resources to producers and consumers. It presupposes the existence of markets where scarcity prices are determined by the interaction between demand and supply. The other fundamental type of resource allocation system employs planning and central co-ordination. The government decides how resources are to be allocated among alternative employments – budget allocation.

Resources or the means of production could be owned predominantly by the public or the private sectors. The prevailing ownership institution may be various private property regimes or the state may be heavily involved in the control of economic resources, either through public enterprises or through the large tax state. Market allocation or budget allocation? Private property regimes or state control or intervention? Real-life politico-economic regimes are combinations of these distinctions, involving mixtures and hybrid examples. In political economy, one finds four ideal types modelling how allocation mechanisms may be combined with ownership structure:

1   Adam Smith: Market allocation based upon private property regimes.
2   Karl Marx: Budget allocation with public ownership.
3   Friedrich List: State intervention into markets with state control of key industries but with little redistribution.
4   Adolf Wagner: Market allocation in combination with budget allocation and state intervention for redistributional purposes.

The traditional contradiction between capitalism and socialism captures only two of the four politico-economic models shown above. Besides Adam Smith's market regime – decentralized capitalism – and Karl Marx's command economy, there are two other ideal types which are highly relevant for the comparative analysis of politico-economic systems, namely Friedrich List's economic nationalism and Adolf Wagner's welfare state.

In the Western world the developments in their politico-economic systems since the Second World War have meant that more and more of budget allocation has been inserted into an economic system that used to be very much based on market allocation and private ownership, as predicted by Wagner (Galbraith, 1969; Johansen, 1977–78). Two different reasons lie behind the seminal process of public sector growth among the rich market economies: public policy in relation to so-called market failures and policy-making with regard to income redistribution (Head, 1974; Wolf, 1988). Budget allocation and market allocation have been combined in more equal doses than was envisaged in the pure model of decentralized capitalism – the so-called mixed economy of the welfare states (Brown and Jackson, 1978; Lybeck, 1986; Lybeck and Henrekson, 1988). At the same time the seminal development in the OECD countries of a process of public sector growth has meant that the public ownership of resources has increased.

The major development in the socialist world up to the collapse of the command economy in 1989 has been the opposite one, i.e. to try to insert more market allocation into a system of public ownership of the means of production (Lindblom, 1977). Is it possible to achieve an introduction of markets into an economic system based on public ownership of the means of production? This is the question about the possibility of so-called market socialism.

All the four models shown above are of relevance to countries in the Third World. The developmental success for the countries in South East Asia is often attributed to their adherence to the state-capitalist model of List. The basic problem of development administration is to make crucial choices about allocation mechanism and ownership structure in order to promote development goals (Hirschman, 1958; Verma and Sharma, 1984). Which politico-economic regime is the best one in promoting development? Are welfare regimes possible, except within rich countries?

Smith: the market economy and efficiency

The concept of efficiency in resource allocation has a precise and specific meaning (Layard and Walters, 1978; Bohm, 1986). Three conditions are sufficient and necessary for an allocation system to be efficient:

1 *Efficiency in consumption*: on the demand side of the economy, consumers trade with each other in order to maximize their individual utilities. An allocation is efficient if it is not possible after a trade to retrade and arrive at a position where the utility of at least one consumer can be increased and the utility of no other consumer be decreased.

2 *Efficiency in production*: on the supply side of the economy producers deliver goods and services. An allocation is efficient if it is not possible to increase the supply of at least one good while the supply of other goods remains constant.

   Efficiency in production means that it is not possible to increase output by changing the composition of the factors of production employed. Overall efficiency also requires that efficiency in consumption matches efficiency in production, i.e. we have:

3 *Product-mix efficiency*: the value to the consumer of a good equals its marginal cost.

It is possible to show that a market economy may under certain conditions fulfil these efficiency requirements by the employment of the price mechanism as the allocation instrument (Arrow and Scitovsky, 1972; Mishan, 1981; Eatwell *et al.*, 1987, 1989a, 1989b). Given a set of competitive prices concerning goods and factors of production, the market mechanism will arrive at a situation where there is efficiency in consumption and in production as well as in the overall economic sense (Debreu, 1959; Lachman, 1986).

These efficiency conditions apply under certain conditions which render the market appropriate for certain types of goods and not for others. The market is suitable for the allocation of private consumer goods, i.e. divisible goods that have few externalities and are characterized by rivalry or no-jointedness (Bator, 1958; Head, 1974; Musgrave and Musgrave, 1980). The market economy faces severe problems when it comes to indivisible goods or public goods and externalities. Moreover, the market is not able to handle overall macro-economic decisions like consumption versus investments. Finally, the problem of determining the distribution of incomes is not solved. We may apply an independent criterion of justice to the outcomes of the operation of the market forces (Nath, 1969; Rawls, 1971).

The basic problem in a market economy is not its internal functioning. On the contrary, if the conditions for market allocation are satisfied there is no cause for concern as the efficiency requirement is met. Problematic in relation to market allocation is its applicability, as the conditions for a perfectly functioning market economy are narrow (Buchanan, 1985). Wolf identifies four sources of so-called market failure or situations where the typical conditions for the successful operation of markets do not apply. They include: (i) externalities and public goods; (ii) increasing returns to scale or jointedness; (iii) market imperfections in terms of actor misinformation or factor inflexibility, often called internalities; (iv) distributional equity (Wolf, 1988: 20–9). The situation with regard to a command economy is the very opposite one, as it is the internal mechanics of such a resource allocation system that are problematic.

Theoretically it is possible to prove that the employment of competitive prices in markets with perfect competition and adequate production technology results in allocative outcomes that satisfy the necessary and sufficient conditions for efficiency. But this is all just theory. The practical institutions of market regimes involve much more than simply perfectly competitive markets. Oliver E. Williamson states:

> Firms, markets, and relational contracting are important economic institutions. They are also the evolutionary product of a fascinating series of organizational innovations. The study of the economic institutions of capitalism has not, however, occupied a position of importance on the social science research agenda. (Williamson, 1985: 15)

The practical feasibility of market allocation is bound together with the occurrence of market failure. The new transaction approach within economics emphasizes that basic contractual problems of asymmetrical information, moral hazard and adverse selection limit the applicability of market exchange and that they may be handled in terms of a variety of institutional responses (Williamson, 1986; Mueller, 1986; Ricketts, 1987).

How widespread market failure is depends on both the evaluation of externalities and inequities in market outcomes and the occurrence of internalities and inefficiencies in market operations, but it also depends on the probability that government action and bureaucratic implementation constitute a real alternative to market failure. The Coase theorem implies that market failure may not be a condition for state intervention, if the likelihood of government failure is even larger (Buchanan, J. M., 1986).

Thus the practicality of a market-oriented society is tied into the fundamental problem of a demarcation line between the private and the public sectors in societies with extensive private property institutions. Budget allocation of resources or budget redistribution of income ameliorate market failure, but there are limits to the size of the public sector when economic efficiency is considered.

Marx: the command economy and inefficiency

The allocation mechanism in a command economy is the command or directive stemming from the authority of the state. The ministry of production in a command economy faces the same requirements for efficiency in consumption and production as is handled by the market with an invisible hand. How is it possible for a command economy to meet the efficiency requirement in consumption and production? It is necessary to distinguish between two problems in relation to a command economy. The first problem is one of *theoretical possibility*: could a command economy satisfy the general conditions for efficiency in resource allocation? The second problem concerns *practical feasibility*: is it possible in a real world sense to devise a system of resource allocation that satisfies the efficiency conditions although it allocates resources by command?

It has been argued that the ministry of production could create a type of information system as well as a type of allocation system that means it would be able to allocate goods and factors of production to consumers and producers in a way that meets the efficiency criteria (Barone, 1935). However, although this may theoretically be possible, its practical feasibility is in question (Hayek, 1935; Bergson, 1981). When looking at the existing examples of command economies it seems as if the practical problems are enormous (Eatwell *et al.*, 1990; Eatwell *et al.*, 1991). Before we begin the empirical evaluation of the model of a command economy, we will look at some of the difficulties from a theoretical point of view.

The practical problem for the central planning board in a command economy is to build up an information system so vast that allocation becomes efficient (Kornai and Liptak, 1962; Heal, 1973; Eatwell *et al.*, 1987, 1989a). The basic idea is that government proposes an allocation of all the goods and services in the economy amongst various uses – the plan. Then, it collects information to make it possible to assess the marginal contribution to social welfare that a good or service makes in each of its uses, but according to whose preferences – the consumers' or the planners'. Then, the next step would be that having derived these marginal contributions, government calculates a new plan in which inputs have been shifted from uses where their marginal values are low to uses where their marginal values are high (Heal, 1973: 156).

Grave doubts have always been raised as to the practical feasibility of this planning model. How could any central authority store or master knowledge about the marginal productivities in a total economy? This is not possible in a changing world (Mises, 1936; Caiden and Wildavsky, 1974). Even if the *information problem* could be solved in a small economy the *incentive problem* would still remain. Since it would be rational for each producer to disguise their information about technologies a strategic game would result. Participants would try to promote their interests by providing biased information. If the ministry of production attempts to force the directives on producers, then there is no incentive to search for a rational technology.

A command economy may use prices instead of explicit commands as in a war economy, but these prices would not constitute market prices. Prices may be employed for several purposes (Johansen, 1977). They may reflect the interaction between demand and supply, but they may also express central authority directives. In a command economy, prices have the function of conveying to the participants in the economy the conditions for their activity as the central authority considers the situation. The prices of goods and services as well as of the factors of production are strictly controlled, meaning that they express the intentions of the central planning board, not the demand and supply of consumers and producers – administrative prices. It has been suggested that this could be resolved by a sort of Groves–Ledyard mechanism (Varian, 1984; Eatwell *et al.*, 1987, 1989a), but whether this is practical remains to be seen.

The advantages of a command economy are that it may make certain types of planning easy. The state could decide the overall direction of the economy. Macro-economic planning that made distinctions between consumption and investment as well as between collective goods and consumer goods would become much easier as the amount of central control is so much larger. The central planning model emphasizes knowledge of technological factors for the governance of the economy in accordance with the preferences of the central planning board (Dobb, 1940).

The disadvantages of the command economy derive from the fact that it tends to be badly inefficient with regard to the allocation of consumer goods or capital. Although it is true that the ministry of finance or the budgetary authority could, in principle, employ efficient shadow prices or exchange ratios between different kinds of resources of production factors, the practical feasibility of such a mechanism is open to doubt. Controlling prices and employing them as tools for commanding the economic decisions of consumers and producers means most probably that neither efficiency in consumption nor efficiency in production will be met. In practical situations we find the curious expressions of a command economy: severe shortages for some goods, enormous overproduction of other goods, mismanagement of capital resources and a peculiar allocation of the labour force (Zaleski, 1980; Kornai, 1986).

These difficulties are well known from studies of the East European systems (Ellman, 1979; Nove, 1986; Åslund, 1995). A huge planning bureau uses prices to allocate resources, but these prices do not reflect changes in demand and supply. They are cost-plus prices, meaning that they are based on the average unit production cost in enterprises producing a good (Eidem and Viotti, 1978). The planning bureaux base their administrative decisions on available technology in terms of how much of the input resources are needed to produce an output unit, given the existing knowledge about production functions. Moreover, the planning bureaux may also adjust these prices in accordance with national priorities concerning the goods that should be produced, replacing consumer sovereignty with collective preferences interpreted by a group of planners (Spulber, 1969; Dyker, 1976; Bergson and Levine, 1983).

In an ideal command economy there would be no need for prices. The state would know the relative value of each good in terms of preferences. No existing economy could, however, be governed in this way. Although, for example, the Soviet economy was basically run by means of a large planning framework – allocating resources to various regions, factories and consumers – it employed a type of price: administrative prices (Dyker, 1976; McAuley, 1979). The single units in the Soviet economy were given a budget within which to make economic decisions about resources. This did not mean that these decisions guided resource allocation, but simply that there was a limit as to how far planning could proceed. The economic decisions of consumers and producers were still largely determined by the plan.

Major economic changes, then, also have to come from the plan. The administrators of the economy must employ various devices in order to gather information about how to increase efficiency. The state has to remain alert to various signals from producers and consumers that the allocation of resources must be changed – queues, overproduction, misallocation, wastage. On the one hand, the state must be able to co-ordinate and process a vast amount of knowledge. The problems with a planning system are that the state may not get the right information from producers and consumers and that the state may not be able to process such a vast amount of information. There are limits to the capacity of any group of actors to control social systems, in particular economic ones. On the other hand, there is the serious incentive problem: what is the reward for the various participants in a planned economy – consumers, producers and administrators – when they search for and transmit the best available knowledge?

Change in production and management becomes particularly difficult in a command economy as there is little scope for innovation and few rewards for individual initiatives. To devise a number of performance indicators does not help as they may be strategically manipulated in a system based on hierarchical control (Leeman, 1963). The sudden and almost dramatic collapse of the East European command economies in the late 1980s appears to have been a mature reaction to long-term system problems of the kind outlined above (Davis and Scase, 1985).

The serious problem of efficiency in a command economy resulted in a search for another resource allocation model. It would be based less on planning and would recognize the fundamental importance of prices – scarcity prices – see Brus and Laski (1990). The socialist models of Lange, Taylor and Lerner are based on an attempt to combine public ownership with market prices (Lange, 1936–37; Lippincott, 1938; Lange and Taylor, 1964; Lerner, A. P., 1944; Mandel, 1986).

The competitive socialist model

The so-called Lange–Taylor model is interesting as it explicitly tries to accommodate a socialist system of resource allocation within the standard efficiency criteria. It is not based on the notion of a command economy with a huge planning office directing the economy by means of state authority. The Lange–Taylor model attempts to combine the trial-and-error procedure of a competitive price mechanism with public ownership of production. The assumptions of the model include: (i) The allocation of capital is to be based on administrative criteria. (ii) The allocation of labour and consumption of goods is to be determined by the interaction between demand and supply in free markets. (iii) The producers of goods are to be instructed to obey the following rules: (a) to choose the combination of factors which minimize the average cost of production; (b) the scale of output is to be determined where marginal cost is equal to the price of the product (Lange and Taylor, 1964).

Given these initial conditions, the state authorities are to start the trial-and-error process by arbitrarily setting the prices for goods and labour. The interaction between consumers and producers on various markets will then in successive stages lead to a state where the prices are adjusted by the price board until the efficiency conditions are met. Thus, a socialist economy could be using real prices and achieve an efficient allocation of resources.

Two detailed models of resource allocation in a socialist economy employing scarcity prices have been developed. The so-called Lange–Arrow–Hurwicz (LAH) model is an attempt to copy the competitive mechanism of a market economy in a socialist system (Arrow and Hurwicz, 1960). The LAH planning procedure may be outlined as a replica of Walras' *tantonnement* process:

> At a given distribution of resources amongst consumers, the central planning board (CPB) quotes a vector of prices. Producers then calculate the production programmes that would maximize profits at these prices, and inform the centre of the supplies, demands and profits that would result. The profits are distributed as the centre may see fit amongst consumers, who then, facing given profit shares and wage rates, choose their most preferred consumption bundles, and inform the CPB of these. The centre now acts as an auctioneer, raising prices of goods in excess demand, and vice versa: and so the process continues. (Heal, 1973: 79)

An alternative to the LAH model is the so-called Malinvaud process where the centre employs a competitive price mechanism in order to arrive at knowledge about the production possibilities of the firms which may be used to determine an efficiency locus. The Malinvaud model places a much stronger role with the CPB (Malinvaud, 1967).

It has been argued that the trial-and-error method suggested in the LAH model of a socialist system of resource allocation will face severe practical information problems. Will the successive reconsideration of prices by a state board really work? Would there not be too slow a process of price adaptation to information about the relationship between demand and supply? How is the remuneration to labour to be decided? Is it really possible to have an equal distribution of income at the same time as the wages are to be determined in the market? According to Hayek, the iterative revision of prices to be fed into market operations would require a board of supermen, with perfect knowledge about all production technologies and the behaviour of managers (Hayek, 1996). It has also been argued that the so-called competitive solution would not handle macro-economic disturbances well (Dobb, 1940; Wright, 1947). The Malinvaud process has been criticized as requiring too much co-ordination between producers.

Another basic problem in the competitive solution remains to be pointed out: the incentive problem. Why would managers in the various production units follow the assumptions of the model, meaning that they would have to be socially rational without any remuneration? Why would it not be possible that the managers of production might try to influence the price board to set the prices in such a way that any losses will be recovered? Why would managers attempt to minimize costs if they are not allowed to capitalize on the profits? If the profits are to be returned to the price board, why would managers care about production costs?

The socialist bias in the LAH model is apparent in the restrictions on capital. Capital would be owned and controlled by the state and profits, interests and rents earned in government enterprises would be distributed as a sort of social dividend unrelated to labour income. But how could there be efficiency in capital allocation given these restrictions? What is the exact meaning of competition in the LAH model? Could there really be competition on either side of the economy if severe socialist restrictions concerning wages and ownership were upheld? It may be argued that from a static point of view the competitive solution might achieve efficiency, but how about a dynamic perspective? Why would managers care about the introduction of new technology if the profits are not to be capitalized in one way or another? According to the Austrian school, there will be no stationary solution as the economy is always in a process of change and adaptation. If risk and uncertainty is inherent in management, then the incentive problem will be most severe as there would be no reward for the embarkment on a process of innovation (Schumpeter, 1944). What is really the difference between the central planning solution and the competitive solution?

The competitive solution suggested by Lange, Taylor and Lerner is an attempt to solve the efficiency equations by means of the market mechanism instead of the administrative solution in the central planning model. The administrative solution is deficient because there is no such vast and reliable information system available as required. The competitive solution aims at replacing the administrative mechanism with a trial-and-error mechanism in combination with some severe socialist restrictions. What is the difference in reality?

It would seem that the competitive solution downgrades the tasks of the ministry of production from those of a giant comprehensive planning body to those of a small price board making adjustments here and there. This is not so, however. The price board in the competitive solution would need extensive knowledge – pure information undisturbed by tactical considerations – in order to control the behaviour of managers. Is average cost really minimized? Is price really equal to marginal cost? Why could not various managers co-operate and try to influence the price or hide information about the cost function? Who could judge whether there really is free entry to the market in a socialist state where the state controls access to capital? Is it not conceivable that it will be difficult to operate markets where the availability of capital is not free?

Some goods may display economies of scale, meaning that there will be losses for the managers when price is set equal to marginal costs. If the price board is asked to change the price so that losses are eliminated, then why could not the board be equally willing to change the prices for other goods? Would it not require the same amount of extensive information as in the command economy to be able to judge the cost function of various enterprises? It seems as if the competitive solution also requires a CPB.

The information requirements are no less formidable in the competitive solution than in the central planning solution. And both face the same incentive problem: how could the participants in this type of resource allocation be trusted with an ambition to act according to the rules? Just as there would be an advantage for managers in a command economy to misrepresent costs in order to maximize their own advantage, so there would be no incentive for managers in the competitive solution to minimize costs, if they could not count on some of the profits being made available to them.

The difference between a CPB and a price board would in effect be marginal. No CPB would ever be able to allocate all resources without the use of some price mechanism. And no price board would ever reach an efficient allocative state if it did not have access to comprehensive knowledge about production possibilities as well as making the correct decisions about the release of the socially owned capital resources.

The zest for a fundamental but still socialist reform of the command economies in Eastern Europe and in mainland China cropped up now and then as a reaction to the rigidities, shortages and inefficiencies of the command economies (Ellman, 1979; Kornai, 1979, 1986; Åslund, 1989).

However, these reform movements in the command economies accomplished less than was hoped for and this is the reason that in 1989 the East European countries decided to look for alternative economic systems outside the various socialist models. What is the basic difficulty in the theoretical argument for a new kind of socialist politico-economic regime – market socialism (Nove, 1983; Le Grand and Estrin, 1989)?

Market socialism

The idea of market socialism was launched as a result of the inefficiency problems of a centrally planned economy. The informational requirements on a CPB would simply be too great to handle by any social organization. However, the proposals for or models of a combination of markets and a socialist economy are ambiguous with regard to two basic problems, the position of a co-ordinating body and the range of the use of markets to allocate resources. From a theoretical point of view we may predict serious difficulties in implementing market socialism in an existing politico-economic system. Let us pinpoint these problems which are relevant to the understanding of mainland China.

All models of market socialism assume some co-ordinating board, but the scope of its operations and its power differs. Given the fact that the co-ordinating board has the responsibility for allocative efficiency it seems difficult indeed to restrict its operations. Even if it employs competitive prices it would still face the requirement that it itself operates rationally. What mechanism in market socialism would guarantee that the co-ordinators make the correct decisions? It seems as if the theories of market socialism simply assume that the co-ordinating board will consist of highly competent people that are unambiguously devoted to the efficiency goal. But why would this be the case? *Sed quis custodiet ipsos Custodes*?

The incentive problem recurs at the management level (Bergson, 1981). There is no mechanism that will reward the managers to act in a way that is socially productive as long as profits cannot be capitalized by the managers. The same problem appears again with regard to labour. If wages are to be set on the basis of an equality requirement, then it is difficult to see why labour would behave in a way that is conducive to collective rationality.

On the consumption side market socialism was meant to strengthen the principle of consumer sovereignty in socialist economies. The use of administrative prices in command economies means that effective demand may show up in ways other than via the price mechanism. There is a constant danger in a command economy of replacing consumer preferences with the preferences of the co-ordinators. Not even market socialism could accept the principle of consumer sovereignty as the co-ordinators would make crucial choices about the division between consumption and investment as well as the long-range orientation of the overall economy. What would be the incentives for co-ordinators to make the correct decisions?

The incentive problem is the most difficult problem that market socialism faces. How is it to be solved given the tension between the use of market prices on the one hand and the restrictions of a socialist economy on the other? The literature on capitalism versus socialism tends to focus on the information problem that emerges as markets are replaced by planning, but the incentive problem is more severe. It accounts for the widespread feeling of apathy in several socialist countries where reforms aiming at market socialism have been tried but where the incentive problem has not been resolved. It also explains the development of a sharp tension between the official economy and the unofficial or black economy in socialist systems.

Could a socialist production system be efficient? What amount of market-type operations and mechanisms could be inserted into a socialist economy in order to raise productivity and affluence? These questions have been much debated by economists over the last 50 years. The debate was clearly relevant to the attempts in the communist world to promote efficiency in their economies. The practical lessons are that a socialist economy is possible but not efficient. In order to promote efficiency the price mechanism has to be resorted to in the sense that prices reflect scarcity of values. This in turn requires that the reward function of the price system is recognized in the *incentive system* of the society, meaning that it will pay for the participants to communicate truthfully and behave rationally in relation to economic parameters.

Only if a socialist state allows private incentives is it possible to employ the price system to allocate resources in an efficient way. The socialist restrictions of the Lange–Taylor model means that the competitive solution will be a variant of the command economy model. How could there be efficiency in production if managers are not allowed access to a capital market as well as being permitted to capitalize profits without the intervention of the state?

How far is it possible to accommodate private incentives without breaking the socialist assumptions of the economic system? The debate about the possibility and efficiency of a socialist economy has focused far too much on abstract equilibrium conditions and has been bypassing crucial institutional problems. The basic difficulty in a socialist economy is not to derive a set of solutions to the standard efficiency conditions but to devise and maintain institutions that implement these solutions in the short run as well as in the long run. It seems as if the two models of a socialist economy – the competitive model as well as the central planning model – make far too strong or simplistic institutional assumptions about the practicability of managing a large economy along socialist lines.

It is impossible to discuss the possibility of change in the allocation mechanism without taking the institutional structure for ownership into account. If market mechanisms are to be employed instead of planning or administration, then private ownership must be allowed. If one favours efficiency in resource allocation, then one has to accept the institutional requirements and consequences of the working of the market. The fact that a country has an ownership structure that is fundamentally public implies that there are definite limits to the scope for the operation of the market mechanism, as in China today.

The introduction of market socialism in communist systems is always of limited significance and is restricted to various types of divisible goods. Often it is accompanied by a process in which attempts to broaden the relevance of the market mechanism are curtailed by a fear for the consequences for the structure of ownership and property rights. Public ownership limits the use of the market mechanism to such an extent as to make the whole idea of market socialism not viable in the long run.

Looking at the various attempts at some type of market socialism in what used to be the communist world – in the Soviet Union, Hungary, Yugoslavia, China – we may predict on theoretical reasons that these reforms will pass through an ambiguous process of implementation characterized by opposite forces. Either the reforms will be curtailed after a while or they will be restricted to a narrow sector of the economy. Or there will be a severe incentive problem as apathy will be the response to a situation where private initiatives are allowed but not rewarded. Or, finally, the communist state has to recognize private initiative to an extent that must have system power implications which call for a delicate balance between the established order and the new initiatives – China tommorrow.

The relevance of market socialism to developing countries is limited due to the fundamental contradictions between the need to maintain control and the pressure to extend market operations. It is symptomatic that the economies characterized by rapid and steady growth have not attempted to adopt the model of market socialism. On the contrary, the economies of the Pacific area have successfully tried a model of capitalism introduced and supervised by government (Zysman, 1983; Sheridan, 1998).

It is often stated that Yugoslavia and Hungary are the only countries where market socialism has been tried on a significant scale (Brus and Laski, 1990). There was a mix of regime reforms in Yugoslavia, all of which can hardly be subsumed under the label of market socialism (Singleton and Carter, 1982; Estrin, 1983; Lydall, 1986). The participatory schemes for workers attracted international attention as a way to reform the rigid bureaucratic nature of the command economy (Dahl, 1985), but it is an open question as to what extent these participatory reforms imply market socialism. The reform of the Hungarian economy away from the common model towards the market socialism model never managed to introduce real market mechanisms as the enterprises remained dependent on the state. However, China today must be regarded as having a market socialism regime, or to be practising market communism. The scale of the Chinese experiment is such that it must give conclusive evidence about the pros and cons of this regime mixture in the short and long run.

Wagner: budget allocation, redistribution and the mixed economy

Extensive budget allocation instead of market allocation in a system with considerable private ownership of the means of production and consumption has become typical in the OECD countries. The relevance of budget allocation has been on the increase in capitalist systems for several decades, transforming these private societies into mixed economies, although the seminal process of public sector expansion has now come to a halt (Webber and Wildavsky, 1986; Wildavsky, 1976, 2nd edn., 1986). It would appear there is a limit to the process of public sector growth. The distinction between a mixed economy and a command economy is a qualitative one. And the transformation of a society with strong private ownership and existing market mechanisms into a system oriented towards the planning mechanism would require structural changes that are far more encompassing than yearly increments in a slow process of public sector growth.

Budget allocation takes place in the yearly budgetary process where requests seek appropriations and appropriations result from the consideration of competing requests (Wildavsky, 1964, 2nd edn., 1984, 1988). The principal tool for deciding which requests will be which appropriations is the authority of government, not the voluntary agreement between producers and consumers. Budget allocation is characterized by considerable stability in that there is a short-term plan about how resources are to be employed and for what purposes which is of a determinate form.

The mechanism of allocation in the budgetary process is not based on competition and exchange but rests on the authority of government to decide on the basis of cost calculations from one supplier, the bureau. Budget allocation is a strategic game between two actors, the government demanding a service and the bureau supplying the service on the condition that total costs will be covered. Thus, we have the typical feature of the budgetary process that programme quantity will not be set where marginal value equals marginal cost (Niskanen, 1971).

Budget allocation is based on monopoly and hierarchy. Goods and services are produced by one supplier and consumed by the citizens without any choice of an alternative. Quantity is determined by the authorities on the basis on various considerations including citizen preferences as revealed in some political process or collective preferences as defined by some authority. The programme is uniformly provided by the authority to be consumed in equal ways by its clients. Quantity is determined in the budgetary process as a result of the game interaction between government demanding a programme and the bureau supplying the programme. There is large scope for negotiation and strategic behaviour in the budgetary process as described by Aaron Wildavsky in a series of studies of the budgetary process (Wildavsky, 1964, 1976, 1984, 1986, 1988).

Price and cost in budget allocation serve administrative functions. On the one hand, the appropriation informs the bureaux about the amount of resources they are entitled to use. On the other hand, the authority mobilizes resources in the form of either taxes or charges. Producer costs are the appropriations which reflect the bargaining power of the two principal actors in the budgetary process. Consumer prices or user fees may be fixed on a variety of grounds from allocative efficiency to redistributional criteria. Labour costs are a function of the bargaining power of the public employees in relation to government, whereas capital costs are handled by means of various administrative criteria. What is lacking is searcity value, the willingness to pay and criteria of profitability.

The basic principles of public administration structure budget allocation. The means and ends of programmes are determined in a plan document which singles out the supplier and identifies the production functions. There is a predetermined structure of monopoly suppliers, the bureaucracy. There is no competition between the bureaux as they have been assigned long-term tasks which are unique for each bureau. Clear standards for the operation of the bureau are laid down and the output of the bureau is regulated by means of technical and legal criteria. Complaint is to be expressed by means of voice, not exit.

As Hirschman argued, the difference between *budget and market allocation* appears most clearly in the handling of allocation failures and the expression of dissatisfaction. Whereas the consumer may exit from the market when faced with a product or service he/she dislikes, the citizen in a voting context has no such powerful tool at his/her disposal. Instead the dissatisfied citizen has to go through the tiresome and lengthy process of complaining to those responsible for the provision of the good or the service, which is a lot less efficient than simply turning to a competitor in the market (Hirschman, 1970).

Long-term planning in a mixed economy is of a different nature. It is also based on a plan document but it lacks the determinate form. It is more of a projection and a guess than a real commitment as to the path to be travelled. Short-term budget allocation and long-term planning have certain advantages which may make them attractive alternatives to market allocation. However, there are certain disadvantages which have become more apparent in the era of big government.

The government budget is a promise about who can expect what money. It is a real commitment that there is a high probability that resources will be forthcoming, particularly in rich countries. In his comparative model of the budgetary process, Wildavsky employs two conceptual pairs in order to derive four ideal types. On the one hand, we have the predictability of the budgetary process as to whether its appropriations will lead to safe expenditure in accordance with what was planned, or the state budget is characterized by instability in that budgets are remade continuously. On the other hand, there is the environment of budget-making – how rich or poor the economy is that supports the public sector. Typical of the *incremental* budgetary fashion that has been prevalent in the mixed economies is the combination of stability and affluence, whereas *repetitive* budgeting typical of Third World countries takes place in a poor environment where the budgetary process tends towards instability (Wildavsky, 1976).

The variation among the so-called rich market economies may be further explained by looking more closely at the budgetary contexts in the leading OECD countries. Wildavsky explains the variation in budget size by the interaction between the containment of conflict and the support for spending on various items in the budget where the first factor reduces whereas the second factor enhances budget-making (Wildavsky, 1986). The question of variation in the public finances is one of the core problems of political economy. We will deal with this problem of the size and orientation of the public budget in empirical analyses of both the variation within the OECD set of countries and the variation between rich market economies, communist systems and Third World countries.

Budgetary stability has a one-year periodicity. Typical of short-term budget allocation, however, is that the one-year periodicity tends to extend to a long-term stability as stated in the theory about incrementalism. Once appropriations are fixed they are non-negotiable. People can predict what services and goods are forthcoming and employees may trust that their salaries will be paid (Rose, 1984, 1989). The budget document is transformed into expenditure decisions which may be called upon in due time. Uncertainty is minimized, predictability maximized.

Stability when considered advantageous tends to characterize the development of the budget, meaning that yearly changes will only be marginal. The theory of incrementalism used to be the established explanation of the short-term budgetary process. It was considered valid until budget-making became more erratic and shifting as a reaction to a more volatile environment. Yearly changes became non-marginal and programmes were really extinguished. Budgetary theory must recognize non-marginal budget-making amounting to a real change, because it is simply the exception that confirms the rule. The relevance of incrementalism hinges on the interpretation of the concept of marginal changes as well as the occurrence of changes in appropriations. It could be the case that incrementalism overemphasized the extent of stability that used to take place before the turmoil of the early 1980s or that the 1980s really meant a decisive break with the past.

A society that trusts budget allocation for a large number of services and goods values control and predictability highly. Government lays down what to expect for one year for a wide variety of utilities. This enhances security of employment and makes it possible to control outputs in accordance with regulations. Short-term cost efficiency is traded for long-term stability and predictability. Budget allocation is the attempt to make the future controllable and predictable in terms of predetermined criteria. The information contained in the budget is a one-way communication that states what will take place and how. Budget allocation is the authoritative allocation of values for a society. And authority if benevolent may accomplish beneficial outcomes.

Budget allocation enhances similarity. The emphasis on similarity follows from two sources: technical rationality and a preference for equality. Budget allocation is a method to inform about how resources are to be used to accomplish a number of goals. And such information has its own requirements. In a system of big government it becomes impossible to take each and every factor into account and to treat each appropriation differently – hence the need for standardization and similarity. To allocate by means of a budget is to employ rules and rules are expedient if they are universal with as few exceptions as possible. The drive for similarity is further strengthened by the preference for similarity in societies with big government. Big government is both an effect and a cause of the trend towards similarity. In relation to the set of public goods there can be no choice between budget and market allocation, because there is so-called market failure. However, in relation to other kinds of goods and services there is a real choice between politics or markets. Often budget allocation is preferred to market allocation because it makes possible the control of outputs which in turn makes standardization possible at the same time as it further enhances similarity for its own reasons.

Budget allocation initiates a need for yet more budget allocation. Budget allocation creates clients who tend to hang on to their appropriations and if possible extend them further. And people are always looking for new appropriations to become clients of budgetary programmes. Budget allocation has its adherents among those who favour stability and value predictability. Once an item of expenditure is accepted on the budget it has a strong probability of remaining there for long periods of time. A variety of arguments have been put forward to account for the expansion of budget allocation (Tarschys, 1975; Larkey *et al.*, 1981; Rose, 1984; Wildavsky, 1985).

The growth of the state is essentially a political process through which the budget has driven out the market as the mechanism of allocation. The process is a universal one in systems with a structure of predominantly privately owned means of production. It is considered that a number of problems and deficiencies may be better attacked by the use of the budget instrument – public policy solutions to market failure. Essentially, it is a preference for stability and predictability as well as similarity. The mixed economy or the bargaining society (Johansen, 1979) means that allocative processes comprise a limited number of choice participants as well as that allocation decisions may be predicted and controlled by government and its bureaux.

Whereas there was a search in communist systems for more market allocation and its derivatives – rapid adjustment, flexibility and mutual adaptation – the opposite tendency has characterized the development of the political economies of the OECD countries. One has resorted to government in order to allocate the welfare state goods and services, although neither could these goods and services be classified as pure public goods nor is budget allocation often based on the occurrence of externalities or economies of scale. The budget instrument has been considered superior to market allocation in relation to a number of basically private goods and services where the elements of jointness and non-excludability have not been conspicuous. In relation to health, social services and education, predictability and similarity have been deemed more important than flexibility or efficiency.

Hierarchy has replaced markets in the economies with extensive private ownership. The budget instrument appears to handle the transaction costs in a complex society characterized by bounded rationality and opportunism with a small number of powerful actors better than the market does. Internal organization will drive out market exchange systems when these conditions obtain (Williamson, 1975) whether in the private sector or in society in general. Combining the transaction argument with the stability and similarity argument, there is a strong case for budget allocation in relation to semi-public goods.

However, there are institutional limits to the expansion of the budget. The structure of privately owned means of production implies some amount of individual choice which works against the expansion of budget allocation. Budget expansion may be conducive to quality but it basically means that resources are allocated by one actor – government – in accordance with standardized rules. Regulation is typical of budget allocation, but there is a limit to the regulative capacity of government in market systems with extensive private ownership. When take-home pay goes down the period of budget expansion is bound to come to an end in systems with private ownership (Rose, 1985). The larger the budget the more serious the efficiency problems.

On the one hand, governments may regulate the private sector in a way that restricts competition (Buchanan *et al.*, 1980; Spulber, 1989). On the other hand, budget allocation of resources may involve budget-maximizing bureaucrats (Niskanen, 1971). A large public sector may involve both extensive regulation and huge public resource allocation by means of bureaux. Budget allocation presupposes bureaucracy. And the problem of efficiency and productivity in budget allocation is very much tied up with the problem of bureaucracy. The distrust of the early 1990s in bureaux as producers of goods and services applies not only to the rich market economies or the so-called mixed economies but equally to the Third World countries where there has been a reassessment of planning and bureaucracy as the tool for managing development objectives.

It has been argued that the welfare state could be dismantled in favour of market allocation with regard to welfare state goods and services (Buchanan, 1986). This presupposes considerable transfer payments in order to maintain a minimum level of income equality. Such a society would constitute a market society that would maximize individual choice and private preferences if transactions costs were not to become staggering. It would be a more volatile society in contradistinction to an economy with a large public sector. Planning, if it works, operates differently, as it is conducive to stability and predictability as well as to control and similarity, at least in theory.

A very salient problem in political economy is to identify criteria for the determination of the size of the allocative and redistributive budget. Such criteria may be either normative, looking for an optimal size of budget allocation and budget redistribution (Margolis and Guitton, 1969; Stiglitz, 1999), or they may be empirical, i.e. they may be the actual factors that explain the variation in the size of the public sector and the welfare state commitments, among the nations, in the world (Wilensky, 1975; Castles, 1982, 1998; Wildavsky, 1986).

The mixed economies of the OECD countries differ, however, in terms of both size and orientation – why? How can we account for the strong variation in welfare state commitments among rich and Third World countries in terms of an empirical analysis? The convergence hypothesis was suggested in the 1960s as a prediction to the effect that welfare state expenditures between market countries and communist systems would become more and more similar (Tinbergen, 1967; Galbraith, 1969). However, it turned out to be wrong. Is it really true that public policies tend to grow more similar between countries as the level of affluence increases, as Wagner's law entails? Perhaps politics matter for public policy outputs or outcomes as discussed in the literature on policy determinants (Danziger, 1978; Sharpe and Newton, 1984)? A number of important questions for research may be identified in relation to the Wagnerian model of the welfare state. Is public sector growth always related to the state of the economy: affluence (Wilensky, 1975)? How far is it possible to expand budget allocation within the confines of extensive private ownership of the means of production? How does public sector expansion affect economic growth?

List: economic nationalism and development planning

The model of economic development suggested by Friedrich List in 1837 designs a major role for the state, but more in terms of guidance or planning than ownership with the exception for key industries which should be controlled by the state (List, (1837) 1983). It has been claimed that the List model played an important role not only in European countries such as Germany and France but also in Japan (Johnson, 1984) and in South East Asia in general with the exception of Hong Kong – what is referred to as the 'governed market theory of East Asian success' (GM theory) (Wade, 1990). What then is developmental planning?

Planning is typically resorted to for a different reason than to keep the public household going, namely to plan the overall development of resources in society. Planning for the long-term development of the economy is a mixture of projection and decision. Planning both attempts to predict the future development of markets and their outcomes and to influence the working of markets in a manner that is conducive to macro-economic objectives. Short-term planning of the economy or budget allocation is often based on long-run planning although the link is far less tight then was once expected. Planning is considered advantageous because it could contribute to stability and predictability. And planning procedures are strong in societies where stability and predictability are highly valued. There is, however, a limit to how much planning can be combined with a structure of private ownership.

The concept of planning is often employed in discussions about politico-economic systems. How does it relate to the concepts discussed so far? Actually, it is far from clear what is meant by 'planning' (Wildavsky, 1973). Several distinctions may be made between different kinds of planning (Johansen, 1977–78). Thus, we have: macro-economic planning = the regulation by the state of fiscal, monetary and trade parameters in order to influence macro-economic targets; micro-economic planning = the control of the state of basic decision parameters; comprehensive planning = the attempt to control the whole economy in more or less detail; indicative planning = the effort to influence the economy by means of selective measures that work out their own consequences.

In a market economy some kinds of macro-economic planning by means of indicative planning mechanisms had been considered relevant after the great depression in the 1930s. Yet, macro-economic planning began to be questioned in the 1970s, as there was a reaction in several OECD nations against a too optimistic and perhaps naïve adherence to Keynesian macro-economic principles (Sawyer, 1989). Micro-economic planning is not in agreement with a market economy as it is characteristic of budget allocation. Comprehensive planning was typical of command economies.

Whereas planning may be employed both in systems based on market allocation as well as in socialist economies although differently, the distinction between competition and budget allocation as the medium of allocation is a sharp one. Budget allocation occurs in both socialist and market economies although in quite different amounts. Whereas budget allocation in socialist systems covered almost all types of goods, in market economies it used to be confined to the provision of public goods. In a system where the state or the public owns most of the means of production market socialism favours the use of competitive prices.

Is it possible to employ market-type decision mechanisms and achieve planning although different from comprehensive planning in a command economy (Tinbergen, 1967)? In any economic structure the role of prices is crucial, but we must distinguish between competitive prices and administrative prices. The South East Asian model attempted to combine markets with strategic state planning, developing infant industries. The Indian debate, for example, about the place of planning in an economy with large-scale private ownership is also highly relevant in this context (Bardhan, 1984; Mareshwari, 1984) – development administration.

Planning may be increased to a certain extent within a system of privately owned resources. In a process of public sector growth where more and more resources are allocated by government, planning is bound to increase. There is a need for planning the development of the public household above and beyond what is possible in market allocation and the strong increase in the public sector calls for a co-ordinating mechanism in relation to the market system. However, there comes a point when planning takes over the basic decision functions of the market. Markets and planning may coexist to some degree only. The continued existence of privately owned means of production presents a challenge to planning systems as they reject the drive for control and predictability. The tension between planning and markets implies that either there will be even more planning or that one has to accept that planning may not work efficiently due to the unpredictable and uncontrollable interaction with markets.

Planning became as popular in rich as in poor countries after the Second World War, identifying almost all kinds of budget-making and administration with planning (Wildavsky, 1973). In the Third World outside the communist systems there was a strong belief in combining planning with market allocation as a way to bypass the conflict between capitalism and communism (Caiden and Wildavsky, 1974). Developmental planning was the technique to steer the economy towards the goals of five-year plans stating collective objectives. It motivated the expansion of the role of the state in society calling for a number of political and administrative measures. Not only would the economy grow but developmental planning would assure the right kind of economic growth. The strength of these planning techniques varied from country to country. India is perhaps the most well-known example of developmental planning with a strong socialist dose, although maintaining a structure of private ownership (Little, 1982). Its role and outcomes in the South East Asian miracles has been a contested issue (Krugman, 1994).

The many failures of developmental planning have resulted in a reconsideration of the place of market forces in processes of development as well as in the form of a strategic instrument to bring about economic growth (Toye, 1987; Balassa, 1989).

The key problem in all forms of economic nationalism – the South East Asia model, state-capitalism, industrial policies – is that of picking the winners. How can government and its bureaucracy do this? Economic nationalism using important substitution measures or export orientation measures also comes into conflict with the rules of the global market economy.

Conclusion

In classical political economy it was asked whether the market or the state performed the best. However, in a comparative perspective it seems important to separate between various kinds of capitalist regimes and attempt to evaluate how they perform on political economy criteria. Thus the so-called capitalist economies perform very differently in terms of such a crucial criterion of evaluation as average economic growth. How can we in a general way enquire into performance differences among different politico-economic systems? We need to proceed from the pure theoretical argument about the superiority of competitive market allocation in combination with capitalist institutions to empirical research into the similarities and differences between various politico-economic systems. One tentative distinction is that between decentralized capitalist, capitalist-state and mixed-capitalist systems on the one hand and socialist regimes on the other hand. Another approach is to classify countries according to the degree of economic freedom characteristic of their institutions.

A research programme examining the outcomes of politico-economic regions involves an analysis of other performance dimensions besides the differential rates of economic development of politico-economic systems. Thus one may ask how an economic regime of one kind or another impacts upon politics, e.g. democracy. In the next chapter we will look at real-life economic regimes and evaluate their economic, social and political outcomes. Such a research effort is only feasible if one moves away from the simple dichotomy of the Great Debate: market or state.

CHAPTER 7

Politico-economic Regimes: An Evaluation

Introduction

In a framework for the analysis of economic systems one may employ a typology based upon four basic features in which each has at least two modes: (i) organization of decision-making: centralization and decentralization; (ii) provision of information and co-ordination: market or plan; (iii) property rights: private, co-operative and public; (iv) the incentive system: moral or material (Gregory and Stuart 1987). These categories can be employed to derive three main types of politico-economic regimes: capitalism, market socialism and planned socialism.

The performance of these three types of economic systems can be analysed by means of data on a set of outcomes: affluence, economic growth, inflation, income distribution, and democracy. The overall finding tends to be the precedence of the capitalist type on these evaluation criteria in relation to the others. However, can we really speak of one and only one capitalist regime and are there actually existing market socialist regimes? Is there some kind of pure model of capitalism which contain the essence of all non-socialist systems or should we recognize the existence of different kinds of capitalist politico-economic regimes? In order to evaluate how various types of politico-economic systems do in the real world one could employ both economic and political evaluation criteria.

In this chapter we evaluate politico-economic regimes by means of developmental criteria derived from the distinction between economic output and rights. Politico-economic regimes may achieve a high level of affluence (production) or secure democracy and human rights, or both. We make two analyses, one covering the pre-1989 world and the other the early 1990s, in order to take into account the extensive changes taking place in the structure of the political economies after 1989 as part of the general move towards more of markets and less of state intervention. And we will consider the following performance dimensions of a politico-economic regime: economic growth, inflation, civil and political rights as well as the extent ʌality in the distribution of income.

Regimes, evaluation criteria and the data

Let us first discuss alternative classifications of economic regimes. Any such classification must take real-life transformations into account. Thus the year 1989 is critical for the correctness of an empirical taxonomy of economic regimes.

Gastil's framework, presented in *Freedom in the World* (1987) is a more refined one for classifying economic regimes around the world. Gastil categorizes politico-economic systems in the following way: (a) *capitalist*: a high degree of economic freedom and relatively little market intervention by the state; (b) *capitalist-statist*: substantial state intervention in markets and large public sectors, although the state remains committed to the institutions of private property; (c) *mixed capitalist*: an activist state with income redistribution, market intervention and regulation although the size of direct budget allocation of resources is not that large; (d) *mixed socialist*: some economic freedom, private property and individual initiative within the framework of a socialist economy; (e) *socialist systems*: basically command economies with little economic freedom, private property and individual initiative. Gastil classifies a large number of countries with the following politico-economic categories:

> *Capitalist economies*: Australia, Belgium, Bhutan, Botswana, Cameroon, Canada, Chad, Chile, Colombia, Costa Rica, Côte d'Ivoire, Dominican Republic, Ecuador, El Salvador, Gabon, Germany, Guatemala, Haiti, Honduras, Iceland, Ireland, Japan, Jordan, Kenya, Lebanon, Lesotho, Liberia, Luxembourg, Malawi, Malaysia, Mauritius, Nepal, New Zealand, Niger, Papua New Guinea, Sierra Leone, Spain, Switzerland, Thailand, the USA.

> *Capitalist-statist economies*: Argentina, Bangladesh, Bolivia, Brazil, Central African Republic, Congo-Kinshasa, Ghana, India, Indonesia, Iran, Italy, Jamaica, South Korea, Kuwait, Mauritania, Mexico, Morocco, Nigeria, Oman, Pakistan, Panama, Paraguay, Peru, Philippines, Saudi Arabia, South Africa, Sri Lanka, Taiwan, Trinidad and Tobago, Turkey, Uganda, United Arab Emirates, Venezuela.

> *Mixed capitalist economies*: Austria, Burundi, Denmark, Egypt, Finland, France, Greece, Guinea, Israel, the Netherlands, Nicaragua, Norway, Portugal, Senegal, Singapore, Sudan, Sweden, Tunisia, the UK, Uruguay, Zimbabwe.

> *Mixed socialist economies*: Burkina Faso, Burma-Myanmar, China, CongoBrazzaville, Libya, Madagascar, Mali, Poland, Rwanda, Somalia, Syria, Togo, Yugoslavia, Zambia,

> *Socialist economies*: Afghanistan, Albania, Algeria, Angola, Benin, Bulgaria, Cambodia, Cuba, Czech Republic, Ethiopia, Hungary, Iraq, North Korea, Laos, Mongolia, Mozambique, Romania, Tanzania, the USSR, Vietnam.

There are problems in relation to the Gastil framework, even when one recognizes that he deals with the realities of the early 1980s. First, are the categories really conceptually distinct? Whereas it may be empirically feasible to distinguish the decentralized capitalist systems from the mixed capitalist ones, the distinction between mixed socialist and socialist is troublesome to apply. Similarly, the separation between pure capitalist and capitalist-statist is not easy to handle.

Second, any classification of countries into types of politico-economic regimes is bound to be time dependent. Gastil's classification refers to the late 1970s and early 1980s but politico-economic structures are not invariant over time. If the effort is to evaluate the performance of politico-economic regimes over time during the post-Second World War period, then the classification has to be reworked for the time period after 1989 which initiates the dismantling of the command economies.

The evaluation of politico-economic regimes below will be done by using evaluation criteria that can be derived from the developmental perspective that runs through the entire volume: economic development, social development and political development. The average rate of economic growth over a number of years taps a dynamic aspect of politico-economic regimes whereas the average yearly rate of inflation captures a stability aspect. The evaluation criteria in a democracy index identify several crucial performance aspects in relation to human rights such as freedom and equality before the law. Finally, there is the inequality dimension to be measured by an indicator on the skewedness in the distribution of income which is a standard criterion on social development. These evaluation criteria – economic, political and social – have been measured on various data sources.

We now turn to an analysis of variance in order to find out whether it is true that one kind of politico-economic regime – capitalism – performed better than its main competitor – socialism, as long as the command economies were in place. How can we test this hypothesis? If it were true that capitalism did better than socialism, then performance data – economic growth and inflation, human rights and inequality – would differentiate between regimes. Is this the case? Since the dichotomy between capitalism and socialism is too crude we compare three types of capitalist regimes with the socialist type of politico-economic system in relation to performance data covering the post-war period up until about 1989. We finish this chapter by looking at evaluation from the 1990s, but then we must employ a different method of classifying economic regimes.

Politico-economic evaluation pre-1989

Table 7.1 presents a tentative classification of politico-economic types that suits the world before the 1989 downfall of the command economy. Since politico-economic regimes tend to remain fairly stable over long periods of

Table 7.1 Classification of politico-economic regimes 1960–85

Capitalist	Mixed capitalist	Capitalist-statist	Socialist
Australia	Austria	Argentina	Afghanistan
Cameroon	Belgium	Bolivia	Algeria
Canada	Denmark	Brazil	Benin
Chad	Finland	Congo-Kinshasa	Bulgaria
Chile	France	Ghana	Burkina Faso
Colombia	Germany	India	Burma-Myanmar
Costa Rica	Ireland	Indonesia	China
Côte d'Ivoire	Italy	Iran	Czech Republic
Dominican Republic	Netherlands	Mexico	Egypt
Ecuador	Norway	Morocco	GDR
El Salvador	Sweden	Nigeria	Hungary
Gabon	UK	Pakistan	Iraq
Greece		Panama	North Korea
Guatemala		Paraguay	Libya
Honduras		Peru	Madagascar
Japan		Philippines	Poland
Jordan		Portugal	Romania
Kenya		Spain	Sudan
South Korea		Sri Lanka	Tanzania
Liberia		Turkey	USSR
Malawi		Uganda	Yugoslavia
Malaysia		Venezuela	Zambia
New Zealand			
Niger			
Sierra Leone			
Singapore			
Switzerland			
Taiwan			
Thailand			
USA			

time, one may dare to suggest that these categories cover the 1960s, 1970s and 1980s. By examining if different policy outputs and outcomes measured by means of average scores characterize these politico-economic regimes one would have indications about which regimes are attended by what results.

Starting from the Gastil framework we have done some changes when classifying countries into sets of politico-economic regimes. On the one hand, a few countries have been classified somewhat differently; Italy, for example, has been placed among the mixed capitalist systems and not as a capitalist-statist system. On the other hand, the two categories of mixed socialist and socialist have been combined into one single category. The set of socialist regimes includes countries that have had a planned economy and a one-party state for a long period during the post-war period, although some of these countries abandoned the communist regime type in 1989 or 1990. We have reduced the number of countries ($N = 84$) included in the analysis of variance of the performance scores, concentrating mainly on large countries. The classification has been checked with *The Economist Atlas* and *Political Systems of the World.*

Gastil's description of the Federal Republic of Germany as only capitalist must be questioned given the strong tradition towards the welfare state already present in the 1949 constitution. Similarly, Portugal and Spain should be regrouped in the light of the strong state involvement in these societies, at least during the fascist period. The more detailed description of some African and Asian countries is open to discussion. Table 7.1 presents a tentative classification.

Among the *capitalist* systems we find both OECD countries and Third World countries. This category is to be found on all the continents as it includes the USA and Canada, Ecuador and Chile, Greece and Switzerland, Niger, Ivory Coast and Kenya, Jordan, Thailand and Malaysia as well as Japan, and finally Australia and New Zealand.

The *capitalist-statist* type covers politico-economic regimes where the state plays a large role within the framework of an extensive private property system and market allocation. This category includes mainly Third World countries in Latin America: Argentina, Brazil, Mexico and Venezuela, or in Africa: Uganda, Morocco and Nigeria, as well as in Asia: the Philippines and Indonesia. The critical question in relation to this category is whether the Baby Tigers of South East Asia are to be placed here (Wade, 1990; Krugman, 1994). Since South Korea, Taiwan and Singapore rather early left import substitution in favour of an export orientation we place them here in the capitalist camp. How to apply this category in connection with OECD countries is debatable. Turkey is often designated as capitalist-statist, but how about Spain and Portugal with regard to their fascist heritage, meaning here economic nationalism?

There are several OECD countries in the set of *mixed capitalist* systems. Actually, most of the West European nations enter this category because of their welfare state orientation. Whether we also find some Third World countries in this category is to be doubted as welfare state spending is low among poor countries.

The category of *socialist* countries covers a few Third World communist regimes besides the East European countries that adhered to a Leninist model of a politico-economic regime up until 1989–90. Thus all politico-economic regime types besides the mixed capitalist category include both rich and poor countries. Wagner's law entails that a necessary but not sufficiency condition for welfare state spending on a grand scale – big government without socialism – is a rich economy.

We will start with the economic dimension, including indices that measure the level of affluence and the average economic growth for various time periods during the post-Second World War period as well as an indicator on the extent of inflation during 1980–85. Then we will bring up the political and social evaluation criteria.

Below we report on the findings from an analysis of variance of the performance data on these four sets of regimes. Some statistics are rendered for each of the evaluation criteria: mean values, the eta-squared statistic and the corresponding level of significance. We are interested in how these different groups of politico-economic regimes perform in relation to each other as well as how much variation there is within the various groups of regimes. The basic question is this: is there more variation *between* the four sets of regimes than *within* these four subsets themselves? If the eta-squared statistic shows scores that are larger than 0.5, then we may conclude that the distinctions between the four politico-economic regimes are real. If, on the contrary, the eta-squared statistic is lower than 0.5, then there is more variation within these categories, meaning that the regime property itself does not matter for the variation in performance.

Level of affluence

Table 7.2 confirms the general impression that capitalism performs better than socialism in terms of economic prosperity, but we must take a closer look at various kinds of capitalist regimes, comparing each of them with the socialist regimes. Let us look at estimates for 1960 and 1985 (Table 7.2).

Fifteen years after the end of the Second World War the capitalist and mixed capitalist regimes had a higher level of affluence on an average than the socialist type of regimes. Since the mixed capitalist type does not cover any Third World country, the distance between the average score for the mixed capitalist regime is far higher than the average affluence scores of the capitalist and the socialist regimes. Yet, the average real GDP per capita was higher in the capitalist set of countries than in the set of socialist countries. The difference was not striking, or $1872 versus $1708 on an average. The variation as measured by the CV scores was quite extensive among both capitalist and socialist regimes as opposed to the fairly homogeneous set of mixed capitalist regimes which are mainly welfare states in Western Europe.

Moreover, the variation within the four sets of politico-economic regimes is substantial. The eta-squared score indicate that the variation within the

Table 7.2 Real GDP per capita in regime sets 1960 and 1985

Economic system	Real GDP/cap 1960	N	Real GDP/cap 1985	N
Capitalist	1872	30	3811	30
Mixed capitalist	4427	12	9358	12
Capitalist-statist	1359	21	2172	22
Socialist	1708	19	3009	20
Mean/total	2077	82	3983	84
Eta square	0.295		0.401	
Sig.	0.000		0.000	

Source: Summers and Heston (1988)

groups is larger than the variation between the groups. This finding is supported by the very high CV scores measuring the within-group variation. The socialist regimes and the capitalist-statist regimes tend to have a lower level of affluence when mean values are focused on. We also note that the maximum values in these two sets are high, as well as that there are low scoring countries in all four sets of politico-economic regimes.

During the 1970s and early 1980s the country mean average income measures rose, although not as rapidly as during the 1950s and 1960s. The increase was, however, weak among the capitalist-statist regimes, which begun to lag behind. Actually, the average level of affluence among the capitalist-statist regimes was reduced in the early 1980s. The other major finding is the poor development in the socialist group of countries, which no longer kept pace with the group of capitalist or mixed capitalist regimes.

The general finding is that the gap between the capitalist and mixed capitalist regimes on the one hand and the socialist and capitalist-statist sets of regimes on the other hand has increased since the 1960s. Looking at country mean values the mixed capitalist regimes in 1985 had a level of affluence three times that of the capitalist-statist regimes as well as that of the socialist regimes, whereas the set of capitalist regimes displayed twice as high average income values as these two politico-economic regimes that lag behind. More specifically, it is found that politico-economic regimes that involve the state to a large extent controlling the actual operations of the economy do worse than politico-economic regimes that trust markets more.

Interestingly, the higher eta-squared statistic for the 1985 data indicate that politico-economic regime does matter somewhat. The within-group variation is only slightly larger than the between-group variation. The mixed capitalist regime does much better than the other systems, partly because it is to be found among rich countries. The socialist regimes, although they tend to have a higher level of affluence than the capitalist-statist regimes, cannot compete with the capitalist ones or the mixed capitalist regimes. Thus, we may conclude that a socialist regime and a capitalist-statist regime meant less of economic affluence than a pure capitalist or mixed capitalist regime. The strong drive towards more of markets at the end of the 1980s and early 1990s appear understandable given these performance data.

Economic growth

The gap between the set of socialist politico-economic systems and two of the capitalist types of systems increased in terms of GDP per capita since 1960. Can we conclude that the rate of economic growth was persistently higher among these two types of capitalist regimes than in the set of socialist regimes? No, there is too much variation between the countries within all three sets to permit any such general conclusion that capitalism always performed better than socialism with regard to yearly economic growth rates. Table 7.3 has the data for 1973–85.

Table 7.3 Economic growth among regime sets 1973–85

Economic system	GDP/capita growth 1973–85	N
Capitalist	1.2	28
Mixed capitalist	1.7	12
Capitalist-statist	0.5	20
Socialist	1.3	13
Mean/total	1.1	73
Eta square	0.031	
Sig.	0.541	

Source: *World Bank Atlas*, 1987 (Washington, DC, World Bank)

Any simple generalization about politico-economic systems fails to do justice to the real-world differences in average growth rates. There are examples of very high average growth rates among capitalist, capitalist-statist and socialist regimes just as there exist cases of very negative growth rates in the same categories of politico-economic regimes. We cannot say that, generally speaking, capitalism all the time and everywhere did better than socialism in terms of economic growth. Some pure capitalist and capitalist-statist regimes did very badly for some time periods.

Inflation

It is possible to broaden the evaluation of various politico-economic regimes by bringing in additional economic evaluation criteria. Here we will look at inflation. The yearly rate of inflation has come to be regarded as a more and more important sign of stability in economic systems as the disruptive consequences of hyperinflation are feared. Are there any systematic differences tied to the various types of politico-economic regimes in terms of average level of inflation in the early 1980s? Table 7.4 indicates how price stability varied in politico-economic regimes.

The overall finding is that it is not possible to trace a special pattern of inflation among the four categories or groups of politico-economic regimes,

Table 7.4 Average rate of inflation 1970–80

Economic system	Inflation rate 1970–80	N
Capitalist	17.6	28
Mixed capitalist	10.2	12
Capitalist-statist	24.8	22
Socialist	12.6	12
Mean/total	17.7	74
Eta square	0.046	
Sig.	0.342	

Source: World Bank (1987)

although the set of mixed capitalist systems is different. Hyperinflation has been a problem in mainly capitalist-statist regimes, but also pure capitalist and socialist regimes have experienced high levels of inflation. Let us turn to other evaluation criteria than simply economic developmental ones.

Human rights

Since there is no standard measure of democracy we rely on indices that attempt to rank countries on the basis of various legal and political rights considerations. There are here striking differences between the four politico-economic regimes, as the country variation around 1980 with regard to democracy is more tied to the between-group variation than what was true of the economic evaluation criteria. The eta-squared score is much higher than was noticed in the analysis of economic evaluation criteria (Table 7.5).

In the mid-1980s democratic political rights occurred mainly among the mixed capitalist regime type. Here we have a number of countries that scored very high on the Humana democracy index. The mean value for the capitalist or capitalist-statist is consistently lower, although these regime categories include countries that score high on the index: New Zealand, Australia, Japan among the capitalist regimes and India in the category of capitalist-statist regimes. The democracy score among the three types of capitalistic regimes is higher than that of the socialist type of regime, but there exist some highly undemocratic regimes also in the set of capitalist and capitalist-statist regimes.

The major finding is that this political evaluation criterion does discriminate between the various politico-economic regimes. The capitalist-statist and the socialist regime types displayed much lower values than the mixed capitalist. It is true that the capitalist regime kind scored higher than the socialist regime type on this measure, but this type also includes countries with low democracy scores, for example, Chile, Chad and Nigeria, not to speak of the Baby Tigers in South East Asia.

Table 7.5   Human rights among regime sets 1980

Economic system	Human rights scores	N
Capitalist	72.7	16
Mixed capitalist	92.2	12
Capitalist-statist	62.6	18
Socialist	44.5	15
Mean/total	66.6	61
Eta square	0.526	
Sig.	0.000	

Note: The Humana index ranges from 0 to 100 and is based mainly on the occurrence of human rights, including political rights (Humana, 1983)

Table 7.6 Income inequality 1970s

Economic system	Gini index 1970s	N
Capitalist	39.9	18
Mixed capitalist	32.3	11
Capitalist-statist	44.0	15
Socialist	32.3	87
Mean/total	38.3	52
Eta square	0.281	
Sig.	0.001	

Note: The estimates of the Gini index stems from Deininger and Squire (1997)

Income inequality

There is a large number of potentially relevant outcome measures that may be employed for the evaluation of politico-economic regimes. Perhaps the extent of income inequality is one of the most sensitive evaluation criteria, because it has figured so prominently in the ideologies tied to the distinction between capitalism and socialism. Is it true, may we ask, that various politico-economic regimes promote income equality differently? Table 7.6 provides some clues to the problem of how and if politico-economic systems are characterized by different structures of income distribution. The data available for socialist regimes is meagre.

The eta-squared statistic being smaller than 0.5 indicates that the variation within the four fundamental categories is larger than the variation between these four sets of systems. However, there is one major finding: it is not the case that a socialist regime resulted in the highest level of income equality, as the mixed capitalist regime type displayed lower scores on all the statistics employed here. In the mixed capitalist systems a combination of economic affluence and political ambitions at redistributing income has resulted in much lower levels of income inequality than in other types of politico-economic regimes. Not very surprisingly, income inequality tended to be sharp in most capitalist-statist and some pure capitalist countries.

Summing up

The performance of politico-economic regimes may be measured by a comparative analysis based on economic, social and political evaluation criteria. The major institutional reforms initiated around 1990 may be seen as a search for a more effective politico-economic regime. What lessons could be learned from the operation of four different politico-economic regimes during the post-Second World War period up to the demise of the socialist systems? A first step towards a refined assessment of the politico-economic performance of various countries is to employ categories like capitalist, mixed capitalist, capitalist-statist and socialist regimes on the basis of how the state recognizes the institutions of private property and of how much space there is for voluntary exchange in the allocation of resources.

The mixed capitalist tends to perform better on all evaluation criteria than the other regime types. The socialist regime type as well as the capitalist-statist regime type tend to lag behind the other two types of capitalist regimes on the evaluation criteria employed here, in particular the average level of affluence measured by the GDP/capita indicator. Politico-economic systems where markets are given a prominent role tend to do better than politico-economic systems where the state is heavily involved in directing the economy.

The failure of the socialist regime type to keep pace with the development rate among the two capitalist types of regimes is apparent already by 1970. One brand of a capitalist regime – capitalist-statist regimes – performs as badly as the socialist kind of regime. Yet, there are straightforward examples of failures even among the decentralized capitalist regimes. What is the situation like in the early 1990s with substantial pressures being mounted for spreading the institutions of the market economy?

Politico-economic evaluation post-1989

The extensive institutional changes started in 1989 make it even more difficult to apply the politico-economic regime concepts. The shift from one regime to another may be a transparent move with a clear-cut transformation from one type to another. Or countries attempting to change their economic institutions may partly fail, meaning that the country ends up having some mixture of institutions from the old and new regimes. Let us go around the world to see how things stand at the moment, employing two new sources offering classifications of politico-economic regimes in the 1990s. Following *Economic Freedom of the World 1975–1995* (Gwartney *et al.*, 1996) as well as 'The world survey of economic freedom' (Messick, 1996), we arrive at Table 7.7.

According to the criteria offered by J. Gwartney, R. Lawson and W. Block (1996) and Messick (1996), most of the countries of the world must be classified as having either a capitalist-statist regime or a post-communist regime. Messick speaks of countries as Free, Partly Free, Mostly Not Free and Not Free – all in all, some 80 countries are ranked from 16 to 0. In *Economic Freedom of the World 1975–1995* (Gwartney *et al.*) there is first an area rating for four sectors of the economy and second a summary index ranging from 8 to 0, classifying some 100 countries. There are some discrepancies between the two country rankings, as their correlation is r = 62). Using these two sources we arrive at the following is in which we indicate the economic regime of the country, ze population-wise in millions of inhabitants around 1995: ominant orientation of the countries on the American continent

Table 7.7 Classification of politico-economic regimes after 1989

Capitalist	Mixed capitalist	Capitalist-statist	Post-communist
Argentina	Austria	Bangladesh	Afghanistan
Australia	Belgium	Bhutan	Albania
Bolivia	Denmark	Botswana	Algeria
Canada	Finland	Brazil	Angola
Chile	France	Burma-Myanmar	Armenia
Colombia	Germany	Burundi	Azerbaijan
Costa Rica	Greece	Cameroon	Belarus
Czech Republic	Iceland	Central African Republic	Benin
Estonia	Ireland	Chad	Bosnia and Herzegovina
Ghana	Israel	Congo, Brazzaville	Bulgaria
Guatemala	Italy	Congo-Kinshasa	Burkina Faso
Hong Kong	Luxembourg	Cote d'Ivoire	Cambodia
Jamaica	Netherlands	Dominican Republic	China
Japan	Norway	Ecuador	Croatia
South Korea	Portugal	Egypt	Cuba
Malaysia	Spain	El Salvador	Ethiopia
Mauritius	Sweden	Gabon	Georgia
New Zealand	Switzerland	Guinea	Hungary
Panama		Haiti	Kazakhstan
Poland		Honduras	North Korea
Singapore		India	Kyrgyz Republic
South Africa		Indonesia	Laos
Taiwan		Iran	Latvia
Thailand		Iraq	Libya
Trinidad and Tobago		Jordan	Lithuania
UK		Kenya	Macedonia
USA		Kuwait	Moldova
Uruguay		Lebanon	Mongolia
		Lesotho	Mozambique
		Liberia	Nicaragua
		Madagascar	Romania
		Malawi	Russia
		Mali	Slovak Republic
		Mauritania	Slovenia
		Mexico	Tajikistan
		Morocco	Tanzania
		Namibia	Turkmenistan
		Nepal	Ukraine
		Niger	Uzbekistan
		Nigeria	Vietnam
		Oman	Yugoslavia
		Pakistan	
		Papua New Guinea	
		Paraguay	
		Peru	
		Philippines	
		Rwanda	
		Saudi Arabia	
		Senegal	
		Sierra Leone	
		Somalia	
		Sri Lanka	
		Sudan	
		Syria	
		Togo	
		Tunisia	
		Turkey	
		Uganda	
		United Arab Emirates	
		Venezuela	
		Yemen, Republic	
		Zambia	
		Zimbabwe	

Note: The classification is based upon Gwartney *et al.*, (1996) and Messick (1996) which are not always in agreement as to how a country is to be classified towards some type of capitalist politico-economic regime is obvious in the 1990s, but are there regimes today other than pure capitalism here? It is true that the only examples of a socialist politico-economic regime – Cuba (11 million) today and possibly still Nicaragua (4.2) – are small states when compared with the giant capitalist nations in this hemisphere. As one may argue that there is hardly real welfare state or a mixed capitalist regime in America, the basic division among the countries on the American continent is that between two types of capitalist regimes, decentralized capitalist and capitalist-statist regimes. Besides Canada (28.5), the USA (264) belongs to the former category where also two Latin American countries could be placed in the 1990s: Argentina (34) and Chile (14). Also Costa Rica (3.4) and Panama (2.7) may be classified as market economies as well as perhaps Guatemala (11). The remaining countries in Central America belong to the capitalist-statist set, although a few have moved towards the market economy: El Salvador (5.9), Dominican Republic (8), Honduras (5.5) with the exception of Trinidad/Tobago (1.2). Despite the institutional reforms in the early 1990s most Latin American countries should still be classified as capitalist-statist, considering the importance of so-called para-statals in their economies. Here, we have two of the giant countries in Latin America: Mexico (94) and Brazil (161). Into the same type of politico-economic systems enters a number of countries with fairly large populations: Venezuela (21), Peru (24), Ecuador (11), Bolivia (8), Paraguay (5.4) and Uruguay (3.2), some of which have moved towards the market economy in the early 1990s, notably Bolivia, Uruguay and Colombia.

On the African continent one used to find a complex pattern of a blend of capitalist-statist and socialist regimes, often existing side by side. Large-scale institutional changes have been attempted in the late 1980s and early 1990s, but it is difficult to assess how much has been accomplished in reality. Pressure to install the institutions of the market economy has come not only from the demise of the socialist economy but also from the IMF-World Bank side structural-adjustment policies, criticizing the capitalist-statist economy. When the socialist economy is to be dismantled, then a country most often ends up in the capitalist-statist regime.

In the north there is Morocco (29) which is a capitalist state coexisting with a number of more or less socialist-oriented regimes in Algeria (28.5), Libya (5.2), Egypt (62.4), Sudan (30) and Ethiopia (56). How these former socialist regimes are to be described today is not clear, as perhaps Libya has the only remaining socialist regime. Algeria moved towards more of capitalism during the 1980s as did Sudan. Tunisia (9) is difficult to place, Gastil suggesting that it belonged to the mixed capitalist type, which is hardly correct, as it is not a welfare state. Probably all these countries practise a capitalist-statist regime as there is much government intervention in the economy.

In West Africa the prevailing regime types is capitalism-statism, reflecting how dominant the *para-statals* tend to be. Here we have the following countries: Senegal (9), Sierra Leone (4.7), Ivory Coast (15), Niger (9.3), Chad (5.6), Togo (4.4), Nigeria (101), and Cameroon (13.5). Among these capitalist-oriented regimes there used to exist a few socialist-oriented regimes: Guinea (6.5), Benin (5.5), Mali (9.4) and Burkina Faso (10.4), but they have now changed their economic system. Probably Ghana (17.8) is the only country that could qualify as a market regime today.

Moving to the Central and Southern parts on the African continent, the question is now what has happened to the several socialist regimes, some of which used to adhere to the notion of an African version of socialism. On the socialist side we had the following regimes: Congo (2.5), Tanzania (29), Angola (10), Zambia (9.5), Zimbabwe (11), Mozambique (18) and Madagascar (14). These countries have moved towards more of a market economy, but the state involvement in the economy remains large by means of a few dominating para-statals, which need not be privatized when socialism is given up. The countries that have a politico-economic regime oriented towards a type of capitalism-statism involve: Central African Republic (3.2), giant Zaire (44), Malawi (9.8), Kenya (29) and Uganda (19.6). South Africa (45) has an advanced capitalist economy, emerging from the capitalist-statist regime that was practised under the Apartheid era. Like Botswana (1.4), it may qualify as a market economy, which is also true of the island of Mauritius. One must remember that several of the Central and Southern African counties have experienced civil war, destroying the opportunities for economic growth.

The populous nations on the Asian continent including Australia and New Zealand belong either to the set of capitalist or capitalist-statist regimes with the exception of a few remaining socialist regimes. In Asia Minor there is a number of capitalist-statist countries: Jordan (4.1), Saudi Arabia (18.8), United Arab Emirates (3), Oman (2.1), Yemen (14.7), Kuwait (1.8) and Iran (65). The classification of these countries is not unproblematic as their persistent war involvement has had an impact on these societies, increasing state involvement in the economy. What remains of the socialist type in the following countries – Syria (15.5) and Iraq (20.6) – is not clear. How Israel (5.1) is to be described is an open question: mixed capitalist, capitalist-statist or market economy? In the Gulf States the state is heavily involved in the oil sector.

In East Asia we find the giant countries of the world, and they are either socialist, capitalist or capitalist-statist. Thus, there is huge India (937) which used to be identified as capitalist-statist but it has changed towards decentralized capitalism in the early 1990s. Pakistan (132), Sri Lanka (18.3) and Bangladesh (128) remain capitalist-statist whereas Burma or Myanmar (45) is still a socialist regime. Examples of a capitalist politico-economic regime are to be found in Thailand (60.3), Malaysia (19.7), South Korea (45.6), Taiwan (21.5), Japan (126), Australia (18.3) and New Zealand (3.4), the latter two countries moving towards the set of market economies and away from the welfare state regime.

Again, how to separate a capitalist regime from a capitalist-statist regime in this part of the world is not always easy. Thus, it has been argued that capitalist Singapore (2.9) belongs to the mixed capitalist type, which is very debatable. Populous Indonesia (204) should be designated capitalist-statist, as should the Philippines (73). Whether the Baby Tigers really are examples of a decentralized market economy has been contested, with the exception of Hong Kong, although it is not a state (Krugman, 1994). Into the set of socialist politico-economic regimes enter Mainland China (1200), North Korea (24), Mongolia (2.5), Vietnam (74.4), Cambodia (10.6) and Laos (4.8). But in some of these countries extensive market reforms have been implemented which question the applicability of the socialist regime type.

It remains to look at politico-economic performance in the old world, here covering both Western and Eastern Europe including Russia and Turkey. On the European continent in this wide sense all the various politico-economic regime types used to be present. But now only bits and pieces remain of the command economy in the former communist countries. Socialism in the form of communism is of little relevance in Europe, but what kind of capitalism will replace socialism? It is far from easy to draw a sharp dividing line between the various kinds of capitalist regimes in Europe in the 1990s.

To the set of mixed capitalist systems should be counted all countries with a strong welfare state combined with extensive market allocation. The set of mixed capitalist regimes includes several small and a few large countries: Norway (4.3), Finland (5.1), Sweden (8.8), Denmark (5.2), Iceland (0.3), Netherlands (15.5), Belgium (10.1), the UK (58.3), Ireland (3.5), the Federal Republic of Germany (81.4), Austria (8) and France (58.1). Perhaps one may argue that Italy (58.3) could be placed among the capitalist-statist regimes, but this applies only if the time period studied is the 1950s or 1960s. Equally debatable is the classification of Spain (39.4) and Portugal (10.6) which are here placed among the set of mixed capitalist regimes as we refer to the early 1990s. Into the category of mixed capitalist regimes we enter only Luxembourg (0.4 million), Switzerland (7.1) and Greece (10.6). Turkey is a border case (63.4), as one could argue that Turkey could be placed among the capitalist-statist regimes.

Up until 1989 the socialist regime type covered the entire Eastern Europe including the USSR. Thus, there existed a number of fairly populous socialist countries and one giant such system. The command economies belong now to history, as all countries have moved away from this economic regime. Some have come close to the market regime whereas others seem stuck in a capitalist-statist type of regime. Here we have: Poland (38.8), the Czech Republic (10.4), Slovakia (5.4), Hungary (10.3), Romania (23.2), Bulgaria (8.8), Yugoslavia (11.1), Slovenia (2.1), Croatia (4.7), Albania (3.4) and Russia (150). Today the Czech Republic and Estonia must be placed in the capitalist set. But things are far less clear in relation to the other East European countries. Russia still operates a quasi-socialist economy, which is also true of the Ukraine (52) and the so-called Khanates: Uzbekistan (23), Kazakhstan (17.4) and Tajikistan (6.2). Poland and Slovenia has moved towards pure capitalism but a capitalism-statist regime seems to replace socialism in other parts of Eastern Europe, which is also true of the Baltic states except Estonia.

Evaluation of politico-economic regimes in the 1990s

In the 1990s the relevance of the traditional distinction between capitalism versus socialism was even less than before the system changes initiated in 1989. In order to understand the variation in politico-economic regimes we need to distinguish between three types of capitalist regimes, leaving the post-communist systems as a residual where it is an open question in relation to several of them how they will transform themselves, i.e. which type of capitalist regime they will end up with.

As things now stand, the politico-economic regime with the best performance record is the mixed capitalist regime – the same finding as above. The average scores for the welfare states are very high on all evaluation dimensions except economic growth. Capitalist regimes do better on economic growth than the mixed economies, but their records on inflation, democracy and inequality are worse than the numbers for the welfare states. The economic regimes where the state is much more involved – the state-capitalist and the post-communist countries – do much worse on all evaluation criteria (Table 7.8).

One clearly observes the crisis for the capitalist-statist systems and post-communist countries in the data in Table 7.8. The prominent place afforded the institutions of the market economy is understandable when one sees the huge differences in performance records between the two types of capitalist regimes that honour the market and the two types of politico-economic regimes in which the state dominates over the market.

However, the eta-squared scores in Table 7.8 indicates that this is not the entire story, because there is more variation within the categories than

Table 7.8 Regime performance around 1990

Economic system	Affluence	N	Growth	N	Inflation	N	Human rights	N	Inequality	N
Capitalist	11257	25	2.1	27	30.4	27	77.0	25	39.9	18
Mixed capitalist	18650	18	1.8	18	6.2	18	93.4	16	31.2	8
Capitalist-statist	3158	48	−0.09	57	43.4	56	52.8	45	45.0	25
Post-communist	2930	24	−4.0	29	11.9	30	50.3	18	32.2	12
Average/total	7296	115	−0.2	131	51.3	131	64.5	104	39.3	63
Eta square	0.627		0.308		0.056		0.467		0.305	
Sig.	0.000		0.000		0.060		0.000		0.000	

Sources: Affluence 1994: World Bank (1996); Growth 1985–94: World Bank (1996); Inflation 1985–94: World Bank (1996); Human rights 1991: Humana (1992); Income inequality or Gini: Deininger and Squire (1997)

Table 7.9   Economic freedom in macro regions

Region	Economic freedom indices 1990–2001							
	Index 1990	*N*	*Index 1995*	*N*	*Index 1997*	*N*	*Index 2001*	*N*
Occidental	5.9	22	14.7	21	8.2	23	4.1	23
CEE and CIS	2.4	5	8.6	16	5.8	13	3.0	25
Central and Latin America	4.8	21	9.7	13	7.3	22	3.3	20
Sub-Saharan Africa	3.6	28	8.1	9	5.2	29	3.0	30
Arab World	3.7	8	5.7	7	6.1	11	2.9	15
South Asia	3.9	5	5.3	4	5.1	6	2.8	7
South East Asia	6.8	9	8.1	12	7.7	11	3.3	16
Average/total	4.6	98	9.8	82	6.6	115	3.3	136

Sources: Gwartney *et al.*, 1996 (Index 1990); Messick, 1996 (Index 1995); Gwartney and Lawson, 2000 (Index 1997); and O'Driscoll *et al.*, 2000 (Index 2001)

among the categories, with the exception of affluence and possibly democracy. There are capitalist-statist countries with a much better performance record than the average numbers of that category. Generally, the CV scores for each evaluation dimension indicate immense variation within the four categories.

One may also look at the country ratings suggested by the Fraser Institute (Gwartney *et al.*, 1996, Gwartney and Lawson, 2000), by the Freedom House (Messick, 1996) and by the Heritage Foundation (O'Driscoll *et al.*, 2000). Let us first look at how these scores vary according to macro regions of the world (Table 7.9).

Economic freedom is according to these rankings high in the occidental world and in South East Asia. Does the degree of economic freedom matter for outcomes? Economic freedom is consistently correlated with positive outcomes such as high affluence, growth, democracy and low inflation. Table 7.10 shows in reduced form evidence for the theory that economic freedom matters positively for outcomes.

The reduced form evidence in Table 7.10 strongly confirms that free economic institutions increase the probability of democracy, economic growth and income equality.

Conclusion

A classical question in political economy is the performance of different kinds of politico-economic regimes. The problem used to be framed as the contest between capitalism and socialism, but it was readily realized that this dichotomy was too blunt a tool for classifying the politico-economic regimes of the world. If two categories are not enough, then how many?

One may employ alternative theories of the role of government in economic development in order to derive a classification of four types of

Table 7.10 Economic freedom and politico-economic outcomes: correlation analysis

Economic freedom	Coeffs	Politico-economic outcomes				
		Affluence	Growth	Inflation	Human rights	Inequality
Index 1990	r	0.67	0.48	−0.32	0.39	−0.12
	Sig.	0.000	0.000	0.001	0.000	0.205
	N	90	97	96	85	53
Index 1995	r	0.73	0.25	−0.07	0.87	−0.08
	Sig.	0.000	0.017	0.274	0.000	0.321
	N	69	75	76	88	41
Index 1997	r	0.73	0.47	−0.001	0.57	−0.205
	Sig.	0.000	0.000	0.462	0.000	0.063
	N	101	110	108	91	57
Index 2001	r	0.65	0.25	−0.11	0.672	−0.102
	Sig.	0.000	0.003	0.110	0.000	0.218
	N	108	121	122	96	60

Sources: See Tables 7.8 and 7.9

politico-economic regimes: (i) decentralized capitalism (Adam Smith); (ii) state-capitalism (Friedrich List); (iii) command economy (Karl Marx); and (iv) mixed economy or the welfare state (Adolf Wagner, John Maynard Keynes). It is not a straightforward task to apply the system categories derived from these alternative theories about the role of the state in economic development to the real world, especially when the world changes rapidly as after 1989.

The basic finding in the two evaluations made above based upon different classifications of countries according to these four ideal types is that the mixed economy does well on all evaluation criteria with the possible exception of economic growth. Decentralized capitalism seems to be more dynamic than the welfare states, but it does not always go together with high scores on democracy, low inflation and income equality. Capitalist-statist systems as well as post-communist countries face tremendous difficulties in their overall performance records, although there were exceptions such as the Japan and the South East Asian Tigers practising economic nationalism at least in the 1950s, 1960s, 1970s and 1980s. Economic freedom matters positively for both economic and political outcomes. When the economic regime is described by a scale measuring the degree of economic freedom according to a composite index, then the evidence suggests again that the economic regime matters for outcomes.

CHAPTER 8

Reneging and its Implications

Introduction

It is a simple fact of human societies that the behaviour of people is heavily orientated in terms of rules of interaction. Why is this so? According to one theory, suggested by Hayek, individual actors identify the norms they wish to live in accordance with by means of spontaneous interaction. Thus, the rules of the human game such as, for instance, the market constitute *spontaneous orders*. As we noted in chapter 1, the market is a heavily institutionalized phenomenon. If Hayek's theory about spontaneous order is correct, then the implication is that markets arrive at their rules step by step without state intervention. Markets can work with a minimum of politics, Hayek argued in his campaign against government, the public sector and the West European welfare state (Hayek, 1996). We will argue that this theory is seriously deficient on both theoretical and empirical grounds. Markets without politics are impossible and exchange without authority does not work.

Before we state the argument that politics is necessarily married with economics, or that economic life cannot flourish without the state, we will briefly make an overview of theories that arrive at the same conclusion as Hayek, although without his special assumptions about the limited cognitive capacity of human beings derived from the so-called Austrian school of economics (Hayek and Klein, 1992). One may argue that markets are superior to governments and that the role of governments should be as small as possible in the economy without committing oneself to any assumptions about man's or woman's limited cognitive abilities. One may claim that markets operate in an optimal manner, if left to themselves, using a rational choice model of human decision-making (Friedman, 1962; Stigler, 1986; Demsetz, 1991). Let us try this approach to markets and see where it will lead us when applied consistently to the classical problem in political economy: state or market.

Walrasian co-ordination

Human beings pursue interests based upon their preferences. The strategies they develop in order to reach their goals depend upon the ambition to further their interests, meaning that they choose in accordance with their preferences. In addition, they take the rules of the game into consideration as different institutions call for a variation in tactics. Now, the interests or preferences of men and women can be self-centred, group oriented or altruistic. Some interests individuals may accomplish on their own whereas other interests they share with a group of people. Altruistic preferences involve the wish to further interests of others. Below we will only discuss whether voluntary exchange in markets is the best mechanism for people to further their self-interests or collective interests.

The invisible hand of Adam Smith makes government – the visible hand – superfluous, as markets can handle all kinds of human interaction that result in the allocation of goods and services. Two questions arise in relation to this argument that the invisible hand is superior to the visible hand. First, what is the invisible hand? Second, does the argument relate to each and every type of human interaction, i.e. also in relation to collective action in groups with a large number of participants?

Markets co-ordinate by means of voluntary exchange, whereas governments co-ordinate by means of politics. The prevailing opinion today is that voluntary exchange is more efficient than state authority. What needs to be clarified in order to make voluntary exchange work is rights, especially property rights. The critical importance of rights to the functioning of markets appears when common pool resources are to be used. Could voluntary exchange but not markets handle common pool resources when property rights have not been introduced?

Co-ordination in a market comes from the interaction between buyers and sellers in various markets. In any economy there must exist some form of co-ordination between demand and supply, whatever the good or service involved. Adam Smith stated the case for *laissez-faire* or *laissez-aller*, meaning that government would not be responsible for economic co-ordination. Instead so-called market forces would accomplish this co-ordination in various kinds of markets, and it would be better the less government interfered in these markets. This is not the place to discuss the origins of this theory, whether it comes from the so-called physiocrats or whether Adam Smith truly invented it. What we wish to focus upon is what this hand could be that both co-ordinates but remains invisible.

The invisible hand must accomplish at least one thing, namely linking demand with supply. If government were not going to do it by means of an order, then prices would be the only other alternative. Competitive prices react in a predictable manner towards excess or too little demand and supply as well as to changes in demand and supply. Prices are competitive when they are not decided by anyone, market players or government. Prices are competitive when they only result from the unregulated interaction of demand and supply. Why?

A competitive price is the outcome of the free interaction between demand and supply. Thus, individuals may act solely on the basis of their self-interests, bidding up or down the price in accordance with their preferences to buy or sell. When the bears meet the bulls, then everyone walks away pleased with the result. Or?

The competitive price is a mechanism of interaction that allows for the co-ordination of human efforts. But it is certainly not institution-free. Individuals may gain more by bypassing this mechanism. Its existence depends upon the rules of the games. Thus, we are led back to the simple question: Who puts the games in place and who guards their implementation?

Suppose we have a standard Walrasian situation, described in Figure 8.1, where lots of people interact in order to buy and sell a simple private good with no economies of scale or externalities. The market outcome of the process of *tâtonnement* or auctioning is that the market supplies quantity Q at price P – Pareto-optimal outcomes. At the same time, this is the best outcome for both the buyers and the sellers. Since the sellers cannot co-ordinate their action, they would not be able to supply less and charge a higher price. Similarly the buyers could not force the sellers to lower their price and sell more at a loss (Bilas, 1971).

Figure 8.1 displays how both the industry and the firm reacts to a rise in demand. In the short term the price increases but in the long term output will increase, reducing price.

The rules of the competitive market force each individual to accept the price of Walras's auctioneer. Thus, their best strategy individually (Nash equilibrium) is also the Pareto-optimal allocation. But it is in the self-interest of sellers to co-ordinate to limit the offer and it is in the self-interest of buyers to force the seller to sell at loss-making prices. Only if the rules are

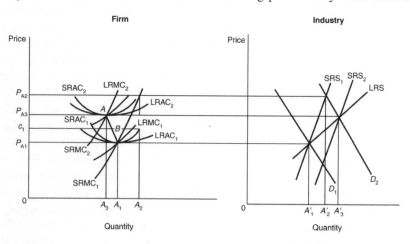

Figure 8.1   Competitive markets – firm and industry equilibria
Note: SRAC = short-term average cost; SRMC = short-term marginal cost; LRMC = long-term marginal cost; LRAC = long-term average cost; D = demand; SRS = short-term supply; LRS = long-term supply

absolutely firm and unambiguous will the invisible hand guide the self-interests towards the best outcome from the collective point of view.

We will argue that it is the state that guarantees the rules that lead to this result when combined with the self-interest seeking of buyers and sellers. These rules include contractual honesty as well as private property rights. If they are not in place, then the probability of reneging will rise dramatically. If players can do better by going into the crime economy, then they will do so. Several arguments suggest that the role of the state in making the market economy possible is not that large. It is suggested that the market institutions tend to emerge over time in their own fashion and that they can be implemented without governments. As long as people can exchange, all problems of human interaction can be handled. These arguments fail to extract the full implications of the problem of reneging in relation to rules.

Before stating what reneging entails for the exchange mechanism, we will show that players using the market mechanism may very well find their Nash equilibrium but they may at the same time fail to promote the Pareto-optimal outcome. Actually, when they pursue their self-interests within the voluntary exchange mechanism, they may promote the most disastrous consequences.

Markets co-ordinate well when their institutional foundations have been implemented. It is the state that does this, not the market itself. Reneging would destroy markets immediately if governments did not police reneging. Lots of what governments do is specifically reducing the probability of reneging as well as limiting its consequences when it occurs. Thus, in political economy it is not market *or* state but market *and* state.

Rent dissipation

If institutions are necessary for economic games, then how are institutions decided upon and introduced as well as maintained in social life? If self-interest – the Adam Smith explanation of the superiority of markets – is not enough, then where does the missing link – rules – come from? Adherents of economic decision theory would be inclined to answer: self-interest again.

Demsetz has argued along these lines when he stated that men and women search for the economic institutions that maximize their self-interest. One version of this argument targets so-called transaction costs, which are assumed to be minimized when individuals are allowed to decide upon which rules to abide by in economic life. Another version of the same argument explains the same phenomenon by referring to the ambition of each and everyone always to capture potential gains, even if it comes at the cost of institutional change (Demsetz, 1967; Libecap, 1993; Barzel, 1997).

The approach to derive not only market outcomes from the maximization of self-interest but also the market regime itself from the same basis proceeds from the observation that people sometimes can agree upon the rules by which they are going to live. Once accepted, such institutions become part of the established order or system of norms that people willingly accept without much argument. However, much more is involved in Demsetz's solution, as the argument is not only that people develop norms to stabilize interaction but that such norms tend to be efficiency-enhancing.

When people interact, then they look out for their best outcomes. If the rules do not promote this search, then people willingly change the institutions in order to put in place the rules that enhance efficiency the most. Thus, people not only look out for their best outcomes but they also search for the institutions that allow them to maximize output. As market rules enhance economic efficiency, the conclusion from this approach must clearly be that people invent and implement the institutions of the market.

Demsetz finds many forms of empirical evidence that support this claim. Resources will always be put to the best use, because people who benefit from the use of these resources will at the end of the day acquire them and put them into operation. If the rules hinder this search for rents, then the rules will be changed one way or the other. Thus, land will be cultivated in such a manner that output is maximized. Mineral resources will be found and owned in such a form that enhances their useful employment. Labour legislation will change, reflecting the efficient use of manpower, etc.

According to Demsetz, people will search for the institutions that maximize output, even when this involves changing the existing rules by means of the investment into costly efforts aimed at affecting government or the judiciary. Thus, when certain forms of private property rules hinder the exploitation of resources, then people will be prepared to pay for having these rules changed. Either people who can employ such resources better than others, meaning presenting them with a higher return, will take over such resources by buying them up, or they will lobby for institutional changes by means of legislation or judicial precedents.

This is a version of the basic argument in *Law and Economics* (Cooter and Ulen, 1999), namely that legal rules for the economic game will take economic efficiency into account to a large extent – the Calabresi argument concerning the evolution of common law (Calabresi, 1985). As long as the investments in institutional change pay off in a higher output in the future, players will be prepared to spend considerable money to change the rules of the game.

One could argue that the Demsetz theory about optimal institutions is merely a version of institutional teleology, meaning a hypothesis to the effect that rules search for economic efficiency. However, the underlying idea is that people like Schumpeterian entrepreneurs are always eager to search for profits, even when it includes searching for institutional changes. Be that as it may, the weakness of the Demsetz argument lies elsewhere, namely in the neglect of the role of the state in defining the economic institutions, in changing them and in implementing them.

The role of government is especially important when it comes to the access and utilization of minerals and resources like gas and oil. Governments may decide that the effective exploitation of such non-renewable resources requires government involvement in various forms. In one version, governments consider that such resources belong to the state and that they cannot be exploited without the state granting rights of exploitation. In another version, governments are to be involved in how such resources can be exploited, even though they are considered to be privately owned. Thus, the exploitation of such resources is often far from a market decision or a private choice. Nor are the rules concerning their exploitation decided merely on the basis of the profit maximization motive.

Governments decide upon economic institutions on the basis of several considerations, one of which is the ambition to maximize output or economic gain. Relevant interests pertain to the protection of national assets, the search for state revenues and stable development. Governments may even decide that the existing rules for the exploitation of such resources are not efficient, meaning that they will intervene in market forces. Natural resources enter into the extensive physical planning schemes created by the state. Although one cannot interpret their existence as evidence to the effect that governments can exploit these resources better than markets, physical or geographical planning indicates that deciding over natural resources is not left to the market, in terms of either their exploitation or the rules that guide their exploitation.

The dynamic theory of institutional evolution as the search for economic efficiency has been applied in the explanation of changes in property rights that did enhance output. However, it fails in relation to the phenomenon of resource depletion and the dissipation of rents. Voluntary exchange seems extremely weak as a mechanism for handling the tragedy of the commons, or the rapid depletion of resources without owners. But even if voluntary exchange may sometimes deliver a set of rules which protect non-renewable resources or resources which may be driven to extinction by over-utilization, it is still the case that voluntary exchange will dissipate rents whenever the number of players is large.

Markets may exist which do not result in the maximization of the gains of the players. Markets may exist where the players fail to find the institutions that enhance Pareto-optimal outcomes. Markets may exist which destroy themselves without voluntary exchange helping at all. When people seek to maximize their self-interests (Nash equilibrium), then they do always end up with a Pareto-optimal outcome.

In the Walrasian market individual rationality and collective rationality go hand in hand, as both are maximized. When there is rent dissipation, individual rationality pulls the players away from collective rationality. Figure 8.2 shows how a group of players – fishermen – may be led by self-interest to catch more than the amount of fish that maximizes the revenues of the group (Ramade, 1995; Tietenberg, 2000).

The Pareto-optimal outcome is E^e where the marginal revenue equals the

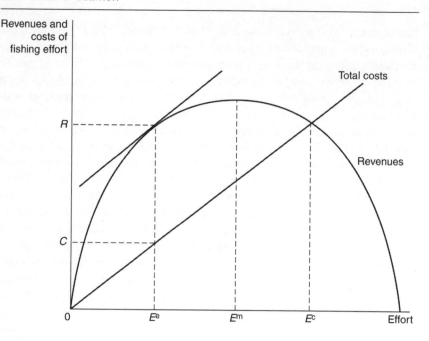

Figure 8.2 Dissipation of rents

marginal cost of catching another fish. But since the price paid for another fish – average revenue – is higher than marginal cost, all fishermen are led to catch a higher quantity. In the end they will catch the quantity E^c if no restrictions on catch are forthcoming. At the catch E^c, there are no profits, as the entire economic rent has become dissipated after catching more than E^e.

This is collective foolishness driven by individual rationality. Each fisherman has an incentive to catch as much as possible as long as his/her costs are covered, even if a higher catch lowers the price for all the fishermen. Since each fisherman cannot control what the other fishermen catch, he gains nothing from abstaining from catching as long as he can sell what he brings up from the sea. The voluntary exchange approach to this collective action problem is to make agreements among the players about quotas that would restrict fishing to the catch E^e. However, these agreements are vulnerable to reneging.

Actually, the collective action problems could be much worse than what emerges from Figure 8.2. In the analysis of the tendency towards over-fishing there is the additional problem of arriving at a catch that is sustainable in the long run. Suppose that the catch E^e is the sustainable catch but that the catch E^c involves a non-sustainable catch with the entailment that the fishing stocks will be reduced to zero in the long run. When the catch is at E^c in Figure 8.2, then this solution is foolish not only for the community of fishermen but also for the consumers as a group.

Thus, the dissipation of rents creates an extremely grave situation when it occurs with extinguishable resources. Excess depletion then becomes irreversible, resulting in the extinction of the resource in question.

The total benefits within fishery in Figure 8.2 are simply price, assumed constant, times catch, which gives revenue. Hence marginal revenue and average revenue may be identified, where AR = price or demand. The downward sloping marginal revenue curve is not the result of market power (which it is in monopolies, but not here). The marginal revenue is the derivative of revenue with respect to effort.

For the fishing community, the Pareto-optimal outcome is MR = MC, i.e. E^e. However, the Nash equilibrium is at AR = MC, i.e. at E^c, as long as there is open access. When price is constant, it implies a horizontal demand curve. Producer surplus would be zero. What happens is that consumer surplus gets shifted to current generations from future ones, as the stock is consumed now rather than conserved. That means that in the price-changing model consumer surplus is increased for current generations due to the lower prices promoted by drawing down the stock.

When there is a scarce resource that has a supply that cannot be expanded, this will give rise to scarcity rent. Unlike the temporary profit that is associated with a normal produced good, this rent cannot be bid away by competition since the supply is fixed. This rent is efficient and serves a social purpose signalling scarcity. In the fishery rents are dissipated by excessive entry, which is inefficient. One would be better off charging for a fishing licence.

Monopoly rent, on the other hand, is created by an artificial or contrived scarcity. Supply could be expanded, but it is not because the firm restricts supply to raise prices artificially. Hence when that scarcity is eliminated, society benefits. In summary, in the first case society loses by dissipation; in the second case, society gains from dissipation.

With respect to monopoly rents, rents create an incentive to invest in inefficient ways to acquire those rents, so-called 'rent-seeking behaviour'. Who captures the rent is, almost by definition, irrelevant to economic efficiency. But if the rent can be captured, or transferred, then this will create incentives to try to acquire it. But this investment in trying to acquire a pure rent is then inefficient. There are those that argue that the deadweight loss underestimates the true efficiency loss of the monopoly since the presence of total monopoly profits induces people to try to capture them, thereby 'wasting' resources.

Although the problem posed in Figure 8.2 is well known today where over fishing with new technology that allows a much higher catch at a lower cost than previously has reduced various fishing stocks to extremely low levels, there is no solution to the situation. Again, the key problem is reneging. Since fishing in the high seas occurs at no man's land, even state intervention does not help. Agreements between states are extremely vulnerable to reneging, as there is no independent authority to check whether agreements are implemented or not, or to police a party that reneges.

We may conclude that people do not all the time easily arrive at institutions that maximize the the gain from economic activity, in either the short or the long run. If people act upon their self-interests, then markets may lead to irrational outcomes, such as rent dissipation and resource depletion. Perhaps it is one of the roles of the state to counteract such perverse market tendencies?

What we are talking about is collective action problems and free riding. Despite the problems that surface when a group of people are to set up rules that bring individual rationality in line with collective rationality, it has been suggested that groups can overcome collective action problems through voluntary co-operation using the exchange mechanism. Let us proceed to analyse this argument that groups can allocate collective goods by means of market-like mechanisms such as exchange.

Free riding

The argument that groups may protect their common resources by means of voluntary agreements about how to use these resources would entail that state action is not necessary in order to protect common pool resources. Groups could themselves make arrangements for a sustainable use of such resources and they may decide to allocate the use of these resources to individuals or smaller groups in accordance with a system of quotas. Two questions come to one's mind: (1) When will such voluntary schemes work? (2) Are they better than state-operated schemes that do the same thing, namely protect the common pool resources?

Protecting a common resource is a public good for the group in question. Groups can allocate a public good by means of collective action, if it can overcome the typical collective action problems. Protecting a common pool resource is only one form of public good. The general theory of collective action is stated in the theory of clubs. It looks upon a group of people as having a common interest in providing something that benefits all. And the basic problem is how people in that group can co-ordinate to pay for the allocation of the collective good. There are two approaches in the literature, one based upon co-operative game theory and the other based upon non-co-operative game theory.

Optimal clubs

It is in the interest of a group to provide a common or collective good when the average benefits to its members are larger than the average costs to its members. One can determine the optimal size of a group by such an argument about average benefits and average costs. Figure 8.3 shows the optimal size of a group, given the average benefits B and average costs C to the group.

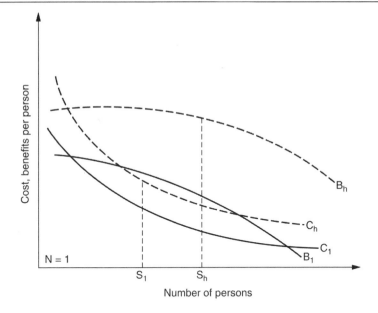

Figure 8.3 Optimal size of a group

The optimal size of a group providing a public good is at the point N along the membership continuum where the difference between average benefits and average costs is maximized.

It is in the interest of the group to take on more members when B > C and also to see that people leave when C > B. The average benefits B depend upon the size N of the group, which is also true of the costs C. As more people join the group, N getting larger, the benefits taper off, whereas the costs decline when more people share the total costs.

Using the same approach one may also derive the optimum size of the common good allocated to the group. Figure 8.4 shows how the average benefits B and average costs C develop as a function of the increase in the collective good provided to the group.

The average cost C of a collective good goes up the more of it is allocated, whereas the average benefits B display a curvature. The optimum quantity Q is determined by the maximum difference between B and C.

When a group has come to understand these two solutions, N and Q corresponding to Figures 8.3 and 8.4, then the group can decide to implement these Pareto-optimal solutions. But why do people create clubs? This theory about clubs and an optimal allocation of a collective good lacks an incentive mechanism that will lead people to become members of clubs. In non-co-operative game theory no assumption to the effect that Pareto-optimal allocations are always forthcoming is made.

Assume, thus, that free riding is possible, i.e. that an individual can get the benefits B without having to take the costs C. Since in a large group N an

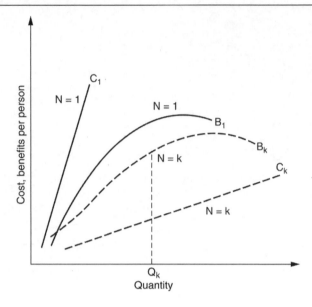

Figure 8.4   Optimal size of the good for a group

individual N-1 is always better off free riding, he or she will free ride since this is the individually rational strategy. In a large group one individual matters little, so the supply of the public good is not affected by one person free riding. However, it follows that free riding is also the Nash equilibrium for the individual N-1-1, etc. The group collapses, although this is not in the best interest of the group as a whole.

Free riding can take place when a group cannot exclude non-members. Sometimes excludability is not a major problem, as groups develop mechanisms for identifying and implementing membership. However, when excludability is impossible or too costly for the group to accomplish by various devices, then free riding will occur. Free riding could be seen as a form of reneging, because it can be interpreted as the breaking of an implicit contract or a silent contract. However, the standard meaning of free riding is not the violation of a contract as with theft. Free riding occurs when a person enjoys something without paying for it although he or she is not breaking the law.

The problem of voluntary exchange provisions of common pool resources is that of free riding. When a group establishes a scheme for the utilization of a common pool resource in accordance with the requirements of Pareto optimality, then insiders or outsiders can free ride on the scheme and benefit without participating in the scheme. If the group can exclude all free riding by outsiders and police all free riding by insiders, then optimal groups will be forthcoming through the membership mechanism. When free riding is possible, then the situation is best modelled by means of non-co-operative game theory.

Table 8.1 Collective action

	Co-operation	*Defection*
Co-operation	5, 5	−4, 6
Defection	6, −4	−3, −3

Non-co-operative game theory

If one relaxes the assumption that people keep their agreement or if one assumes that they can state their benefits wrongly, then the voluntary exchange mechanism will not lead to the establishment of clubs that allocate an optimum amount of a public good. Instead there will be massive collective action problems. Participating in collective action becomes a prisoner's dilemma game – see Table 8.1.

Defection may take many forms. Whether it is simply refusing to pay a membership fee, or even never accepting to pay anything, it is still the case that defection is the best strategy for an individual – his/her Nash equilibrium.

All forms of collective action where free riding is possible involve a contradiction between the Nash equilibrium and the Pareto-optimal solution. Olson applied this problem to the formation of interest groups in society, arriving at the conclusion that they could only form if a few persons were willing to take on the supply of the entire public good. According to the logic of a non-co-operative game only a suboptimal amount will be forthcoming because this is in the interest of one key person. The others will simply free ride upon this person. This solution is far from optimal, as all would have benefited from the supply of the amount E of the collective good. The basic equation governing collective action and free riding for any individual i is:

(1) $MU_i > MC$, for the entire collective good.

Thus, when (1) holds for one individual, then all the others free ride. And when it does not hold for any individual, then no collective action occurs.

Starting from non-co-operative game theory, the only way to stop free riding is to put up a fence somehow. When some form of a fence is in place, then free riding stops automatically, as only people who pay get past the fence. Such a fence may take may forms: (i) memberships fees; (ii) joint effort; (iii) selective incentives, etc (Olson, 1965).

Markets handle free riding by prices. However, when prices cannot be charged or when prices are not respected, then the state is the only mechanism against free riding. Since states have limited jurisdiction, there is no effective mechanism against free riding when it occurs on *Terra Nullius*. Intergovernmental organizations or supra-governmental organizations can be employed against free riding but they are far less effective than nation-states. In reality, states may free ride in relation to international regimes, as when they accept the killing of endangered species or at least do not intervene against this. States handle free riding by means of its unique authority – the Hobbesian position. Before we discuss this approach to free riding which in effect changes the game in Figure 8.1, we will bring up another approach, namely co-operative game theory.

Co-operative game theory

The mechanism used in co-operative game theory is the voluntary agreement between the interacting players. Thus, group decisions can be based upon binding agreements between group members. The key assumption here is that people wish to co-operate and that they implement the terms of agreements automatically. Defection does not occur because it is assumed away. What are the implications for collective action?

The optimal club is now forthcoming on the basis of agreements among the group members linking their participation with their individual willingness to pay. The basic logic in a co-operative approach is contained in the following equations:

$$(1) \quad \sum_{i=1,2...}^{n} MU_i = MC \text{ (collective rationality)}$$

(2) $MU_i > MC_i$ (individual rationality).

The co-operative solution to allocating a collective good allows for groups to create and maintain optimal clubs by the voluntary mechanism of exchange, resulting in agreements that are enforced. But how is enforcement going to be forthcoming, if free riding is possible? The only mechanism in order to arrive at self-enforcement is the Lindahl mechanism, if one does not assume altruistic interests among the players.

Lindahl's mechanism

Markets cannot provide public goods like law and order or defence, because the self-interests of the individuals would not lead them to provide a Pareto-optimal supply of public goods. The difficulty is free riding, which lures people away from participating in collective action. The larger the group, the more difficult becomes the problem of handling free riding by means of voluntary exchange. Consider the so-called Lindahl model of public goods in Figure 8.5, where a group of three players would arrive at the supply of a public good by means of voluntary exchange.

Three individuals want to provide themselves with a public good G, which they all can consume without reducing the consumption of each other. They have different preferences for G, as indicated by their individual demand

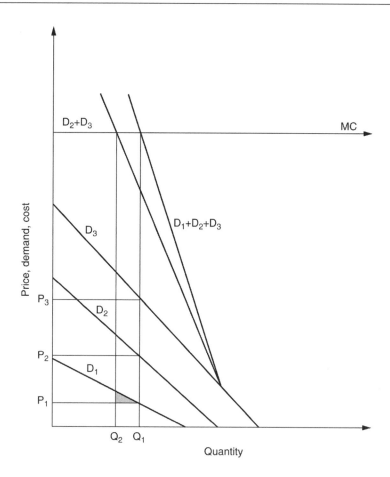

Figure 8.5   Public goods and free riding

curves: D_1, D_2 and D_3. The construction of G is assumed to display constant returns to scale, meaning a constant marginal cost curve. The optimal allocation of G is the quantity of the public good where the combined willingness to pay equals the total cost. In Figure 8.5 this is where the vertically summed preferences of the players cut the marginal cost curve, or at Q. The three players would contribute to the payment of the cost for G in accordance with their preferences for G. These prices – P_1, P_2, P_3 – are so-called Lindahl tax prices.

However, a player can do better than co-operating under the Lindahl scheme and thus reach a better outcome than paying, for instance, P_3 and sharing in G with the others. How? The answer is: By reneging. If player 3 misrepresents his preference for G, stating no preference at all or indifference, then he/she can still share in the allocation of G although at a somewhat lower quantity. The gain in not paying the Lindahl price P_3 is more than the cost of a reduction in the quantity of G.

A voluntary exchange mechanism now requires that the other two players can retaliate against player 3 or renegotiate the entire deal. The risk is then that also players 1 and 2 renege, with the implication that voluntary exchange fails, as no public good would be forthcoming. This is the rational reason for the state allocating public goods, as the probability of reneging decreases.

Collective action and transaction costs

When a group of people provides themselves with something they all can share in, then we have a public good for that group. Public goods can be of various kinds, depending upon the nature and the size of the group in question. What is typical of a public good is that people share the costs of the good and they share in the benefits of the good. It is not divisible and it is lumpy. A voluntary exchange approach involves that the group can co-ordinate the individuals by means of agreements about how the costs and benefits are to be divided. The probability of a successful group action, meaning that an optimal supply of the public good would come forth, depends critically upon the size of the group, N. Compare the following two situations:

> CASE 1.   A three-person group. Suppose that they each have an income of $20,000 and that they pay the following prices reflecting different preferences to cover the cost of a lumpy public good at $20,000: A = $10,000; B = $6,000; and C = $4,000. Each person is thus critical to the allocation of the public good, and their contribution amounts to the following shares of the total cost: A = 50%; B = 30%; C = 20%. Free riding is excluded since the project would have to be broken off if all do not participate.

> CASE 2.   A one-thousand person group: Again we assume that they have an average income of $20,000. The cost of the lumpy good is now assumed to be 2 million dollars, which when shared by all equally becomes $2,000. The share of the individual contribution is now 1/1000, or 0.01 per cent. For the individual the contribution takes a 10 per cent share of his/her income but that constitutes an infinitesimal part of the payment for the lumpy good.

As the group grows bigger, the cost for the public good goes up. But this has entirely different implications for the individual. His/her contribution will still take a substantial part of his/her income, but the part of the contribution to covering the whole cost approaches zero quite rapidly. No one will have an incentive to pay for the public goods of a group when N becomes large. Although his/her contribution is costly for him/her, it means virtually nothing for the group. Why, then, contribute?

The paradox of collective action is that the individual counts for nothing but all individuals are still extremely important. Only the state can overcome this paradox by means of its authority to act, it is often argued when suggesting the so-called Hobbesian state as the ultimate solution to free riding. Thus, free riding is ruled out by means of legislation. People have to pay taxes and people who deliberately avoid doing so run a great risk of

Table 8.2 The assurance game

		A	
		Co-operation	Defection
B	Co-operation	2.2	0.0
	Defection	0.0	1.1

going to jail. Thus, there is no free riding any longer but illegal reneging. The individual faces a game against nature, where the probability of getting caught times the cost of being convicted will be compared with the probability of succeeding with tax evasion times the gain from such action. Many people will decide this game by relying on their sense of solidarity with their country.

Hobbes's solution

One suggested solution to the prisoner's dilemma game is to call up the government, as it is argued that only states can handle free riding effectively in the last resort. What governments do is simply to change the payoffs in a prisoner's dilemma game so that it becomes a game of assurance. This entails that defection is no longer an option – see Table 8.2.

Here, there are two Nash equilibria, of which 2.2 is the Pareto-optimal outcome. However, once a Hobbesian state is in place, then governments may use the state mechanism for other purposes than protecting groups and individuals against free riding. It may itself engage in free riding in the sense that it grabs without paying or violates various kinds of law. Hobbes may have wished to call such a predicament a stateless society, though. It is true that free riding is no longer an option, if collective action has the structure of an assurance game. At the same time the voluntary exchange mechanism typical of agreements and markets has been replaced by a coercive mechanism – the state. Is there no alternative?

The argument that voluntary exchange may handle collective action and free riding has been developed recently both theoretically and empirically. The focus is not upon one kind of voluntary exchange, namely markets, and their use of prices as the mechanism of exclusion. This requires the use of private property rights, which is exactly what is missing with common pool resources. Instead the focus is upon agreements and solidarity. Let us examine the argument of Elinor Ostrom, who has developed the theory that people may introduce regimes that counteract the free riding on such resources.

Ostrom's theory deals with 'CPR' meaning: 'a natural or man-made resource system that is sufficiently large as to make it costly (but not impossible) to exclude potential beneficiaries from obtaining benefits from its use' (Ostrom, 1990: 30). Since these common pool resources bring benefits to people and their usage involves organization meaning costs, the problem of co-ordination arises. Markets cannot work since it is explicitly laid down that free riding is not only feasible but also probable. Thus, private property rights cannot be fully implemented or policed. What to do?

Let us quote again from Ostrom when she gives examples of CPRs: 'fishing grounds, groundwater basins, grazing areas, irrigation, canals, bridges, parking garages, mainframe computers, and streams, lakes, oceans, and other bodies of water' (Ostrom, 1990: 30). Since excludability is not feasible, free riding will result in suboptimal outcomes, usually analysed as resulting from a confrontation between individual and collective rationality. In the worse case scenario we have the depletion situation whereby the common pool resources are destroyed literally. Co-ordination is thus necessary to overcome such collective action difficulties. But co-ordination how? Ostrom suggests: self-organization or self-governance on a local scale, which is basically the use of a voluntary exchange approach involving the making of agreements among players and the monitoring of these agreements. She states that self-organization is a method of co-ordination when:

> a group of principals who are in an interdependent situation can organise and govern themselves to obtain continuing joint benefits when all face temptations to free-ride, shirk, or otherwise act opportunistically. (Ostrom, 1990: 29)

She opposes self-organization to market organization (property rights) and state organization (centralization). Whereas the first may be impossible, the latter would involve relying upon coercion, meaning that the outcomes could be even worse than collective action failures.

It is not clear why one form of state organization, viz. local governments, could not constitute a possible governance mechanism in this case, if the emphasis is upon self-rule and local goods. Local governments could be seen merely as clubs for the provision of goods and services in accordance with Figures 8.3 and 8.4. Local governments resolve the threatening consequences of opportunistic behaviour in relation to CPRs by putting up fences, for instance in the form of strict membership criteria implemented by state power. However, Ostrom wishes to rely upon a mechanism of co-ordination that is outside a so-called *Leviathan* approach. She writes about the state as 'a ruler who recognises that substantial benefits can be obtained by organising some activities'. But the drawback of the state mechanism is that: 'There is no mechanism, such as a competitive market, that would exert pressure on the ruler to design efficient institutions' (Ostrom, 1990: 41). Really? Ostrom seems blind to the very strong possibility of having a *demos* as the ruler and use the Downsian competitive mechanism of elections and party rule. A *Leviathan* state would not resolve the prisoner's dilemma problem, as people could free ride upon government.

In any case, let us briefly look at the empirical examples of self-governance of CPRs that Ostrom describes. We wish to know: Is the *Leviathan* really absent? Of the 14 cases of voluntary provision of a common pool regime that she investigated, only six could be unambiguously described as working or 'robust'. Typical of these six success stories are clear boundaries and membership on the one hand and recognized rights to organize on the other hand. The first derives from private law arrangements, backed indirectly by the state, whereas the second involves the direct backing of a government. All the failure cases lack either the first feature – clear boundaries – or the second feature – recognized rights to organize. A purely voluntary exchange arrangement for a CPR would have to grapple with exactly these two features enhancing free riding which indicate the total absence of a state.

From what has been said above, it is apparent that free riding is based upon and exploits to a maximum the lack of property rights. The state can handle free riding to a certain extent, but it fails when free riding takes place in areas where state control is either impossible (oceans) or not practicable (poaching). When property rights are missing, then the market also fails. Let us look at a theory that clearly links the use of voluntary exchange as a tool of co-ordination with the existence of property rights.

Coase's theorem: creating property rights

The present market euphoria, propagated by key organizations and academic economists, pays little attention to the serious problems that arise when the institutional conditions for a market economy are not met. Markets may destroy themselves when, for instance, property rights do not exist. Or markets may degenerate into the crime economy when it becomes more lucrative to make money by violating the rules of game than by abiding by them. States make the market economy possible, leaving governments with many tasks involved in putting into place a *Leviathan* for the economy. The abandonment of the command economy has in no way reduced the need for a Hobbesian state.

The state is a collective action enterprise. It cannot be supplied by voluntary exchange. However, it can be governed democratically. It makes not only the market economy possible but can also facilitate broader schemes of voluntary exchange such as self-governance regimes. Theories about the distinction between the market and the state focus upon private property rights, transaction costs and the advantages of voluntary exchange. We argue that reneging is the basic problem, which necessitates the use of government authority, i.e. the state. When governments supply law and order, then they make the market possible. Law and order is a public good, which cannot be supplied by means of voluntary exchange.

The state is not vulnerable to the kind of free riding that occurs under voluntary exchange schemes. Public goods would be forthcoming, but the allocation of G would not necessarily satisfy the conditions for Pareto optimality. One group could end up having more or less of G than it wants or having to pay more or less than it should. When governments take on the responsibility for the allocation of public goods by means of the authority of the state, then voting in government becomes the critical and decisive element for allocative outcomes.

Coase links the market as well as voluntary exchange with transaction costs (Coase, 1988). We argue, however, that it is reneging that is the key to explaining when markets work and do not work or when the voluntary exchange mechanism leads to efficient outcomes. Coase's theorem states that two or more players will always find the Pareto-optimal outcomes in economic interaction when they can negotiate freely and at zero transaction costs. Property rights do not matter, because the players will find and implement any Pareto-optimal outcome, whatever the property rights are.

The applicability of Coase's theorem has been much discussed, especially in relation to common pool resources like environmental protection in various forms. The standard interpretation is that the theorem proves that state action is not necessary as voluntary exchange may handle collective action problems like limiting pollution or depletion. What government bureaucracies do ineffectively and at high internal costs, the parties concerned can achieve more efficiently by simply bargaining about the costs involved in pollution or depletion. Figure 8.6 shows the Coase mechanism for arriving at an optimal decision concerning the pollution (as an externality) a firm may cause a community.

If property rights are placed with the polluting firm, then the community will pay the firm for stopping pollution at HE_1, paying at least Z but not

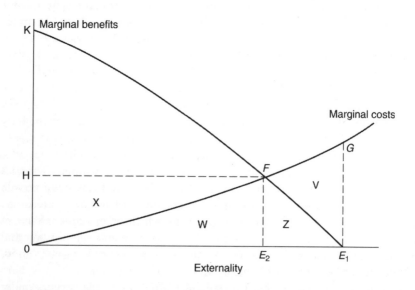

Figure 8.6 Coase's solution for a good with external effects

more than Z and V. If on the other hand, property rights are placed with the community, then the firm could compensate the community by paying, for instance, W and X. In both cases the Pareto-optimal quantity is forthcoming at HE_1.

The assumption about zero transaction costs makes the Coasean model amorphous. It is very difficult to measure transaction costs, meaning that one can never really tell whether they are zero, small or huge. Moreover, one cannot tell whether the transaction costs arise because the players first have to decide upon the allocation of the property rights or whether they concern only the efforts at bargaining after property rights have been clarified. Coase's model clearly assumes that property rights have been established one way or the other. His basic idea is that how this matter is resolved does not hinder the arrival of the players at a Pareto-optimal outcome.

The implication for the state is that it should be active in identifying property rights and in reducing transaction costs. What Coase is really saying is that governments should take the institutions of the market economy seriously by carefully putting into place the five institutions listed in Chapter 1 and monitoring their observation closely. This is a weak interpretation of Coase's theorem.

A strong interpretation of the Coasean theorem says that all forms of collective action problems can be resolved by voluntary exchange as long as property rights are transparently defined and transaction costs are zero. When these two conditions do not apply, then voluntary exchange will not arrive at Pareto-optimal outcomes. The Coase requirements of low transaction costs and property rights restrict, if true, the optimism of Ostrom concerning self-organization or self-governance. Yet, the Coasean theorem in no way reduces the importance of the state to the market economy. Using a Coasean mechanism for handling pollution, namely litigation, presupposes the existence of a state that prevents reneging.

Monopoly and oligopoly

The conventional theory about market entails that governments may intervene when market failures occur. Market failures constitute a necessary but not a sufficient condition for state intervention. If governments decide to intervene when there is market failure, then there is no assurance that government will do better than a market that operates badly. Some scholars call this the risk of state failure. One kind of market failure is market power, which makes possible monopolies. Market power implies that firms are no longer price takers but price setters, meaning that they can reduce output in order to maximize their revenues. This violates the requirement of markets to fulfil Pareto optimality.

Monopolies deviate from the ideal model of the competitive market, launched by the Lausanne School. This is as true today as it was yesterday. But why is this then a problem? Because we do not know for sure whether real markets adhere more to the monopoly model than to the competitive model. Perhaps the real world of economics is inhabited by neither perfectly competitive markets nor monopoly markets but something in between, called 'oligopoly' and 'monopolistics competition'.

The basic problem today in market economics is not the theoretical one of modelling the properties of ideal type market. Rather it is the empirical one of finding out whether the markets that we use on an everyday basis are close or far away from the four basic ideal types: (i) perfect competition; (ii) monopoly; (iii) oligopoly; and (iv) monopolistic competition. It is far from clear how one decides an empirical question like that. And we shall see that economists have widely different views upon the subject. We will focus upon the implication of the *Chicago School Economics* that all markets tend towards the competitive model, if left to themselves, meaning no government intervention.

Market power stems from economies of scale, i.e. the first kind of market failure identified in chapter 6. When one firm may supply the whole market, then the Walras mechanism does not work. There will not be a million suppliers and a million buyers bidding up or down the price in relation to the signals of the Walras auctioneer. When firms have market power, then they can determine how much to supply – quantities – by deciding upon their prices so as to maximize their profits. Market power is either total meaning that the market is a virtual monopoly or the market is shared among a few firms creating an oligopoly. We must ask the basic question: Economies of scale – do they exist naturally or can they be manufactured by institutions?

Are there natural monopolies?

It used to be accepted that some markets could never be Walrasian ones. These markets are the ones where nature has created a special situation, namely economies of scale without any limit. Thus, increasing returns to scale lead to a situation where one firm may allocate the Pareto-optimal amount but several firms cannot. This is a natural monopoly situation and the policy implication if any is that governments should not attempt to promote competition, since it would be a pure waste in the case of several suppliers. Figure 8.7 outlines this predicament where competition would not work (Sherman, 1989; Carlton and Perloff, 1999).

The logic in relation to the overwhelming economies of scale in Figure 8.7 is impeccable. If the market is divided among two small firms producing together at Q_2, then they will supply the whole market, but prices will be higher than if one firm supplied the whole market at Q_1. Thus, perfect competition does not lead to a Pareto-optimal outcome, because the prices charged at P_2 would be exorbitant in relation to the price that one firm would charge, or P_1. The reason is the overinvestment in fixed costs, which implies that the considerable increasing returns to scale are not captured by

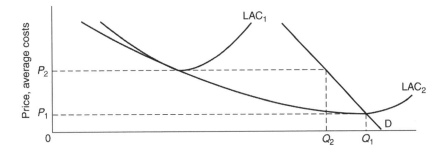

Figure 8.7   Natural monopoly

any firm. Conclusion: It is better that one firm supplies the whole market at
Q_1 charging price P_1.

The situation in Figure 8.7 is described as natural monopoly. If the
market starts from zero, then it will arrive at a monopoly but only at the
cost of senseless competition, which by its own logic will result in one firm
taking the whole market. The policy conclusion is then that governments
should promote a monopoly from the beginning, stopping competition that
cannot work and formalizing the natural monopoly into a legal monopoly.

The traditional theory of public regulation started from a situation like
that of Figure 8.7 and came to the conclusion that state intervention in one
form or another was necessary, since arriving at an outcome like quantity Q_2
and price P_2 was nothing but a market failure. The theory of public
regulation not only developed a number of hypotheses about how
government could promote efficiency in a situation like that in Figure 8.7
where marginal cost pricing could involve a loss to the firm supplying Q_1,
but it also argued that large parts of the economy were characterized by
economies of scale to this high extent.

The natural monopoly theory covered almost all kinds of infrastructure,
which could amount to some 10 per cent of the economy in an industrialized
and urbanized world. Thus, one important sector of the economy would be
dominated by a few large firms, supplying the whole market with their
products and having thousands of employees. However, one difficulty
remains to be solved, if one accepts the basic assumption that infrastructure
displays immense increasing returns to scale due to the crucial role that nets
play in the allocation of such services. It is easy to argue that only one net is
feasible from an economic point of view, given the existing technology, that
is.

The difficulty can be stated in game theory terms: the Pareto optimal
output Q is not the Nash equilibrium of the firm operating in that market
environment. The motivation of a firm supplying the whole market in
accordance with the market environment in Figure 8.7 is to behave like a
monopolist would do, i.e. maximizing profits by restricting output to the
quantity where the marginal revenue equals the marginal cost. The Nash

equilibrium in Figure 8.7 is the monopoly output, which involves a huge rent to the firm, the larger the rent the more inelastic the demand.

The traditional theory of regulation now calls upon government again, this time to undo the monopoly. Policy could be used, it is claimed, to negotiate a deal with the firm that involves a higher output and a lower price. If these negotiations do not meet with success, then the policy conclusion would be to nationalize the firm, transforming it into a public enterprise. Here we have the contrast between American versus the European policies in relation to infrastructure: the public utilities model on the one hand and the public enterprise model on the other.

Public regulation could thus be employed to move the economy out of a market failure and state intervention in one form or another would be called upon for efficiency reasons. The Chicago School now questions both links in this argument for policy. First, it rejects that that policy works by arguing that the firm, whether private or public, will place itself at the monopoly point whatever government does. Second, the only way to leave this legal monopoly that government has created by means of its regulatory ambitions is to allow competitive markets to operate in the normal way (Stigler, 1988).

Asymmetric information, stated within a principal–agent approach, explains why public regulation fails. When a private firm is regulated, then the excess rent ends up with the shareholders. But when a public enterprise has a legal monopoly, then the rent is dissipated in the form of excess costs, i.e. X-inefficiency. Governments are much too feeble to accomplish any other solution than Qmon. The bargaining game is won all the time by those that are being regulated, because they have an information advantage about the market situation.

The policy conclusion is then: Deregulate! But one must show that deregulation will bring about a Pareto improvement, which can only come through competitive pressures pushing firms to lower their prices and allocate more. Where is contestation going to come from in a market situation like that in Figure 8.7? Answer: From changing the only component that is characterized by increasing returns to scale in infrastructure, namely the net. Who will do that? Reply: Governments.

Contestability can always be contrived

According to the prevailing market philosophy, no markets are naturally monopolies. Contestation is always forthcoming when there are profits to be made as long as entry is not blocked. Thus, what is critical is contestability and the removal of barriers to entry. This is the George Stigler position which may be interpreted as a combination between Walrasian economics and Schumpeterian economics.

The capitalist entrepreneur is always looking for a profit to be made. He/ she will start up economic activities whenever it is lucrative. When markets are mature and profit margins have been pushed so low that price equals cost of producing, then the entrepreneur will go somewhere else. He/she is the revolutionary force in the economy, searching for new markets where profit levels are substantial. What is essential then is entry to markets, not the number of players in itself. It is sufficient for there to be one entrepreneur challenging a monopoly in order to bring down price and increase output. Thus, Walrasian markets need to be contestable by one entrepreneur and not necessarily competitive by millions of buyers and sellers.

Infrastructure presents one major obstacle to entry in the form of a huge net where the possession of it presents the owner with enormous market power. He/she may decide price both upstream and downstream, affecting the whole chain of production within an infrastructure domain. Competition can only be created if the barriers to entry that stem from net control can be bypassed. How?

Here the link between the state and institutional change becomes crystal-clear. The institutions of the market economy include private ownership. The search for affluence makes people look for those institutions that enhance wealth. However, in relation to the allocation of infrastructure this kind of institutional teleology fails as private ownership is part of the problem and not the solution. It is when one of the players in the market for infrastructure controls the net that monopoly is the natural outcome. Thus, government is needed to prevent vertical integration, which is exactly what firms search for in infrastructure. This is government creating contestability by means of institutional changes affecting ownership and competition. And it is a kind of institutional change that players searching for profits would not easily figure out or wish to try.

The net must be separated from the production and distribution of the infrastructure good or service. When the net is placed with an independent operator that has no profit motive, the access to the net can be rented out on a per minute basis. An alternative solution is to introduce various principles concerning the use of a net by outside operators such as third-party access and essential facility. When the use of the net can be bought on a per minute, per day, per month or per year basis, then competition is possible.

A variety of solutions are feasible. For electricity, for example, it is convenient to introduce a *bourse* where excess supply and demand meet, employing the net to transport the produced quantities to consumers anywhere in the country. In other kinds of infrastructure, a leasing arrangement appears more convenient such as long-term rental arrangements of between ten and 20 years, as, for example, in water allocation. The principle of third-party access can be used in telecommunications as well as gas to enhance contestability.

What one arrives at is a total transformation of the market situation. Instead of Figure 8.7, we have a situation where cost curves have the normal curvature and where a large number of small supplies can supply the whole market at reasonable prices. There is no longer any economies of scale.

Public regulation does not work, meaning that prices will still be too high and output too low (Stigler, 1988) and the net is the only element in infrastructure that displays increasing returns to scale (Demsetz, 1988). The conclusion must then be that what is needed is an institutional reform creating one form or another of tendering/bidding for the net. We argue that it is the state who can do this institutional reform, governments learning how to operate such schemes. When governments do not have this power to introduce tendering/bidding and thus elicit contestability, then how can market power be undone?

One school of economic thought has long argued that real-life markets tend not to be Walrasian-type markets. Instead firms claim, with considerable success, market power. Most markets are imperfect competition markets: monopolies, oligopolies, monopsony or monopolistic competition. The standard models in micro-economic theory show how such markets with imperfect competition deviates from the ideal market type: pure or perfect competition. However, what economic theory does not inform about is how close reality is to the one or to the other.

How is one to judge whether a firm has market power or not? It seems that most company products have substitutes, meaning that there are few real monopolies except when government has created them as legal monopolies. However, the Cambridge School of economic thought argues that companies use their brands together with excessive advertising in order to arrive at market power. Look at the classical model by Chamberlain concerning monopolistic competition – Figure 8.8 (Bilas, 1971).

This is neither monopoly nor perfect competition. Firms have a certain amount of market power meaning that they can find their Nash equilibrium of setting marginal revenue equal to marginal cost. But in the long run high profits will stimulate competitors to enter, which lower the demand for the product, sending profits downwards. If different brands are close substitutes, then profits will be driven down until price equals cost. However, firms may use advertising to create an image that brands are truly different and that a consumer may well benefit from paying for price differences between various brands.

It is exactly here that it becomes extremely difficult to decide whether a market is perfectly competitive or imperfectly competitive. A number of empirical criteria has been developed to measure market power as well as profit levels. However, these studies are not conclusive in their findings. When globalization is taken into account, then the issue becomes even more difficult. Firms may use sales in many countries in order to capture economies of scale when launching a brand as a special product. If consumers in several countries look upon the firm brand as virtually without substitutes, then market power can be exercised at the same time as production is large enough to capture the possible economies of scale.

Stigler challenged the model of imperfect competition stating that existing markets are more close to the ideal of perfect competition than to Figure

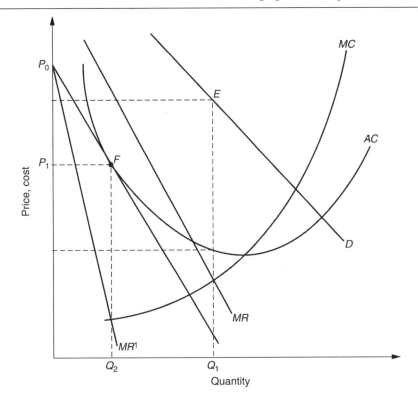

Figure 8.8   Monopolistic competition

8.8. above. Imperfect competition raises a number of policy concerns about the role of advertising in the economy. Even if imperfect competition only delivers above normal profits in the short run, it challenges one essential condition for market perfection, namely symmetrical knowledge between seller and buyer. Imperfect competition is only possible if consumers believe the message of massive advertising, namely that products are different. If this message is wrong, then sellers are misleading consumers – the condition (3) in chapter 6.

There has always been two contrasting views about the market, one positive and the other negative. One of the key arguments for the negative view concerns imperfections in knowledge on the consumer side. Consumers are being misled by firms – this is a basic theme from Veblen to Galbraith. When one party has more knowledge than the other, then interesting strategic interaction may follow, from which the first gains more than the other. But is this a problem of economic efficiency or is it a distributional matter? Imperfect competition according to Chamberlain poses a problem for economic efficiency only in the short run. In the long run firms will produce where price equals cost.

Imperfect competition does not present a serious problem of economic efficiency as long as the imperfection in Figure 8.8 is of a short-term nature. However, this may take considerable time and firms may invest heavily in advertising, sending the message that the firm's products have no substitutes. If this strategy is successful, then governments may wish to consider doing something to improve consumer information. A number of policies can be used to enhance the symmetry between producers and consumers.

What happens if the consumers have a complete disbelief in what producers want to sell? An extreme model of information asymmetry is the Akerloff model of 'any market for lemons' allocation. Here the market can only allocate a fraction of the supply, as there is no market clearing price for the rest of the units that sellers wish to sell and buyers want to buy. Asymmetric knowledge can have enormous consequences upon markets, which call for policy. Increasing consumer awareness and removing information asymmetries are not small tasks for government. The market for used cars is a good example where state intervention helps make markets more efficient. Policies to make consumers less vulnerable to firm abuse of information cover a number of areas today, such as health care, insurance and second-hand markets besides the introduction of general principles of consumer regret, one weak trial, etc. Perhaps firm advertising is not such a threat after all? How, then, about cartels? Do they exist?

Cartels are not stable

The organization of a cartel is considered a threat against the market economy because it involves monopoly. A few producers collude in order to contrive a monopoly, allowing them to earn super-normal profits at the expense of the consumers. This can only be done by market power which is used to restrict output, causing a deadweight loss to the entire economy. It was always open to debate whether any form of monopoly was bad because of the efficiency reason (deadweight loss) or for distributional concerns (economic rents).

Cartels are cause for public concern, it is widely believed. And governments engage in policy against cartels, called anti-trust policy-making. There are two models of state intervention. On the one hand there is the American Sherman Act system which makes collusion a crime for which persons could be sent to jail. On the other hand there is the EU system which employs administrative law against collusion, imposing fines upon persons who create or maintain cartels. Both the US system and the EU system allow government to require that a cartel is broken up, which may entail that a company be split into two.

One may distinguish between horizontal and vertical cartels, depending upon how the integration takes place. Horizontally, a cartel may cover the same producers all over a country or the world. Vertically, a cartel may be collusion between various stages in the process from production to distribution. The EU system accepts horizontal integration more than vertical integration, whereas the opposite tends to be true of the American system. Globalization affects cartels in two opposite ways. On the one hand globalization makes cartels more difficult to put in place and maintain, because there are many more players in the market place. On the other hand the gains from colluding increases when a cartel could operate on the entire global market. The most successful cartel is after all the OPEC.

Collusion presents government with two key questions: (1) Does anti-trust work? (2) Is anti-trust worth the effort? Whereas adherents of *Cambridge Economics* unambiguously reply YES to both these two questions, people with a leaning for the Chicago School approach are more hesitant. Demsetz, for instance, argued forcefully that anti-trust is not worth the effort. However, there is an even more subtle argument against state intervention, namely that trusts undo themselves. One may also simply argue that anti-trust does not bite. Let us discuss these three responses to anti-trust policy-making: (i) not useful; (ii) not effective; (iii) not necessary.

Demsetz offers an alternative interpretation of the firm with market power. He argues that such a position reveals strength, not corrupt practices. When firms make super-normal profits, then their products are highly demanded and they have a cost advantage. Using anti-trust to force them to break up could spell higher costs for consumers. Firms with horizontal or vertical integration can capture economies of scale, allowing them to supply a huge part of the market by pricing lower than competitors. This is good for the consumer in the short run. The long-run implications of market power are undone by the market itself, since new entrepreneurs will enter the market sooner or later, challenging the monopoly position of the firm or cartel. One could even argue that the lack of competition reflects that no entrepreneur wants to enter because it would not be profitable. Thus, from the existence of market power for a firm one cannot conclude that there is a cartel or a monopoly.

Here we have the crux of the matter: How is one to detect collusion? It will never take the form of written documents, as mere implicit collusion is enough to bring about higher prices and lower quantities. But how does one reveal implicit or silent contracts? Interestingly, the anti-trust authorities in the USA employ a version of the prisoner's dilemma game to get at collusion. By promising almost acquittal to the party that confesses collusion, one targets the other party with a high sentence. But where does one find the indicators on the existence of restrictive practices, if not merely in firm size or firm profits?

Anti-trust investigations are often used when firms attempt to merge. Thus, firms need government approval in order to merge their businesses both in the USA and the EU. These investigations take time and often result in certain conditions for merger, like, for example, the shedding of certain parts of the new company. However, the general experience with anti-trust decision-making is that mergers are very difficult to stop because of the pressures being levied at the anti-trust boards. Only rarely do anti-trust decisions go against the interests of the firms.

Yet, the most profound argument against using anti-trust to undo collusion comes from the theory that predicts that cartels collapse by themselves because they cannot handle their own collective action problem, namely free riding. Let us discuss this argument at greater length as it takes us into some of the most interesting aspects of game theory.

A cartel is a collusion among two or more players who wish to derive profit from organizing themselves as a monopoly. Thus, they must agree upon price and quantity. But how can they do this if such agreements cannot be policed or litigated? The difficulty was first pointed out by Cournot in the nineteenth century who showed that the Pareto-optimal outcomes for the cartel as a whole may be not be the Nash equilibrium of each of the single players. A cartel must take two decisions: (i) to limit production to Qmon and to raise price to Pmon; and (ii) to divide internally what is going to supply what given that the total supply is Qmon. However, each player can gain more by reneging on this agreement and sell more than its quota, since it would increase its profits. If all do this, then the cartel breaks down.

The problem of a cartel can be visualized by means of the interaction between two players who collude about prices and quantities in a market where a cartel of the two may supply the whole market. Suppose that the two firms accept the price which maximizes profits but dispute who is going to supply the most output. The Pareto-optimal deal between the two firms is any agreement which divides Qmon between the two players – a task for negotiation. But when negotiation fails, then their Nash equilibrium is to supply output in accordance with their anticipation of what the other player is going to supply. Thus, we arrive at the famous reaction functions of Cournot and Stackelberg – leader and follower – see Figure 8.9 (Bilas, 1971).

If the cartel can behave as one firm, then it can set $MR = MC$ and restrict output. If the cartel is two colluding firms dividing the monopoly rent m equally, then either Cournot or Stackelberg strategies are more likely. If the two firms start a price war – Bertrand's strategy – then price will be driven down to MC.

Implications for regulation and anti-trust

The Chicago School of Economics directs a clear message against state intervention, whether in the form of public regulation or in the form of anti-trust. This may sound like a paradox, but it is not. The Stigler–Demsetz position is consistent, following from a firm belief that all real markets are very close to the Walrasian market ideal and that state intervention can do nothing to enhance efficiency. Monopolies are only manufactured by government and cartels are unstable. Thus, markets are competitive markets when left alone to the invisible hand.

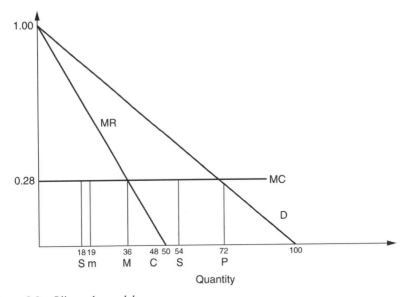

Figure 8.9 Oligopoly models
Note: D = demand; MC = marginal cost; MR = marginal revenue; P = Pareto-optimal; C = Cournot; M = Monopoly; S = Stackelberg; B = Bertrand; M = Perfect Collusion
Source: Carlton and Perloff (1999)

Many scholars wish to accept one part of the market philosophy and still hold on to a major role for state intervention. They wish to reserve anti-trust as a major task for government. Thus, they state the need for strong government surveillance of the economy in order to detect and destroy cartels. Anti-trust can call for large bureaux at various levels of government. One telling case is the EU Commission where several commissioners work more or less with competition policy besides the many national governments who also conduct anti-trust policies.

One could debate whether the US model of anti-trust policy is better than the model that is used in the competition bureaux of the EU, meaning more efficient in hindering or removing oligopolies. The EU Competition Commissioner has an impressive 500 members of staff, including almost 100 in the so-called merger task force, and they appear to wield more powers than regulators in the USA, at least on paper. Since the EU anti-trust is based upon an administrative ruling by the Commission, the Commission officials are simultaneously prosecutors, judges and jurors. The only way to undo a decision by the Commission on trust practices of various forms is to go to the European Court of Justice, where it takes a long time to appeal a decision.

In the USA the regulator has to go to an ordinary court in order to implement an anti-trust decision, as trust practices imply a violation of the penal code. The outcome of such a ruling could be a prison sentence.

However, in reality it is far from certain that the US practice is weaker than the European one. This issue involves difficult problems concerning the efficacy of common law practices as compared with civil law practices, but what is accomplished by means of many administrative decisions can often be reached by one single ruling in a case, which becomes a precedent. It may well be the case that several and different administrative rulings bite less than one sharp ruling on an important case.

If one adheres to a market philosophy looking upon markets as being more efficient than governments, then one would be inclined to look upon anti-trust policy-making as an additional tool that fits nicely into an emphasis upon markets. Socialists may have given up on state allocation, but they may wish to emphasize anti-trust. However, this combination is not logical from the point of view of Stigler–Demsetz. Let us pinpoint this as clearly as possible, outlining various forms of state intervention into the market.

In the idea of a European regulatory state, launched by G. Majone, we find a very strong belief in the possibility and desirability of government intervention in markets, either in the form of regulation or in the form of anti-trust. Majone speaks for governing the economy by means of regulators, either single ones or regulatory boards. The problem is only that regulators may not always do the best things for the economy. And they impose a cost which can become considerable if the number of regulatory bodies start multiplying, as in the UK during the 1990s.

We have looked at two classical arguments for state intervention. On the one hand there is the entire theory of traditional public regulation, focusing upon natural monopolies and legal monopolies. On the other hand there is the argument in favour of anti-trust policy-making, targeting cartels as well as horizontal and vertical integration. The strong deregulation phase of public policy-making has left anti-trust as the main form of state intervention in the market. The purpose of anti-trust is entirely different from traditional public regulation as it aims to increase competition and not stifle it by various kinds of barriers to entry, including legal monopolies, licences, etc.

Reregulation is seen as expanding anti-trust into new dimensions where it becomes so important that it gives rise to a regulatory state that can take over many tasks that were earlier placed upon the shoulders of government, including the allocation of services. A regulatory board can do lots of things in a market economy: control quality, investigate collusion, check prices, enhance competition, arrange auctions and tournaments, hear customer complaints, etc.

The Chicago position is the one that is logically consistent. If real markets tend towards the Walrasian model, then public regulation as well as anti-trust policy-making make little sense. But how is one to show empirically whether markets are competitive or monopolistic? There does not seem to exist a body of empirical evidence that decides conclusively for or against these two positions, the Chicago position and the Cambridge position. And the nature of real markets is in the final resort not a modelling problem but an empirical question.

Conclusion

The invisible hand may very well result in individual utility maximization, but why would it also accomplish the best outcomes for a group of people? Or to use a slightly more technical manner of speaking: If every game has at least one Nash equilibrium, then it does not follow that this outcome or these outcomes are also Pareto optimal. Nash equilibria may occur which are asocial, meaning that individual rationality is conducive to collective irrationality.

Market games may achieve Pareto optimality, but the naked pursuit of self-interest only will not do this. In order for the market economy to channel the maximization of self-interests into Pareto-optimal outcomes certain specific institutions must be guaranteed by the state. These institutions minimize the disruptive consequences of reneging, which if unchecked leads to market breakdown or the dissipation of rents. When reneging is massive, then we have the crime economy.

Markets operate on the basis of voluntary exchange when property rights including the rights of labour are defined and secure. Small groups can handle human interaction if property rights are well defined and the costs of transaction are low – this is what the Coasean theorem shows. When property rights cannot be clarified, then voluntary exchange could sometimes work under a regime of self-governance – the Ostrom argument. However, when property rights are difficult to introduce and enforce as well as when the number of choice participants N becomes large, then there is no alternative to the state.

Government is better suited to handle collective action problems but it is no panacea. Public organization is vulnerable to free riding itself. And when state territory is ill defined or absent, then free riding will occur.

It is the state that guarantees the operation of markets, as it is the guardian of property rights and the enforcer of agreements. It is when states cannot fulfil their tasks as guardians that free riding becomes very difficult to handle. This is so, for instance, with environmental problems of a global nature. The logic of the 'state as the guardian' argument does not mean that governments will concentrate their efforts upon these guardianship tasks of identifying and enforcing rights. Governments can deteriorate into warrior states, using their authority to undo rights, taking the assets of the country for themselves. Such a development is usually the first stage towards a stateless society.

CHAPTER 9

Who is the State?

Introduction

Several theories examined in political economy concerning the demarcation between the state and the market have one thing in common despite their diversity, namely that they search for a positive role of the state in the economy. They differ often very much about both the ends and the means of state intervention, but they take a positive view of policy, its capacity to improve upon things. In essence, these theories are normative ones, outlining how government could contribute to economic efficiency and social justice.

However, one could well ask: Why assume that governments aim at improving the economy? Relaxing this key assumption allows us to enter into totally different kinds of analyses where the state makes use of the economy for its own purposes or even for the private goals of political leaders. Such an approach to the state is a realistic one, attempting to assess what governments actually do to the economy. Instead of assuming benevolent preferences among the political authorities, it starts from the assumption of self-interest among the actors in the public sector. This is the so-called *Public Choice School*, modelling the actions of politicians and their bureaucracies in accordance with the standard assumption of economic choice theory, namely the maximization of egoism.

There is of course no valid *a priori* reason to start the analysis of government and the economy from an assumption that the state is always or most of the time a benefactor of the economy. It is as if the whole debate turns on the question of market perfectability. If markets work in a marvellous manner, then the problem is solved. Governments can sit back and let the markets handle the problems of human interactions. If, on the other hand, markets display failures, then the state must undo them. Yet, what about an approach that starts from the assumption that governments use the economy for their own purposes, be they public or private ones?

The most coherent approach along this perspective is the *Public Choice School*. It starts from one basic assumption, namely that public choice is no different in principle from private choice, meaning that people in government maximize their self-interest to the same extent as people in markets. The differences between state and market stem from the institutional setting, which condition the choice of strategies when players maximize their utility. Let us look at the *Public Choice School* to see what results they arrive at from such a starting point (Brennan and Buchanan, 1980; Buchanan and Musgrave, 1999).

Benevolent sovereigns

The *Public Choice School* developed its theory about the state in the form of a concise criticism of welfare economics and its search for an optimal combination of state and market. Markets do well, according to this theory, when they allocate goods and services that are divisible and involve rivalry as well as excludability. Governments should allocate goods and services when there is so-called market failure, i.e. indivisible goods and services involving jointness in consumption and non-excludability or free riding. The theory of market failures is based upon a hidden assumption, namely that the state has a natural objective to undo such failures with market operations. But where does it come from? The objectives of the state are nothing but what various people in government decide to pursue. And they may be driven by objectives other than altruistic ones. This is the gist of the *Public Choice School* criticism of one branch of economics: welfare economics. Thus, it may well be that markets fail in relation to the allocation of goods and services involving economies of scale or externalities, but why would governments be preoccupied with removing market failures? What motivates governments to try to promote benevolent outcomes?

The *Public Choice* theory of the state comprises two parts. First, we have the assumptions about the key players. Second, we have the deductions from these assumptions containing predictions about real-life outcomes. These implications may be checked against available evidence about the behaviour of politicians and bureaucrats. The key question in relation to the *Public Choice* approach is not whether the model assumptions are correct, but whether these assumptions yield predictions that are on the whole more true than false. The starting point in the evaluation of the *Public Choice School* is the methodological position advocated by Friedman (Friedman, 1953).

If one were to examine the realism of the model assumptions entering into a debate about the typical motives of public actors, then it seems impossible to advocate the one position – benevolence – as against the other – egoism. Interests and preferences vary from one actor to another as well as from one political context to another. How to generalize about the motivation of politicians and bureaucrats?

Besides the assumption of egoism the *Public Choice* framework employs the rational choice assumption that is standard in economic decision-making. Assuming perfect information appears as unrealistic as the assumption that egoism is the sole motive of public officials.

Yet, the standard methodology for testing a theory still applies, as the crucial test is with the confrontation of the model implications with reality.

Below we will look at two well-known *Public Choice* models which take the assumptions of the school to its extreme, predicting highly negative outcomes resulting from the actions of politicians and bureaucrats. Model realism is not the test, although one may wish to counteract that many public officials are truly motivated by the public interest or altruistic assumptions. It is impossible to explain all the variations in reality, as what is at stake are not the exceptions but the general situation which always takes the form of probabilities.

Thus, it is not the truth of the assumptions that is at stake when evaluating the *Public Choice* theory of the state, but the correctness of its predictions about reality. If the predictions turn out to be correct, then this evidence confirms or corroborates the theory but it does not conclusively prove the correctness of the theory. New evidence may appear tomorrow that falsifies the test implications. One may then conclude that the model assumptions are not sufficient for the derivation of correct predictions. Perhaps they are too parsimonious or simple?

Model simplicity is highly valued within the *Public Choice* framework, but the risk is large that a very small set of simplistic assumptions leads to incorrect predictions. The *Public Choice School* focuses almost exclusively upon the explanation of behaviour by means of preferences and information with the actors. What is missing are the institutions that regulate public decision-making. When they are added, then alternative test implications may be derived, even if one maintains the self-interest axiom and rejects the benevolent dictator assumption, typical of welfare economics and its normative solutions about the optimal mix of markets and state.

Modelling collective choice in the public sector requires that one makes clear assumptions not only about the impact of rules – the institutional requirement – but also that one is aware of a principal difficulty in relation to the kinds of interests and preferences that public actors may adhere to. We are referring to the distinction between the state as a legal entity and the persons that occupy positions in government. The self-interest axiom may appear to be relevant in relation to government as people, but it entirely misses the point when applied to the state as a legal corporation. Let us explain.

State and governments: a crucial separation

The state is by definition a legal order, based upon the capacity of governments to legislate. Governments can use this so-called *Leviathan* to promote outcomes that are beneficial to the country or they can use this sovereign power for their own purposes. When one makes an assumption about the benevolence of the public actors, then it is a matter of the public interest. However, one may assume that self-interest plays such a major role with people in government that the public interest falls by the wayside.

In the theory of the state it has been suggested that states have interests that are different from the personal motives of people in office. Thus, states wish to maintain themselves from an organizational point of view and defend their so-called state interests. This theory of state interests does not entirely coincide with the hypothesis about the public interest, as state interests have been interpreted to include aggressive objectives such as geopolitical goals, or even territorial expansion and the elimination of internal opposition. Yet, however these two conceptions are interpreted – the public interest and the reasons of state – it remains the case that it complicates matters considerably when modelling the behaviour of politicians and bureaucrats.

Even if one regards the assumption of state reasons or the public interest as referring merely to an illusion, it remains the case that public officials refer to altruistic considerations all the time. Thus, the standard stated motivation for public decisions and action does not refer to the self-interest of the players, which does not exclude the possibility that the real driving force is egoism. However, it complicates matters. This is even more the case when one makes the distinction between ends and means.

Politicians and bureaucrats may well be driven by self-interest but they could still promote the public interest because doing so increases their capacity to derive benefit for themselves. Thus, the critical separation between egoism and altruism within the *Public Choice* framework becomes blurred. The formula 'private vices, public virtues' may work also within the state and not merely in markets. Whether the self-interest of politicians and bureaucrats can be channelled towards the promotion of broader collective interests – state reasons or the public interest – depends, we argue, upon the framing of the public institutions.

The *Public Choice School* puts the self-interest assumption exclusively in the centre when approaching the state, which replaces the benevolent dictator assumption of welfare economics. Let us follow this approach and ask: If governments are solely motivated by self-interest, then what would they do to the economy? Let us first deal with the politicians.

A revenues-maximizing *Leviathan*

In a very crude model suggested by Buchanan, governments would preoccupy themselves with capturing a part of the resources of the country by means of taxation. They could well do other things than this, but their primary objective would be to secure a considerable and safe tax return for the state. The reason is of course that this money for the *fisc* could be employed to pay the salaries of the government people. Figure 9.1 shows two reaction functions, one where the tax base offered by the population to the government is almost unrelated to government expenditures, and another which links tax base with expenditures.

Can the population choose the reaction function BB^1 ahead of AA^1? Well, it depends upon the rules of the game. Taxes come from the population and

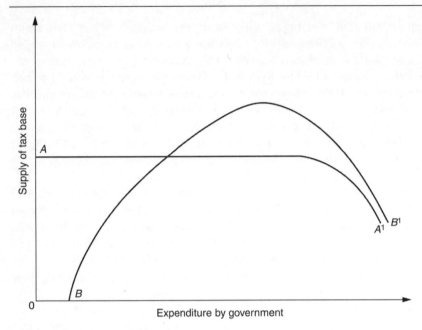

Figure 9.1   A revenue-maximizing *Leviathan*

they would want something in return – a *quid pro quo*. Two regimes are possible in principle: a democratic one and an authoritarian one. The latter is perhaps not so interesting, because the state would merely use its monopoly of violence in order for governments to get the resources they wish to claim. Such a strategy would work as long as the state itself is not called into question.

More interesting is the situation under a democratic regime. Let us assume a Downsian game with two major political parties and a set of institutions securing a majoritarian election procedure. Since such a regime puts competition into place, the opposition could defeat a government by promising lower taxes. And the population would vote rationally by favouring the opposition candidates, if it wished to limit the revenue appetites of the state. As Downs argued, such a competitive regime would force the government to adopt the median voter standpoint on one policy issue or on a set of issues. This means that taxes could be as large as the population wants them to be (Downs, 1957).

Actually, starting from a competitive political mechanism one may arrive at alternative conclusions about the size of government. Downs predicted that the public sector would actually tend to be too small in a democracy, because the electorate is myopic, meaning not fully and rationally informed about the pros and cons linked with public services (Downs, 1960). The opposite prediction is to be found with Stigler, who explained the growth of government in the twentieth century as driven basically by minorities combining in Parliament to defeat the majority.

To arrive at this conclusion that the size of government is too big given the preferences of the electorate one must add an assumption about the deficiency of the competitive mechanism to reveal correctly the dominant preferences in society. Somehow the electoral mechanism fails to disclose fiscal illusions or the strategies of minorities to combine temporarily in order to defeat the majority. It is stated that big government is a huge set of programmes that confer special benefits upon many small groups but distribute the costs on to the silent majority. Fiscal illusions tend to occur especially when the institutions favour the centralization of political power or enhance multi-party-system politics with too many alternatives.

The literature on the growth of government has not come up with a single valid theory about the causes or conditions of government expansion. Since public sector expansion is both a demand and supply phenomenon, one would like to see some form of equilibrium emerging between groups who want public sector expansion and groups who reject higher taxes. At least such an equilibrium should be forthcoming over time. Pursuing a revenues-maximizing strategy would then be difficult, especially when a competitive election mechanism is at work.

Budget-maximizing bureacracies

Another model with the same twist is the Niskanen model of a budget-maximizing bureaucracy. Again we start from the assumption of self-interest in the state, but this time the focus is upon civil servants. They would maximize their budgets in order to receive the best possible working conditions. And they would succeed by not revealing the marginal value and the marginal cost of what they are providing – see Figure 9.2.

Again, the conclusion depends upon the basic rules of the political game. In a democracy the bureaux are paid for by the public. Thus, it could put pressure upon governments to economize by, for instance, not playing Niskanen games but using an alternative funding method. In reality, it is the government who pays for the inefficiencies that result from budget-maximizing strategies by the bureaucrats. What governments need to do is to change the budgetary process so that marginal value and marginal costs are revealed. This can be done if the government employs another decision mechanism than bureaucracy.

New Public Management (NPM) offers a set of institutions which would limit the occurrence of Niskanen inefficiencies – too big supply. NPM replaces the funding principle of budget allocation with a tendering/bidding mechanism which when working would reveal marginal benefits and marginal costs in relation to public programmes. Thus, governments need not play Niskanen games where they set the total budget equal to the total cost. By tendering public services governments may compare alternative bids on the basis of marginal benefits and marginal costs, arriving at efficiency in allocation.

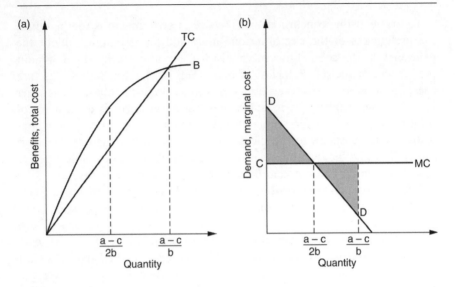

Figure 9.2   Niskanen's budget-maximizing model

The conclusion is again an institutional one, namely that a competitive mechanism could force governments to deal with market failures and attempts to resolve them in such a way that output is maximized. This time the competitive mechanism is not the market but democratic politics. One may arrive at the same result even in an authoritarian regime, if the government opts for maximizing its revenues through an economic policy that emphasizes economic growth. In so-called rentier states, governments put a premium upon economic performance, as it provides them with sufficient resources to meet the demands of their populations without using taxes, which could offset a claim for voting rights, or democracy.

Rentier states

Why would governments have an interest in inefficient and costly operations in the public sector? Since this is the main conclusion in the *Public Choice School*, one would wish to know why it is considered by scholars like Buchanan, Tullock and Frey as a conclusion that is almost beyond all reasonable doubt. Is there empirical evidence enough to warrant the conclusion that all governments are inefficient and behave like a bad agent in relation to their principal, the population?

It must be emphasized that the *Public Choice* argument that governments are inefficient and maximize their revenues from their principals is an empirical one. It is not a logical deduction from any general theory about principal–agent interaction, because the outcomes will vary depending upon the choice of strategies as well as the institutions in place that regulate this interaction. Thus, it is a straightforward conclusion from the workings of a competitive democracy that both sitting governments and the opposition have an interest in not wasting the resources of the state upon projects that do not pay off in terms of either electoral support or financial support. This is the Peltzman restriction upon rent-seeking activities of whatever kind they may be. It does not follow from a Peltzman mechanism that governments must be efficient for the entire society (Pareto-optimal) but they surely would be interested in using their money wisely from their own point of view (Stigler, 1998).

It is an open question whether politicians who pursue their self-interest favour or counteract waste in government. This is so because any strategy to the one side or to the other could be a success or a failure depending upon the reaction of the electorate.

Perhaps matters are entirely different in authoritarian regimes? Democratic regimes appear to offer both incentives and institutions which dampen the consequences of rent-seeking in the public sector. How far they hold is an empirical question. What we wish to discuss now is whether all authoritarian regimes would favour inefficient government operations.

It is interesting to examine the so-called rentier states in this connection. These are the states on the Arab peninsula where governments can use the enormous revenues from the production of oil to pay for government operations and services. A rentier state possesses such vast revenues from the windfall profits within oil extraction that they do not have to engage in revenue-maximizing strategies targeting various forms of taxation. We are of course referring to Saudi Arabia, Kuwait, Bahrain, Qatar, Oman and the United Arab Emirates, although not all of the seven emirates have oil.

The rentier states provide a range of public services to their citizens who accept the governments as legitimate as part of the *quid pro quo*. There are, apparently, no taxes in these countries, or at least they constitute a minor burden for the population. To get this equation going, the governments can hardly afford much of inefficiencies in public programmes.

State failures

Yet one cannot deny that many governments are part of the problem and not the solution to the situation of a country. The list of state failures may be made into a comprehensive one, comprising not only the mistakes of many governments but also the vicious actions of some governments to grab the resources of the country and even destroy them, including minorities in the population.

One must here distinguish between the state and governments. The state is a specific organization whose distinctive attribute is the possession of a vast capacity to control people and their lives through the use of its machineries: police, the military forces and the judicial apparatus. Governments are the key political actors in the state who decide over the state, for instance what its personnel should do and how its operations should be structured.

When there is talk about state failure, then it is really governments and how they act that is at stake. When states engage in atrocities, then there are people responsible behind these things. Often the perpetrators are linked with governments, the police or the army or the civil service. However, there is one case where it is correct to speak of state failure, namely when the state collapses more or less as with anarchy or civil war.

However, this is not the kind of state failure that figures prominently in mainstream public choice theory. State failure is here conceived as so-called *internalities* or internal organization difficulties that increase the costs of government operations and make them inefficient. Internalities do not involve complete state breakdown, but they make the government less attractive as a provider of goods and services in comparison with the market.

The idea behind the concept of state failure is that public organization has an in-built tendency to result in inefficiency. Public choice scholars are sometimes willing to concede that markets also can deliver inefficient outcomes – *externalities*. But having conceded this they usually add that the costs from internalities tend to be far larger than the costs from externalities. Thus, markets should prevail over governments.

Inefficiency in government may take two very different forms. One is simply oversupply, as more quantities of goods and services are provided because normal demand restrictions do not apply for some reason. Budget constraints are much weaker in the public sector, as it is not really the consuming citizen who pays but the anonymous taxpayer. This is the Niskanen position.

Another kind of inefficiency is too high unit costs – X-inefficiency. Waste or slack can occur when the quantity supplied is too low or the quantity supplied is too high – X-inefficiency can occur both in monopoly situations (too low output) and in the Niskanen situation (too much output). Why, then, would X-inefficiency be such a paramount problem in government? Can it not occur also in private firms to the same extent?

Poor states or states in poor countries

In a global market economy the problem of state failure takes on a global dimension. In Third World countries markets often work with difficulties. But where is improvement going to originate from? State intervention to make markets work better seems very improbable when the state is mismanaged by corrupt or incompetent governments. Poverty in the Third World works against efficient governments. It makes governments lack resources which pulls politicians and bureaucrats into the dangers of corruption.

In several Third World states one frequently observes revenue-maximization strategies on the part of governments. The state becomes a burden upon society as it is seen as the sole source of income in a meagre civil society.

When the environment is characterized by *prebendalism*, then the logic of state intervention must make state failure very likely and governmental efforts to improve upon market operations futile. However, the *Public Choice* analysis of state failure does not target Third World governments. It is a theory about First World states. Empirical evidence suggests that state failures of the kind that the *Public Choice School* speaks of do occur but they are hardly omnipresent. Perhaps the closest approximation to the massive state failure outlined in the model of a revenue-maximizing *Leviathan* or a budget-maximizing bureaucracy is the present situation in several parts of Sub-Saharan Africa, as analysed in the 1997 book *La criminalisation de l'Etat en Afrique* (Bayart *et al.*, 1997).

Thus far we have looked at the *Public Choice School* that questions a basic assumption in all discussions about the distinction between state and market, namely that governments have clear and social objectives. What the *Public Choice School* aims its criticism at is what is called 'welfare economics' in economic literature. The attack upon welfare economics is certainly not without foundation as it does start from the idea of a benevolent government trying to achieve Pareto optimality in allocation. Now, welfare economics and its suggestions about market failures and rational state intervention constitute normative theory, as it basically deals with ideal solutions. It does not predict how real governments will behave, whether in the First or the Third World. What comes out of welfare economics is a set of guidelines about how governments may wish to define the relationship between state and market in their countries. These normative criteria may be used or they may not be employed. They may be correct or they may be incorrect. But they cannot be judged according to their capacity to predict empirically what governments around the world are actually doing in terms of state intervention. Let us move to another theory about state failure, which is very much applicable to all states. We are referring to the theory that states that governments are completely powerless in relation to markets.

Do markets outsmart governments?

Governments have since the heyday of Keynesian economics reserved for themselves a special domain of decision-making, namely macro-economic policy-making. Even if it is true that state intervention in the micro parts of the economy does not make sense, governments have been much less inclined to give up macro-economic intervention. However, it is now argued that macro-economic policy-making is without teeth. The various ideas in the leading macro-economic school – encompassed by rational expectations theory – imply that governments are powerless when they attempt to impact upon the major aggregates of the economy. Yet, governments make this kind of state intervention all the time, especially when markets appear to falter. Thus, the Asian crisis, for instance, was resolved at least to some extent through various kinds of state intervention (Krugman, 2000).

The state acts in relation to the macro economy in various ways. Thus, central banks monitor the economy on an almost daily basis, checking interest rates affecting currencies and investigating the money supply. The ministry of finance presents a yearly budget which includes many decisions concerning taxing and spending. Yet, the prevailing macro-economic theory implies that all this has little impact (if any) upon the economy. Instead it argues that markets anticipate government policies and often cancel out their impact.

Governments may influence the economy by long-run policies or short-run policies. The long-run perspective involves the making of policies which affect positively the key factors that enhance economic development, or economic growth. The standard way of modelling economic growth in the long-run perspective is to employ the so-called Solow growth model, which links balanced economic development with three factors, namely increases in capital and labour as well as technological innovations. Thus, we have:

(1) $Y = F(C, L, T)$.

Solow stated a few conditions for the growth in output to be balanced in the long run, meaning that national income Y would grow at about 2–4 per cent a year. The identification of the relationships in the Solow model is done by means of a so-called Cobb–Douglas production function of the type:

(2) $Y = AL^aC^b$

where A = technology.

This approach allows one to estimate the contribution of each factor to output, which is essential if one wishes to understand the distribution of income between capital and labour as well as the capital base for the yearly output – the capital/output ratio. Here, we will not look into these matters, but simply point out that many government programmes have an impact upon these three variables: A, L and C. Thus, publicly supplied education and health care affects the supply of labour. Public investments in infrastructure affects capital, which is also true of decisions facilitating investments. Finally, government can create a climate that is friendly to innovations, meaning that technology is also affected by state intervention.

This is not to suggest that governments may direct or govern the economy by means of industrial policies picking winners. Economic nationalism or the so-called South East Asian model of economic development is not what is intended here. The argument is merely that even within a Western-type market economy, government policies in relation to labour, capital and technology may have long-run consequences promoting economic efficiency or increasing total output. However trivial this kind of state intervention may be, it is still worth emphasizing. Yet, the focus of macro-economic theorizing is upon the short-run changes in the economy, especially the economic fluctuations that we attribute to the business cycle.

The business cycle and Keynesianism

The basic image of the business cycle is that the yearly output fluctuates strongly around the long-run growth path with swings of various sizes between depression and over-heating. The duration of these swings varies from one period to another, as some depressions are longer or deeper than others and some forms of over-heating more grave than others. Since the loss in economic output as measured by the distance between the long-run path and the depths of depressions can be substantial, macroeconomics developed a theory about how government could make the swings less sharp by using counter-cyclical measures that smooth out the fluctuations. Two questions arise: (1) Does any form of macro-economic policy work? (2) Which one is the most efficient macro-economic policy, assuming more than one policy works?

It is a basic belief among economists of whatever orientation they adhere to that the business cycle fluctuations heal, meaning that the economy returns to balanced growth after a period of depression or over-heating. Thus, the economy is like a self-equilibrating mechanism where forces offset each other so that adjustment takes place sooner or later. Thus, the economy returns to full output after a period of adjustment to a shock. What is contested is, however, the length of the adjustment process as well as the capacity of governments to improve upon adjustment.

Business fluctuations have been looked upon somewhat differently by economists. To some, recessions were aberrations as they took the economy off its natural growth path, resulting in misery and losses. To others, however, recessions were as natural as the path of development that they diverged from. Recessions constituted a healing process for the economy where mistakes were undone and the future growth path was secured. The most articulated interpretation of recessions as natural was launched by J. Schumpeter. It may be seen as the anti-interventionist argument whereas of course the Keynesian contains the pro-interventionist argument. This is also how Schumpeter himself conceived of the situation while he was alive.

The famous expression '*creative destruction*' of Schumpeter indicates the basic idea in his theory of the business cycle, viz. that recessions help sorting out winners and losers. The entire business cycle with its fluctuations around an expansionary path can be linked with the role of the entrepreneur in the economy. In Schumpeterian economics emerging from the so-called Austrian approach the driving force in a capitalist economy stems from the ambition of the entrepreneur to find new ways of making profit. Thus he/she launches new products that people willingly buy because they stem from innovations or improvements in existing products. The reward for pushing the economy ahead lies in the profit that an entrepreneur can make for a while until competitors enter the race. In periods of over-heating there is overshooting which is corrected for by means of recessions when weak competitors are eliminated. In such a Darwinian perspective upon the business cycle there is little room for state intervention to heal the economy.

In Schumpeter's view, recessions in the short run help the economy in the long run as those efforts that are not so creative are forced into bankruptcy and liquidation whereas more creative projects stay in the race. If one takes the other view that recessions impose a cost upon the economy in the form of lost output, then there is a role for governments to play. They could, for instance, try to reduce the length of the recession as well as make it less profound. This view would probably claim that the loss in output is so costly that the gains from creative destruction do not warrant that the recession goes on any longer than necessary. The pro-interventionist theory would strengthen its claims if it could also show that the adjustment process is slow and comprises a number of mechanisms that protract the length of adjustment such as sticky prices, rigid wages and the liquidity trap.

Let us look at what role the Keynesian approach provides for government when it takes a pro-interventionist stance. Suppose the 'animal spirits' of Keynes drive the economy off its equilibrium growth path where all resources are employed due to the occurrence of a shock that no one anticipated. What can governments do and what should they do to the economy?

Keynesian macroeconomics dominated the theory about state intervention in relation to the business cycle from the end of the Second World War to the advent of monetarism around 1970. For some time it seemed as if one had to choose between either Kenysianism or monetarism, but since the 1980s there has been a proliferation of new ideas about what the state can and should do in relation to the business cycle, some of which are labelled New Classical Economics, indicating a wish to return to pre-Keynesian theories. The situation today is very complex, including as it does new Keynesian schools of thought (McCandless, 1991).

What is Keynesianism? This question is impossible to answer within the framework of this volume, but the main ideas imply that government could and should play an active role in reducing the fluctuations in the business cycle and thus mitigate their consequences upon economic activity. Keynesianism comprises both fiscal and monetary policies, and it has leanings towards discretionary intervention over rule-based intervention. The basic model is the so-called Keynesian cross linking planned demand with actual output or income Y. Thus we have in a simple version:

(K) $Y = C + I + G + (E - I)$

where Y = national income, C = consumption, I = investment, G = public spending, E = exports, I = imports.

This is a model of the real economy, where it does not matter in what monetary unit these variables are measured – the neutrality of money argument. If output is at a lower level than full employment income, then government can use either fiscal or monetary policy, or both, to boost the economy and push it towards its full employment output, since resources are idle. A full specification of how this may be done according to various Keynesian schools of thought would require a separate volume, introducing, for instance, the so-called IS-LM models.

Here, we target the policy implications of the Keynesian framework in order to discuss whether they are implementable or should be implemented. The Keynesian position in relation to activist macro-economic intervention is clear, despite all criticism against his foundations as, for instance, the nature of the consumption function C. Since in Keynes's view the economy may stay for quite some time below its full employment output level due to a fundamental lack of rapid adjustment in key parameters such as wages and prices, it is the task of government to intervene and simulate the economy. The rejection of Keynesianism is based upon the argument that this cannot be done. Why? Three mains reasons may be distilled from the debate *pro et contra* Keynesianism.

(*1*) *The NAIRU argument*: A fundamental objection against Keynesianism concerns the nature of the total demand and supply curves in any macro-economic model. These prices–output curves are not normal micro-economic curves, as they refer to the aggregates over all markets. Thus, it is possible that they look differently from Walrasian demand and supply curves. The difficulty is the nature of the supply curve for the entire economy, which must be vertical, at least in the long run (see Figure 9.3).

When the economy is at Y_1 in Figure 9.3, then any state intervention increasing demand can only result in inflation with no impact upon real output. Even if the economy is at Y_0, the attempt to boost demand will bring about a rise in output but prices will also rise. Keynesian policy-making seems to suggest a trade-off between output or full employment on the one hand and rising prices or inflation on the other hand.

However, there is a more fundamental objection, as one may ask quite seriously: If the economy is at its full employment level, then is it at Y_0 or Y_1? There is a basic ambiguity in the concept of full employment, which is the target in Keynesianism. Is it 1 per cent, or 2 per cent, or X per cent ... unemployment? The reply was that government should only intervene so as to keep the economy at its NAIRU level, meaning the non-accelerating inflation level of unemployment (Sawyer, 1989; Marin, 1992). It was suggested that it could be located somewhere around 6 per cent unemployment.

(*2*) *Expectations*: The Keynesian model K has a very simple mechanism built into it, as it is believed that government can increase and decrease the aggregates on the right-hand side in order to arrive at a change in total output or national income on the left-hand side. However, when

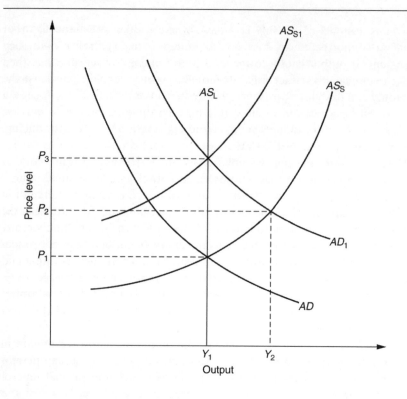

Figure 9.3   Macro-economic equilibria – short and long term
Note: AD = aggregate demand; AS = aggregate supply; Y = national income

government takes its decisions about its policy instruments – fiscal or monetary policy, then the impact of these instruments upon the market economy is not simple causation, as if one were pulling threads or pushing balls. Fiscal and monetary policy are transmitted from government to the economy through various mechanisms that work on the basis of the expectations of the players in the market. Once expectations are added to macro-economic decision-making, then the model in K is much too naïve. Researching expectations has become a major field in macroeconomics, as they are highly relevant for how the basic parameters in the economy – prices, wages, interest rates, bank lending, etc. – react to government stimuli in the form of fiscal and monetary policy. These expectations have been modelled differently, from adaptive expectations to rational ones. The publication by J. Muth of the first paper in rational expectations theory stimulated the emergence of a whole new way of thinking about macroeconomics, elaborated especially by Robert Lucas (see Romer, 1996; Romp, 1997).

The relevance of adding expectations, adaptive or rational ones, to the model K appears when one realizes that expectations can undo the policy impact aimed at by government. How this happens will become transparent when we move to the early criticism of Keynesianism in the form of monetarism. Government may try to impact upon expectations but then government needs a strategy against the players in the market economy, with the implications that macroeconomics becomes applied game theory. Especially fascinating is the question whether government should employ a rule-based strategy or a discretionary strategy or mix the two. Actually, government may have a larger impact upon the economy if it lets the players guess what strategy it will choose, as unanticipated policy changes have a larger effect than anticipated ones.

(3) *Financial markets*: The model K is a model of the real economy, identifying how total production is determined. Much of the economy belongs, however, to the financial economy, i.e. the markets for exchange, equity and bonds. Surely, the financial economy has an impact upon the real economy. But why is it not then included somehow in the model determining total output? Money figures prominently in the financial economy, but it hardly even occurs in the simple Keynesian model K. Even when extended by means of the LM schedule – the demand and supply of money – there is still little attention paid to the impact of financial markets upon the real economy.

Yet the financial economy is far from a mere mirror of the real economy. Its scope has become so huge that it has a profound impact upon the real economy, sometimes driving it. Globalization started with trade in the real economy but has moved to a much bigger dimension by means of the integration of the financial economies of the advanced countries. Here capital flows in the financial economy are today larger than the GDP of a country, which has enormous macro-economic consequences.

The flow of currencies from one country to another is thus only partly linked with the expansion of world trade. It is true that international trade has grown each year since the end of the Second World War, being responsible for much of the growth in affluence around the world, but capital flows attain their huge sizes today due to either long-term direct foreign investments (FDIs) or short-term financial investments in bonds, stocks and currencies. Macro-economic modelling today targets an open economy where the restrictions deriving from the need for external balance are very real ones, and where external restrictions on currencies set clear limits as to what can be done domestically. Here we have the argument of the irreconcilable triangle, meaning that governments cannot have much freedom of action on monetary policy when the policy is also pegging the currency at the same time as there are free capital flows. If capital flows are as important as the global economy implies and money plays a crucial role in the economy, as witnessed in the financial markets, then perhaps macroeconomics should include a theory about money and its macro-economic role. Let us move to monetarism.

Monetarism and new classical economics

It was when Keynesianism ran into mounting problems in the early 1970s that an alternative framework for macro-economic intervention was suggested. Actually, the basic framework had been around for some time but it was when Milton Friedman put it to use that it became highly relevant. It has been suggested that already David Hume had an understanding of the mechanism outlined in the monetarist model F:

(F) M X V = P X Y

where M = money supply, V = the velocity of transaction of money, P = the price level and Y = total output.

The model (F) played a prominent role already in *Cambridge Economics* but it was Friedman who pulled the policy implications out of the model. What Friedman suggested was that government policies were likely to have an impact upon M on the left-hand side in (F), but that impact would not likely in its turn move Y on the right-hand side of F. Instead, changes in M would lead to changes in P, especially inflation. This is not the place to enter into the various variations on the themes that can be elaborated upon, using the framework (F). What we must discuss is their policy implications for state intervention in relation to business cycle fluctuations. The most discussed application was the Friedman criticism of the Phillips curve, which had become central in Keynesianism as it developed in the 1950s and 1960s, but also his argument in favour of floating exchange rates became very influential.

For our purposes, we can examine two facets of monetarism that are relevant in a policy perspective. On the one hand, there is the negative argument that activist and discretionary policy-making only accomplishes inflation. On the other hand, there is the positive argument that rule-based policy targeting the level of inflation can reduce the fluctuations in the business cycle.

The Phillips curve: The idea that there is a trade-off between unemployment and inflation became very popular when such a relationship was statistically established by Phillips in an empirical study. Its theoretical foundations were more shaky, but it could be included in a Keynesian revised macro model where finally money was given a larger role to play. It was already understood that total output was linked to employment in a direct way – Okun's Law. And one could interpret the interaction of macro demand and supply curves in such a way that output could in the short run be pushed higher by demand policies but it would lead to some degree of inflation.

The nature of the Phillips curve is such that it presents a number of policy options for governments when conducting macro-economic policy. In principle, government could choose any combination of inflation and unemployment suggested by the negative relationship in Figure 9.4.

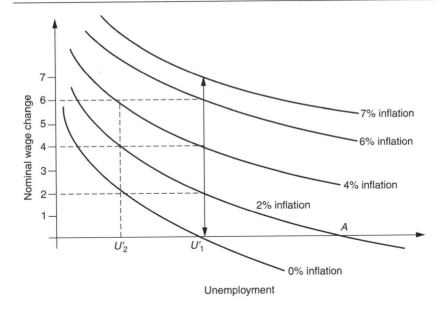

Figure 9.4 The Phillips curve

Thus, starting from Figure 9.4 it has been suggested that right-wing governments would pursue a policy mix of low inflation and high unemployment whereas a socialist government would have the opposite preferences, or a policy mix of inflation and unemployment. The Friedman analysis by including adaptive expectations of the players came up with an entirely different conclusion, which shook Keynesianism in its foundations.

In an expectations-augmented macro-economic model, government policies will only have an impact as long as the players in the economy have not had time to react. Once they realize what is going on, they may take action that more or less undoes the impact of the policy. Friedman suggested that the economy moves from, for instance, a to b after a government stimulus but then reverts back to c due to the reactions of the players in the economy once they realize what is going on. Since the real wage, w/p, has fallen due to the rise in inflation, unemployment will return to its starting point before the stimulus. A new attempt to reduce unemployment would only involve a similar travel, from c to d to e – the Phillips curve is in reality a straight vertical line starting from the NAIRU equilibrium.

This approach to state intervention is much less optimistic than the Keynesian framework is. Governments can have little impact upon total output and they risk inducing inflation in the economy, which is a negative because it reduces economic activity, all other things being equal. The launch of this approach could not have been more timely, as many economies of the world were faced with the new phenomenon of stagflation, i.e. both high inflation and high unemployment, which was due not only to the oil crises but also to failed Keynesian policy-making. Let us turn to the positive argument within monetarism, which actually turned out to be less well founded than the negative argument.

The Money Supply Rules: Friedman had in mind a very simple relationship between money supply and economic activity, which was implemented institutionally in the form of strong and independent central banks. An economy needs a certain amount of cash in order to make transactions possible, given a fixed rate of velocity of money. When too much money is injected into the economy by the Monetary Authority, then the risk of inflation is high, especially if also the velocity of transactions goes up. On the other hand, when too little money is around, then output falls – the Great Depression. Conclusion: Create a fixed policy rule which links the creation of money with the increase in GDP.

Monetarism as a policy regime at first worked marvellously but after a while problems emerged, some of which were severe in nature. On the one hand, it became increasingly difficult to tell what money was and how its supply should be measured and monitored. Alternative concepts of money were suggested but it did not really help to have a choice between M1 and M6, if neither of them could effectively be monitored. If the measurement of money proved such a daunting task, then how could it effectively be controlled? At the end of the day, monetarism went back to the standard monetary policy techniques of interest rate manipulation, either directly or by open market operations.

Monetarism seems to suffer from a certain degree of triviality, in saying that money and output are correlated. Well, this is hardly a profound truth since output is measured in, transacted by and stored by means of money. Thus, when little money is around, output falls. And when a lot of money is around, people want to buy so much that prices rise. A more consistent alternative to Keynesianism was to be found in *New Classical Economics*, which also suggests entirely different policy recommendations.

Strictly speaking, state intervention in relation to the business cycle is neither necessary nor desirable if one adheres to the perspective on the economy that adherents of New Classical Economics propagate. Although this school involves a clear return to ways of thinking before the so-called Keynesian revolution, it contains a wide variety of new ideas coming out of rational expectations economics. The strong belief that markets always clear, finding their equilibria after a disturbance, typical of classical economics, is here combined with the idea that players are driven by rational expectations. Thus, markets will adjust much more quickly than in classical economics and with much less pain.

In the Lucas interpretation of New Classical Economics the business cycle is not simply ignored or explained away. Business cycles are not conceived of as monetary aberrations nor as Schumpeterian selection processes. The business cycle is real in the sense that output changes due to unanticipated shocks. However, once these are fully realized the players in the economy take the necessary steps, meaning that markets will clear and there will be no involuntary unemployment. There is no need for government intervention, even if it were the case that state intervention works. The Lucas position in macroeconomics presents the most systematic rejection of any conception of government as fine-tuning the economy. In the short-run perspective, governments are weak in relation to the economy, as the key variables are determined by market forces. The whole idea of counter-cyclical policy-making is unworkable.

Does inflation matter?

Let us look at the key factor in both monetarism and New Classical Economics, namely inflation. Both monetarism and New Classical Economics connect good economic performance with a low level of inflation. How can this claim be supported by evidence? First we describe the country variation in inflation rates. How does inflation occur around the world? Table 9.1 suggests a few clues as to how inflation differs between economies.

The country variation is substantial, as some countries display very low numbers whereas others experience hyperinflation. Hyperinflation is characteristic of Latin America, the former Soviet Union countries and Sub-Saharan Africa. Low levels of inflation are to be found in occidental countries. We ask secondly if inflation matters, and Table 9.2 has the relevant data on this question.

The correlations in Table 9.2 give a weak support for the key hypothesis that inflation is negative for economic development. This is all reduced-form evidence, indicating that the higher the inflation rate the worse economic performance tends to be.

One may use two basic types of empirical evidence to test the inflation

Table 9.1 Inflation 1961–98 based on yearly averages

Region	1961–73	1973–90	1990–98	1995–98
Occidental	5.0	13.8	3.8	–
CEE and CIS	–	35.4	161.7	53.4
Central and Latin America	11.1	188.7	124.2	16.2
Sub-Saharan Africa	4.0	17.5	15.6	145.5
Arab World	4.0	16.4	23.2	19.3
South Asia	5.3	10.5	12.6	12.6
South East Asia	31.2	8.7	8.5	11.8
Mean	9.1	54.5	41.6	45.7
N	64	88	95	117
Eta square	0.124	0.156	0.146	0.033
Significance	0.250	0.029	0.027	0.711

Source: World Bank (2000a)

Table 9.2 Inflation and economic outcomes: correlations

Economic outcomes	Coeffs	Inflation: 1961–73		Inflation: 1973–90		Inflation: 1990–98		Inflation: 1995–98	
		Total	Excluded	Total	Excluded	Total	Excluded	Total	Excluded
GNP/capita growth	r	−0.17	−0.29	−0.35	−0.19	−0.04	−0.05	−0.26	−0.38
	sig	0.102	0.019	0.001	0.048	0.358	0.320	0.003	0.000
GNP/capita (Atlas)	r	−0.14	−0.07	−0.15	−0.21	−0.12	−0.37	−0.098	−0.38
	sig	0.147	0.307	0.089	0.031	0.131	0.000	0.171	0.000
GNP/capita (PPP)	r	−0.15	−0.05	−0.15	−0.17	−0.11	−0.36	−0.11	−0.37
	sig	0.123	0.356	0.093	0.071	0.159	0.000	0.127	0.000

Note: Total column = includes all cases. Excluded column = cases with hyperinflation, i.e. higher than 100% is excluded from the correlation analysis

argument. First, *structural model evidence* examines whether one variable affects another by using a model suggesting a channel through which this variable affects the other. Second, there is *reduced-form evidence* concerning whether one variable has an effect on another and it refers directly to the relationship between the two variables. The structural model approach offers an understanding of how the connection between two variables (inflation/output) works. If the structure is correct, i.e. it contains the entire transmission mechanism linking two variables, then the structural model approach has a major advantage over the reduced-form approach. Thus, the approach is better than the reduced-form approach if the correct structure of the model is known. However, structural model evidence is only as good as the structural model it is based on. Structural models about inflation and input state the transmission mechanisms wrongly, bypassing, for example, important factors. In other words, one may reject the interpretation of evidence from many structural models because one believes that the channels of the influence of inflation upon the economy are not known (Mishkin, 1998).

The main advantage of *reduced-form evidence* is that no restrictions are imposed upon the way inflation affects the economy. If the transmission mechanism is not fully known, then one may still observe the effect of inflation by looking at whether changes in inflation correlate highly with changes in affluence and economic growth.

The key objection to reduced-form evidence is that it may misleadingly suggest that changes in inflation cause changes in, for example, economic growth when that is not the case. Correlations do not necessarily imply causation. The fact that the change in one variable is linked to another does not necessarily mean that one variable causes the other. There may be reverse causation and this can lead to misleading conclusions when interpreting correlations. Another possibility is that an outside factor, yet unknown, could be the driving force behind two variables that move together.

One cannot say that reduced-form evidence is preferable to structural model evidence or vice versa. The structural model approach used offers an understanding of how the economy works. If the structure of the model is not correctly specified, leaving out important parts of the transmission mechanism, then it is more misleading than illuminating. The reduced-form approach does not restrict the way inflation affects the economy and may be more likely to see the full effect of inflation upon other economic aggregates. However, reduced-form evidence cannot rule out reverse causation or the possibility that an outside factor drives changes in both output and money.

Conclusion

In political economy the state is given certain functions or roles in the economy. However, what is the motivation that drives governments to accomplish these in the best manner possible? Do governments have knowledge enough? And do governments really wish to achieve optimal solutions? Asking questions like these leads to the opposition between two models of the state: welfare economics and the *Public Choice* approach. Since state action is always what behaviour governments decide to engage in, the problem of the motivation of politicians is crucial for how governments impact upon the economy. However, even when governments wish to improve upon economic performance it is far from certain that their policies have the intended effects.

Governments can have a positive impact upon the economy in the long run by creating a favourable climate for economic development in accordance with a model of sustainable and balanced growth underlining state spending. However, governments cannot undo the business cycle or change economic output in the short run. However, the opposite is not true, namely that governments cannot harm the economy. When governments act to stimulate the economy, then they will only increase the level of inflation. When they act to disinflate the economy, then their actions are already anticipated by the market.

The extremely negative view of the state in some recent literature is, in our view, more relevant to Third World governments than to First World countries. In several countries in Africa, Asia and Latin America one observes governments that conduct revenue-maximizing strategies with often disastrous long-term effects on the economy and the country. However, tax or budget-maximizing strategies work only in the short run, as their negative implications also hurt governments in the long run. In democracies with well-institutionalized party competition, there are brakes upon these strategies of politicians and bureaucrats.

The interaction between government and markets is now modelled as a game, both in New Classical Economics and New Keynsian Economics

(Romp, 1997). The problem concerns the co-ordination between government and the firms in terms of expectations about unemployment and inflation both in the short-run and the long-run perspectives. Failure to co-ordinate may result from time inconsistency i.e. the contradiction between expections about the short-run and long-run perspectives. In a global market economy co-ordination becomes even more difficult as governments become interdependent in their policies.

It remains an issue whether government can increase macro efficiency in the market economy. A recent argument maintains, however, that

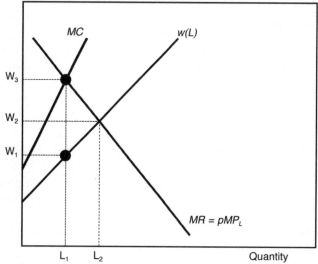

Figure 9.5   Monopsony

government can undo one form of micro efficiency, monopsony (Figure 9.5). If there is one buyer of labour, then he/she would buy L_1 amount and pay the salary W_1. Government can intervene and introduce a minimum wage at W_2, although not increasing the number of employed to L_2.

PART III

Governance and Globalization

The state appears in many forms. In classical political economy the separation between the Guardian State, the Infrastructure State and the Welfare State was much discussed with the view to demarcate what was to be done by government and what could be left to the market. The theory of socialism added the provision of private goods to this framework without delivering a convincing theory of how governments could operate the necessary production systems. Finally, German political economy identified state-led economic development as an additional theory about the public and the private. Where do these ideas about state and market leave us today when the economies of the world are interwoven into a global market economy?

In a global perspective the command economy as well as the model of South East Asian development belong to the past. Globalization is at odds with the strong autarchy typical of the command economy as well as with the state intervention of the economic nationalism characteristic of the South East Asian model. In a global market economy borders have to be open, the playing field must be levelled and government cannot direct the economy in any other way than guaranteeing the rules of the game impartially. Governments cannot give favours to their own enterprises and they cannot pick the winners by means of an industrial policy. Countries that significantly retain such practices will lose out.

Adapting to the global market economy is often a difficult process for the governments of the world. The lead of the occidental world (Western Europe, North America and Oceania) derives much from the fact that these states have come far in this adaptation process. Latin America has taken giant strides during the 1990s, whereas Africa and the Arab World lag behind. Interestingly, globalization with its principles of no discrimination, state neutrality and free capital flows presents a formidable challenge to South East Asia, where remnants of both the command economy and economic nationalism are to be found. Can market socialism in China really continue as it does now with formidable economic growth? One may ask this, especially as China seeks entrance to the organizations of the global market economy. And the transformation of the economies of Japan, Taiwan, South Korea, Singapore and Malaysia after the Asian crisis in 1997 away from *state dirigism* is still unfinished at the turn of the century.

The next three chapters will analyse global governance. They deal with challenges, responses and reforms of global political coordination.

CHAPTER 10

Challenges to Governments from Globalization

Introduction

Just as the domestic market economy, the global market economy needs state governance. In reality, the challenges to governance become even bigger when the market is truly global. On the one hand the need for co-ordination increases as the market economy becomes global. On the other hand political co-ordination becomes more difficult as complexity increases. Thus, trade and investments link the country economies more and more. Financial integration has benefited immensely from the New Economy and the interlinkages between the stock markets of the world. How, then, about political co-ordination among the governments of the states of the world?

Governments in the states of the world acting as the guarantor of the global market economy must restrain the crime economy, facilitate exchanges across borders, reduce the threat and disruptive consequences from war as well as mitigate the burdens of world poverty. At their disposal they have certain national resources but also the system of international organizations of various kinds. Let us talk first about the challenges and then examine the remedies.

Restraining the crime economy

The logic of reneging entails that one can do better in the crime economy than in the market economy. As the borderline between honest and corrupt business is floating, especially in the global market economy, the temptation to cross into the crime economy is truly large. Sometimes the market economy itself is described with characteristics that apply more to the crime economy, which is hardly clarifying. Thus, it is said that world capitalism is a casino economy where illegal or amoral practices are very much occurring (Strange, 1997), as states have retreated leaving the field open to markets (Strange, 1996), driven by mad money (Strange, 1998).

Yet, business is not crime and the global market economy is not wild capitalism. The global market economy faces a number of challenges, one of which is to make the border between legal and illegal practices more transparent. This may include making countries less vulnerable to speculative attacks against their currencies, but financial opportunism is not a crime. The problems stemming from the crime economy are of such a size that they call for attention by governments, especially when crime is organized internationally. The global economy makes international crime easier, not because it is mainly illegal activities itself but because economic activities become more difficult to supervise.

One may speak of the international crime economy, as people are based in one country but conduct their illegal business in other countries. Cross-border crime becomes very lucrative, as the probability of getting caught reduces when a border is crossed before or after the crime. This applies especially to money laundering as well as to the smuggling of people, but it is also true of theft, for instance the organized stealing of luxury cars. Some types of crime activity have always had this migratory character, such as drug trafficking, which may involve the transfer of drugs from one airport to another before it ends up on the street.

International crime takes place because for a certain group of people it pays more to operate in the illegal economy than in the legal one. With globalization the stakes increase, as profits from illegal business go up while the probability of getting caught goes down. When there is more money to get hold of, more people join in. Thus, the global crime economy includes not only petty theft, but the main players are organized crime syndicates, sometimes with links to politicians, trade unions and even army officials. Corruption is affected by the growth of the international crime economy, as organized crime may use the support or negligence of officials in order to facilitate their business.

The state response to international crime has not been entirely efficient, mainly because states have to respect country borders. It is true that co-operation between the police of various countries has increased considerably. A special organization has been set up for facilitating cross-border collaboration – Interpol.

Facilitating exchange

When economic activities do not take place in the underground economy or (worse) in the crime economy, they enter the domestic economies or the global market economy. The separation between domestic activities and global activities used to refer to the occurrence of trade across borders. In the global market economy this separation has become much less connected with the movement of goods across borders than with creating a global market economy run by similar rules. Although trade in goods represents a large proportion of world trade, the trade in services across borders is rapidly becoming a huge section in the global market economy. How is exchange in the global market economy to be organized from an institutional point of view, especially the trade in services?

Institutionalizing trade has come a long way during the post-war period, culminating in the creation of the Word Trade Organization (WTO) in 1995, located in Geneva. The WTO system came out of the General Agreement on Tariffs and Trade (GATT) framework, which started in 1967 with ongoing deliberations about the conditions for world trade, aimed at the lowering of barriers to trade. The GATT rounds ended with the conclusion of a comprehensive document on world trade in goods, to be implemented by the WTO. The institutionalization of trade in services remains to be done. Its relevance is growing with the speed with which the Internet economy grows.

One spectacular kind of internationalization of services is the widespread use of franchises. Franchising used to occur mainly in the food industry, but it has now spread to demographics, business services and the Internet. The largest franchiser in the world is the McDonald's Corporation with some 25,000 outlets in 119 countries. In the USA the number of franchisers is estimated at 3000, whereas France has 520 and Germany 500. Franchising is rapidly spreading to the Third World and it includes such activities as cleaning, food delivery and Internet services. Franchisers are thus using their websites to communicate with their franchisees and to seek out new ones.

Sometimes this interaction between franchiser and franchisee fails, as when it took McDonald's four years to remove its Paris franchisee. Franchising is a form of intellectual property right, which calls for international regulation, as it can be used to expand operations very quickly, in contrast to investing in new physical premises for starting your own operation which can be very time-consuming. Creating international rules for interaction between franchisers and franchisees is only one aspect that must be included in the regulation of services.

The WTO has taken on the task of facilitating exchange by creating and policing global norms for trade. It and its predecessor – the GATT framework – have accomplished much in lowering tariffs and abolishing quotas in relation to trade with goods, which was estimated at a staggering 5.5 billion dollars in 1999. The challenge for the WTO is now to attempt to extend free trade to the huge area of services, where trade was estimated at 1.3 billion dollars in 1999. An agreement – *Accord général sur le commerce des services* (AGCS) – was signed in Marrakesh in 1995, which invited the member countries of the WTO to discuss an approach for opening up free trade in a number of services.

Interestingly, the agreement mentions one area that is to be excluded, namely the services that are provided as part of the exercise of government power. Although one may discuss which services are truly part of government, the liberalization of services would comprise a number of services, both private and public. One set of services is to be found in infrastructure where, for instance, electricity supply could become the target for successful liberalization, but it requires rules not only about market access but also about state subventions. Another set of services with a large potential for liberalization is the health care area, but this forms part of government in several countries. The health care market is already very large within the countries that make up the WTO (roughly 2 trillion dollars), which makes it very attractive for liberalization, but about 76 per cent of the money comes from state budgets in one form or another.

The liberalization of services within the private sector has already advanced in certain areas, such as insurance and the banking sector. However, one is far away from a system where services can move freely across borders or people can move freely from a service in one country to a service in another, enjoying the same standard in each, for instance. The approach chosen in the *AGCS* is to distinguish between (i) the cross-border supply of services, (ii) the consumption of services abroad, (iii) the commercial presence of a service provider and (iv) the presence of physical persons in another country supplying services. To achieve a considerable amount of liberalization in all these aspects of the provision of services requires the resolution of many questions concerning common rules and standards.

Avoiding war

Economic activity is a form of peaceful interaction between buyers and sellers. It may well concern military hardware, as in the case of countries that are exporting a great deal of military equipment to other countries. The buying and selling of arms has increased steadily and is worth billions of dollars now. There are some chief exporting countries and some troubled areas of the world where countries import a lot of military hardware. This is trade, not war, but the risk is of course that all the weapons will be used one day for destructive purposes.

Peace not war promotes affluence. Periods of war bring about immense destruction of capital with the consequence that output falls dramatically. The long period of peace after the Second World War has been accompanied by a steady rise of output in the world economy – see Figure 10.1.

With an average growth rate in output in the world economy of about 3–4 per cent per year, the world economy is bound to double quickly. Figure 10.2 shows how output has grown almost seven times since 1970.

For the countries that have been to war during the post-war period the consequences have been dire indeed. Thus, the loss in affluence in Iraq, Serbia and many parts of Africa has been quite substantial. The theory that world capitalism feeds upon the buying and selling of arms to such an extent that war is necessary to keep the wheels going amounts to a gross exaggeration. Affluence results first and foremost from peace and trade.

The growth in output according to Figure 10.2 is closely connected with the steady growth in world trade. Along with the growth in output of the world economy, imports and exports have taken an increasingly larger part of the GDP of the countries of the world. Thus, the impex indicator measuring the size of imports and exports of GDP has risen step by step

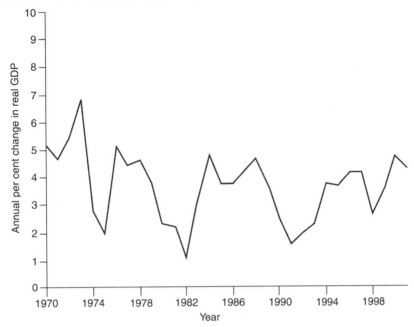

Figure 10.1 Expansion of the world economy 1970–2000: yearly GDP growth
Source: WEO data, September 2000

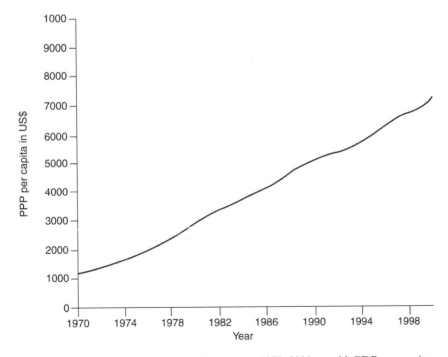

Figure 10.2 Expansion of the world economy 1970–2000: world GDP per capita
Source: WEO data, September 2000

from 20 to 50 per cent – see chapter 2. The importance of trade liberalization cannot be doubted. One may disagree about the choice of strategy for accomplishing it, the WTO framework being based upon multilateral reductions whereas bilateral agreements also constitute a possibility. The great advances made in the long negotiations leading up to the GATT agreement were made possible through the multilateral approach. However, trade liberalization has also been accomplished through the bilateral approach, used extensively by Great Powers such as the USA and the EU. The most conspicuous evidence in favour of trade liberalization is to be found in the development in world trade. Every year since 1950 world trade has increased in volume.

Recent developments in trade theory focus much upon the distinction between inter-industry trade and intra-industry trade. Whereas traditional trade theory using comparative advantage or factor endowment theory emphasized the benefits from inter-industry trade, more recent theory of international trade deals with intra-industry trade based upon economies of scale and imperfect competition. World trade data supports the intra-industry argument, as trade is most extensive between industrial nations trading similar goods with each other. One understands the worry of Third World countries when they look at data indicating the dominance of trade between the so-called TRIANGLE, or North America, the EU and South East Asia. The role of Africa in international trade is vanishingly small, considering that it harbours some 650 million people.

The market economy is so large that civil expenditures outweigh military ones. It was when Japan turned away from military adventures and focused upon becoming an economic superpower that the affluence of the country started to increase dramatically, taking Japan to the heights of inclusion in the set of rich countries. The same is true of China, which can only close some of the gap with Japan if it stays away from high military risks. This is not to deny that several giant firms are heavily involved in defence contracts that provide for thousands of jobs. And the line of separation between military and civil expenditures is far from transparent, even in Western Europe where, for instance, the aeronautics industry takes both civil and military contracts.

What is crystal-clear is that large-scale war would be extremely damaging to the world economy. The dismantling of the Soviet Union has eliminated the risk of a new world war, but there are several areas in the world where major wars could erupt: the Middle East, Central Africa, the Horn of Africa, Pakistan-India and South East Asia. In addition, there are areas where chronic civil wars are conducted: Colombia, West Africa, Angola, and Central Asia. In all these cases war brings destruction and economic decline.

When a war would threaten the supplies of vital resources such as oil, then its negative impact upon the economy can be observed in the dramatic swings on the financial markets at the major bourses of the world. Such wars have such a profound impact upon the world economy that they could trigger a world depression. The critical question for the global market economy is whether there is enough world governance in place to prevent major wars from occurring in places that are critical for the world economy. This is, first, a matter for the United Nations and its Security Council and, second, for the international community.

According to one theory, war and political instability is driven mainly by the inegalitarian distribution of wealth in the world. Thus, civil wars occur in the poor countries of the world. Sometimes the crime economy and civil war join forces as in the case of whole countries being drawn into drug trafficking. The emergence of the new feudalism consisting of warlords in Africa and Asia is also linked with world poverty, as the only occupation for far too many is to carry arms and use them to get revenues. Personal ties threaten the state in many places in the world, where poverty feeds clientelism. When one speaks of the distribution of resources and the 'division of the cake' in the world economy, then one is confronted with the precariousness of the situation of labour in Third World countries.

Protecting labour

The revenues that economic activity generates can be divided between the so-called factors of production – land, capital and labour – in very different ways. In an advanced economy a huge part of the 'cake' that each country 'bakes' every year ends up with labour. This generates purchasing power and stimulates economic progress. The division between labour and capital reflects their respective contribution to the GDP, which can be derived from a so-called Cobb–Douglas production function of the type discussed in chapter 9. About 70 per cent of the GDP goes to labour whereas 30 per cent ends up as payments to capital and land, generally speaking. In Third World countries the division is slightly different, as wages constitute a smaller cost than the costs for capital or land.

The weakness of labour outside the advanced economies of the world is the major factor in explaining poverty. As long as millions work at low wages there is little hope for an improvement in living standards. Although unemployment and exclusion account for much of world poverty, it is the low salary levels among those working in Third World countries which is the main cause of poverty. If purchasing power were stronger with those who have a job, their spending would trickle down and generate economic development. Wages are low in the Third World because work is simple, the supply of labour is enormous and the working classes are not organized.

It is true that wages will reflect the market value of its marginal product. Thus, if what labour produces are low-quality simple products, then salaries will stay at a low level. Wages will be driven down when work is so simple that anyone can do it. With millions of people looking for a job in Third World countries, salaries must be driven downwards by competition.

Table 10.1 Human rights conventions: number of conventions where countries are a party in 1999

Macro region	ILO conventions: Number	Human right conventions: Number
Occidental	4.2	18.1
CEE and CIS	3.1	14.3
Central and Latin America	4.4	18.0
Sub-Saharan Africa	4.2	17.9
Arab World	3.3	14.6
South Asia	3.9	16.3
South East Asia	4.1	17.7
Mean	3.9	16.8

Note: The maximum number of ILO conventions covered here is six; the total number of human rights conventions covered here is 24
Source: US State Department (2000), Appendix C

However, wages need not be exploitation salaries, if labour can make its voice heard. Crucial for a fair division of the 'cake' is the permission of trade unions to be active. Trade unions aim at raising salaries and preventing exploitation. They meet with varying degrees of success in their work, depending upon the morale of the trade union as well as the resistance from the employers. In many Third World countries the rights of labour are not recognized. Some regimes actively persecute trade union people whereas others just see to it that free trade unions are not organized. Table 10.1 presents data that measures the respect for trade union rights as they are reflected in the acceptance of a number of ILO conventions, as well as the number of human rights conventions which countries are parties to around the globe. Signing is one thing, implementing another.

Merely organizing labour in the Third World will not increase salaries by much, but it could counteract the tendencies towards exploitation of children and women as well as reduce the frequency of injuries in working life. It has been argued that trade unions belong to the Western culture and that they are at odds with other systems of values such as Islam, Hinduism or Asian values. Such rhetoric is often just a rationalization of the unwillingness of those in power to face the legitimate claims of organized labour. Improving the conditions under which trade unions may work is an imperative for raising the standard of living in the Third World.

Fighting poverty

Much is said about fighting poverty in the world. But there is little evidence to the effect that poverty is decreasing. By 'poverty' we mean absolute poverty, or the number of people who live under a certain level of income, which is necessary for an acceptable quality of life – the poverty line. Income

Table 10.2 Human poverty by macro regions

Region	HPI1–99	HPI1–00	HPI2–99	HPI2–00
Occidental			12.1	11.2
CEE and CIS				
Central and Latin America	15.7	15.1		
Sub-Saharan Africa	41.2	39.4		
Arab World	24.7	24.4		
South Asia	38.4	36.9		
South East Asia	23.3	20.6	12.0	11.2
Mean	29.5	27.9	12.1	11.2

Sources: UNDP (1999) and (2000)

differences in the relative sense of 'poverty' can never be eradicated simply because it is a relative measure. A number of measures including the Gini index have been constructed to tap how gross national income is divided in a country. What we will speak of here attempts to measure poverty more properly, however.

First we rely on the human poverty index developed by UNDP – see Table 10.2. The human poverty index (HPI) brings together four basic dimensions of human life – a long and healthy life, knowledge, economic provisioning and social inclusion. The higher the value of the index, the larger the proportion of people living in poverty. The UNDP has developed two separate indexes, one covering the developing countries (HPI1) and the other one covering the industrialized countries (HPI2). Massive poverty is a characteristic feature of Sub-Saharan Africa and South Asia, where almost half the population lives in dismal conditions. Also Arab countries have considerable poverty.

Another way of approaching human poverty is to consider the proportion of the population in a country having an income below what is considered to be the poverty line. Again it is necessary to distinguish between developing countries (Natpov1) and industrialized countries (Natpov2). The data presented in Table 10.3 thus only gives a very crude picture of people living in poverty, since the poverty lines defined may vary substantially across countries. Still it is apparent that poverty is much more of a reality in Sub-Saharan Africa than is the case in the industrialized countries, even when one considers the various contexts.

In several countries, close to half of the population lives under or at this poverty line. These countries include several African ones, India, Pakistan, Bangladesh and Indonesia, as well as the Philippines and some Latin American countries including Brazil. The difference between these many millions of people and the very rich people in the advanced countries is such that redistribution becomes a global issue. But how could this redistribution be done? The case for direct redistribution in the form of foreign aid has been met with less and less acceptance. However, there are certain policies that could help. One strategy is debt forgiveness.

Table 10.3 Population living below certain income poverty lines as a percentage of the population

Region	Natpov1–99	Natpov1–00	Natpov2–99	Natpov2–00
Occidental			10.7	10.7
CEE and CIS			37.1	37.1
Central and Latin America	31.6	32.4		
Sub-Saharan Africa	42.5	45.2		
Arab World	13.8	20.5		
South Asia	32.5	34.7		
South East Asia	27.8	23.0	3.7	3.7
Mean	33.0	34.9	23.7	23.7

Sources: UNDP (1999) and (2000)

The debt burden is a real problem for many Third World countries, as indicated by the ratio between debt and GDP as well as between debt payments and export income – see Table 10.4. The two indicators employed here – EDT = total debt stock and INT = interest payments – in relation to GDP and exports of goods and services displays no major changes for the period covered here, i.e. from 1980 and the 1990s. One may observe that the debt burden has increased continuously in order to double in about 20 years. However, debt payments have not gone up as much. Debt payments tend to constitute about 7 per cent of the export value of goods and services.

The accumulated debt in some countries is so huge that debt can no longer be serviced. When this is true, donor countries could just as well write off the entire debt. Several Third World countries have to use a large part of

Table 10.4 Debt indicators for the developing countries

Year	EDT/GNP	INT/GNP	EDT/XGS	INT/XGS
1980	20.30	1.60	88.40	7.10
1988	35.10	2.10	176.90	10.60
1989	33.90	1.90	169.90	9.30
1990	34.20	1.70	162.50	7.80
1991	37.80	1.80	171.20	8.00
1992	38.10	1.60	170.90	7.20
1993	40.10	1.60	177.20	6.90
1994	40.30	1.60	168.00	6.60
1995	38.90	1.80	149.10	6.90
1996	36.00	1.70	137.40	6.40
1997	34.90	1.60	129.00	6.10
1998	42.10	2.00	147.90	7.00
1999	41.50	2.20	136.60	7.20

Note: EDT = total debt stocks; INT = debt payments; GNP = Gross National Product; XGS = exports of goods and services
Sources: World Bank (various years): *Global Development Finance*

their export incomes upon the service of foreign debt. A generous policy of debt forgiveness would allow these countries to use these resources for other purposes, e.g. investments in infrastructure.

Another strategy is to improve the terms of trade between advanced countries and Third World countries. This can only come about through the removal of hindrances to trade. If Third World countries could have complete access to the markets of the advanced countries for all their products, then they would be able to export much more, specialize more and earn more income. Further reductions of tariffs and quotas in agricultural products and textiles are essential to several Third World countries, especially if dumping practices of advanced countries are to be avoided.

Finally, there is foreign aid. The target of 1 per cent of GDP to be given by a donor country to a receiver country has never been met in practice, as very few countries have displayed this kind of generosity. Many rich countries provide substantially less foreign aid and they also 'attach strings' to whatever assistance they provide. Table 10.5 provides a listing of the DAC member-countries in accordance with the foreign aid they provide, where 'DAC' stands for the Development Assistance Committee within the OECD.

Table 10.5   Foreign aid (as a percentage of GNP) 1996–99: DAC member-countries

Country	1996	1997	1998	1999
Australia	0.28	0.28	0.27	0.26
Austria	0.24	0.26	0.22	0.24
Belgium	0.34	0.31	0.35	0.30
Canada	0.32	0.34	0.29	0.28
Denmark	1.04	0.97	0.99	1.00
Finland	0.34	0.33	0.32	0.32
France	0.48	0.45	0.40	0.38
Germany	0.32	0.28	0.26	0.26
Greece	–	–	0.15	0.21
Ireland	0.31	0.31	0.30	0.31
Italy	0.20	0.11	0.20	0.15
Japan	0.20	0.22	0.28	0.35
Luxembourg	0.43	0.55	0.65	0.64
Netherlands	0.81	0.81	0.80	0.79
New Zealand	0.21	0.26	0.27	0.27
Norway	0.85	0.86	0.91	0.91
Portugal	0.21	0.25	0.24	0.25
Spain	0.22	0.24	0.24	0.23
Sweden	0.84	0.79	0.72	0.70
Switzerland	0.34	0.34	0.32	0.35
UK	0.27	0.26	0.27	0.23
USA	0.12	0.09	0.10	0.10
Total DAC	0.25	0.22	0.23	0.24

Source: DAC data (OECD, 2000)

The international community has been more willing to engage in specific actions that help under specified circumstances. Thus, a number of operations have been conducted against famines and natural catastrophes. It seems as if the fight against poverty lacks an understanding of both ends and means as rich countries hesitate simply to provide resources without any conditions. All the facts indicate that poverty is increasing, not decreasing.

Yet there is lots of cynicism tied up with world poverty. Everyone is concerned but few are willing to do something and even fewer know what to do. Can one blame poverty upon poor people, when they take actions, which increase the probability of more of poverty? Can outsiders take action against poverty when the country with poverty does little or nothing? Perhaps these questions are merely posed in such a manner as to call for a negative attitude towards intervention. But poverty is a challenge to the whole world and its consequences are felt all over the globe. The problem is only that the instruments are not available when it comes to doing something, especially for governments outside the country in question.

The other side of the coin is, of course, the affluence of the rich countries. Poverty in the sense of the Third World context does not exist in the advanced world. It is not absolute poverty which is at stake in the rich countries, but relative poverty or the skewed distribution of income and wealth. Within a country one can ask whether a policy of redistribution may meet with sufficient approval from a majority of the electorate. One may also ask whether policies of redistribution work, in the sense that they really accomplish changes in the distribution of income and wealth to the benefit of the poor. In any case, these questions are hardly relevant in a global context today, where there is little sympathy for global redistribution. Any improvement of the condition of the poor countries must come from their own efforts at reintegration in the world economy, although rich countries may help in various ways.

Resources: the energy problem

The earth hosts more than 6 billion people. At least half of them live in what we have called absolute poverty, struggling every day to survive. Less than 1 billion live in rich countries. The difference in average living standards between the rich countries and the poor countries is such that were all the people in poverty to live like the people in affluence, then the resources of the earth would be used up within a time period of roughly ten years. Thus, poverty is built into the entire economic system of the globe in the sense that absolute poverty can only be eradicated by the most far-reaching changes in the global market economy, involving – it seems – a lowering of the consumption levels in the rich countries.

The scarcity problem number one is not food as in the neo-Malthusian approach but energy, more specifically petrol. The world energy consumption is still very much relying upon the use of oil in various ways, but oil is

Table 10.6 World crude oil reserves 1999 (billion barrels)

Region and country	Oil & Gas Journal	World Oil
North America	**76.8**	**55.0**
Mexico	47.8	28.4
USA	21.0	21.0
Central and South America	**89.5**	**63.4**
Venezuela	72.6	45.5
Western Europe	**18.9**	**19.8**
Norway	10.9	11.9
UK	5.2	5.2
Eastern Europe and Former USSR	**58.9**	**67.9**
Russia	48.6	55.1
Middle East	**673.6**	**627.1**
Iran	89.7	92.9
Iraq	112.5	99.0
Kuwait	96.5	94.7
Saudi Arabia	261.5	261.4
United Arab Emirates	97.8	63.9
Africa	**75.4**	**77.2**
Libya	29.5	26.9
Nigeria	22.5	22.5
Far East and Oceania	**43.0**	**57.1**
China	24.0	33.5
World	**1033.2**	**967.5**

Source: Energy Information Administration, 2000a: 277

an exhaustible resource, which is rapidly being exhausted. For each 4 litres of petrol that are consumed only 1 new litre is found. The price of petrol must go up in the future. The question then becomes whether the global economy is strong enough to find alternative sources of energy as well as to economize upon energy better. Table 10.6 has information about the oil resources, known and estimated unknown, according to different estimates.

Almost 30 per cent of known world oil resources are to be found in Saudi Arabia. Other countries with considerable oil reserves are Iran, Iraq, Kuwait, the United Arab Emirates, Russia, Venezuela and China.

Total production stood at 65 million barrels a day, which could be sold at the going market price. This is a sharp increase from 20 million barrels a day since 1960. Who produces all this petrol? Table 10.7 has information about this.

Although Saudi Arabia is the largest producer of oil, it is still a fact that the OPEC countries together produce less than 50 per cent. Table 10.8 shows where this oil ends up, which is very much in the advanced world and in China. The United States consumes 25% of world total consumption but it no longer has huge reserves.

Assume that the estimates in the *International Energy Outlook 2000* (Energy Information Administration, 2000b) of the forthcoming increase in

Table 10.7   World crude oil production 1960–99 (million barrels per day)

Country/Organization	1960	1965	1970	1975	1980	1985	1990	1995	1999
Total OPEC	**8.70**	**14.35**	**23.30**	**26.77**	**26.61**	**16.18**	**23.20**	**26.00**	**27.64**
Kuwait	1.69	2.36	2.99	2.08	1.66	1.02	1.18	2.06	1.90
United Arab Emirates	0	0.28	0.78	1.66	1.71	1.19	2.12	2.23	2.17
Saudi Arabia	1.31	2.21	3.80	7.08	9.90	3.39	6.41	8.23	7.83
Nigeria	0.02	0.27	1.08	1.76	2.06	1.50	1.81	1.99	2.13
Venezuela	2.85	3.47	3.71	2.35	2.17	1.68	2.14	2.75	2.83
Total Non-OPEC	**12.29**	**15.98**	**22.59**	**26.60**	**32.99**	**37.80**	**37.37**	**36.33**	**38.02**
Norway	0	0	0	0.19	0.53	0.79	1.70	2.77	3.02
Former Soviet Union/ Russia	2.91	4.79	6.99	9.52	11.71	11.59	10.98	6.00	6.07
USA	7.04	7.80	9.64	8.37	8.60	8.97	7.36	6.56	5.93
World	**20.99**	**30.33**	**45.89**	**52.83**	**59.60**	**53.98**	**60.57**	**62.33**	**65.66**

Source: Energy Information Administration, 2000a: 279

Table 10.8   World petroleum consumption 1960–99 (million barrels per day)

Country/Organization	1960	1965	1970	1975	1980	1985	1990	1995	1998
Total OECD	**15.78**	**22.81**	**34.49**	**38.82**	**41.41**	**37.23**	**40.82**	**44.96**	**46.98**
Germany	0.63	1.61	2.83	2.96	3.08	2.70	2.66	2.88	2.92
Japan	0.66	1.74	3.82	4.62	4.96	4.38	5.14	5.71	5.51
South Korea	0.01	0.03	0.20	0.31	0.54	0.57	1.03	2.03	2.00
UK	0.94	1.49	2.10	1.91	1.73	1.63	1.75	1.85	1.78
USA	9.80	11.51	14.70	16.32	17.06	15.73	16.99	17.72	18.92
Total Non-OECD	**5.56**	**8.33**	**12.32**	**17.38**	**21.66**	**22.87**	**25.06**	**24.91**	**26.66**
China	0.17	0.23	0.62	1.36	1.77	1.89	2.30	3.36	4.11
India	0.16	0.25	0.40	0.50	0.64	0.90	1.17	1.58	1.84
Former Soviet Union/ Russia	2.38	3.61	5.31	7.52	9.00	8.95	8.39	2.98	2.46
World	**21.34**	**31.14**	**46.81**	**56.20**	**63.07**	**60.10**	**65.98**	**69.87**	**73.64**

Source: Energy Information Administration, 2000b: 289

consumption of oil going from 73 million of barrels per day in 1997 to 112.8 million of barrels per day in 2020, and assume that the known reserves of oil in 1999 should be 1,000,000 million barrels are correct. Then by year 2020 slightly less than 70 per cent of these reserves would be used. Whether these different estimates are reasonably correct or not is difficult for us to have any opinion on. But what these figures suggest is that we are coming closer to a stage when we may foresee the end of mass use of oil, and unless alternative resources are found to replace oil, there will be serious implications for communications based upon oil and the industries producing vehicles for communication.

When comparing where the 77 billion barrels of oil are produced with where that oil is consumed one realizes quickly the dilemma of the Western powers, who have made themselves increasingly dependent upon supplies of petrol from Third World countries. It is true that the two oil crises in the 1970s made Western countries look for substitutes to petrol, but the increased dependency of the USA upon import of oil has not been sufficiently compensated by the production of North Sea oil.

Oil is certainly one source of energy. A considerable part of the energy supply of the world comes from other sources such as atomic energy, electricity (water), wind power, solar energy, etc. It has been estimated that energy from oil represents about 40 per cent of all the energy used. The implication is crystal-clear; namely that the world must find more oil resources in the near future, which cannot be done without collaboration between firms and governments. If the consumption of petrol stays at today's level, then it will take another 30 to 50 years before the oil resources have been completely exhausted. However, that will not happen, as the price adjustments will call forth a lower consumption of petrol as well as a more intensive search for new petrol. What is the role of the market, on the one hand and governments on the other hand in this process?

The market for petrol handles the short-term allocation of oil on the basis of the interaction of supply and demand, whereas the major production firms take the long-term decisions about the search for new wells. The governments in the oil-producing countries are very much involved in both decision-making in the short term and the long term. Many of the oil-producing firms are state enterprises or public joint-stock companies where the state is a majority shareholder. Policy-making in relation to the oil sector involves taking a vast set of considerations into account, covering everything from the drilling of oil to the selling of petrol. These matters are so important that governments do not leave them to market forces. These decisions have clear implications for peace and war between nations.

The global environment

The problems surrounding energy relate not only to securing a safe supply of it at reasonable prices. They also involve crucial questions concerning the environment. In a global perspective a number of environmental issues have received increasing attention during the last decade, some of which concern the use of combustibles for a variety of purposes. Global warming is one of the key problems of global environmental concern. A second one is the reduction in the ozone layer. Finally, there is the increasing pollution and destruction of wildlife and the oceans of the world – the tragedy of the commons.

The search for cheap energy explains a lot about global warming, as it is driven by the carbon dioxide emissions from the burning of fuel and coal. Paradoxically, the only solution to the problem with carbon dioxide emissions could be that the world runs out of petrol reserves, which may happen towards the end of the twenty-first century. The hole in the ozone layer depends again upon the emissions into the atmosphere of dangerous substances. The hole has now widened to such an extent that its reduction poses a real threat to mankind, because the ozone is necessary for keeping down the radiation from the sun, high levels of which can cause cancer in human beings. Should the hole widen dramatically, then mankind could face extinction.

The pressure from a huge world population upon nature and its wildlife has increased step by step. Thus, a number of animal species are close to extinction. The instrumental use of natural resources puts water in danger of being massively polluted. This is true for both the scarce water resources that are used for drinking purposes and for the oceans of salt water, which have become increasingly polluted.

Figures 10.3 to 10.4 display information about changes in the global environment over time, from 1970 to the end of the twentieth century.

There is no sign of any end to the increase in carbon emissions, which since 1970 have gone up by about 50 per cent. Two countries have exceptionally high emissions, namely the USA and China. Attempts at an international regulation of carbon emissions has so far proved unsuccessful, by means of, for example, the Kyoto Protocol.

The immense carbon emissions result in higher and higher concentration of toxic materials in the air – see, for example, Table 10.4 concerning the

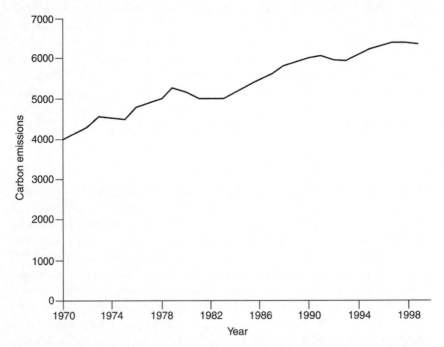

Figure 10.3   World carbon emission from fossil fuel burning (millions of tons of carbon)
Source: Brown *et al.*, 2000: 67

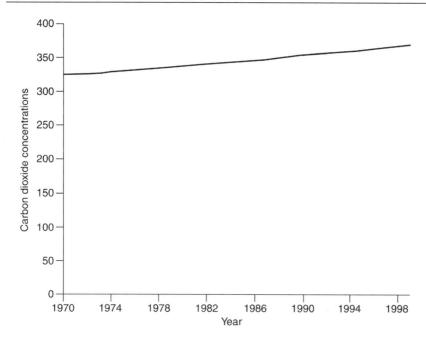

Figure 10.4 Atmospheric concentration of carbon dioxide in parts per million volume (ppmv) 1970–99
Source: Same as Figure 10.3

occurrence of carbon dioxide. This in turn drives the entire process of global warming, which is beginning to have such disastrous consequences for world climate.

The Intergovernmental Panel on Climate Change (IPCC) found in their 2000 report that the already existing negative predictions about the state of the global environment must be further emphasized. The average global temperature stands at about 14°C. The IPCC state that one may foresee the following:

1   Temperature increase in 2100 compared with 1990: 1.5–6.0 degrees.
2   Concentration of CO_2 in the atmosphere: 540–970 ppm.
3   Increase in the temperature of the globe: 0.4–0.8°C.
4   Higher sea and ocean level: 0.14–0.80 m.

With regard to global warming this amounts to a strong warning, as it had earlier been predicted that there would only be an increase of between 1–3.5°C. At the same time, the problem of the shrinking ozone layer is not going away. The hole in the ozone layer is large enough to threaten higher cancer risks for several countries.

Environmental problems have become politicized in almost all countries where free debate is institutionalized. Many countries have put in place ambitious environmental policies, meeting in some cases with a high degree of policy success in terms of concrete outcomes. One example that may be mentioned is the State of California where the fragile nature of this part of the USA has been protected through a variety of policies. However, this bright picture is not true of the situation in Eastern Europe or in many Third World countries. The key problem is represented by the collective action difficulties that were analysed in chapter 8.

Even if collective action problems can be overcome within a country, calling for a positive contribution from local and regional governments as well as central government, the most alarming signs of environmental degradation perhaps come from the measures of the global environment.

There have been two standpoints concerning the data presented above. On the one hand, it is argued that global warming and the holes in the ozone layer are not a cause of concern. The picture is far from as clear-cut as some people claim that these increases could be temporary. On the other hand, many people regard these phenomena as the major future challenges for the world community besides wars and poverty. It seems as if the last standpoint received a definitive confirmation by the disclosures in 2000 from a broad expert committee within the United Nations.

There is little else to do than to put one's faith into those responsible for international solutions to global environmental problems. Major agreements have been struck but they remain to be put into effect. Thus, conventions have been made at the Rio de Janeiro meeting in 1992 as well as at the Kyoto meeting in 1997. However, not much has been accomplished. The technical approach to the emissions of CO_2 amounts to a Coasean method based upon the allocation of specified limited rights to such emissions. When made operational, such rights could be traded between countries that pollute a lot and countries that pollute little. Such a market for emissions would ultimately reveal costs and be conducive to the use of techniques to control emissions.

Yet, the problem is reneging in the form of free riding as well as negligence in relation to treaties or agreements. How is one to implement such measures when free riding is a real possibility, not only for individuals but also for states? How are international solutions to global problems to be implemented when there is no world federation?

Conclusion

It is not difficult to list a set of major problems for the earth as it enters the period of globalization. Perhaps many more should be added to the list above. However, from our perspective – the governance of the global economy – the emphasis upon the problems in relation to just exchange, consumer purchasing power, the rights of labour, the growing energy scarcity and world pollution seems justified. They have in common that they affect the operations of the world markets and they call for state intervention in order to be handled, if not resolved.

The market mechanism is a very powerful tool for managing the allocation of certain resources. But its precious mechanism – voluntary exchange – needs state protection. When the markets become global, then some form of global state governance is necessary to facilitate exchange and block the spread of the crime economy. Labour is a key production factor in the market economy, but the circumstances under which workers participate in the global market place leave much that can be improved upon. Whether the global market economy can achieve not only efficiency but also justice depends to a large extent upon how this problem is handled. The difference between wild capitalism and the institutionalized market economy is closely connected with how labour is treated. It also has a bearing upon the burning problem of world poverty.

Yet there are limits to what the world markets can accomplish. The poverty question in the sense of absolute poverty or famines requires state intervention, at least in order to give access to the markets of the rich countries for the products from the poor countries of the world. Markets can handle the energy question only by allowing price to go up as scarcity increases. Government action may help in this adaptation process. The environmental problems of the globe are entirely outside the confines of the market economy, as the tragedy of the commons calls for global state intervention, but by which state? Finally, the global market place rests upon peace, but the hope for eternal peace on the earth remains just that, a wish.

CHAPTER 11

Structures of Global Governance

Introduction

Global governance is today entrusted to a patchwork of institutions comprising the nation-states on the one hand and the international organizations on the other. These institutions have emerged from separate developments in the past, each part having its own genesis. The key question is whether this pattern of different institutions for different world problems is enough to provide governance for the global market economy in the future. If changes are considered necessary, then one must also raise the question of the feasibility of various alternative governance schemes.

We will look at four of the key institutions for global governance. First, there is the regulation of war and peace within the United Nations (UN) framework and additional treaties. Second, three economic organizations are responsible for economic governance: the World Bank (WB), the International Monetary Fund (IMF) and the World Trade Organization (WTO). Third, regional governance has become an alternative to state and global governance, especially in Western Europe. Besides these three key elements in global governance, there is a whole set of international regimes and organizations, each looking into its own special matters. All of this amounts to a loosely structured system, which reflects the basic fact that nation-states are still the key players on the global political scene.

We will argue that this patchy framework has its own logic and that further advances in state integration are very difficult to achieve. The idea of a world federation is not a viable one, given all the diversity in ethnicity, religion and values between the states of the world. However, states may increasingly co-ordinate in order to protect the global market economy from which they derive so many benefits. Global governance is driven by considerations of both efficiency and equity according to the two main scholarly traditions in international politics, the Hobbesian perspective and the Grotius approach.

The goals of international co-ordination can be identified in two entirely different ways. On the one hand, one may look at the needs of mankind for collaboration between the states of the world – the Grotius approach. Here we find a number of important objectives from facilitating the operations of the world market place to protecting mankind from environmental disaster and dismal poverty like the occurrence of famines. On the other hand, world governance rests upon the key players in the global arena, the nation-states. And they have objectives of their own such as security and independence. This is the basic approach of Hobbes. The international legal order may be interpreted as a compromise between Grotius's and Hobbes's ideas, which involves a tension between altruistic mankind and selfish states that is at the core of today's efforts to further extend and deepen world governance.

Grotius's and Hobbes's perspectives

Today public international law contains a broad set of rules regulating the behaviour of the states of the world. Since states are to a considerable extent both the subjects and the objects of this legal regulation, one may argue that public international law is as intimately connected with the concept of the state as is municipal or national law. The political theory of public international law emerges with Grotius in the form of an argument about *Jus Gentium* at the very same time as the political philosophy of the state takes definitive form with Hobbes, focusing upon positive law as the commands of the sovereign. Grotius and Hobbes were preoccupied with interpreting the very same organization, Grotius looking at it from the point view of its external relations – other states – whereas Hobbes examined it from the point of view of its internal relations – the subjects of society.

Public international law is the regulation of state relations, which regulation has seen a sharp increase in both depth and scope since the end of the Second World War (Brownlie, 1998; Combacau and Sur, 1999). Public international law contains today a bulk of rules that bind the states and which, to a large extent, originate from agreements between the governments of these states. Thus, states accept to bind themselves for reasons, we argue, of either expediency or justice, according to the interpretation of the government making the contract in question.

Public international law involves the activities of international regimes. It is often stated that international reciprocity has replaced state autonomy, as mutual obligations create a world legal order – a giant international code for the Rule of Law among states, managed by numerous international organizations, the number and activities of which have increased correspondingly to the proliferation of rules. Can we conclude that Grotius has finally defeated Hobbes, that the state *Leviathan* has been chained by an international *Rechtsgesellschaft* guarded by effective custodians – so-called international regimes? Not quite, because public international law as it stands today is in several ways in line with a Hobbesian perspective on unlimited state sovereignty, which shows up in its critical weaknesses: the implementation deficit. Travelling along a Kantian approach to international regimes, connecting domestic and international order offers a plausible approach to the implementation deficit.

Expediency versus equity as a foundation for public international law

First and foremost it must be clearly stated that public international law is mainly contract law between sovereign states. Thousands of agreements lie at the core of this international legal order, made at specific points of time by the legal representatives of the states, i.e. their governments, and later often ratified by the national assemblies of these countries. The legal assumption is that governments or Parliaments by accepting these agreements commit the state that they represent to stick to them for as long as the agreements are effective. Public international law stems from contracting behaviour between governments, which contracts are then applied to the state in question. Through these numerous contracts, states create duties and rights between them concerning various matters, following either what expediency dictates or justice ordains. Whether the future governments in the contracting states will implement the contracts is an open question and creates the implementation risk. Now, which contracts would governments wish to sign?

Thus, public international law originates in contracts between states as well as in customs and precedents, reflecting considerations of both *equity* and *expediency*. The rules contained in these agreements – 'laws in the books' – constitute 'law in action' only in so far as there is a high probability of the continued observation of the terms of the contracts agreed upon and their implications. In this respect – efficacy of legal rules – there is no difference in principle between rules in agreements between states and rules enacted by national assemblies: in order to be effective these rules must have a certain likelihood of being respected, or when not respected of being enforced.

Thus, there must exist a *pacta sunt servanda* orientation among the states of the world, or at least the vast majority of them, in order to have an international legal order. But where does it come from? Are the agreements that found public international law self-enforceable in the sense that persons often find it advantageous to stick to agreements already made or to respect them as a matter of honesty? Why would governments make agreements if their immediate inclination were to violate them? Bilateral agreements or agreements made in a small group of states could enjoy self-enforceability, as cheating would perhaps be easily discovered and possibly punished.

Self-enforcement of rules in public international law could be forthcoming due to the nature of the contracts made between governments in the name of states. There are two grounds only: either the agreements are made because they are in the self-interest of states – expediency – or they are made because they are self-evidently just – equity? We will call the first motive the Hobbesian foundation of public international law and the second motive the Grotius foundation of public international law. Yet, neither expediency nor equity as the motive for making the agreements among states entails that each and every government of a state that signed the agreement will follow the contracts. Enforcement of public international rules is problematic, as will be discussed below. Public international regimes face various problems of enforcement, from intentional violation, to straightforward cheating, to sloppy observance, to benign negligence, to a lack of knowledge about what is required. These international rules of state conduct are for their continued validity dependent upon the activities of the various international regimes that have been instructed to implement the principles of public international law. Thus, there arise the two basic problems in the political theory of international regimes, which hang together: (i) What international agreements are sovereign states willing to accept, i.e. which rules do they enact together? (ii) When are states willing to respect the international rules within their respective jurisdictions?

The setting up of an international regime as an enforcement mechanism for public international law offers only an intermediate solution to the implementation problem, because first one needs to understand why states proceed to establish these agencies and second one needs a theory that explains why the activities of these agencies are accepted by the states. If the purpose of international regimes is to force states to respect public international law, then why do states accept to be thus restrained in the first place? And even if they voluntarily agree to set these regimes up, then why would they accept any activity of these regimes that constrain them when respect for public international law means the existence of law that sooner or later constitutes restrictions upon state behaviour? The question about the origin of public international law as well as the question of observation of public international law is, in fact, the very same problem about motivation: What motivates the governments of states to agree to or to respect public international law? Rationality, i.e. expediency, or justice, i.e. equity?

The contractual difficulties in international law were fully realized for the first time in the wake of the Grotius–Hobbes revolution in political theory. And they are still with us, because designing mechanisms that implement public international law still poses unresolved problems. Yet, these problems have to be tackled with a view to finding new and more effective tools for the implementation of the rules governing the conduct of states, as the concerns of humanity are at stake. Perhaps it is also urgent to find ways and means of strengthening the principles of public international law, for instance with regard to genocide.

The problem of the foundation of public international law may be stated by putting Hobbes up against Grotius, i.e. pitting sovereignty theory against the theory of the international community or, in a slightly different form, rational choice theory against moral reasoning. The problem of the implementation deficit in public international law can be analysed as the search for a mechanism that would possess enough legitimacy to bring a state back to co-operation, when its government has defected from what international principles of state conduct requires.

Here, we will first discuss two things. First, we show how the public international law perspective arises even within a pure Hobbesian approach to the state. Second, we will focus in particular upon one piece of public international law where Grotius's equity basis of public international law becomes apparent, the protection of mankind or humanity. After this, we bring up the implementation problem, which arises in relation to both the Hobbesian and Grotius's perspectives on public international law, as self-enforceability cannot be secured.

Although a number of international regimes are in operation today, it may be argued that they face a twofold deficit, which needs to be addressed as in the light of a new century. First, the international regimes deal with the difficult problem of enforceability of norms, as international agreements *qua* contracts are not self-enforceable. Governments may fail to respect the norms arrived at, as defection is sometimes a more rational strategy. Second, governments may not wish to agree to the making of new norms, suggested by the international organization, that are complementing already existing norms in order to better protect humanity. We will argue that the implementation deficit arises with a vengeance not only when one remains within a Hobbesian or a rational choice perspective on international regimes, but also because international regimes are equally vulnerable to the enforcement problem under a Grotius justice conception.

Hobbes's position: expediency

Since Hobbes the focus in the normative theories of politics has been the state and its specific characteristics, i.e. its sovereignty over a clearly specified territory. The first identification by Jean Bodin of this public power or legislative supremacy that constitutes the body politic posed further questions that were to occupy the great theorists in the centuries to come. What is the nature of this *potestas*? Can a legal framework restrain it at the same time as the state is unlimited in terms of its capacity to make law? Should it be exercised by some specific person or a group of persons at the same time as its objective is the interests of the people? Political theory after Hobbes becomes almost exclusively state theory.

In political theory the Hobbesian focus upon the state and its so-called interests to the exclusion of every other consideration was immediately contested by scholars, who pointed out the conflict between the so-called reasons of the state (*Staatsräson*) – Machiavellianism – and the vital concerns of humanity (Meinecke, 1962, 1963). Before Hobbes there was a general acceptance that political power was bound by universal moral principles. We need only to go back to Catholic political theory in the High Medieval period or Roman Stoicism to find a coherent theory to the effect that rulers or the public authorities were bound by basic principles governing mankind. A most coherent theory to that effect was launched just 26 years before *Leviathan* (1651) by Grotius, whose *On Law in Peace and War* from 1625 is in effect a summary of the entire classical and Christian reflection upon political authority or worldly powers in relation to humanity.

There is only one place in *Leviathan* where Hobbes explicitly addresses the issue of relations between states. In part I, chapter XIII ('Of the Natural Condition'), the twelfth paragraph, he says three things. First, he says that states are placed in a state of nature, and that the system of states is anarchy. Second, as a result of this, the relations between states are tense and the leaders of states will all the time make preparations for defending their respective interests by means of force. Third, this situation does not, however, cause the same concern as anarchy and conflict within the states does. While intra-national anarchy has all the awful consequences described vividly by Hobbes, it does not follow, says Hobbes, that the same kind of misery results from international anarchy.

It is the last assumption which explains why Hobbes sees no need for a world government or international legal regimes. One may certainly argue against Hobbes that he is mistaken in his complacent view of international anarchy. At any rate, one may criticize him for paying far too little attention to the international situation. He gives no evidence for his conclusion. Thus, Hobbes's argument in favour of this unlimited power of the state is entirely founded upon his reasoning about the need for internal order and the rule of law within a country. But how about the dangers of an *Omnium Bellum Contra Omnes* between states? In modern political theory one employs the prisoner's dilemma game in order to portray the logic of the Hobbesian argument in favour of the existence of a sovereign (Mueller, 1989). But the same dilemma arises not only in the internal affairs of countries but also in their external relations, i.e. in the interaction between states. If states cannot come to an agreement about the rules of the game, or if they do not respect the rules of the game that have been identified in mutual contracts, then the risk of war is imminent, which may also hurt the internal safety of a country. Can there be internal peace if there is external war?

The external safety problem arises with a vengeance from within a Hobbesian approach to government. Can states solve this problem simply by resorting to the driving force that to Hobbes is the central motivation of actors, i.e. self-interest? Or is something additional needed that is outside the Hobbesian framework, namely moral norms? If states make contracts about how they wish to live together in an international environment and move on to set up regimes that somehow police these contracts, then sovereign states have agreed to limit their own power, which would amount to auto-limitation. But is auto-limitation the sole foundation for public international law? Taking a rational choice approach (Laver, 1997), this is the sole possibility for avoiding international anarchy. But does auto-limitation really work? And does it result in morally acceptable solutions?

One must not believe that there would be no international legal order if one starts from a rational choice perspective. In a world of sovereign states there would arise a common interest in the regulation of mutual matters among governments. Although the principle of state sovereignty excludes any mutual regulation of internal state matters, immediately one recognizes that it is often in the self-interest of governments to negotiate agreements with other governments about the *modus vivendi* between the states in question. Thus, one government would wish to receive the acceptance of its sovereignty of other states in exchange for a similar recognition of the other states, which in turn calls for a mutual settlement of the terms of interaction among sovereign states. It takes little imagination to realize that these questions about state interaction become very rapidly not only numerous but also very complex.

Starting from the Hobbesian predicament of sovereign states, public international law can be interpreted as the rational outcome of processes of negotiation among states. This entails that public international law would embody not the Grotius fundamental principles of equity but the rational principles that states decide to accept. These rules resolve merely the interaction problems that are bound to arise once one accepts state sovereignty. Public international law would under a rational choice interpretation hand down the institutions that states agree to accept, because the contracting governments regard them as promoting the self-interest of the country. Since contracting parties tend to accept Pareto-optimal solutions, and Pareto-optimal solutions may be self-enforceable, public international regimes are actually far more stable than envisaged and rely not only upon the enforcement mechanism devised in relation to the rules.

State sovereignty versus state reciprocities has been one major way of posing the problem of the nature of public international law, especially if one takes a so-called dualistic approach to how national law relates to international law (Kelsen, 1961). However, instead of the prevailing model of a confrontation between the idea of state sovereignty and the notion of public international law, one could regard public international law as a necessary complement to national law. The concept of state sovereignty does not make sense if one does not clarify how one sovereign state is to relate to another sovereign state. Thus, national and international law are closely linked, as in the so-called monist approach. It is in the self-interest of states not only to legislate internally but also to legislate externally, which it can only do by means of agreements with other states. Thus arises the rational choice approach to public international law as the search for the equilibrium institutions that rational governments would accept.

Let us ask: What rules of interaction would governments tend rationally to accept, if they know that they will interact with an ocean of states under a time frame that involves almost infinity, and knowing that the institutional solution agreed upon will be attributed to the state that the government represents? Any government, except one that is totally committed to warfare, would realize that certain common principles of conduct are needed for the regulation of the many different forms of interaction with other states. Even an opportunistic and myopic government would choose the co-operation alternative in relation to other states, if it can predict that other governments would effectively retaliate if there is no peaceful agreement – at least in the first rounds of interaction.

Under a Hobbesian concept of the state, each and every government would insist that it gets an opportunity to negotiate and accept these rules of common conduct, which it would stipulate that all must accept as a condition for their own co-operation. Such a minimum state regulation that most governments would self-interestedly seek would cover the identification of a state, the relations of peace and war with other states as well as the space on earth that cannot be identified as state territory. Many rules in public international law could actually be interpreted as flowing from a series of bilateral contractual agreements between governments. But the content of many of these agreements would soon fall under the requirement of universilizability (Hare, 1967), meaning that several of the principles agreed to appear to be rationally acceptable only if they apply in the same manner to all other states. Not only state co-operation but also the universilization of the institutions arrived at would stem from contracts that rational governments decide to endorse. Whether they also stick to them is another question, however. Government can agree to many things, and yet not enforce the agreements although these are made in the name of the state which they represent.

Thus, it would often be in the best self-interest of governments to negotiate treaties with other governments, arriving at mutually valid rules of state interaction. These rules would authorize not only rightful conduct in relation to matters that go beyond the concept of state sovereignty such as the oceans, the rivers and migrating animals. First and foremost public international law would safeguard the states themselves by rules about state integrity and rules about protection against unlawful attacks. As a matter of fact, the opposition between state sovereignty and international regime is only partially a real one, because much public international law results from a voluntary exchange approach between governments in which states regulate their mutual interests to their advantage.

Much of the rules of public international law, based upon a great number of treaties, constitute transparent examples of how players negotiate rational institutions searching for a Pareto-optimal solution to collective action problems involving a long-term time horizon. Governments, having realized that they have more to gain from peaceful co-operation than defection involving the risk of war or sanctions, have set up an impressive body of international regulations. Moreover, they have made a kind of supreme laying down of mutual rules about these agreed upon rules in the Vienna Convention on the Law of Treaties from 1969. In this major piece of public international law, governments commit their states to the meta-rule principles of *Pacta Sunt Servanda* and *Good Faith*. Public international law thus has some self-enforcement force that is derived from a rational choice approach with each government. Why agree to anything in a contract, if the intention would be to cheat immediately? Some international law principles are even considered to have become *Jus Cogens*, which may lead to the nullification of agreements that contradict public international law, thus safeguarding the *Pacta Sunt Servanda* principle. However, there is no complete or automatic self-enforcement, which remains the weakness in public international law leading to its implementation deficit, as governments may fail to honour their agreements or the agreements that prior governments of the same state have concluded.

Public international law and the state – two entities with complex connections. One may start from the latter and derive the former: the classical, auto-limitation approach. Or one may begin from the former and identify the state: the residual approach. Under the auto-limitation framework states possess complete sovereignty but hand over powers to international regimes, whereas under the residual approach the international community identifies the degrees of freedom of state action. The relationship between national and international law is typically discussed under the monist versus the dualist conceptions, but it is to a large extent a problem similar to that of the hen and the egg: which comes first?

What we now need to find out, however, is whether public international law is not also to be understood as a set of ultimate moral principles which governments – willingly or unwillingly – accept as ultimate values – the Grotius position. The Grotius position is the exact opposite to the Hobbesian one where the rules of public international law would constitute a set of rationally negotiated principles that are accepted because they are expedient – the rational choice position. However, under both interpretations there is the implementation deficit.

Grotius's position: equity

Grotius argues the case for *Jus Gentium* by means of abstract principles of right reason, drawn from the collective experience of civilized humanity. To him states stand in homology to man, because both single individuals and organized collectivities have to recognize certain just principles of conduct that justly restrict their discretion. In the same way that men and women realize that one is entitled to defend oneself but not to attack others, so must governments reason. However, one does not need the entire theory of natural rights in order to arrive at a regulation of state behaviour. States facing each other in a Hobbesian predicament would rationally negotiate expedient solutions to their interaction problems. What more, then, than expedient rules does equity as the foundation for public international law entail in terms of restrictions upon the behaviour of governments?

States exercising their sovereign power would rationally agree and thus bind themselves to what? If state autonomy would be conceived of as producing international order, then how far would self-limitation go as the foundation for public international law? Which rules would a state willingly and rationally accept, given that other states do the same? If there is a discrepancy between rules so derived and the existing body of public international law, then expediency cannot explain everything; equity must also count.

Reading *On Law in Peace and War* and comparing it with other major works in the normative theory of public international law like those by Pufendorf or Wolff, one is struck by the astonishing fact of how much Grotius relies upon the ancients when deriving his theory about the natural limits on state activities. All the time he refers to the main lines of thought about the requirements of humanity stemming from the Greek-Roman tradition and Christian thought. Evidently, to Grotius the distinction between right reason or the eternal truths of humanity and the Stoicist-Christian legacy was a very fine one indeed.

Grotius's entire argument is based upon a homology between individuals and states, as they have the same motivation and they abide by the same normative rules. Thus, Grotius starts from the Epicurean assumption that man and woman pursues his/her self-interests, especially in relation to fungible assets. Man and woman are not only able to grab what naturally comes his/her way but also able to protect what has been acquired against invaders, if necessary by means of force. Since man and woman naturally want more of things that bring pleasure, the question arises whether man or woman can attack others to grab even more, even if self-defence is not at all involved. Grotius's *chef d'œuvre* actually employs an entire volume (Volume I) to establish this symmetry between persons and states, when seen from a legal point of view.

Grotius combines his Epicurean starting point with a Stoicist-Christian ethics, which accepts defence against attacks but never allows attacks in the first place. Thus, the fundamental motivation includes acquisitiveness but not attacks. Reason, says Grotius, provides man with the principles of mankind, which also God endorses because they constitute natural justice. These principles of right reason include that one speaks the truth, that one keeps one's promises and that one respects others, compensating them when one has caused damage against other people as well as that each punishment requires a proportionate crime. These precepts of justice make life in human societies possible, everyone realizes. What is true of man and women is also true of the most powerful of human organizations, the state. Thus, when states interact they must stick to the same precepts.

From this Epicurean-Stoicist-Christian starting point Grotius suggested in Volume II an elaborate set of international rules in order to control the behaviour of states and constrain them to pursue certain paths of activity and have them abstain from others. Here we meet a number of key elements in public international law today: the rights of Embassies, the duties in relation to burial places, the rejection of unjust wars, rules about the proper conduct of just wars, the respect for treaties, the right to self-defence, the rejection of genocide, the respect for civilians and the duty to take care of prisoners of war as well as the lawful implications of victory in wars. Grotius argues in favour of these rules, not with reference to the self-interests of governments or states but on the basis of justice considerations.

However, it should be pointed out that Grotius also derived other principles limiting the degrees of freedom of states from his framework, namely the maxims of *terra nullius* and the freedom of the seas, but in so doing he relies more upon expediency – states simply cannot control space entirely. The key question is, of course, the one that Grotius did not even bring up in order to debate: the implementation of these maxims – what agency will constitute an enforcement mechanism of Grotius principles of mankind? Is it the case, one may ask, that the enforcement problem is even larger under a Grotius approach than under a Hobbesian approach? There would at least be a minimum amount of self-enforceability when parties make agreements based on self-interests. Yet, cheating is always a problem in any contractual relation, as long as there is no mechanism for enforcement built into the contract. The problem has been well modelled as a prisoner's dilemma game, where collaboration among states as well as respect for agreements is not self-enforceable.

The implementation deficit

Grotius looks upon states as strictly homological to men and women, and the critical problem is the very same one: how to admit the role of self-interest and restrict it so that it does not result in mere aggression. If there are eternal maxims guiding mankind when men and women interact, then these maxims also guide states – to the same extent. But, if this is the construction, then how can these maxims be implemented? To Grotius, the most profound principle guiding men, women and states is that agreement must be fulfilled – *Pacta Sunt Servanda*. But as Hobbes points out, this basic principle is not self-enforceable. Since it is the task of the state to guarantee this fundamental principle of mankind with its sovereign power, one arrives logically at the Hobbesian position, meaning there is no additional authority available to see to it that also governments maintain the natural precepts of reason when they act, for instance, in relation to each other. Thus, the homology breaks down, as states are different from men and women.

The problem of enforceability of rules of state behaviour is the critical question in relation to public international law. Public international law has expanded tremendously after the Second World War ended in 1945, covering more and more aspects of the interaction among governments. But how can one make sure that all these agreements are honoured, meaning that the principles of public international law are obeyed? The implementation deficit remains immense in public international law and it concerns all aspects of implementation, i.e. the observation of clear rules as well as the interpretation and adjudication of contested rules and the employment of correction measures. Let us show why.

The more states interact, the more rapidly will public international law tend to increase. As a result of the process of internationalization or globalization during the post-war period, public international law has grown immensely. One may argue that the notion of state sovereignty has lost its meaning today. But one must remember that public international law is basically treaty law, stemming from the voluntary acceptance by states of contracts. Independently of what takes precedence – state autonomy or reciprocity between states – international law is based upon consent by governments. It is founded upon state sovereignty. States acting upon the basis of sovereignty would voluntarily agree to certain regulations. Which ones would be the most urgent? Perhaps the rules that regulate the existence of the state itself, its peace, survival and borders?

One could point out that states would have no objection to private international law, because economic interaction between individuals across borders runs into the problem of conflict of laws easily. States may be less inclined to accept international restrictions upon the making of internal law, such as economic legislation deriving from the mutual needs of economic interaction across borders. Yet, the core of public international law lies elsewhere, namely in the voluntary agreement among states about restrictions upon their degrees of freedom when interacting with each other in public matters. But does such law also possess efficacy, meaning that its rules are observed or implemented?

For the purpose of exposition, one could – somewhat superficially it may certainly be said – divide public international law into at least three kinds of regulatory frameworks: (i) rules about the integrity of the state, including war; (ii) rules about space, including *terra nullius*; and finally (iii) rules about citizenship, treatment of foreigners and refugees, including rules against genocide. In order to bolster these regulatory schemes there are, in addition, rules about state responsibility and rules about international adjudication, including the operation of numerous international regimes. International regimes are one mechanism for making sure that effectiveness and generalizability are achieved. Yet, these three sets of rules are somewhat different when it comes to the reasons why states would adhere to them, i.e. co-operate.

Rules about state integrity and war

The idea of a norm against war emerges at the same time as the governments enter into a vast regulation of their relationships in the form of the Westphalia Peace. The medieval idea of a Christian community is replaced by an international regime of states bound by agreements that governments commit themselves to respect – the *Pacta Sunt Servanda* principle. A hierarchy of men and women arranged in the two subcommunities, the worldly (*imperium*) and the sacred orders (*ecclesia*), is replaced by a set of sovereign states, interacting with each other on the basis of their self-interests: *ragione di stato*. In such a predicament of many states, a government when maximizing its self-interests would pursue a line of maximin, safeguarding whatever assets they have and avoiding their worst outcome in the form of an annihilation of their state. If states are risk avoiding, then devising as well as agreeing upon rules against war becomes a serious strategic option.

The short-term gains from public international law are quite substantial to the state, as several of its principles identify the basic rights and obligations of states such as the impossibility to violate its territory, the non-interference in its internal affairs and its rights to independence. What public international law does first is to specify what 'sovereignty' refers to from a legal point of view. Thus, public international law may not only restrain states but also actually increase their powers. Moreover, it may be very attractive for a state to be recognized as having legal equality with other states. The problem in relation to such rules, which appear to be beneficial to all states that accept them, is what happens if cheating takes place. If the circumstances change, then the self-interests of governments may dictate a strategy that involves violation of the accords. Thus, an external enforcement mechanism needs to be provided, preferably at the time the agreements are signed.

Against the relevance of public international law it is sometimes argued that its list of fundamental state rights and duties are very lofty and lack precision. However, one observes that in a rather concrete manner these concepts are very important for simple mundane matters such as the legal status in one country of people representing another country, as formulated in numerous conventions. This focus upon the inviolability of such persons with diplomatic status includes the representatives of international regimes. Under certain circumstances a government may engage in a strategy that runs counter to the agreements its state has signed, although it may claim that it is not cheating. Hence, an external interpretation mechanism and transparency requirements need to be provided, preferably at the time the agreements are signed.

Of course, it is a rational strategy from governments that they would want to have a principle of non-interference laid down, all other things being equal. But they would have to face the fact that public international law always contains principles that oppose each other. Thus, a government cannot ask for non-interference or non-intervention in circumstances when other principles are relevant to which a state has also committed itself; for instance, principles laid down in other international agreements concerning human rights. If it is expediency which drives governments to accept rules against state interference like warfare, then what motivates them to accept rules that may be the foundation for interference into another country? When there is conflict among the rules in public international law, then an external adjudication mechanism needs to be provided, perhaps at the time the agreements are signed.

Some governments often question the long-term advantages of rules against war, including disarmament. They believe that they can somehow improve their international position by not committing their states or consider that they need the war option in order to claim what is due to them, for instance undoing old injustices or securing an effective defence if other governments attack. When it comes to negotiations about rules banning the use of certain weapons, the logic of state behaviour seems to follow deliberations about short-term versus long-term advantages in accordance with the so-called chicken game, i.e. accepting binding rules while at the same time minimizing the disadvantages of committing the state to something that may turn out to be a strait-jacket in the future. At the same time, humanitarian reasons cannot be ruled out as totally unimportant in relation to state self-interest. This applies to the efforts to control weapons that are especially dangerous to the population of the country, such as biochemical weapons or land mines. The logic of nuclear arms control seems more driven by expediency than equity, however, as the implication for strategic behaviour is the old lesson: arm if you want peace. International agreements about arms control are only stable if the agreements can be policed. Thus, an external surveillance mechanism needs to be provided, preferably at the time the agreements are signed.

Rules about space

As the state is based upon a principle of territoriality, it follows that the division of the earth becomes a vital concern for states, with regard to surface, coastal regions and the air. It is in the self-interest of governments to set up rules about how the state space is to be managed. Two rational reasons stand out. First, a state would want to exercise control not only over its land space but also over its rivers and coastal regions. That the state claims absolute control over its air space is obvious for security reasons, but immediately a state must accept rules that allow other countries' aircraft access to that space. International air traffic could not work if there was not an international regime setting and policing standards about private air traffic around the globe. It is not in the self-interest of states to put up hindrances against international traffic. Thus, expediency dictates rules and the behaviour of international regimes about air, land and maritime traffic.

Second, a state wants to make sure that the resources available in its coastal areas benefit the country, although it has to accept the principle of the high seas as a natural limitation for how far it could claim control. Actually, one of the first theoreticians to identify the principle of *mare liberum* of oceans was Grotius in a separate treatise. States have after the Second World War actively sought and successfully extended their legitimate control over their coastal regions, including the new concept of the exclusive economic zone. As a matter of fact, controlling these economic zones and the state's continental platform may be not only in the public interest of the country but also in the narrow fiscal interests of governments, as this space may harbour rich natural resources.

Again, we note that self-interest is not the sole reason for the regulation of the high seas, the coastal areas and the river basins between several states. There is also a set of principles of equity involved, allocating rights to utilization as well as duties in relation to utilization. However, the expediency reasons are dominant in so far as states may claim control over a space at a reasonable cost. When this is no longer possible, then there is a tendency for the area to be placed in the public domain under the control of an international regime. As costs of policing and controlling become excessive, then the management of the area requires international co-operation, where the terms of utilization will be set by the rational considerations of the states *primo*, and *secundo* by certain equity principles, such as the rights of navigation for instance. The special international regimes of the Suez and the Panama canals are examples of how the interests of governments in revenues and territorial control are confronted by the interests of the international community in securing safe and effective navigation routes.

Rules about individuals

It is when we enter the regulation of individual beings in public international law that the rational choice approach appears much less applicable. Why would states voluntarily hand over regulatory competence to an external body by means of international agreements when it comes to the specification of human rights in a broad sense, including the treatment of refugees? The reasons provided by Grotius are much more at the forefront here than the Hobbesian ones, as this regulation enters into the entire set of human rights rules, covering not only all kinds of civil and political rights but also a prohibition against genocide. Since it is not self-interest that is at stake when governments voluntarily contract about these limitations upon their behaviour, then any tendency towards self-enforcement would have to be based upon humanitarian motivation with governments, if there is not an explicit implementation mechanism devised when the agreements are made. The implication is that any contract about human rights without a mechanism for surveillance, adjudication and enforcement is an incomplete contract.

One basic principle of public international law as well as of the functioning of international regimes is that the agents of law are the respective states. It is the states that commit themselves in relation to each other. Thus, they are the so-called subjects of this kind of international law and internal subjects – citizens – in each country can only be the objects of public international law. Then, if these conditions were the given premises for the making of public international law as well as for the activities of international regimes, then why would governments accept external policing of the rights of their citizens? They may agree to the signing of contracts about human rights, but why implement such contracts, except when it is in the self-interest of governments to do so, for instance when faced with external pressures from other states or an international organization? The mere passage in time between the signing of an accord and the fulfilment of the accord augments the implementation deficit, as not only the possibility of explicit cheating becomes a real one but also the likelihood of simply negligence taking place becomes more feasible.

Government could have a self-interest in seeing to it that foreign populations are treated in an acceptable manner, if, for instance, these populations include relatives of the people in the state concerned, for instance where they constitute minorities of other nations. Often governments see themselves as the protector of minorities in neighbouring countries when these minorities share common characteristics with the people living in the state ruled by a certain government. If such protection could be universalized in the form of human rights or prohibition against genocide, then so much the better. At the same time universalization entails weaker protection due to the enforcement problem. Self-interest seems a much too narrow concern when it comes to explaining the large parts of public international law that deal with human rights, i.e. not states but individuals. Correspondingly, these agreements need to be complete in the sense that an enforcement mechanism has to be devised at the time the contracts are signed. Otherwise, there is a large risk that they will remain merely paper rules.

The political theory of human rights has enormous consequences not only for internal state constitutional law, but also for external state international law. One may perhaps say that it unifies the two perspectives on law, the positivistic approach underlining the supremacy of the state, and the natural law perspective emphasizing that states have to act in respect of right reason, when they make law. Human rights enter not only the constitutions of single states, but make up a sizeable portion of public international law. At the time of Grotius, this connection was not clear, as he focused upon the implications of *Jus Gentium* for deriving limitations upon states in their behaviour concerning peace and war, while at the same time rejecting any relevance of human rights for constitutionalism within the state.

Thus, the rules about individuals in public international law can only to a limited extent be derived from the rational reasons of states. Even when governments have committed themselves to human rights frameworks, they still tend to react very negatively when called upon to respect these rights by another government or an international regime. The basic legitimization of international rules about individuals stems from the equity foundation of public international law. But how can they then be enforced?

The enforcement problem

Governments have agreed in numerous conventions to create an international legal order, carrying rights and duties of states towards each other and towards individual beings including rights of groups such as national minorities. The rational choice approach outlining the self-interest of states in erecting public international law can only to a limited extent deliver an answer to the question of how the contracts agreed to are to be implemented, since any tendency towards self-enforcement of contracts is not enough. There must be policing activities of international regimes set up either in connection with the treaties or immediately after.

In addition to the reasons listed above that create the implementation deficit for public international law – cheating, negligence, ambiguity, opportunism – one would wish to mention also universalization: a government would accept an international regime so long as all other governments do the same. As long as the rules of the international community are implemented in a general fashion, applying to all, then the best strategy of each government is to co-operate and not defect. But this requires that defection be penalized either by an international organization, which can if allowed be highly instrumental in punishing defection, or by actions of other governments directly.

Yet, public international organizations have not been given strong enforcement competencies. Since the states are the contracting parties, it is a general presumption that it is the governments of the contracting states that are to initiate action when defection takes place as well as implement the corrections that an international organization may decide upon. Thus, from whichever angle we approach the international legal order, the self-enforcement problem arises: Will the governments of the states that signed the treaties from which the international rules emerge also either implement them themselves or call for the implementation of the rules? Perhaps, when it is a matter of rules that were made on the basis of self-interest, but how about the equity rules?

Unconditional norms for state conduct come from justice considerations. If there are basic principles of mankind that states have to respect, then that respect must be forthcoming whether these rules are in the national interest of a state in question or not. And these rules have to be obeyed, whether or not there is an international regime that can punish defection. However, the risk for a conflict of interest between the principles of humanity and state reasons is obvious, and there is often little an international regime can do when a state defects from the norms of mankind. Grotius delivered a number of key norms belonging to *Jus Gentium*, which concerned the rights of people in war, including the rights of prisoners of war, the protection of the population and the status of women and children. It is here that the rules against genocide enter. When a government kills people in its population who have no military function, then it commits a crime against mankind.

The reason that a state does so is to be found in the Hobbesian perspective on state sovereignty and state interests. Here, the conflict between the interests of state and the concerns of humanity is clear-cut. Self-enforceability of the rules about individuals will not automatically be forthcoming, and an international regime has to be set up to protect the norms of humanity.

Perhaps one could say that public international law rests upon incomplete contracting in the same sense that all contracts leave open certain possibilities: co-operation or defection. On the one hand, one must assume that in a voluntary exchange approach the contracting parties consent to the rules in the contract, because they accept and approve of them. On the other hand, the parties have incentives explicitly to violate the agreements and implicitly neglect them, when defection is a more dominant strategy over co-operation. The only solution possible to this dilemma is to contract an enforcement mechanism at the same time as the contract is drawn up (Eatwell *et al.*, 1989a). Often this has been done, but the mechanism designed has not been given leverage, because at the end of the day the international legal order restricting states remains the patrimony of the very same states.

International regimes and world governance

After the Second World War international regimes have expanded in number as well as scope reflecting the enormous growth in public international law. The political theory of the international order needs to assess these developments. One approach would be to use the perspectives from the history of political thought. Whether one, as in jurisprudence, models the relations between states and the international community in a monistic or a dualistic fashion, it remains impossible to have the one without the other. Two principles of orientation are conceivable: (i) Hobbesian self-interests; (ii) Grotius morality concerns stemming from the needs of mankind. In public international law and in the activities of the various international regimes, these two foundations interact.

The great problem, however, remains the enforceability problem, as defection from contracts agreed upon may present the rational strategy for governments. One finds the same problem in other forms of international law, for instance trade agreements or conventions. The only way, given the present system of states constituting the international community, is that the international rules be protected by means of a set of international courts or dispute settlement tribunals. The increase in activities by international lawyers is most welcome if one takes a Grotius perspective upon the state and the international community.

One may interpret public international law as resting upon incomplete contracts. Sometimes conventions are signed without any explicit design of a mechanism for enforcement of the contract. Sometimes the agreements among states do contain an enforcement mechanism that is part of the contract, but it tends to be all too weak. As long as the contracts remain incomplete, one is bound to have opportunistic behaviour by actors who wish to capture the opportunities for separate gains that the incompleteness provides. The conclusion must be that one designs better contracts between states where the agreements involve a commitment to accept strong enforcement.

The enforcement question may be considered the most critical one when it comes to the possibility of global governance in terms of rationally instituted rules. Rules without enforcement do not make up institutions. Thus, we must ask: Who will enforce the institutions in global governance?

When studying international organizations it may be appropriate to introduce a few distinctions. First, one may ask how an organization operating globally is related to the state or a government. Organizations co-operating at the international level with close relations to government bodies may be called intergovernmental organizations or IGOs. On the other hand, organizations that stand free from governmental bodies are called non-governmental organizations or NGOs. Table 11.1 contains estimates of the number of international organizations during the twentieth century as presented by the Union of International Associations (UIA).

Second, another distinction may be made by separating conventional international bodies from all other kinds of international organizations. Typical examples of conventional IGOs are the UN, ILO, EU, NAFTA and ASEAN whereas a conventional NGO would be Amnesty International. As non-conventional IGOs we would count the IMF and the World Bank. As non-conventional NGOs we may identify organizations such as Greenpeace International or the WWF – the World Wide Fund For Nature, formerly known as World Wildlife Fund.

It is quite obvious from the numbers of international organizations estimated in Table 11.1 that there has been a huge growth in the number of organizations during the twentieth century. In particular this holds true for non-conventional NGOs numbering some 40,000 in the year 2000. The number of IGOs has not increased that much. Actually, looking at the conventional IGOs we may note a slight decline in their numbers during the 1990s.

We will now look at a few of these international organizations. Below we examine the UN system with its core institutions concerning war and peace. In the next chapter we will look at a few IGOs and some NGOs too.

Intergovernmental organizations: the UN system

Let us start our review of a few major IGOs by looking at the UN. The UN was established on 24 October 1945 by 51 member-countries. Following the decolonization process as well as later the break-up of the former Soviet Union there has been a growth in the number of member-countries,

Table 11.1 International organizations 1909–2000: estimated numbers

Year	Conventional bodies		All types of bodies	
	IGO	NGO	IGO	NGO
1909	37	176	37	176
1951	123	832	123	832
1954	118	997	118	1008
1956	132	973	132	985
1958	149	1060	149	1073
1962	163	1324	163	1552
1964	179	1470	179	1718
1966	199	1675	199	2830
1970	242	1993	242	3379
1972	280	2173	280	3733
1976	252	2502	252	6222
1978	289	2420	289	9521
1981	337	4263	1039	13232
1984	365	4615	2842	19614
1985	378	4676	3546	20634
1987	311	4235	3897	23248
1988	309	4518	4038	24902
1989	300	4621	4068	20063
1991	297	4620	4565	23635
1992	286	4696	4878	27190
1993	272	4830	5103	28901
1995	266	5121	5668	36054
1996	260	5472	5885	38243
1997	258	5585	6115	40306
1998	254	5766	6250	42100
1999	251	5825	6415	43958
2000	241	5936	6556	45674

Sources: UIA (1999, 2000)

reaching 100 in 1961 and going up to 189 members in the year 2000. This process of growth is displayed in Figure 11.1.

From the beginning the aims of the UN have been to maintain international peace and security, and to develop international co-operation in economic, social, cultural and humanitarian areas. In order to implement such aims the UN has developed an internal organization attempting to balance the influence of the many small member-countries and the few major states taking their place as permanent members of the Security Council.

To be able to run the organization the UN is in need of financial support from the member-countries. In 1946 the yearly appropriation was in the region of US$ 19,390,000. In 1974 the yearly appropriation was changed to bienniums and for the first biennium the appropriation was in the region of US$ 606,033,000. In 2000–2001 this had reached the sum of US$

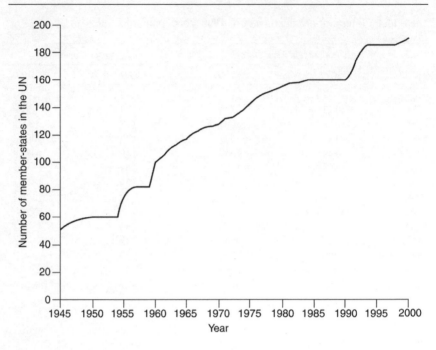

Figure 11.1   Growth in UN member-states: 1945–2000
Source: UN (2000)

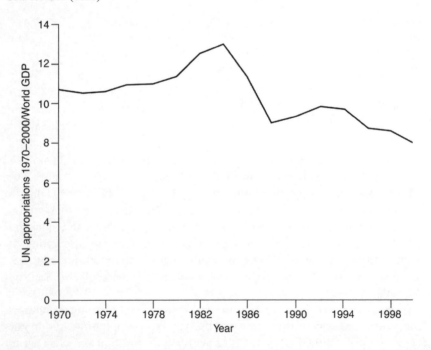

Figure 11.2   Biennial appropriations for the UN in relation to Gross World Product
Sources: *Europa World Yearbook* (various years)

Table 11.2   Member-countries contributing more than 1% of the UN appropriations 1985–98

Contributions 1985		Contributions 1994		Contributions 1998	
Country	%	Country	%	Country	%
USA	25.00	USA	25.00	USA	25.00
USSR	11.10	Japan	12.45	Japan	17.98
Japan	9.58	Germany	8.93	Germany	9.63
Germany FR	8.31	Russia	6.71	France	6.49
France	6.26	France	6.00	UK	5.08
UK	4.46	UK	5.02	Russia	2.87
Italy	3.45	Canada	3.11	Canada	2.83
Canada	3.28	Spain	1.98	Spain	2.57
Australia	1.83	Ukraine	1.87	Netherlands	1.62
Spain	1.70	Brazil	1.59	Brazil	1.51
Netherlands	1.63	Australia	1.51	Australia	1.47
China	1.62	Netherlands	1.50	Belgium	1.10
Ukraine	1.46	Sweden	1.11	Sweden	1.10
Germany, DR	1.39	Belgium	1.06		
Sweden	1.31				
Brazil	1.27				
Poland	1.24				
Belgium	1.22				

Sources: *Europa World Yearbook* (various years)

2,536,000,000. Figure 11.2 attempts to indicate the relation between UN biennial budgets and Gross World Products from 1970 to 2000. Although the figures displayed are very crude, they do indicate that the financial support for the UN has declined over time. Indeed the 1990s was a period of financial crisis for the UN.

The size of the contributions from the member-countries is decided by the General Assembly on the recommendation of its Committee on Contributions. In 1972 a ceiling was introduced, meaning that no member should contribute more than 25 per cent of the contributions, which change only affected the USA. Its share was to begin with a high 39.89 per cent. In 1985 18 members where expected to pay more than 1 per cent of the contributions but this number decreased to 14 members in 1998. Since not every member pays its dues, this contributes to the financial crisis, not least since the USA is one of the members not fully paying its dues (Table 11.2).

Ever since the establishment of the UN there have been proposals for reform of the organization. During the 1990s we may identify a number of proposals for reform due to a number of reasons. The end of the cold war constitutes one and another was the fiftieth anniversary of the UN in 1995 when reform was again suggested by Boutros Boutros-Ghali in his report entitled *An Agenda for Peace*, which focused on reforms of the peacekeeping work of the UN. In another report, *Our Global Neighbourhood*, from the same year, a Commission on Global Governance headed by the then Swedish Prime Minister Ingvar Carlsson presented a proposal for comprehensive reform of the UN. The most recent reform proposals stem from Kofi Annan. It was released in July 1997 and was entitled: *Renewing the United Nations: A Programme for Reform.* Yet, none of these proposals has resulted in any major change of the UN. The organization still faces economic problems and the structure of the General Assembly and the Security Council remains basically the same as at the time of the establishment of the UN.

In reality, the UN is a whole system of various organizations that co-operate under the umbrella of the UN. First, we have a number of Regional Commissions like the Economic Commission for Latin America and the Caribbean (ECLAC), including the ECE, ESCAP, ECA and ESWA. Common for these commissions is that they are subsidiaries of the Economic and Social Council. Second, there are other UN bodies that are subsidiaries under either the General Assembly or the Security Council, having the General Secretary as their executive head. Among these organizations we may count the UN Development Programme (UNDP), the UN Environment Programme (UNEP), the UN High Commissioner for Refugees (UNHCR) and the UN Children's Fund (UNICEF). Third, we may distinguish the specialized agencies of the UN. Some of these had predecessor organizations within the League of Nations like the ILO, FAO, UNESCO and WHO. Another category comprises the technical agencies consisting of organizations like the Universal Postal Union (UPU), which had been established earlier in 1875, but also organizations formed under the auspices of the UN like the IMF (1945), ICAO (1947) or WIPO (1970). Another category in this group is the Bretton Woods Institutions or as they also are called the World Bank group which was formed in 1945. Let us take a closer look at some of these subsidiary organizations of the UN: the ILO, IMF and the World Bank.

The institutions of peace and war

Decisions about war have been transferred to the international community who is exercising its authority over the conduct of just wars by means of the UN and its Security Council. Thus, the Security Council can make interventions in zones of conflict and make binding recommendations to states in war. During the post-war period there has been much activity in the Security Council as well as a number of interventions where the UN has enlisted troops for the UN or where the troops of various nations have fulfilled a mandate.

One may have different opinions about whether the UN framework for maintaining peace is effective or not. It has not stopped all wars and the interventions have in certain cases not been successful in stopping war once they have broken out. However, the frequent interventions in conflicts between states as well as in civil wars have contributed to the institutionalization of military conflicts around the world. It is true that this institutionalization is far from complete, as wars go on today in several places without the UN being able to do anything about it.

The UN safeguards peace through both anticipation and reaction. Governments think twice before they start a war, knowing that their actions will be monitored by and discussed in the Security Council. The risk of sanctions is a real one, which could involve anything from military intervention to economic sanction or penalties after war is over. Again, this prevention of war is not absolute, as wars do break out from time to time. Yet, merely the knowledge that a response from the UN is likely makes governments reflect over their options instead of just 'jumping in'.

When it comes to judging or evaluating the capacity of the UN to engage in sanctions after war has broken out, the opinions differ. Some have emphasized that the troops of the UN often do little to resolve a conflict that they often arrive late to. Some peacekeeping missions seem to go on endlessly, whereas a few others have failed miserably. However, it may be too much to demand that operations always meet with success. A few operations have been successful in the sense that the goals of the mission have been to a large extent accomplished. A number of proposals have been put forward to strengthen the capacity of the Security Council to intervene.

The Security Council has a structure, which reflects its origins in the cold war situation after the end of the Second World War. It can only take action if its five permanent members are not against the action plus four more members among the non-permanent ones. All in all, the Security Council has 15 members and a positive decision requires that there is no veto from one of the permanent members, which are the USA, Russia, China, the UK and France. All discussions about changing the Security Council have thus far not resulted in anything other than an increase in the number of non-permanent members from 11 to 15 in 1965.

The wider UN framework

The UN is a vast intergovernmental mechanism with a number of large suborganizations. One can be a member of the UN without being a member of all the suborganizations. Here we find large international regimes or NGOs with considerable staff working for the purposes of mankind such as education (UNESCO), health care (WHO) and the protection of labour (ILO). What distinguishes the Security Council from these suborganizations is the fact that the Security Council has the authority to implement its decisions against the will of a state, whether it is a member or not of the UN. Thus, when it comes to war and peace there is true world governance in the sense of a world government with enforcement power. The suborganizations work on the basis of the voluntary membership principle, meaning that states accept to follow the recommendations of these international bodies.

UNESCO

The United Nations Educational, Scientific and Cultural Organization (UNESCO) was formed in 1946 and has its headquarters in Paris. The purpose of this agency of the UN is to advance co-operation in areas like education, science and culture. Its largest sector of activity is the field of education where it has been active in developing educational systems and undertaking literacy campaigns, in particular among the countries in the Third World. UNESCO also plays a co-ordinating role for the worldwide development of international co-operation within the natural sciences as well as in the social and human sciences. Within the culture area, an important issue has been the attempt to safeguard the cultural heritage of the world. Most countries, being members of the UN, also adhere to UNESCO. There are, however, a few remarkable cases of non-membership in UNESCO. One such is the USA which had withdrawn from UNESCO by the end of 1984 and has so far not re-entered the agency; one year later also the UK left UNESCO because of disagreements with the ideological emphasis of the organization, but the UK re-entered UNESCO in 1997. The biennial budget for 1998–99 was US$ 544 millions.

WHO

The World Health Organization (WHO) was established in 1948 as the central agency within the UN framework directing international health work. The founding charter of WHO was signed by 26 member countries while 50 years later the organization has more than 190 members. Its headquarters are located in Geneva. The main activities of the WHO centres on the control and prevention of diseases. At the present time the prevention of HIV infection has a high priority, while other infectious diseases like tuberculosis, malaria and cholera are still important. Other important activities of the agency are to assist with developing primary health care and health building as well as developing standards for pharmaceutical products. The regular budget for the two-year period 1998–99 amounted to US$ 842 millions, meaning that WHO is one of the larger of the UN specialized agencies.

ILO

The International Labour Organization (ILO) was founded in 1919 and became a specialized agency associated with the UN in 1946. The main objectives of the organization are to promote decent living standards, secure and satisfactory labour standards and adequate employment opportunities. The governing body of ILO contains half government representatives, while the second half is divided equally by representatives of the employers and of the workers. At the time of its foundation the number of member-countries was 44 and this had increased to 64 in 1934. At the time of its refoundation in 1946 the number had decreased to 55. In the year 2000 most of the countries that are members of the UN are also members of the ILO, although there are some exceptions, since the number is 174. Thus, Switzerland is a member of the ILO but not of the UN, whereas the opposite is the case for some micro-states like Andorra, Kiribati, Monaco and Nauru, but also a country like Turkmenistan. The net expenditure for the ILO amounted to US$ 481 millions in 1998–99, and since the 1970s it has reached the level of between 15 and 20 per cent of UN expenditures.

FAO

The Food and Agriculture Organization of the United Nations (FAO) was established in 1945 and it is located in Rome. The FAO serves as a co-ordinating body within the UN system for development programmes in food and agriculture. Its main activities focus on agriculture, fisheries, forestry and environment but it also deals with nutrition and food security. FAO also has a major responsibility for emergency relief around the world due to threatening famines caused by flooding or drought. The biennial budget for FAO in 1998–99 was US$ 650 millions.

Global governance faces the risk of food shortages, as the world population continues to increase rapidly. The neo-Malthusian perspective will be a highly relevant one in the twenty-first century. As Table 11.3 indicates, world food production keeps increasing but will the yearly changes in food output keep up with population growth?

One may observe in Table 11.3 that cereals, root crops and milk have not kept up with the growth in world population. This increases the probability of famines.

Conclusion

Global co-ordination can take place through the global market economy or through the activities of international political organizations. Thus, the key question in political economy comes back in relation to the global market economy: co-ordination by means of voluntary co-operation or through government? If the argument in this book is correct, then economic co-ordination in the global market economy is not enough. However strong world economic integration is, there must be state co-ordination through governmental mechanisms or similar mechanisms. Two kinds of international bodies may be identified: (i) intergovernmental organizations – IGOs – and (ii) non-governmental organizations – NGOs. Together the IGOs and NGOs constitute a patchy system of political co-ordination, which is not sufficient in relation to the global society and economy.

These two types of international governance mechanism have multiplied in numbers after the Second World War in response to the two basic reasons

Table 11.3   World food production per capita 1980–98

Year	Cereals	Root crops	Vegetables	Fruits	Meat	Milk
1980	351.84	120.68	78.97	66.71	29.66	104.88
1981	364.62	122.59	79.12	64.68	29.73	103.66
1982	370.78	120.83	80.33	68.58	29.90	104.22
1983	350.09	119.42	79.32	66.89	30.33	106.59
1984	378.33	124.07	82.91	65.27	30.59	105.73
1985	379.68	120.22	83.49	64.26	31.15	105.60
1986	375.49	114.83	86.13	67.07	31.86	104.70
1987	355.98	114.40	86.49	66.77	32.37	102.73
1988	341.29	110.14	85.64	66.82	33.09	102.46
1989	362.62	111.58	85.94	66.56	33.09	102.09
1990	369.04	108.45	86.85	67.14	33.77	102.92
1991	350.72	107.06	86.28	66.04	33.94	99.84
1992	361.03	110.14	86.00	69.99	34.04	96.96
1993	343.93	114.56	92.09	69.59	34.54	95.10
1994	349.40	107.25	95.19	69.70	35.12	94.47
1995	333.57	110.06	98.88	71.57	35.62	94.21
1996	358.61	114.84	102.58	73.79	35.51	93.38
1997	359.21	107.33	102.73	74.54	36.22	93.12
1998	346.73	105.52	102.29	73.37	36.49	92.06

Note: The per capita measure is arrived at through dividing world production expressed in 1000 MT with world population expressed in millions
Source: FAO (various years): *FAO Yearbook*

for international co-ordination, namely expediency (Hobbes) and equity (Grotius). One may say that generally the IGOs serve the interests of the states in delivering sufficient international co-ordination to protect vital state interests whereas the NGOs are more geared to the protection of the interests of mankind. Everyone seems to agree that the present system of international co-ordination is not enough, despite its strong evolution in recent decades. What are the basic problems in the present system? Can it be improved upon? The next chapter will discuss ways to strengthen political co-ordination globally, reforming the present system of state interaction.

CHAPTER 12

Towards a World Federation?

Introduction

The idea of a world government has taken two forms, historically speaking. On the one hand, we have the dreams of certain major personalities in the history of ideas of one government for the whole of mankind, however naïve such personalities may seem. On the other hand, we have the practical efforts at establishing a system of world dominance, which, however, so far have failed. One may mention the ideas of Kant concerning a *feodum* or a world federation in relation to the first and the concept *Pax Romana* in relation to the second.

Perhaps the time has come to unite the dreams of a world government with the existing practices of international organizations, which taken together offer governance of a number of matters, including the world economy? What is needed is evidently a combination of the dreams about eternal peace, abolition of famines and elimination of racial discrimination with a realistic understanding of what is possible in terms of co-ordination above the main actors, the nation-states.

Two elements will have to be combined in any world government, namely the identification of the true objectives of mankind and a decentralized system of world governance, which promotes these goals. How can this be done? What are the main dangers in setting up a system for world governance? In political thought we find secular ideas about world governance aiming at eternal peace, as with Abbé de Saint-Pierre (1713–1717), Rousseau (1761) and Kant (1795).

The Kantian approach

One way to solve the problem with the implementation deficit in public international law is to use a different institutional mechanism than the international organization, namely a union. A union of states could solve the implementation problem by investing a federation with the requisite powers, and thus in the economists' language, internalizing the public good aspects of producing law and order. Actually, after the Hobbesian revolution in political theory several scholars including Rousseau paid attention to the possibility of creating peace and international order between war-prone states. But they could not come up with an implementation mechanism that would overcome the defection opportunities in relation to international contracts, where it often makes sense to cheat as long as the other states choose the co-operation strategy. It was not until 1795 that Kant found a solution in his *Zum Ewigen Frieden* in the form of a permanent federation of states, albeit somewhat too loose to attract any practical consequences.

With Kant the international norms about individuals involve a claim to morality. They are necessary because they are inherently just. Thus, governments can only violate them by explicitly committing an injustice. And injustices do have to be confronted and if possible rectified. If not, the distinction between right and wrong becomes muddled and the risk for additional violations escalates. What is at stake is *morality* and *publicity*, as Kant would say (Kant, 1991 (1795)). To take one example: as long as the Turkish government refuses to settle the Armenian issue by means of proper legal action, acknowledging its wrongdoings in the same way as the German government has taken responsibility for the Nazi atrocities, Turkey will constitute a challenge to the international community, as the possibility remains that other minorities could be treated in the same manner without consequences.

A state that rejects publicity about its activities does wrong, according to Kant. If the principle that the state follows in its activities is so bad that it cannot be made public, then it cannot possibly survive questioning from the moral standpoint. There is no third possibility. Either a state accepts publicity and then qualifies for morality, or the state hides what it has done and should then meet with the disapproval of the international community. It is difficult to see how Turkey could become a member of the European Union (EU), given the strong commitment of the EU towards the implementation of human rights. With Turkey as a full member of the EU and possibly as its second largest member, the EU would have a morality problem in its own structure.

Self-enforceability does not work at all in relation to morality. The implementation deficit is immense and can only be ameliorated by means of international juridical action. Thus, the international regime focusing upon the International Court in The Hague should be bolstered by new rules against crimes against humanity. As these rules have to struggle against state interests, they can only be argued on the basis of the concerns for justice, i.e. morality in the international community. This is an endless task, the relevance of which is not diminished by its practical difficulties.

The moral theory of an international order orientated towards Kantian ethics may have to struggle with immense practical difficulties, but these do not in the least reduce the equitable nature of the enterprise. If crimes against humanity are to be eliminated from the earth once and for all, then it can only be done by means of collective action, where an international regime is empowered to penalize the ever-present defection alternative. It should be possible to devise implementation *ex ante*, i.e. warnings against such crimes, due to the fact that information about the conditions in the countries of the world is much more accessible now than it used to be, although the fears of states against unlawful interference in their domestic affairs will no doubt be substantial. At the same time implementation *ex post* is absolutely crucial.

The Kantian world federation idea is probably impracticable. Thus, we can only rely upon the existing complex pattern of international organizations. But the competencies of the intergovernmental organizations (IGOs) and the non-governmental organizations (NGOs) can be augmented, both executive and judicial. Besides there are the emerging regional co-ordination mechanisms. The emergence of the EU makes Kant's approach relevant, as the EU raises the hopes of eternal peace, at least in Europe. Kant's argument is, however, not based upon state auto-limitation among governments as actors. It belongs not to the expediency tradition but to the equity legacy, which draws implications about the behaviour of states from normative principles of argument, i.e. what justice requires from governments when they interact with each other.

Kant did not elaborate upon his idea of a world federation in greater detail. Thus, he did not face up to the enforcement problem. What prevents states from entering into an agreement to respect world peace and then reneging on this contract at some later occasion? Without some enforcement mechanism the commitment is not credible, as history has shown time and time again. As emphasized in relation to Grotius, we know much about what morality requires from governments. But it is the Hobbesian problem of incentives that is so crucial. How can the world community establish and maintain organizations through which basic institutions are enforced?

We suggest neither a world government nor one that continues the present system of state co-ordination. Mankind cannot solve the problems of the globe without intergovernmental co-operation. To rely on market co-ordination only is not enough due to global market failures such as externalities, rent dissipation, free riding, market instabilities, etc. But how, then, are the rules of the global society including the global market place to be enforced?

Too much centralization (*Scylla*)

The existing system of world governance is a carpet with many independent pieces between which there is not much co-ordination. This fact reflects both the historical evolution of these bodies, many of which need state approval for their existence, and a deep suspicion against co-ordination at the international level, as states guard their rights.

States will accept international co-ordination under certain conditions. They will not accept a general transfer of power to international bodies when they cannot predict how such powers will be employed. Thus, some competencies have been delegated to certain international bodies, but these are based upon the assent of the states.

States decide to join international bodies and thus they implicitly accept to comply with the decisions and actions of these bodies. If they are not pleased with what these bodies do or say, then they may decide to leave. Nothing forces a state to become a member of the United Nations (UN), the WB, the IMF or the WTO. Entrance to these international organizations is in principle the same as entrance to a club, i.e. it is based upon voluntary exchange. Thus, states enter these bodies because they regard it as being more to their advantage to be in than to be outside the organization in question.

However, the international order that has been created through voluntary assent by states is not merely a set of private agreements. They constitute the bulk of public international law, which is the legal order of mankind, valid for all states whether they are members or not. The international legal order has resulted from the many treaties between states as well as the practice of international bodies together with international jurisprudence delivering principles about Right Reason in relation to mankind.

If states commit actions in violation of the rules of the international legal order, then they may suffer from sanctions from member-states. In the case of peace and war they may even suffer from military retaliation from the international community. Although the enforcement of the institutions of the international legal order is problematic, given the non-existence of a world government, states cannot do as they wish in relation to matters that fall under the jurisdiction of international regimes.

This construction of a system for world governance without one world government reflects the foundations of the existing world order, which rests upon sovereign nation-states. They collaborate when they find it mutually advantageous to do so – Hobbes's perspective. Or they accept restrictions upon their discretion when the needs of mankind impose it upon them – Grotius's perspective.

World governance in this decentralized structure is most probably the only acceptable solution to the states. They will oppose any attempt to create strong governance at the international level. Increased levels of centralization would threaten state interests and could jeopardize the co-ordination that has been achieved.

What can be done in the future is only to strengthen gradually this patchy pattern of international co-ordination. No attempts to create a world order led by one superpower have been successful. This is true of all empires in history. The world will have to live with several governance mechanisms at the international level, which will not be co-ordinated through one mechanism.

Too much centralization would be experienced as a threat towards the states and cultures of the world. It would be rejected as an imperialist attempt. What makes the international legal order a real constraint ensues from the fact that most member-states wish to respect it and are prepared to engage in sanctions in order to make it respectable. Too much centralization would undermine this foundation of international co-ordination as based upon assent.

Too much decentralization (*Charybdis*)

When analysing how international bodies like the UN or international organizations like Interpol operate, then one finds as the general feature the strong fear of rendering competencies to supra-national bodies. This appears also in the EU, although here there has been some movement beyond this fear, at least to some extent. Given the strong emphasis upon the states and the rights of the states, this tendency towards decentralization is no surprise, but it poses several major problems for the governance of the world community.

Too much decentralization implies that international bodies can do little when a few states refuse to go along. The blocking capacity is stronger than the capacity to change in the construction of the bodies responsible for world co-ordination or governance. Any group of choice participants must trade off the capacity of one member to veto any decision by the group against the capacity of the group to get something done. In the international organizations the key players are the nation-states, which guard their right to veto with great care. However, this blocks the international organization's capacity to act.

Blocking power works both *ex ante* and *ex post* in international organizations. First, it makes it difficult to arrive at positive decisions concerning international co-ordination. Since unanimity is an often-employed decision rule for aggregating the opinions of member-states, the veto cast by one government tends to make action impossible. However, if action is taken, then compliance with implementation requires acceptance by the member-states concerned. Governments who face adverse decisions often simply refuse to respect them and then obstruct their implementation. Reneging is the problem and it may occur even when a government is a part of positive decisions but does not really want to implement them – the Japanese policy under the international regime governing whaling, for example.

Blocking *ex ante* a decision or *ex post* a decision makes international co-ordination not very predictable. First, world governance suffers from the enormous difficulties in getting governments to agree on what to do. Second, world governmance has few mechanisms of implementation at its disposal to see to it that decisions do not remain as lofty proclamations. It could be argued that decentralization is too strong in today's world governance structure, which explains why there are so many NGOs also operating besides the main international organizations: the UN, WB, IMF and WTO.

Excessive decentralization is the other side of the coin of fear of centralization, or it is a strong respect of the rights of the nation-states. There needs to be a balancing act between *Scylla* (strong centralization) and

Charybdis (excessive decentralization). Some people may argue that there is a binary choice, meaning that one can only have one or the other. We believe, however, that the possibilities of strengthening world governance have not been fully identified or explored. The margin between *Scylla* and *Charybdis* is potentially larger than has been realized when it comes to avoiding both strong centralization and excessive decentralization.

Increased international co-ordination can be achieved if one were to make use of the existing pattern of a plethora of international organizations, IGOs, NGOs and regional co-ordination mechanisms. What must be changed is the blocking power, both *ex ante* and *ex post*.

Less of veto power but more of sanctions against reneging

The existing system of intergovernmental co-ordination is highly frag-mented, but that acts as a guarantee against excessive centralization. It includes certain enforcement powers which counteract its excessive decentralization. In fact, this is the way to go forward in a pragmatic fashion, learning from each step towards a strengthening of intergovern-mental co-ordination to find out whether it works or not.

Ex ante: To empower these IGOs that already operate, one must relax the unanimity requirement. There are so many different voting rules that one can use besides the perhaps-too-drastic but highly efficient simple majority scheme. International organizations have only begun to reflect over the possibilities of quantitative voting, which, together with inclusive voting rules, can give enough protection for governments against unwanted decisions at the same time at the organization itself is not made totally powerless, as with the veto rule.

Many problems in international governance are more of a legal nature than strictly political. Thus, judges and courts can be used more often and given more competences to judge cases where a state has been negligent or refuses to implement a decision by an international body.

Ex post: Reneging is the great sin in international co-ordination. The possibility of delivering sanctions against a government that reneges must be strengthened. It is true that imposing sanctions is not an easy task in intergovernmental bodies, but it occurs and sometimes it works. Thus, the UN can impose severe sanctions upon a government that threatens the international community or neglects its duties towards other countries. The International Court of Justice in The Hague has not only ruled effectively in many cases involving conflicts between states but also imposed sanctions, sometimes with consequences.

Sometimes the countries of the world that wish to live by the principles of Grotius call themselves the 'international community'. Although this is a very loosely defined group of states where membership is floating and participation changing, it sometimes takes action and imposes sanctions against violations of international law. The international community may create an *ad hoc* war tribunal for crimes against humanity, as with the wars in the Balkans in the 1990s. Or the international community may decide to create a permanent tribunal for such crimes.

Courts can also play an important role in other international bodies and their rulings can be increasingly accepted by member-states due to the legitimacy of judges. One interesting example is the WTO which quite extensively employs court proceedings to arrive at decisions in trade disputes. Such dispute settlement mechanisms could be used much more in IGOs.

Fewer players: State co-ordination is a version of the general problem of collective action where free riding is an option. The greater the number of states that engage in collective action, the more promising the free riding option is. This follows from the typical N-1 and 1/N difficulties that groups comprising N members face. The logical consequence is that collective action would be far easier if there were fewer players, and also if these players had a longer time horizon.

Numbers and discounting have a very negative impact upon the possibility of resolving collective action problems. If the number of players participating in a group is brought down, then free riding could be more easily policed and a player would stand greater risk to lose by not voluntarily participating. The longer the time horizon of the players, the less attractive becomes the free riding option due the future costs of retaliation from group members.

When regional associations of states emerge, then this can be interpreted as a positive development from the perspective of handling collective action problems. Thus, the EU reduces 15 states to one voice which reduces transaction costs considerably when it comes to negotiating and enforcing international agreements. Regional integration in other parts of the world such as North and South America as well as South East Asia can be interpreted in the same vein, as reducing the probability of free riding. However, reducing the number of players in a group does not guarantee that the remaining players will find optimal solutions and also respect them. Big states can still decide to free ride before an agreement is made or by reneging on a final agreement.

International co-ordination is basically a voluntary phenomenon. The state is the organization which possesses a claim to sovereign power, meaning that governments can legislate about the interests of their countries in a manner which can be restricted only through self-regulation. The auto-regulation of the state can take three forms. First, governments bind their states by signing conventions and protocols which contain rules about what states can and should do. Second, governments enter their states into various clubs or IGOs by applying for membership, thus accepting the rules of the international organization. Third, governments may accept the activities of NGOs, thus limiting their own scope of manoeuvring. Let us discuss some examples of the last two forms of international co-ordination. The first kind was examined in chapter 11 in relation to the institutions of war and peace.

The economic governance institutions

Economic co-ordination is carried out by the global market and the international organizations supporting it. These organizations are basically clubs into which states enter through the membership mechanism. However, the world economic organizations are even more contested than the Security Council, especially during the last decade. Although these organizations originated from one framework for world economic regulation – the Bretton Woods System created in 1945 – they may be examined as comprising three separate elements, although interacting frequently:

The World Bank: What distinguishes the World Bank (WB) is its commitment to fostering long-term economic development. It is active in Third World countries, financing investments that are to be paid back over a long period of time, or more than ten years. It raises its capital on the international capital markets and lends it out on favourable terms to the borrowing countries, meaning lower interest rates than could be obtained in the market. The WB has thus far not faced default on any of its many loans.

In the year 2000 the number of countries members of the World Bank was 183. Twenty-five countries took part at its inaugural meeting. In 1947 the number of countries was 47, in 1965, 102 and in 1985, 149. One of the major activities of the WB is to commit loans to developing countries. During the 1990s the total commitments from IBRD (International Bank for Reconstruction and Development (UN)) and IDA (International Development Association (UN)) have ranged between US$ 20 billions (1990) and US$ 29 billions in 1999. Running these programmes, i.e. the total administrative budget, amounted to a cost of 1353 millions in US dollars in 1998.

The WB consists of the IBRD as well as the IDA. The IBRD was established in 1945 while the IDA came into operation as late as 1960. Together with the International Financial Corporation (IFC), the Multilateral Investment Guarantee Agency (MIGA) and the International Centre for Settlement of Investment Disputes (ICSID), these institutions form what is called the World Bank group. Initially, the IBRD focused on post-war reconstruction in Europe, but later its main objective has been to assist the economic development of the member-countries. When the IDA was established in 1960, it aimed to assist the poorer countries among the developing countries. Over the years the WB has changed its investment policy from a focus upon big infrastructure projects to including human capital or social capital projects. Today it finances projects that empower women and that enhance community development. It also engages in projects aiming at public sector reform.

The IMF: The role of the International Monetary Fund (IMF) is entirely different from that of the WB, as it handles short-term problems concerning currency exchange and the balance of payments in member-countries. It is basically a kind of a bank where members may deposit surplus funds, which they may later draw upon when things become tight. The IMF has 140 member-states and it operates a system of drawing rights, which in some cases may include exceptional credits to countries in desperate need for foreign currency.

The IMF was founded in 1945. Representatives from 29 countries signed its founding charter, and when it began its operations in 1946 it had 39 members, which may be compared with its current membership of 183 countries in the year 2000. The objectives of the IMF have primarily been to promote international monetary co-operation and facilitate the expansion and balanced growth of international trade. In practice, much of the work of the IMF has been focused on various kinds of financial assistance or financial crises. Up to now the major beneficiaries have been Mexico, Russia, Korea and Argentina. In the year 2000 the IMF had a total fund credit and loan outstanding amounting to some US$ 66.5 billions. These assets are raised through what are called quota subscriptions, which means that each member-country contributes with a certain sum of money according to its ability. In 1946 this contribution amounted to US$ 7.6 billions but was US$ 193 billions in 1998, or roughly 0.6 per cent of the Gross World Product. These quotas also form the basis for the vote in the governing bodies of the IMF, which means that the major voting powers belong to the USA, Germany, Japan, France and the UK. The IMF is one of the larger international organizations in terms of staff, as it numbers some 2600. The cost of running this organization was in 1998 close to US$ 500 millions, but the IMF has few powers of control as to how its money is spent.

The IMF used to operate on the basis of the gold standard that was reintroduced in the Bretton Woods system, until the USA went off the gold standard in 1971. Since then, the IMF handles a floating exchange system where countries can seek help when their currencies change rapidly. The IMF does not restrict itself to providing reserves but conditions its assistance upon the making of certain policies that may in the long run stabilize the economy of the country. The most-discussed policy has been the so-called structural adjustment policy that the IMF imposed upon the Third World countries during the 1980s and 1990s. The actions of the IMF during the South East Asian crisis have also stimulated much discussion, linked to whether Plan A or Plan B would work the best for saving these economies, the latter but not the former involving the use of capital controls.

The IMF has recently shifted somewhat its orientation from underlining free capital movements and foreign investments to promote social development within the country. Some claim that the IMF bears a large responsibility for aggravating poverty problems in several Third World countries, to which the IMF usually replies that the situation would have been even worse without IMF assistance.

The WTO: Emerging out of the GATT framework, the World Trade Organization (WTO) in Geneva is the forum for the governance of world trade. Its mandate is actually rather large, as it covers not only trade in goods but also trade in services including intellectual property rights. The WTO includes a tribunal which may rule over complaints and which has at its disposal certain sanctions.

The WTO governs a huge agreement among its member-states, covering thousands of pages regulating world trade. This agreement covers not only reductions in tariffs and quotas but also the removal of technical hindrances to trade. Trade easily becomes very technical and a full liberalization of world trade would require extensive harmonization of technical specifications on products. The WTO framework involves strategic action on the part of many countries, which negotiate about market access and reciprocal reductions in barriers to trade. Certain Third World countries have accused the rich countries of using the WTO for enhancing their specific trade interests, whereas the poor countries still suffer from the agricultural policies of the rich countries. Further reductions in tariffs and quotas are still a high priority for the WTO, which, however, is also very interested in extending trade liberalization to services.

Regional governance mechanisms

Another kind of intergovernmental organization is exemplified by the initiatives taken to establish regional economic co-operation in various parts of the world. The EU was the first one of its kind when it started as the European Economic Community in 1957. Beginning as a community to promote a reduction of customs it has developed into an intergovernmental organization co-operating in both the political and economic sphere (but not as yet ending up as a federation).

More or less similar regional initiatives have been set up in South East Asia, North America and South America. The oldest one of these is ASEAN, or the Association of South East Asian Nations, formed in 1967. The founding nations were Indonesia, Malaysia, Philippines, Singapore and Thailand. It has subsequently extended its membership and in the year 2000

Brunei, Cambodia, Laos, Myanmar and Vietnam had joined the ASEAN. In 1993 an ASEAN Regional Forum (ARF) was established with the intention of including the People's Republic of China among its participants. In the year 2000 the ARF membership stands at 22. The main objectives of ASEAN relate to trade and security. Within the trade area the aim is to establish a free trade area within the region by 2008. Since the ASEAN was established during the Vietnam war, the end of the cold war has put new issues on the agenda. The main conflictual problems that this area faces with regard to military security arise from the maritime claims in the South China Sea as well as the control over the potentially oil-rich Spratley and Parcel Islands.

The North American Free Trade Agreement (NAFTA) between the USA and Canada came into effect on 1 January 1989. NAFTA aims at removing most of the restrictions on trade and investments between the countries. NAFTA was extended to include Mexico from November 1993. There have been negotiations with Chile but so far no extension of the membership has taken place.

Finally, we may mention the Southern Common Market, or MERCOSUR (Spanish)/MERCOSUL (Portuguese). It was established in 1991 and its aim was to create a common market for the four member countries: Argentina, Brazil, Paraguay and Uruguay. In 1996 Chile negotiated a free-trade agreement with MERCOSUR, and in 1997 such an agreement was also concluded with Bolivia.

One response to the governance needs in the global period is to put up partial mechanisms, i.e. governmental co-ordination within a specific region of the world. This approach will not solve all problems of governing a global economy because it is not comprehensive enough. There will still be a need for international organizations, which will handle the interaction between these regional 'states' and the rest of the world community of governments. The most advanced experiment with regional co-ordination over the economies of several countries is the EU, which has engaged in a governance of the economy that is far stronger than the other two regional mechanisms, the NAFTA and the ASEAN.

Governing the economies of Western Europe was one of the main reasons for the creation of the European Economic Community in 1958. The EEC started out as a customs union, developed strongly through the creation of an internal market and has today reached the stage of a monetary union with a single currency. The EU includes more than economic governance as it also encompasses foreign policy and defence co-operation as well as police and border control matters. As long as the economic co-ordination is much more extensive than the political co-operation, one can maintain that the EU is more an economic club than a new state in Western Europe.

This is not the place to enter into the debate about the constitutional development of the EU towards a possible federal state for Europe. This involves difficult questions about both the enlargement and the deepening of the union. What needs to be emphasized instead is the amount of economic governance that the EU has accomplished, integrating 15 countries' economies into one single framework. The most conspicuous sign of the institutional integration in Western Europe is the rapid development of EU law, comprising the treaties, the legislation in Brussels and the case law of the European Court of Justice. Much of this law is in reality state governance of the economy.

The development of the EU out of the EEC is the hitherto most successful case of regional co-ordination among states. The EEC started out as a customs union, developed into a common market and has recently introduced a common currency, the euro. It is neither a confederation nor a federation from the point of view of constitutional law. It is stronger than a confederation but weaker than a federation. It has certain state attributes such as law, money and public servants. But it lacks other state attributes such as an army, a police force and implementation organizations at the regional and local levels. The peculiar organization of the EU testifies to the capacity of institutional innovation to go beyond existing practices. World governance may increasingly take the form of regional co-operation in mechanisms to which states delegate competencies.

Ad hoc organizations and their regimes

Besides the major international organization in the UN system or the Bretton Woods institutions, there is an immense variety of smaller organizations, some intergovernmental and some non-governmental. Some serve vital needs of states, such as Interpol, whereas others attempt to further the interests of mankind, such as the Whaling Commission and Amnesty International. Whether these organizations are intergovernmental, semipublic or private matters little for their basic mode of operation, which is restricted by the logic of all kinds of international co-ordination, namely the power of the member-states of the international community.

Interpol

The International Criminal Police Organization (Interpol) is orientated towards facilitating co-operation among the criminal police within more than 125 member-countries in the fight against international crime. It promotes co-operation between police authorities within the limits of the laws in each country. A general secretariat headed by a secretary handles its everyday efforts. Each affiliated country has a domestic clearing house through which its police forces can communicate either with the general secretariat or with the police of other affiliated countries. Interpol is an information centre and not itself a police force.

Interpol operates a giant record of international criminals at its headquarters in Lyon, France. It holds information about their identities, aliases, associates and methods of working, received from the police of member-countries. Interpol is only a concrete instrument for fighting crime through the use of extradition between countries.

Generally speaking, Interpol identifies three kinds of international criminals. First, there are criminals who operate in more than one country: smugglers dealing mainly in gold and narcotics. Second, other criminals who do not travel but their crimes affect other countries – for example a counterfeiter of foreign banknotes. Finally, there are criminals who commit a crime in one country and then go to another. Besides collecting information about these three kinds of criminals, Interpol may ask that a criminal be detained so that extradition proceedings can be initiated. Interpol also collects information about property smuggled out of a country in which a crime was committed as well as about unidentified bodies in order to reveal their identity.

The General Assembly and its Executive Committee are the managing bodies of Interpol, whereas the permanent departments within the General Secretariat attempt to implement what the two deliberative organs decide. The close contacts between the National Central Bureaux (NCBs) of Interpol in the various member-countries and the General Secretariat in Lyon make up the core of Interpol's efforts at crime prevention. The Liaison and Criminal Intelligence Division handles the centralization of police information, managing the computerized processing of police information and the electronic archive system. The Criminal Intelligence Sub-Division is responsible for processing information intended for the NCBs, using up-to-date and sophisticated technology, often responding quickly to requests from NCBs.

The Message Research and Response Branch records police information in accordance with the rules on data protection and the deletion of information. It deals with requests from NCBs and works closely with the Liaison and Criminal Intelligence Division. The International Notices Section drafts and publishes notices at the request of the NCBs, with emphasis on rapid circulation. The files in the General Secretariat's records section are electronically scanned. The Fingerprinting and Identification Department is responsible for processing fingerprints and photographs, and updating their files. The Automated Search and Archives (ASA) Section is engaged in electronically archiving all criminal data received at the General Secretariat and in operating the Automated Search Facility (ASF). This enables the NCBs to have direct access to the database. The Analytical Criminal Intelligence Unit gives to the General Secretariat and Interpol's member-countries tactical and strategic intelligence relating to international crime in order to define criminal networks more accurately, to determine enforcement priorities and to plan effective follow-up enforcement action.

According to Interpol there are three main factors which hamper international co-operation. Different structures of various police forces in some countries make it difficult to know which particular department is empowered to deal with a case or to supply information. Second, the fact that different countries use different languages can become a barrier to communication. Finally, problems arise due to the immense variation in legal systems throughout the world.

Is the work of Interpol sufficient to stem international crime? The NCBs collect criminal intelligence which has a direct bearing on international police co-operation from sources in their own countries, and pass this material on to the other NCBs and the General Secretariat. They try to see to it that police action or operations requested by another country's NCB are carried out on their territory, receiving requests for information, checks, etc. from other NCBs while replying to such requests. Finally, they transmit requests for international co-operation made by their own courts or police departments to the NCBs of other countries. Yet, despite all the work put in by Interpol as well as many national police forces, crime has been on the increase for a long time and it is becoming more and more international. Crime is a threat against the market economy, because in many cases it makes reneging more lucrative than the contractual honesty that is a foundation-stone of the market economy.

The International Whaling Commission

The IWC was set up in 1946 under the International Convention for the Regulation of Whaling. It is an intergovernmental organization that remains outside the UN framework. At the beginning of the twenty-first century, it has 40 countries counted as its members, including whaling countries like Norway, Canada, Japan and Russia as well as non-whaling countries like Austria, Sweden and Switzerland; Iceland left the IWC in 1992.

The basic purpose of the IWC is to work for the conservation of the world stock of whales. This is done through setting up regulations for whaling, and a pause in commercial whaling was introduced between 1985 and 1993 when Norway resumed commercial whaling. The IWC also designates whale sanctuaries in certain parts of the world oceans. In order to be able to fulfil its regulations, the IWC conducts research aimed at estimating the world stock of whales. Due to the difficulties of arriving at reliable estimates, the IWC has not published any estimates of the total whale population since 1989, only for the species where they know they have reliable estimates. Thus they estimate that there are slightly less than 1 million of minke whales which is the kind of species that is hunted by the Norwegians, amounting to a catch of some 500 whales per year at the end of the twentieth century. The other major whale hunting countries are Canada, Russia, Japan as well as USA (Alaska) and Denmark (Greenland).

Non-governmental organizations

Although the total number of NGOs is larger than that of the IGOs, we will here present only a few examples of NGOs. We will briefly comment upon two kinds of NGOs, namely organizations concerned with environment as well as organizations focusing upon human rights. Some of these environmentalist groups may also be called transnational environmental activist groups (TEAGs) and among them we include the Friends of the Earth (FoE) as well as Greenpeace. The World Wide Fund For Nature (WWF) seems, however, to represent a more traditional form of organization. These environmental organizations were established in the early 1960s or in the 1970s. They made themselves known worldwide during the late 1970s but they seem to have peaked in terms of membership already in the early 1990s.

The oldest of these three organizations is WWF, which was founded as a charity in Switzerland in 1961. From the beginning the WWF was headed by various royal celebrities like HRH The Duke of Edinburgh and HRH Prince Bernhard of the Netherlands. From the 1980s and during the 1990s the WWF has collaborated with other organizations like the UNEP and the ICUN (World Conservation Union). Its work is aimed at the preservation of biological diversity as well as the promotion of the concept of sustainable uses of resources and the reduction of wasteful consumption and pollution. In the mid-1990s it claimed almost 5 million supporters and a presence in around 130 countries. The operating expenditure of the organization in 1998 was close to US$ 60 millions.

The Friends of the Earth was founded in 1971 by organizations from France, Sweden, the UK and the USA. By the end of the 1990s it claims to have organizations in 63 countries. The total number of members and supporters of groups adhering to the Friends of the Earth come close to 1 million. The combined annual budget for the FoE groups was estimated to come close to US$ 200 millions. The FoE is thus a network of environmental groups working as a pressure group at the national as well as the international level. The common theme for these groups is campaigning for an environmentally sustainable development.

Greenpeace is probably the best known among the TEAGs. It was founded in Canada in 1971. Its aims were to end nuclear testing but also to halt and reverse the destruction of the biosphere. In the early 1990s it claimed to have more than 4.5 million supporters in 143 countries. At that time it had offices in 30 countries – probably the period when Greenpeace peaked in terms of membership. In 1995 the membership worldwide was down to 2.9 million supporters, and it even went to 2.4 million in 1998 but was again on the rise to 2.5 million supporters in 1999. The same pattern is obvious among the national sections and in Sweden there was a decrease from 110,000 supporters in 1995 to 71,000 in 2000. As a matter of fact, in the USA the organization dropped from 2.3 million supporters in 1990 to 350 thousands in 1998. This slowdown also appears from the reports on total expenditures of Greenpeace 'World Wide' as well as for Greenpeace International. In US dollars there was a decrease from 153 millions in 1995 to 118 millions in 1998 for the 'World Wide' organization, while Greenpeace International decreased from US$ 37 millions in 1995 to US$ 29 millions in 1998.

Among the human rights organizations there are two major ones, namely Amnesty International (AI) and the Human Rights Watch (HRW). AI is the older one of the two as it was founded in 1961 through the initiative of the British lawyer Peter Benenson. From the beginning its objective was to fight for the right of individuals put in prisons for political reasons. The aims of the organization have subsequently been broadened to include campaigns for human rights in general and not least the campaign against the practice of the death penalty. A sign of recognition of its work in the international community was the Nobel Peace Prize in 1977.

Already in 1980 AI had built up a large international network with the establishment of national sections in around 40 countries; its membership figures at that time could be counted in hundreds of thousands. The AI continued to grow also in the 1990s and has claimed a worldwide membership of more than 1 million. At the end of the twentieth century the AI had established national sections in 57 countries and members are present in more than 160 countries. Yet there are signs of a slowdown in its expansion during the last years of the 1990s. From a yearly budget close on £6000 in 1961 it had increased to £10 millions in 1990 and £17.7 millions in 1998 (= US$ 30 millions); if we assume that AI stands for one-third of the expenditures of AI worldwide, then the total expenditures would come close to US$ 90 millions.

The Human Rights Watch was founded as the Helsinki Watch in 1978. Its main objectives at that time were to watch the implementation of the Helsinki Accords agreed upon in 1975. Thus the focus was on the standing of human rights in the Soviet Union and in Eastern Europe. The network of watch committees that had emerged changed its name to Human Rights Watch (HRW) in 1988 to reflect the reorientation of the work of the network to cover human rights globally. The HRW is thus an independent, non-governmental organization relying on contributions from private individuals and foundations and not from government funds. In 1998 its total operating expenses were estimated to be in the region of US$ 12.6 millions.

Comparing the financial resources of the international organizations surveyed, there is no doubt that the IGOs working within the UN system have more resources than the NGOs focusing on environment or human rights. But it also seems to be the case that the environmental NGOs are more resourceful than the human rights NGOs.

A lack of consensus

States react in an ambivalent manner towards international co-ordination. Since they may benefit from it, they favour it. However, as they may suffer from it, they oppose it. Centralization is rejected because it would make the members of the international community – the states of the world – too weak. At the same time complete decentralization is not in the best interests of the states, as it would be conducive to the law of the jungle. In addition, such a Hobbesian predicament where states would be in a constant struggle with each other would be extremely dangerous for the other major party of international co-ordination, namely mankind or the populations in the member-states.

Co-ordinating 195 states, or the governments of these states, entails not only the big numbers problem that is at the core of collective action difficulties. It also involves facing up to immense differences in values among the governments. International co-ordination starts from the whole spectrum of various values, ideologies, ethnicities and religions and has to distil from this variety the common interests of both member-states and mankind.

Governments act in relation to the demand for international co-ordination on the basis of both true long-term state interests and short-term opportunism. Opportunism may occur both before and after the signing of an international treaty. Pre-contractual opportunism results in high transaction costs whereas post-contractual opportunism leads to reneging. One method for strengthening international co-ordination is to steer away from opportunism and hand over a set of issues to judges.

The growing reliance upon courts and judicial action in order to settle political disputes or conflicts is not confined to the domestic arena, where many scholars have pointed out the strong drive towards judicialization. Since domestic issues may prove too difficult to handle or resolve by means of the democratic arena, many groups have turned to litigation as a weapon in the domestic struggle. Judges and courts, however, can be a great deal of use in international governance, as they could be very usefully employed to protect mankind against the worst forms of crimes.

Judicialization: International Criminal Court

Early the UN argued the need to establish an international criminal court to prosecute crimes such as genocide. In resolution 260 of 9 December 1948, adopting the Convention on the Prevention and Punishment of the Crime of Genocide with article I characterizing genocide as 'a crime under international law', article VI provides that persons charged with genocide 'shall be tried by a competent tribunal of the State in the territory of which the act was committed or by such international penal tribunal as may have jurisdiction'. In that same resolution, the General Assembly asked the

International Law Commission to suggest an international judicial organ for the trial of persons charged with genocide. Following the Commission's conclusion about the establishment of an international court to try persons charged with genocide or other crimes of similar gravity, the General Assembly established a committee to prepare proposals relating to the establishment of such a court. The committee prepared a draft statute in 1951 and a revised draft statute in 1953, which, however, was never finally adopted.

Yet, the question of the establishment of an international criminal court resurfaced. In 1989 the General Assembly asked the International Law Commission to resume work on an international criminal court with jurisdiction to include drug trafficking. When the conflict in the former Yugoslavia broke out involving war crimes, crimes against humanity and genocide ('ethnic cleansing') again received international attention. The UN Security Council established the *ad hoc* International Criminal Tribunal for the former Yugoslavia, which has for several years conducted investigations to hold individuals accountable for atrocities of these kinds.

An International Law Commission completed its work on the draft statute for an international criminal court in 1994 and submitted the draft statute to the General Assembly. The General Assembly then established the Ad Hoc Committee on the Establishment of an International Criminal Court and it created the Preparatory Committee on the Establishment of an International Criminal Court which completed the drafting of the text. At its fifty-second session, the General Assembly decided to convene the UN Diplomatic Conference of Plenipotentiaries on the Establishment of an International Criminal Court, subsequently held in Rome in July 1998. It adopted a convention on the establishment of an international criminal court, which will come into effect when it is ratified by more than 60 states.

The establishment of a permanent international criminal court (ICC) is seen as a new step forward in relation to the primary objectives of the UN as securing universal respect for human rights throughout the world. The fight against impunity and the struggle for peace and justice and human rights in conflict situations in today's world is seen as most urgent. Actually, an international criminal court has been called the missing link in the international legal system. The International Court of Justice at The Hague handles only cases between states, not individuals. Without an international criminal court for dealing with individual responsibility as an enforcement mechanism, acts of genocide and egregious violations of human rights often go unpunished. In the last 50 years, there have been many instances of crimes against humanity and war crimes for which no individuals have been held accountable: Cambodia, Rwanda, Congo, etc. Two *ad hoc* international criminal tribunals, one for the former Yugoslavia (as mentioned above) and another for Rwanda, have been created recently, but it has been considered that that only a permanent court can effectively stem these atrocities against mankind. The establishment of an *ad hoc* tribunal entails 'selective justice'. A permanent court would operate in a more consistent way, taking up all relevant cases. Reference has also been made to 'tribunal fatigue', or the delays inherent in setting up an *ad hoc* tribunal, which lead to a situation in which crucial evidence can deteriorate or be destroyed and perpetrators can escape or disappear, etc. The tremendous effort behind *ad hoc* tribunals may soften the political will required to mandate them. Basically, *ad hoc* tribunals are subject to limits of time or place. For instance, the mandate of the Rwanda Tribunal is limited to events that occurred in 1994, but genocide also took place after 1994.

The approach was handed down in the Nuremberg Tribunal, which stated that 'crimes against international law are committed by men, not by abstract entities, and only by punishing individuals who commit such crimes can the provisions of international law be enforced'. This established the principle of individual criminal accountability for all who commit such acts as a corner-stone of international criminal law. According to the Draft Code of Crimes against the Peace and Security of Mankind, completed in 1996 by the International Law Commission at the request of the General Assembly, this principle applies equally and without exception to any individual throughout the governmental hierarchy or military chain of command. Already in 1948 in the Convention on the Prevention and Punishment of the Crime of Genocide the UN laid down that the crime of genocide may be committed by constitutionally responsible rulers, public officials or private individuals.

The states have emphasized all along in the discussion about creating an international criminal court that criminals should in the first place be brought to justice by national institutions. But in times of conflict, whether internal or international, normal state institutions may be either unwilling or unable to act. Governments may lack the political will to prosecute their own citizens, such as bureaucrats or military men, as was the case in the former Yugoslavia. Or state institutions may have collapsed, as in the case of states around the Great Lakes in Africa.

Perpetrators of war crimes and crimes against humanity tend to go unpunished. Despite the military tribunals following the Second World War and the two recent *ad hoc* international criminal tribunals for the former Yugoslavia and for Rwanda, this is also the case today. Effective deterrence would only be possible if an international criminal court is created. The main difficulty in setting up such a court is again the fear among states that they could be forced to hand over persons that they do not wish to see prosecuted and tried – what is referred to as the criteria of admissibility of prosecution. Why would states sign such a treaty that could have negative consequences for them?

The Rome Treaty creating the International Criminal Court will only be ratified if sufficient states feel that they have little to lose in terms of such a mechanism. The Rome Treaty goes to great lengths in seeing to it that democratic states honouring human rights will have nothing to fear. This court will in principle only try cases that are already clearly defined as unacceptable atrocities in 'Rule of Law' countries.

Article 1 introduces the International Criminal Court ('the Court'): 'It shall be a permanent institution and shall have the power to exercise its jurisdiction over persons for the most serious crimes of international concern, as referred to in this Statute, and shall be complementary to national criminal jurisdictions. The jurisdiction and functioning of the Court shall be governed by the provisions of this Statute.'

Article 4 gives the Court on international legal personality: 'It shall have such legal capacity as may be necessary for the exercise of its functions and the fulfilment of its purposes. The Court may exercise its functions and powers, as provided in this Statute, on the territory of any State Party and, by special agreement, on the territory of any other State. The jurisdiction of the Court is limited to what is called the most serious crimes of concern to the international community as a whole: (a) The crime of genocide; (b) Crimes against humanity; (c) War crimes; (d) The crime of aggression.'

In reality, most of the articles of the Rome Treaty deal with the problem of admissibility: When and how can the Court initiate an investigation against persons in a specific country that may lead to prosecution and trial for crime against mankind? The Prosecutor may initiate investigations *proprio motu* on the basis of information on crimes within the jurisdiction of the Court. He or she may seek additional information from states, organs of the United Nations, intergovernmental or non-governmental organizations, or other reliable sources that he or she deems appropriate, and may receive written or oral testimony at the seat of the Court. If the Prosecutor concludes that there is a reasonable basis to proceed with an investigation, he or she shall submit to the Pre-Trial Chamber a request for authorization of an investigation, together with any supporting material collected. Victims may make representations to the Pre-Trial Chamber, in accordance with the Rules of Procedure and Evidence. The Pre-Trial Chamber may upon examination of the request and the supporting material consider that there is a reasonable basis to proceed with an investigation. It shall then authorize the commencement of the investigation, without prejudice to subsequent determinations by the Court with regard to the jurisdiction and admissibility of a case.

The key concept of admissibility or inadmissibility comprises criteria for deciding both when an investigation cannot be initiated and when it should be initiated. Inadmissibility occurs in the following situations:

(i) The case is being investigated or prosecuted by a state which has jurisdiction over it, unless the state is unwilling or unable genuinely to carry out the investigation or prosecution;

(ii) The case has been investigated by a state which has jurisdiction over it and the state has decided not to prosecute the person concerned, unless the decision resulted from the unwillingness or inability of the state genuinely to prosecute;

(iii) The person concerned has already been tried for conduct which is the subject of the complaint, and a trial by the Court is not permitted under article 20, paragraph 3;
(iv) The case is not of sufficient gravity to justify further action by the Court.

Admissibility, on the other hand, occurs when there is unwillingness: the Court has to consider whether one or more of the following exist:

(i) The proceedings were or are being undertaken or the national decision was made for the purpose of shielding the person concerned from criminal responsibility for crimes within the jurisdiction of the Court referred to in article 5;
(ii) There has been an unjustified delay in the proceedings which in the circumstances is inconsistent with an intent to bring the person concerned to justice;
(iii) The proceedings were not or are not being conducted independently or impartially, and they were or are being conducted in a manner which, in the circumstances, is inconsistent with an intent to bring the person concerned to justice.

In addition, there is the so-called exceptional case: In order to determine inability in a particular case, the Court shall consider whether, due to a total or substantial collapse or unavailability of its national judicial system, the state is unable to obtain the accused or the necessary evidence and testimony or is otherwise unable to carry out its proceedings.

Why do some countries object to a permanent international criminal court? They are worried that an unchecked international court could infringe on basic American constitutional rights for fair trials. For instance, they want ironclad guarantees that the Court would never try the soldiers of the country. Thus, even Pentagon officials fear that Americans might be falsely accused of crimes, thus inhibiting US humanitarian military missions. These worries are probably overstated. The tribunal of 18 world jurists may charge only persons who commit crimes that outrage the international community as a whole. And no one can be convicted without clear proof of intent to commit the illegal act. The prosecutor is under both judicial and budgetary controls which promises both competence and objectivity. Each nation retains the primary right to try its own nationals in a fair trial under its own laws. When there are crimes, like, for example, sexual slavery and forced pregnancy, that the treaty covers but which are not specifically enunciated in a country's own military laws and manuals, then the country in question may incorporate these crimes into its laws to assure that any of its military personnel charged with a crime could be tried by the courts of the country.

The introduction of this permanent court would signify that international governance covers the regulation of crimes against humanity. It will not be able to undo such events, but such a court would make their occurrence less frequent. In particular, it would strengthen the resistance to such atrocities and focus the attention of the world upon where they may occur.

Conclusion

Some feel that globalization weakens the state. This is especially true of Third World states. Thus, one observes increasingly how anarchy spreads from one country to another in Africa and some parts of Asia. In these parts of the world the state needs to be rebuilt and strengthened. But the main trust of globalization is different. It results in less of state sovereignty, not anarchy, but it calls for more of interstate co-ordination. Globalization calls for international co-ordination. One very powerful form of global co-ordination of interactions is the global market economy. It has emerged as a highly integrated mechanism in a stunningly short period of time. However, it cannot solely be relied upon. There must also be non-market co-ordination, meaning some form of state authority.

First, the global market economy is vulnerable to reneging, resulting in a growing crime economy. Second, there are severe collective action problems in the global market economy, resulting in rent dissipation, the destruction of common pool resources and massive externalities. Third, the global market economy suffers from instabilities and imbalances in the form of currency crises and debt problems which can be counteracted by international co-ordination. Fourth, the global market economy is characterized by immense differences in socio-economic development, which call for international efforts to help those countries that have been left behind.

But the present system of state co-ordination is fragmented and states face huge difficulties in co-ordinating their action to arrive at acceptable solutions to the problems of the planet. The road ahead must be to strengthen intergovernmental bodies, undoing veto tactics and removing enforcement difficulties. Interstate co-ordination can become much more effective without calling for one-world government, which is hardly desirable, especially if one were to employ courts and judges more.

Conclusion: Size of Government in Globalized Countries

Introduction

State and market are the two principal methods for the allocation of scarce resources to human needs and wants. If a country favours public resource allocation, then it will end up with a large public sector, whereas if it trusts the market the private sector will tend to be larger than the public sector (Hirschman, 1982). Countries differ considerably in their principal choice between state and market. How are we to account for the various ways of combining state and market?

The distinction between the public and private is thus made in different ways in the countries of the world. Some trust public resource allocation, whereas others emphasize the private sector and market allocation. What are the sources of these differences? In the 1970 and 1980s the policy determinant literature searched for models that would explain the variation in public expenditures. One theory suggested by Harold Wilensky focused upon economic resources and modernization in an attempt to revitalize Wagner's law. The contrary theory argued that politics mattered, especially the strength of the Left (Social Democracy and trade unions) in government and society.

Within *Chicago School Economics* the growth of government in countries with a capitalist economy is looked upon as the outcome of democratic politics where minorities combine to defeat majorities temporarily. The goal of minorities is to concentrate benefits for themselves while spreading out the costs upon the majority (Leube and Moore, 1986; Demsetz, 1991). This theory is suggested as an alternative to Wagner's Law claiming that a large public sector is actually what a majority of the population wants.

The various hypotheses explaining both the growth of government in advanced countries and the cross-country differences in the size of the public sector were launched before globalization set in on a major scale. When countries face a global market economy, then a big public sector does not seem as attractive anymore. But there remains a basic need for government.

Does politics matter?

The first attempts to account for the tremendous public sector growth in rich countries took the form of *demand theories* suggesting that socio-economic development of necessity requires public resource allocation (Wagner), that increasing affluence implies larger budgets (Wilensky), that the dominance of the Left in society or government means budget expansion replacing market mechanisms (Schmidt), that a strong position for the Right in government is a negative determinant (Castles), that collectivist ideologies promote public sector expansion (Wilensky), that sudden social shocks necessitate budgetary shift-points towards much higher levels of public spending (Peacock), that technological development pushes industrial societies more towards the public sector to balance the private sector (Galbraith), that welfare spending by the neighbouring state implies a demand for welfare programmes at home (Tarschys), that the increasing openness of the economies of the rich countries of the world create a demand for budgetary stabilization of the erratic fluctuations of markets (Cameron), that all political systems whether capitalist or socialist face the same policy demands for public programmes (Pryor) and that egalitarian values promote big government contrary to individualist cultures (Wildawsky).

The second stage in the debate about public sector growth offered *supply theories*. Here we find the hypotheses that budget-making must mean oversupply (Niskanen), that public spending involves bureaucratic waste (Tullock), that public sector growth is a function of bureau size maximization (Downs), that public sector productivity is negative, claiming more resources every year for the 'same' output (Baumol), that budget-making rests upon fiscal illusions about the relation between cost and benefit (Oates), that budget-making is asymmetrical, meaning that those benefiting from public sector expansion are strategically stronger than those that have to pay (Kristensen), that public officials whether politicians or bureaucrats are motivated by a private interest function tied to the size of the budget, and that it is difficult to close the gap between benefit and cost in the public sector (Wicksell).

We will argue that politics matters in relation to the fundamental choice between public resource allocation and the market. However, politics enters into a context of policy-making which includes other factors that must be taken into account (Danziger, 1978).

Policy-determinant models

According to one seminal theme, *economic* factors are of crucial importance for public policy-making (Wilensky, 1975). A higher level of affluence is supposed to result in more public spending as the supply of, as well as the demand for, public policies increases with more abundant resources –

Wagner's law (Wildavsky, 1985). This does not imply that the higher the economic growth the larger the public sector, only that nations that are more affluent will display a distinction between the public and the private that is different from that of poor nations. In terms of economic growth there is the counter-Wagner Law claiming that rapid economic growth cannot be combined with rapid public sector expansion. Economic hypotheses about the variation in public spending either focus on supply factors or demand factors (Borcherding, 1977, 1984). Some scholars emphasize some special economic variable like the openness of the economy (Cameron, 1978).

According to another seminal theme, slow, broad social change accounts for a reorientation of the distinction between the public and the private. As stated above, it is argued that *social structure* factors such as modernization or urbanization implies more of public spending for both indivisible and divisible goods and services. In a similar vein it is argued that broad demographic changes result in a demand for public policies. According to one hypothesis, the relative proportion of elderly has a definitive impact on various types of welfare spending (Wilensky, 1975). A different hypothesis states the contrary, that rapid social change accounts for public sector expansion. External shocks like war or social upheaval have the result that public expenditures jump to a substantially higher level where they tend to remain – the *displacement hypothesis* (Peacock, 1979).

A third set of hypotheses focus on the impact of *politics* on the distinction between public and private. On the one hand, it has been argued that the political power of parties of the Right is a decisive negative determinant of the size of the public sector (Castles, 1982, 1998). On the other hand, a different argument is that the strength of the position of parties of the Left is conducive to public budget-making (Schmidt, 1982). A variety of indicators may be employed to measure the position of the Left, implying that there is a large number of hypotheses about the implications of politics, some referring to Leftist governments, others to trade-union power or more generally to the power division between the Left and the Right in society, and still others to the relevance of various types of regimes (Weede, 1984; Cameron, 1978, 1984). In addition to the party effect hypothesis one may also include here the *demonstration hypothesis*, which argues that countries take over policies from other countries as partners in a policy diffusion process. According to the argument about institutional sclerosis, we may expect to find extensive policy-making in nations with a long and unbroken tradition of modern public institutions, resulting in various kinds of policies that hamper the free operation of the market (Olson, 1982): the *institutionalization hypothesis*.

Is it then really true that affluence or modernization is such a powerful determinant of public policy-making? Is it really the case that political institutions or political parties matter little? The set of countries included in the empirical analysis below covers three different regimes on a broad basis:

advanced capitalist systems in the form of OECD countries, communist systems as they existed up to the 1989 upheaval in Eastern Europe; and developing countries – both so-called LDCs and NICs.

Size of public expenditures around the world *circa* 1975

Public Expenditures are measured by the total civilian public sector, non-military outlays/GDP, and indicators of subaggregates like defence expenditures, education and health expenditures. The reliability of the data may be questioned for some nations, which also applies to the indicators listed below. The data on public expenditures for the communist countries appear to be most uncertain. We have calculated a ratio between total public budget and net material product which is not identical to GDP to arrive at a measure comparable to total civilian outlays of general government; the data for these countries have, with the exception of Romania, been taken from *Europa Yearbook*. They roughly refer to the mid-1970s.

The economy is measured by the level of economic affluence (GNP/cap.) in 1975, economic growth between 1960 and 1977, as well as the structure of employment in agriculture in 1977. Openness of the economy is tapped by an index measuring the size of exports and imports in relation to the GNP. Modernization refers to the level of modernization to be measured by two kinds of indicators; one refers to material aspects (energy consumption, radio or TV licences, telephones), while the other stands for health (life expectancy for males, proportion of physicians, infant mortality). Broad demographic changes may be described by indicators such as population density, the proportion of the population in major cities.

Politics is tapped by a set of democratically oriented nations which may be identified by means of a human rights index for the late 1970s, and a democracy index for 1960 and 1965. In order to identify a set of communist regimes an index of the strength of the communist parties is employed. It also allows us to classify political systems as to the extent of radicalism. Moreover, we use two other indices of the strength of the Left, an index of the strength of socialist parties as well as the dominance of the Left in governments over the last decades. Social structure refers to a set of indicators that taps the variation in social structure between nations, such as ethnic or religious fragmentation and proportion of Catholics and Moslems. Institutionalization is measured by an index measuring the introduction of modern leadership and modern political institutions.

The regression analysis presented in Table C.1 gives a number of estimates for three sets of nations, from the most inclusive one consisting of 78 countries to the small set of OECD countries numbering 24. The goodness of fit of the models is quite substantial, as the R-squared values indicate.

Wealth and modernity is no doubt a source of policy-making. The state

Table C.1 Determinants of total civilian general government outlays around 1975

Predictors	*(N=78)* Beta-wt	*t*	*(N=70)* Beta-wt	*t*	*(N=24)* Beta-wt	*t*
GNP/cap. 1975	0.13	0.80	0.40	2.17	0.04	0.27
Modernization: health aspects	0.35	2.32	0.07	0.36	0.23	1.90
Economic growth 1960–77	−0.02	−0.25	−0.07	−0.73	−0.16	−1.23
Impex index	0.16	2.05	0.24	2.77	0.34	2.65
Proportion living in cities > 100,000	−0.14	−1.58	−0.19	−1.90	−0.27	−1.94
Social heterogeneity	0.05	0.58	−0.09	−0.86	0.04	0.28
War experience	0.05	0.65	0.16	1.82	−0.04	−0.40
Left dominance in government	0.36	3.91	0.17	1.84	0.35	2.95
Democracy index	−0.21	−2.13	0.11	0.93	0.13	1.02
Time of institutionalization	−0.27	−2.13	−0.19	−1.32	−0.09	−0.76
R^2	0.66		0.79		0.92	
R^2A	0.61		0.63		0.85	

Sources: Total civil general government outlays: Taylor and Hudson (1972) and IMF (1982); GNP/cap. 1975: Taylor (1981); Modernization: health aspects: Taylor (1981); Economic growth: 1960–77: World Bank (1980); Impex index: Taylor (1981): Proportion living in cities > 100,000: Taylor (1981); Social heterogeneity: Taylor and Hudson (1972); War experience: Weede (1984); Left dominance in government: Banks (1978), Delury (1983); Democracy index: Humana (1983); Time of institutionalization: Taylor and Hudson (1972)

must have a certain amount of resources in order to employ public resource allocation for purposes other than those entailed in the minimal state. Public policy-making beyond the provision of pure collective goods is to be found in an economy with abundant resources. In poor countries the state will be smaller than the market.

The implication of wealth, openness of the economy and modernity is clear when it is a matter of comparing all types of nations. The picture is more ambiguous when we look at the really rich nations. It seems as if there is a limit to the opportunities that affluence creates for public resource allocation. Once a nation has passed a certain threshold in terms of affluence public policy-making becomes less relevant. Most interestingly, a high rate of economic growth is negatively associated with total civilian outlays in the set of rich nations.

There can be no doubt about the importance of the political dimension for the overall structuring of the distinction between the public and the private. Whatever the set of nations studied, the position of the Left within government or society has an impact on the division between state and market, as long as we are not trying to account for the narrow variation in the welfare state in Western Europe. It is not only the case that public resource allocation is the only mechanism employed in those systems where the Left has a hegemonic position. It also applies that the stronger the Left is in non-communist regimes the larger the public sector. The hypothesis

Table C.2 Determinants of general government educational expenditures around 1975

Predictors	(N=78) Beta-wt	t	(N=70) Beta-wt	t	(N=24) Beta-wt	t
GNP/cap.1975	0.55	2.71	0.59	2.73	0.28	1.20
Modernization: health aspects	−0.18	−0.92	−0.22	−1.02	−0.37	−1.69
Economic growth 1960–77	−0.18	−1.76	−0.03	−0.25	0.20	0.84
Impex index	0.16	1.66	0.07	0.68	0.23	1.00
Proportion living in cities > 100,000	0.00	0.05	−0.02	−0.20	0.14	0.56
Social heterogeneity	0.02	0.21	0.09	0.71	0.33	1.31
War experience	0.20	2.05	0.18	1.73	0.06	0.33
Left dominance in government	0.34	2.90	0.30	2.76	0.52	2.38
Democracy index	0.21	1.63	0.24	1.68	0.34	1.42
Time of institutionalization	0.14	0.86	0.09	0.53	−0.01	−0.06
R^2	0.45		0.50		0.72	
R^2A	0.37		0.42		0.51	

Sources: Educational expenditures/GDP: Taylor (1981); Sivard (1980); see also Table C.1

about the impact of institutionalization receives support. The longer a nation has been engaged in nation building, the more the state tends to be engaged in extensive policy-making. While it is true that economic resources matter as predicted in the Wagner's Law and the openness of the economy hypothesis, it is far from being the crucial variable. Politics does matter.

Education is a kind of good that tends to be more in demand the more affluence there is. However, this does not mean that there has to be policy programmes providing this good. Affluence also means that citizens have a larger capacity to make their own choices, suggesting that they may use the market to provide themselves with education opportunities. We may expect to find that wealth or modernity explains part of the variation in education expenditures but only a part. The findings in Table C.2 confirm this interpretation.

Poor nations cannot afford to operate extensive programmes in the field of education. Rich nations on the other hand face a choice between public and private as they can afford to allocate resources to various kinds of education. Which mechanism of allocation is resorted to depends on other factors of which politics appears to be the most relevant one. The position of the Left matters very much in relation to public spending for education. It is also the case that democratically structured nations favour public education systems.

The provision of health tends to be larger in richer countries than in poorer ones, but this does not imply that affluence implies public spending for health. Health may be provided for privately in terms of market operations. The results stated in Table C.3 confirm this hypothesis.

Wealth and modernity have a positive impact on health policy-making,

Table C.3 Determinants of general government health expenditures around 1975

Predictors	(N = 78) Beta-wt	t	(N = 70) Beta-wt	t	(N = 24) Beta-wt	t
GNP/cap. 1975	0.32	1.84	0.28	1.50	−0.22	−0.76
Modernization: health aspects	0.14	0.88	0.15	0.80	0.35	1.28
Economic growth 1960–77	−0.13	−1.48	−0.05	−0.58	−0.26	−0.89
Impex index	0.01	0.15	−0.04	−0.43	−0.02	−0.07
Proportion living in cities > 100,000	0.12	1.25	0.12	1.22	0.26	0.84
Social heterogeneity	0.07	0.08	0.13	1.21	0.28	0.90
War experience	−0.02	−0.21	−0.03	−0.35	−0.07	−0.31
Left dominance in government	0.30	3.07	0.27	2.82	0.46	1.68
Democracy index	0.13	1.25	0.12	0.98	0.04	0.13
Time of institutionalization	−0.11	−0.80	−0.16	−1.09	0.17	0.61
R^2	0.61		0.63		0.57	
R^2A	0.55		0.57		0.23	

Sources: Health expenditures/GDP: Taylor (1981); Sivard (1980); see also Table C.1

up to a certain level. Once there is a certain level of public provision of health services, other factors will determine whether there will be public or private provision. Most important is politics, the Left favouring public resource allocation. It may be believed that military spending is more favoured in authoritarian or communist systems than in democratic ones. Table C.4 shows that this is not the case.

What matters with regard to military effort is war experience. Countries that have this kind of experience emphasize military spending. Wealth and modernity have a limited impact, indicating that the richer a nation is the more resources there are available for such purposes, but still the most

Table C.4 Determinants of military expenditures around 1975

Predictors	(N = 78) Beta-wt	t	(N = 70) Beta-wt	t	(N = 24) Beta-wt	t
GNP/cap. 1975	−0.12	−0.59	−0.21	−0.99	−0.37	−1.50
Modernization: health aspects	0.41	2.25	0.58	2.66	0.15	0.66
Economic growth 1960–77	0.15	1.56	0.14	1.29	0.16	0.65
Impex index	0.05	0.55	0.05	0.53	−0.43	−1.76
Proportion living in cities > 100,000	0.02	0.18	0.01	0.11	−0.34	−1.29
Social heterogeneity	0.15	1.39	0.21	1.75	0.10	0.38
War experience	0.62	6.46	0.60	5.87	0.60	3.10
Left dominance in government	0.22	1.97	0.28	2.58	0.28	1.20
Democracy index	−0.05	−0.38	−0.19	−1.32	−0.01	0.05
Time of institutionalization	0.35	2.21	0.34	1.98	−0.36	−1.55
R^2	0.49		0.50		0.69	
R^2A	0.41		0.42		0.45	

Sources: Defence expenditures/GDP: Taylor (1981); Sivard (1980); see also Table C.1

Table C.5. Public expenditures 1980 and 1992 as a percentage of GDP

1980	Total Exp.	Government consumption	Mil. Exp.	Edu. Exp.	Health Exp.
OECD	45.9 (*N*=15)	17.8 (*N*=22)	2.7 (*N*=24)	5.9 (*N*=24)	4.8 (*N*=24)
Third	31.0 (*N*=31)	15.4 (*N*=74)	4.5 (*N*=91)	4.2 (*N*=93)	1.6 (*N*=92)
Comm.	41.7 (*N*=2)	11.8 (*N*=4)	4.6 (*N*=9)	4.1 (*N*=8)	3.5 (*N*=9)
Mean	36.1 (*N*=48)	15.8 (*N*=100)	4.2 (*N*=124)	4.5 (*N*=125)	2.4 (*N*=125)

1992	Total Exp.	Government consumption	Mil. Exp.	Edu. Exp.	Health Exp.
OECD	46.8 (*N*=24)	18.6 (*N*=21)	2.4 (*N*=24)	5.3 (*N*=23)	5.9 (*N*=24)
Third	25.7 (*N*=60)	14.6 (*N*=73)	5.2 (*N*=89)	4.1 (*N*=70)	2.2 (*N*=70)
Post-C.	49.2 (*N*=3)	17.1 (*N*=13)	2.7 (*N*=17)	4.9 (*N*=4)	4.6 (*N*=19)
Mean	32.3 (*N*=87)	15.7 (*N*=107)	4.3 (*N*=130)	4.5 (*N*=97)	3.4 (*N*=113)

Sources: Total expenditures 1980: IMF (1984); Military expenditures 1980: Sivard (1983); Educational expenditures 1980: Sivard (1983); Health expenditures 1980: Sivard (1983); Total expenditures 1992: IMF (1994); Military expenditures 1992: UNDP (1995); Educational expenditures 1992: UNDP (1995); Health expenditures 1992: UNDP (1995)

important determinant is the actual experience of war. Now, do these findings stand up when we look at the evidence from data about the 1990s?

Size of public expenditures around the world *circa* 1994

Government is necessary for social life, but the size of government varies considerably. Why is this so? The literature on the size of the public sector has suggested a few major determinants: (i) affluence; (ii) political preferences; and (iii) the power of producer groups or distributional coalitions. We wish to add (iv) democracy as a major explanatory factor.

Table C.5 shows the basic difference between three kinds of countries in terms of the size of public expenditures 1980 and 1992, i.e. after the measurement point of time for the analysis above.

Measuring the size of the public sector in a command economy is notoriously difficult, since the state in practice dominates society completely, meaning that the private–public distinction loses its import. What has happened in the post-communist countries is an expansion of the private sector together with a reduction in public expenditures, a process that the figures in Table C.5 fail to identify. Outside the command economies public expenditure is one proper measure of the size of the public sector, but within the communist systems the public sector was much larger than public expenditures, as the state controlled the entire economy owning the capital.

Public expenditures as a percentage of GDP is up slightly among the rich countries, whereas things are ambiguous with regard to the Third World countries, as the figures for the 1980s are based on a small sample. Among

Third World countries one can observe both increases and decreases. Some countries have moved in the same direction as the rich countries, i.e. more of public expenditures and a larger public sector. But one can also observe the other process involving a substantial reduction in public expenditures. Countries that have reduced their public sector include among others: Argentina, Dominican Republic, Ecuador, Guatemala, Indonesia, Kenya, Malaysia and Thailand – all countries that have attempted to move out of the state-capitalist regime towards decentralized capitalism. However, we also find Third World countries that have increased their public expenditures, for instance: Brazil, India, Mexico, Paraguay and Uruguay.

We now turn to a regression analysis of the expenditure variation, where we focus upon the differences among the OECD and Third World countries. Thus, we exclude the set of post-communist countries as they are still in the process of bringing down their public sectors, searching for a new public–private mix (Table C.6).

The major finding in Table C.6 is the evidence that points at democracy as a key factor when understanding the public–private sector mix, how it varies around the world. It is not the case that either modernization (GDP/capita) or politics (Left) are the key variables when understanding expenditure variation. Democracy is a more relevant factor than the standard factors listed in the policy determinant literature. It drives up public expenditures in general, especially health care expenditures, and drives down military spending.

In democratic states it is evidently the case that politicians face strong pressure for enhancing citizen well-being by increasing civilian expenditures and holding back military spending – this is the Wagner-inspired interpretation of this finding. An equally plausible supply side interpretation suggested by Chicago School economists may be stated, focusing upon how politicians may resort to employing public expenditure items in order to enhance their popularity with the electorate. In any case, democracy means a larger public sector on the civilian side whereas an authoritarian regime implies more military spending.

Table C.7 gives more recent information about the size of government, focusing upon the size of central government in countries in our macro regions. The size of central or national government is always smaller than measures on general government. We observe that the advanced market economies have the largest public sectors, the data now shows. The size of government has come down in former communist countries. Relatively speaking, central government is half the size of that in advanced countries in all macro regions except the CEE and CIS.

State or market in a country is a real choice opportunity when national public policy-making moves beyond the provision of pure public goods. And this choice opportunity becomes an actuality when nations have been modernized to such an extent that the state has large extractive capacities. Economic development and modernization opens up the possibility of

Table C.6 Regression analysis of public expenditures: OECD and Third World

Total Exp. 1992

	Coeff	*BetaWt*	*t-stat*
LNRGDP	2.14	0.14	0.89
Open80	0.02	0.06	0.65
Left	1.26	0.13	1.28
Demo91	0.30	0.44	3.00
Inst	−0.03	−0.12	−0.79
R^2A	0.50	($N=70$)	

Military Exp. 1992

	Coeff	*BetaWt*	*t-stat*
LNRGDP	2.68	0.66	6.02
Open80	0.01	0.09	1.07
War	−0.12	−0.02	−0.17
Left	0.04	0.01	0.13
Demo91	−0.17	−0.95	−7.74
R^2A	0.48	($N=81$)	

Educational Exp. 1992

	Coeff	*BetaWt*	*t-stat*
LNRGDP	0.45	0.27	1.53
Open80	0.00	0.06	0.45
Left	0.15	0.12	0.84
Demo91	0.02	0.20	1.03
Inst	0.00	0.19	0.91
R^2A	0.10	($N=70$)	

Health Exp. 1992

	Coeff	*BetaWt*	*t-stat*
LNRGDP	0.51	0.25	1.95
Open80	−0.00	−0.03	−0.34
Left	0.02	0.02	0.21
Demo91	0.04	0.45	3.95
Inst	−0.01	−0.21	−1.53
R^2A	0.67	($N=73$)	

Sources: LNRGDP: Summers and Heston (1994); Open80: Summers and Heston (1994); War: Wallensteen and Sollenberg (1995); Left: *Encyclopaedia Britannica* (1995); Democracy 1991: Humana (1992); Institutionalization: Black (1966)

Table C.7 Public sector size as a percentage of GDP by macro-regions 1995 (central government)

Region	CGCON	N	CGEXP	N	CURREV	N	TAXREV	N
Occidental	18.7	23	38.5	23	34.1	23	30.7	23
CEEB and CIS	17.1	24	34.4	13	30.6	13	27.6	13
Central and Latin America	11.5	21	21.8	13	20.1	13	16.9	13
Sub-Saharan Africa	14.9	35	27.0	13	22.6	13	17.9	13
Arab World	17.6	12	32.4	12	26.1	11	15.9	12
South Asia	11.9	6	21.7	6	14.1	6	9.9	6
South East Asia	10.4	14	17.7	9	19.7	9	16.2	9
Mean/total	15.0	135	29.7	89	26.0	88	21.5	89
Eta square	0.20		0.44		0.39		0.48	
Sig.	0.000		0.000		0.000		0.000	

Note: CGCON = central government consumption; CGEXP = central government expenditures; CURREV = central government current revenues; TAXREV = central government tax revenues
Source: World Bank (2000a)

extensive public policy-making – so far Wilensky is right. But the Wilensky mechanism has lost much of its explanatory force, as the variation in public sector size has become more complex and several countries have initiated public sector retrenchments.

Although it is true that as countries modernize resources become available for civil public expenditures, one must ask whether this possibility also becomes a reality in terms of a large public sector. Countries face the basic choice between public resource allocation and market operations as the mechanism for allocating scarce resources. And politics matters very much for the way that choice was resolved in the 1970s. This applies in particular in relation to non-military expenditures which in advanced economies mainly refer to semipublic or private goods. The tendency for public resource allocation to expand as a function of the modernization of the economy expresses a decision to trust one mechanism of allocation more than the other – and this decision is based more on *political considerations* than simply *economic determinism*. And these preferences for public expenditures may be reversed when markets are given a more prominent role. Thus, public sector growth is not inevitable, as the findings above show.

The most interesting finding here is that democracy is a powerful explanatory factor when it comes to public expenditures in the 1990s. The more democratic a country tends to be, the larger the public sector. Public expenditures, especially on health care, are driven up by democratic politics. Economic resources constitute a necessary condition for public expenditures but they do not make up a sufficient condition. In the 1970s it was the position of the Left that was critical, now it is democracy.

Conclusion

Public resource allocation is resorted to as nations grow richer and more modern, but there is a limit to the attractiveness of the state. In several countries the relevance of the market increases as citizens may wish to emphasize exit more than voice (Hirschman, 1970). Public resource allocation may have been a more attractive alternative than market allocation due to non-existence of markets or the need for political control, but there is a limit to the usefulness of this mechanism of collective choice, especially in relation to a global market economy. Technical considerations hardly give public resource allocation an advantage over markets, and as the attractiveness of public resource allocation is founded upon politics it means that the spread of a market ideology can reverse processes of public sector growth. Globalization tends to favour market allocation, but the need for government remains as the global market economy poses new problems calling for political co-ordination.

Government is hardly small in the advanced market economies. One may explain the size of the public sector in these countries either by demand side factors or by supply side factors. In any case, government is vital to the stability of the market economy in these countries. And one may attribute some of the problems in the economies in other parts of the world to the weakness of government, as for instance in Sub-Saharan Africa and South Asia. This is true of the need for government in relation to domestic economy, but what about the custodian or guarantor role of government when the national economies have become open, entering the global market economy?

Global co-ordination between states can be done by government negotiating or collaborating bilaterally. However, such a system would hardly be transaction cost saving. In a world consisting of some 195 states a multilateral approach would seem more efficient and also more equitable (Gilpin, 2000). The multilateral approach, however, requires a system of international organizations – the IGOs – that implement and police such agreements between states. The existing system of intergovernmental mechanisms is too fragmented and weak to effect strong co-ordination between states, which the global market economy calls for. We suggest that one attempts to strengthen government in the global market economy but without creating one world government, which is both impossible and undesirable. What must be done is to reform the present IGOs and empower them, especially by increasing their capacity to take legal action in accordance with public international law.

The emergence of regional state co-ordination helps considerably in reducing transactions costs when negotiating multilateral agreements between governments. Thus, the EU, for instance, increases the likelihood that international agreements can be struck. However, regional co-ordination does not guarantee that reneging or free riding will go away, as the recent experience with the Kyoto Protocol on the global environment indicates. If there would emerge a system of five or six regional blocs at the government level, then it would help but not guarantee the achievement of global governance.

Bibliography

ACDA (US Arms Control and Disarmament Agency) (1985, 1997) *World Military Expenditures and Arms Transfers*, Washington, DC, The Agency.

Adelman, I. and Morris, C. T. (1967) *Society, Politics and Economic Development*, Baltimore, OH, Johns Hopkins University Press (revised edn, 1973).

Ahluwalia, M. (1976) 'Inequality, poverty and development', *Journal of Development Economics*, 3, 4, 307–42.

Akerloff, G. (1970) 'The market for lemons: qualitative uncertainty and the market mechanism', *Quarterly Journal of Economics*, 84, 488–500.

Almond, G. A. and Coleman, J. (eds) (1960) *The Politics of Developing Areas*, Princeton, NJ, Princeton University Press.

Almond, G. A. and Powell, G. B. (1966) *Comparative Politics: A Developmental Approach*, Boston, Little, Brown.

Almond, G. A., Flanagan, S. C. and Mundt, R. J. (eds) (1973) *Crisis, Choice, and Change: Historical Studies of Political Development*, Boston, Little, Brown.

Apter, D. E. (1965) *The Politics of Modernization*, Chicago, University of Chicago Press.

Arat, Z. F. (1991) *Democracy and Human Rights in Developing Countries*, Boulder, CO, Lynne Rienner.

Arrow, K. J. (1963) *Social Choice and Individual Values*, New York, Wiley.

Arrow, K. J. (1983) *General Equilibrium*, Oxford, Basil Blackwell.

Arrow, K. J. and Hurwicz, L. (1960) 'Decentralization and computation in resource allocation', in Pfouts, T. (ed.) *Essays in Economics and Econometrics in Honour of Harold Hotelling*, Chapel Hill, University of North Carolina Press.

Arrow, K. J. and Scitovsky, T. (eds) (1972) *Readings in Welfare Economics*, London, Allen & Unwin.

Åslund, A. (1989) *Gorbachev's Struggle for Economic Reform: The Soviet reform process, 1985–88*, London, Pinter.

Åslund, A. (1995) *How Russia Became a Market Economy*, Washington, DC, Brookings.

Atkinson, A. B. and Stiglitz, J. E. (1980) *Lectures on Public Economics*, Maidenhead, McGraw-Hill.

BAC (US Bureau of Arms Control) (1999) *World Military Expenditures and Arms Transfers*; available at: www.state.gov.www/global/arms/bureauac.htm

Bairoch, P. (1975) *The Economic Development of the Third World since 1900*, Berkeley, University of California Press.

Bairoch, P. (2000) *Le tiers-Monde dans l'impasse*, Gallimard, Paris.

Bairoch, P. and Levy-Leboyer, M. (eds) (1981) *Disparities in Economic Development Since the Industrial Revolution*, London, Macmillan.

Balassa, B. (1989) *Comparative Advantage, Trade Policy and Economic Development*, London, Harvester Wheatsheaf.

Balassa, B. (1991) *Economic Policies in the Pacific Area Developing Countries*, London, Macmillan.

Banks, A. S. (1972) 'Correlates of democratic performance', *Comparative Politics*, 4, 217–30.

Banks, A. S. (ed.) (1978) *Political Handbook of the World: 1978*, New York, McGraw-Hill.

Banks, A. S. (1996) Cross-national Time-series Data Archive, Binghampton, NY, Center for Social Analysis, State University of New York at Binghampton.

Bardhan, P. (1984) *The Political Economy of Development in India*, Oxford, Blackwell.

Bardhan, P. (1988) 'Alternative approaches to development economics', in Chenery, H. and Srinivasan, T. N. (eds) *Handbook of Development Economics*, vol. L.

Barone, E. (1935) 'The ministry of production in a collectivist state', in Hayek, F. A. von (ed.), *Collectivist Economic Planning*, London, Routledge & Kegan Paul.

Barro, R. (1991) 'Economic growth in a cross section of countries', *Quarterly Journal of Economics*, 56, 407–43.

Barsh, R. L. (1993) 'Measuring human rights: problems of methodology and purpose', *Human Rights Quarterly*, 15, 87–121.

Bartelson, J. (2000) 'Three concepts of globalization', *International Sociology*, 15, 180–96.

Barzel, Y. (1997) *Economic Analysis of Property Rights*, Cambridge, Cambridge University Press.

Bator, F. M. (1958) 'The anatomy of market failure', *Quarterly Journal of Economics*, 72, 351–79.

Baumol, W. J. (1965) *Welfare Economics and the Theory of the State*, Cambridge, MA, Harvard University Press.

Bayart, J.-F., Ellis, S. and Hibou, B. (1997) *La criminalisation de l'Etat en Afrique*, Brussels, Editions Complexe.

Beisheim, M, Dreher, S., Walter, G., Zangl, B. and Zürn, M. (1999) *Im Zeitalter der Globalisierung?: Thesen und Daten zur gesellschaftlichen und politischen Denationalisierung*, Baden-Baden, Nomos.

Beynon, J. and Dunkerley, D. (eds) (2001) *Globalization: The reader*, New York, Athlone.

Bergson, A. (1981) *Welfare, Planning and Employment*, Cambridge, MA, MIT Press.

Bergson, A. and Levine, H. S. (eds) (1983) *The Soviet Economy: Toward the year 2000*, London, Allen & Unwin.

Bhagwati, J. N. and Ruggie, J. G. (eds) (1984) *Power, Passions and Purpose: Prospects for North–South negotiations*, Cambridge, MA, MIT Press.

Bigsten, A. (1987) 'Growth and equity in some African and Asian countries', Stockholm, Sida (unpublished manuscript).

Bilas, R. A. (1971) *Microeconomic Theory*, Tokyo, McGraw-Hill.

Binder, L. (1971) 'Crises of political development', in Binder *et al.* (eds) *Crises and Sequences in Political Development*, Princeton, NJ, Princeton University Press.

Binder, L. (1986) 'The natural history of development theory', *Comparative Studies of Society and History*, 28, 3–33.

Binder, L., Coleman, J. S., La Palombara, J., Pye, L. W., Verba, S. and Weiner, M. (eds) (1971) *Crises and Sequences in Political Development*, Princeton, NJ, Princeton University Press.

Black, C. (1966) *The Dynamics of Modernization*, New York, NY, Harper & Row.

Bohm, P. (1986) *Social Efficiency: A concise introduction to welfare economics*, London, Macmillan.

Bollen, K. A. (1979) 'Political democracy and the timing of development', *American Sociological Review*, 44, 572–87.

Bollen, K. A. (1980) 'Issues in the comparative measurement of political democracy', *American Sociological Review*, 45, 370–90.

Bollen, K. A. (1986) 'Political rights and political liberties in nations: an evaluation of human rights measures, 1950 to 1984', *Human Rights Quarterly*, 8, 567–91.

Bollen, K. A. (1990) 'Political democracy: conceptual and measurement traps', *Studies in Comparative International Development*, 25, 7–24.

Bollen, K. A. (1993) 'Liberal democracy: validity and method factors in cross-national measures', *American Journal of Political Science*, 37, 1207–30.

Bollen, K. A. and Grandjean, J. (1981) 'The dimension(s) of democracy: further issues in the measurement and effects of political democracy', *American Sociological Review*, 46, 65, 1–9.

Bollen, K. A. and Jackman, R. W. (1985) 'Political democracy and the size distribution of income', *American Sociological Review*, 50, 438–57.

Bollen, K. A. and Jackman, R. W. (1989) 'Democracy, stability and dichotomies', *American Sociological Review*, 54, 612–21.

Borcherding, T. E. (1977) *Budgets and Bureaucrats: the Sources of Government Growth*, Durham, NC, Duke University Press.

Borcherding, T. E. (1984) 'A survey of empirical studies about causes of the growth of government', paper presented to the Nobel Symposium on the Growth of Government, Stockholm.

Brandt Report (1980) *North-South: A programme for survival*, London, Pan Books.

Braudel, F. (1993) *Civilisation, économie et capitalisme, XVe–XVIIIe siècle*, Armand Colin, Paris.

Brennan, G. and Buchanan, J. M. (1980) *The Power to Tax*, Cambridge, Cambridge University Press.

Brown, C. W. and Jackson, P. M. (1978) *Public Sector Economics*, Oxford, Martin Robertson.

Brown, L. R., Renner, M. and Halwell, B. (eds) (2000) *Vital Signs: The environmental trends that are shaping our future*, New York, NY, Norton.

Brownlie, I. (1998) *Principles of Public International Law* (5th edn), Oxford, Oxford University Press.

Brunner, R. D. and Brewer, G. D. (1971) *Organized Complexity: Empirical Theories of Political Development*, New York, Free Press.

Brus, W. and Laski, K. (1990) *From Marx to the Market: Socialism in Search of an Economic System*, Oxford, Clarendon Press.

Buchanan, A. (1985) *Ethics, Efficiency and the Market*, Oxford, Clarendon Press.

Buchanan, J. M. (1967) *Public Finance in Democratic Process*, Chapel Hill, University of North Carolina Press.

Buchanan, J. M. (1986) *Liberty, Market and State: Political Economy in the 80s*, London, Harvester Wheatsheaf.

Buchanan, J. M. and Musgrave, R. A. (1999) *Public Finance and Public Choice – Two Contrasting Visions of the State*, Cambridge, MA, MIT Press.

Buchanan, J. M., Tollison, R. D. and Tullock, G. (eds) (1980) *Toward a Theory of the Rent-seeking Society*, College Station, Texas, A & M University Press.

Caiden, N. and Wildavsky, A. (1974) *Planning and Budgeting in Poor Countries*, New York, Wiley.

Calabresi, G. (1985) *Common Law for the Age of Statutes*, Cambridge, MA, Harvard University Press.

Cameron, D. (1978) 'The expansion of the public economy: a comparative analysis', *American Political Science Review*, 72, 1243–61.

Cameron, D. (1984) 'Impact of political institutions on public sector expansion', paper presented to the Nobel Symposium on the growth of Government, Stockholm.

Carlton, D. W. and Perloff, J. M. (1999) *Modern Industrial Organization*, Harlow, Addison Wesley Longman.

Castells, M. (1998) *The Information Age: Economy, Society and Culture: Volume III: End of Millennium*, Oxford, Blackwells.

Castles, F. G. (ed.) (1982) *The Impact of Parties: Politics and Policies in Democratic Capitalist States*, London, Sage.

Caves, R. E. and Jones, R. W. (1985) *World Trade and Payments*, Boston, Little, Brown.

Cerny, P. G. (1997) 'Paradoxes of the competition state: The dynamics of political globalization', *Government and Opposition*, 32, 251–74.

Chacholiades, M. (1985) *International Trade: Theory and Policy*, London, McGraw-Hill.

Chaudhuri, P. (1989) *The Economic Theory of Growth*, London, Harvester Wheatsheaf.

Chenery, H. and Srinivasan, T. N. (eds) (1988) *Handbook of Development Economics*, Vol. I, Amsterdam, North-Holland.

Chenery, H. and Srinivasan, T. N. (eds) (1989) *Handbook of Development Economics*, Vol. II, Amsterdam, North-Holland.

Chilcote, R. H. and Johnson, D. L. (eds) (1983) *Theories of Development*, Beverly Hills, CA, Sage.

Choi, K. (1983) 'A statistical test of Olson's model' in Mueller, D.C. (ed.) *The Political Economy of Growth*, New Haven, CT, Yale University Press, pp. 57–78.

Choksi, A. M. and Papageorghiou, D. (eds) (1986) *Economic Liberalization in Developing Countries*, Oxford, Blackwell.

Chow, G.C. (1994) *Understanding China's Economy*, New York: World Scientific Publishing.

Coase, R. H. (1988) *The Firm, the Market and the Law*, Chicago, University of Chicago Press.

Coleman, J. S. (ed.) (1965) *Education and Political Development*, Princeton, NJ, Princeton University Press.

Collier, D. (1978) 'Industrial modernization and political change: a Latin American perspective', *World Politics*, 30, 593–614.

Combacan, J. and Sur, S. (1999) *Droit International Public* (4th edn), Paris, Montchrestien.

Cooter, R. and Ulen, T. (1999) *Law and Economics*, Harlow, Longman Higher Education.

Coppedge, M. and Reinicke, W. H. (1990) 'Measuring polyarchy', *Studies in Comparative International Development*, 25, 51–72.

Crisp, J. (1999) 'Who has counted the refugees? UNHCR and the politics of the numbers', Geneva, UNHCR (UNHCR Working Paper 12).

Cutright, R (1963) 'National political development: measurement and analysis', *American Sociological Review*, 28, 253–64.

Dahl, R. A. (1971) *Polyarchy*, New Haven, CT, Yale University Press.

Dahl, R. A. (1985) *A Preface to an Economic Theory of Democracy*, Cambridge, Polity Press.

Danziger, J. N. (1978) *Making Budgets: Public Resource Allocation*, Beverly Hills, CA, Sage.

Davis, H. and Scase, R. (1985) *Western Capitalism and State Socialism*, Oxford, Blackwell.

de Carvalho, J. A. M. and Wood, G. H. (1978) 'Mortality, income distribution and rural–urban residence in Brazil', *Population and Development Review*, 4, 3, 405–20.

Debreu, G. (1959) *Theory of Value*, New York, Wiley.

Deininger, K. and Squire L. (1997) *The Deininger-Squire data set*; available at: www.worldbank.org/research/growth/dddeisqu.htm

Delury, T. E. (ed.) (1983) *World Encyclopedia of Political Systems*, Harlow, Longman.

Demsetz, H. (1967) 'Towards a theory of property rights', *American Economic Review*, 57, 347–59.

Demsetz, H. (1988) 'Why regulate utilities?', in Stigler, G. (ed.) *Studies in Political Economy*, Chicago, University of Chicago Press, pp. 267–69.

Demsetz, H. (1991) *Efficiency Competition and Policy*, Cambridge, MA, Blackwell.

Deutsch, K. K. (1961) 'Social mobilization and political development', *American Political Science Review*, 55, 493–514.

Diamond, L. (1992) 'Economic development and democracy reconsidered', *American Behavioral Scientist*, 35, 450–99.

Dobb, M. (1940) *Political Economy and Capitalism*, London, Routledge & Kegan Paul.

Downs, A. (1957) *An Economic Theory of Democracy*, New York, Harper & Row.

Downs, A. (1960) 'Why the government is too small in a democracy', *World Politics*, 12, 541–63.

Dyker, D. A. (1976) *The Future of the Soviet Planning System*, Cambridge, Cambridge University Press.

Easton, D. (1965) *A Systems Analysis of Political Life*, New York, Wiley.

Eatwell, J., Milgate, M. and Newman, P. (eds) (1987) *The Invisible Hand*, London, Macmillan.

Eatwell, J., Milgate, M. and Newman, P. (eds) (1989a) *Allocation, Information and Markets*, London, Macmillan.

Eatwell, J., Milgate, M. and Newman, P. (eds) (1989b) *General Equilibrium*, London, Macmillan.

Eatwell, J., Milgate, M. and Newman, P. (eds) (1990) *Problems of the Planned Economy*, London, Macmillan.

Eatwell, J., Milgate, M. and Newman, P. (1991) *Economic Development*, London, Macmillan.

Eckstein, A. (ed.) (1971) *Comparison of Economic Systems: Theoretical and Methodological Approaches*, Berkeley, University of California Press.

Eggertson, T. (1990) *Economic Behaviour and Institutions*, Cambridge, Cambridge University Press.

Eidem, R. and Viotti, S. (1978) *Economic Systems*, London, Martin Robertson.

Eisenstadt, S. N. (1966) *Modernization*, Englewood Cliffs, NJ, Prentice Hall.

Ellman, M. (1979) *Socialist Planning*, Cambridge, Cambridge University Press.

Encyclopaedia Britannica (annually) *Britannica World Data*, Chicago, Encyclopaedia Britannica.

Energy Information Administration (2000a) *Annual Energy Review 1999*, Washington, DC, US Department of Energy.

Energy Information Adminstration (2000b) *International Energy Outlook 2000*, Washington, DC, US Department of Energy.

Estrin, S. (1983) *Self-management: Economic Theory and Yugoslav Practice*, Cambridge, Cambridge University Press.

Europa World Yearbook (various years) London, Europa Publications.

FAO (various years) *FAO Yearbook*, Rome, Food and Agriculture Organization of the United Nations.

Firebaugh, G. (1999) 'Empirics of world income inequality', *American Journal of Sociology*, 104, 1597–1630.

Fischer Weltalmanach (various years) Frankfurt-on-Main, Fischer Taschenbuch Verlag.

Frank, A. G. (1967) *Capitalism and Underdevelopment in Latin America: Historical Studies of Chile and Brazil*, New York, Monthly Review Press.

Freedom House (1999) *Freedom in the World: The annual survey of political rights and civil liberties, 1998–1999*, New Brunswick, NJ, Transaction.

Freedom House (2000) *Annual Survey of Freedom House Country Scores 1972–73 to 1999–00*; available at: www.freedomhouse.org/ratings/

Friedman, M. (1953) *Essays in Positive Economics*, Chicago, IL, University of Chicago Press.

Friedman, M. (1962) *Capitalism and Freedom*, Chicago, IL, University of Chicago Press.

Galbraith, J. K. (1969) *The New Industrial State*, Harmondsworth, Pelican.

Gastil, R. D. (1986) *Freedom in the World: Political rights and civil liberties 1985–1986*, Westport, CT, Greenwood Press.

Gastil, R. D. (1987) *Freedom in the World: Political rights and civil liberties 1986–1987*, Westport, CT, Greenwood Press.

Gersovitz, M. E., Diaz-Alejandro, G. R., Ranis, G. and Rozenzweig, M. R. (eds) (1982) *The Theory and Experience of Economic Development: Essays in Honor of Sir W Arthur Lewis*, London, Allen & Unwin.

Gilpin, R. (2000) *The Challenge of Global Capitalism*, Princeton, Princeton University Press.

Gregory, P. R. and Stuart, R. C. (1989) *Comparative Economic Systems*, Boston, Houghton Mifflin.

Grier, K. B. and Tullock, G. (1989) 'An empirical analysis of cross-national economic growth, 1951–80', *Journal of Monetary Economics*, 24, 259–76.

Gurr, T. R. (1990) *Polity II: Political Structures and Regime Change, 1800–1986* (Computer file), Boulder, CO, Center for Comparative Politics (producer), *1989*, Ann Arbor, MI, Inter-university Consortium for Political and Social Research (distributor), *1990*.

Gwartney, J. and Lawson, R. (2000) *Economic Freedom of the World: 2000 Annual Report*, Vancouver, Fraser Institute.

Gwartney, J., Lawson, R. and Block, W. (1996) *Economic Freedom of the World 1975–1995*, Vancouver, Fraser Institute.

Hadenius, A. (1992) *Democracy and Development*, Cambridge, Cambridge University Press.

Hare, R. M. (1967) *The Language of Morals*, Oxford, Oxford University Press.

Harrie, C. (ed.) (2000) *Contemporary Developments and Issues in China's Economic Transition*, New York: St Martin's Press.

Hayek, F. A. von (1996) *Individualism and Economic Order*, Chicago, University of Chicago Press.

Hayek, F. A. von (ed.) (1935) *Collectivist Economic Planning*, London, Routledge & Kegan Paul.

Hayek, F. A. von and Klein, P. G. (eds) (1992) *The Fortunes of Liberalism, Vol. 4: Essays on Austrian Economics and the Ideas of Freedom*, London, Routledge.

Head, J. G. (1974) *Public Goods and Public Welfare*, Durham, NC, Duke University Press.

Heal, G. M. (1973) *The Theory of Economic Planning*, Amsterdam, North-Holland.

Held, D., McGrew, A., Goldblatt, D. and Perraton, J. (1999) *Global Transformations: Politics, economics and culture*, Cambridge, Polity.

Higgott, R. A. (1983) *Political Development Theory*, London, Croom Helm.

Hirschman, A. O. (1958) *Strategy of Economic Development*, New Haven, CT, Yale University Press.

Hirschman, A. O. (1970) *Exit, Voice and Loyalty: Responses to decline in firms, organizations and states*, Cambridge, MA, Harvard University Press.

Hirschman, A. O. (1982) *Shifting Involvements: Private Interests and Public Action*, Princeton, NJ, Princeton University Press.

Hirst, P. and G. Thompson (1996) *Globalization in Question: The international economy and the possibility of governance*, Cambridge, Polity.

Holm, H. H. and Sorensen, G. (1995) *Whose World Order? Uneven Globalization and the End of the Cold War*, Boulder, CO, Westview Press.

Humana, C. (1983) *World Human Rights Guide*, London, Hutchinson.

Humana, C. (1986) *World Human Rights Guide*, (2nd edn), London, Economist Publications.

Humana, C. (1992) *World Human Rights Guide* (3rd edn), New York, Oxford University Press.

Huntington, S. P. (1965) 'Political development and political decay', *World Politics*, 17, 386–430.

Huntington, S. P. (1991) *The Third Wave: Democratization in the late twentieth century*, Norman, OK, University of Oklahoma Press.

International Monetary Fund (IMF) (1982) *Government Finance Statistics Yearbook 1982*, Washington, DC, IMF.

International Monetary Fund (IMF) (1984) *Government Finance Statistics Yearbook 1984*, Washington, DC, IMF.

International Monetary Fund (IMF) (1994) *Government Finance Statistics Yearbook 1994*, Washington, DC, IMF.

International Monetary Fund (IMF) (1997) *World Economic Outlook*, May, Washington, DC, IMF.

International Monetary Fund (IMF) (2000) 'World Economic Outlook database: September 2000'; available at: www.imf.org/

International Monetary Fund (IMF) (various years) *Direction of Trade Statistics Yearbook*, Washington, DC, IMF.

Internet Software Consortium (2000) 'Internet domain survey'; available at: www.isc.org/ds/

Jackman, R. W. (1975) *Politics and Social Equality: A Comparative Analysis*, New York, Wiley.

Johansen, L. (1977) *Public Economics*, Amsterdam, North-Holland.

Johansen, L. (1977–78) *Lectures on Macroeconomic Planning I–II*, Amsterdam, North-Holland.

Johansen, L. (1979) 'The bargaining society and the inefficiency of bargaining', *Kyklos*, 32, 497–522.

Johnson, C. (ed.) (1984) *The Industrial Policy Debate*, San Francisco, Jossey-Bass.

Johnson, H. (1958) *International Trade and Economic Growth*, London, Allen & Unwin.

Johnson, H. G. (1975) *Technology and Economic Interdependence*, London, Macmillan.

Jones, R. W. and Kenen, P. B. (eds) (1984) *Handbook of International Economics*, Amsterdam, North-Holland.

Kant, I. (1991) (1795) *Vers la paix pérpetuelle. Que signifie s'orienter dans les pensées? Qu'est-ce que Les Lumières*, Paris, Flammarion.

Katzenstein, P. (1985) *Small States in World Markets*, Ithaca, NY, Cornell University Press.

Kelsen, H. (1961) *General Theory of Law and State*, New York, NY, Russell & Russell.

Kiely, R. and Marfleet, P. (eds) (1998) *Globalization and the Third World*, London, Routledge.

Kormendi, R. C. and Meguire, R. G. (1985) 'Macroeconomic determinants of growth: cross-country evidence', *Journal of Monetary Economics*, 16, 141–63.

Kornai, J. (1980) *Economics of Shortage*, Amsterdam, North-Holland.

Kornai, J. (1986) *Contradictions and Dilemmas. Studies on the Socialist Economy and Society*, Cambridge, MA, MIT Press.

Kornai, J. and Liptak, T. (1962) 'A mathematical investigation of some economic effects of profit sharing', *Econometrica*, 30, 140–61.

Korzeniewicz, R. R. and Moran, T. P. (1997) 'World-economic trends in the distribution of income', *American Journal of Sociology*, 102, 1000–39.

Kreuger, A. O. (1978) *Liberalization Attempts and Consequences*, New York, National Bureau of Economic Research.

Krugman, P. (1994) 'The myth of Asia's miracle', *Foreign Affairs*, 73, 6, 62–78.

Krugman, P. (2000) *The Return of Depression Economics*, Harmondsworth, Penguin.

Krugman, P. R. and Obstfeld, M. (2000) *International Economics*, Reading, MA, Addison-Wesley.

Kuznets, S. (1955) 'Economic growth and income inequality', *American Economic Review*, 45, 18–25.

Kuznets, S. (1965) *Economic Growth and Structure*, New York, Norton.

Kuznets, S. (1966) *Modern Economic Growth*, New Haven, CT, Yale University Press.

Kuznets, S. (1968) *Toward a Theory of Economic Growth*, New York, Norton.

Lachman, L. M. (1986) *The Market as an Economic Process*, Oxford, Blackwell.

Lal, D. (1983) *The Poverty of 'Development Economics'*, London, Institute of Economic Affairs.

Lange, O. (1936–37) 'On the economic theory of socialism', *Review of Economic Studies*, 4, 53–71, 123–42.

Lange, O. and Taylor, F. M. (1964) *On the Economic Theory of Socialism*, Minneapolis, University of Minnesota Press.

Larkey, P., Stolp, L. and Winer, M. (1981) 'Theorizing about the growth of government: a research assessment', *Journal of Public Policy*, 2, 157–220.

Laver, M. (1997) *Private Desires, Political Action*, London, Sage.

Layard, R. R. B. and Walters, A. A. (1978) *Microeconomic Theory*, New York, McGraw-Hill.

Le Grand, J. and Estrin, S. (eds) (1989) *Market Socialism*, Oxford, Clarendon.

Leeman, J. W. (ed.) (1963) *Capitalism, Market Socialism and Central Planning*, Boston, Houghton Mifflin.

Leftwich, A. (1990) 'Politics and development studies', in Leftwich, A. (ed.) *New Developments in Political Science*, London, Edward Elgar.

Leftwich, A. (1994) 'States of Underdevelopment', *Journal of Theoretical Politics*, 6, 1, 55–74.

Lerner, A. P. (1944) *The Economics of Control*, New York, Macmillan.

Lerner, D. (1958) *The Passing of Traditional Society: Modernizing the Middle East*, New York, Free Press.

Levine, R. and Renelt, D. (1992) 'A sensitivity analysis of cross-country growth regressions', *American Economic Review*, 82, 942–63.

Levy, M. J. (1952) *The Structure of Society*, Princeton, NJ, Princeton University Press.

Lewis, W. A. (1988) 'The roots of development theory', in Chenery, H. and Srinivasan, T. N. (eds) *Handbook of Development Economics*, Vol. I, Amsterdam, North-Holland.

Libecap, G. D. (1993) *Contracting for Property Rights*, Cambridge, Cambridge University Press.

Lindblom, C. (1977) *Politics and Markets*, New York, Basic Books.

Lippincott, B. E. (ed.) (1938) *On the Economic Theory of Socialism*, Minneapolis, University of Minnesota Press.

Lipset, S. M. (1959) 'Some social requisites of democracy: economic development and political legitimacy', *American Political Science Review*, 53, 69–105.

Lipset, S. M. (1994) 'The social requisites of democracy revisited', *American Sociological Review*, 88, 4, 903–10.

Lipset, S. M., Seong, K. Y. and Torres, J. C. (1993) '*A* comparative analysis of the social requisites of democracy', *International Social Science Journal*, 45, 2, 155–75.

List, F. (1983) *The Natural System of Political Economy*, London, Frank Cass (originally published 1837).

Little, L. M. (1982) *Economic Development – Theory, Policy, and International Relations*, New York, Basic Books.

Little, L. M. D., Scitovsky, T. and Scott, M. (1970) *Industry and Trade in Some Developing Countries*, Oxford, Oxford University Press.

Lybeck, J. A. (1986) *The Growth of Government in Developed Economies*, London, Gower.

Lybeck, J. A. and Henrekson, M. (eds) (1988) *Explaining the Growth of Government*, Amsterdam, North-Holland.

Lydall, H. (1986) *Yugoslav Socialism*, Oxford, Clarendon Press.

McAuley, A. (1979) *Economic Welfare in the Soviet Union*, London, Allen & Unwin.

McCandless, G. T. Jr. (1991) *Macroeconomic Theory*, Englewood Cliffs, Prentice-Hall International Inc.

McCormick, B. J. (1988) *The World Economy: Patterns of growth and change*, Deddington, Philip Allan.

McGrew, A. (1992) 'The third world in the new global order', in Allen, T. and A. Thomas (eds) *Poverty and Development in the 1990s*, Oxford, Oxford University Press, pp. 255–72.

Maddison, A. (1995) *Monitoring the World Economy 1820–1992*, Paris, OECD.

Malinvaud, E. (1967) 'Decentralized procedures for planning', in Malinvaud, E. and Bacharach, M. (eds) *Activity Analysis in the Theory of Growth and Planning*, New York, Macmillan & Co.

Mandel, E. (1986) 'A critique of market socialism', *New Left Review*, 159, 5–37.

Mankiew, N. G, Romer, D. and Weil, D. N. (1992) 'A contribution to the empirics of economic growth', *Quarterly Journal of Economics*, 57, 407–37.

Mann, M. (1997) 'Has globalization ended the rise and rise of the nation-state?', *Review of International Political Economy*, 4, 472–96.

Mareshwari, S. R. (1984) *Rural Development in India*, New Delhi, Sage.

Margolis, J. and Guitton, H. (eds) (1969) *Public Economics: An Analysis of Public Production and Consumption and their Relations to the Private Sector*, London, Macmillan.

Marin, A. (1992) *Macroeconomic Policy*, London, Routledge.

Mathur, A. (1983) 'Regional development and income disparities in India: a sectorial analysis', *Economic Development and Cultural Change*, 31, 475–505.

Meier, G. M. (ed.) (1984) *Leading Issues in Economic Development*, New York, Oxford University Press.

Meinecke, F. (1962) *Weltbürgertum and Nationalstaat*, Munich, R. Oldenbourg Verlag.

Meinecke, F. (1963) *Die Idee der Straatsräson in Neueren Geschichte*, Munich, R. Oldenbourg Verlag.

Messick, R. E. (1996) 'The world survey of economic freedom', *Freedom Review*, 27, 2, 7–17.

Meyer, J. W. (2000) 'Globalization: sources and effects on national states and societies', *International Sociology*, 15, 233–48.

Mises, L. von (1936) *Socialism: An economic and sociological analysis*, London, Cape.

Mishan, E. J. (1981) *Introduction to Normative Economics*, Oxford, Oxford University Press.

Mishkin, F. S. (1998) *The Economics of Money, Banking, and Financial Markets*, New York: Addison-Wesley.

Morris, M. D. (1979) *Measuring the Conditions of the World's Poor: The physical quality of life index*, New York, Pergamon Press.

Mueller, D. C. (1986) *The Modern Corporation*, London, Harvester Wheatsheaf.

Mueller, D. C. (1989) *Public Choice II* (2nd edn), Cambridge, Cambridge University Press.

Mueller, D. C. (ed.) (1983) *The Political Economy of Growth*, New Haven, CT, Yale University Press.

Muller, E. (1988) 'Democracy, economic development, and income inequality', *American Sociological Review*, 53, 50–68.

Musgrave, R. A. and Musgrave, R. (1980) *Public Finance in Theory and Practice*, New York, McGraw-Hill.

Myrdal, G. (1957) *Economic Theory and Underdeveloped Regions*, London, Duckworth.

Myrdal, G. (1968) *Asian Drama I–III*, New York, Pantheon Books.

Myrdal, G. (1970) *Objectivity in Social Research*, London, Duckworth.

Nath, S. K. (1969) *A Reappraisal of Welfare Economics*, London, Routledge & Kegan Paul.

Neubauer, D. E. (1967) 'Some conditions of democracy', *American Political Science Review*, 61, 1002–9.

Niskanen, W. E. (1971) *Bureaucracy and Representative Government*, Chicago, Aldine Publishing Company.

North, D. C. (1990) *Institutions, Institutional Change and Economic Performance*, Cambridge, Cambridge University Press.

Nove, A. (1983) *The Economics of Feasible Socialism*, London, Allen & Unwin.

Nove, A. (1986) *The Soviet Economic System*, Boston, Allen & Unwin.

Nua Internet Surveys (2000) 'How many online?'; available at: nua.ie/surveys/

Nurkse, R. (1961) *Equilibrium and Growth in the World Economy*, Cambridge, MA, Harvard University Press.

O'Driscoll, G. P., Holmes, K. R. and Kirkpatrick, M. (2000) *The 2001 Index of Economic Freedom*, Washington, DC, Heritage Foundation.

O'Brien, D. C. (1972) 'Modernization, order, and the erosion of a democratic ideal: American political science 1960–70', *Journal of Development Studies*, 8, 4, 351–78.

Ocampo, J. R. and Johnson, D. L. (1972) 'The concept of political development', in Cockroft, J. D., Frank, A. G. and Johnson, D. L. (eds) *Dependence and Underdevelopment: Latin America's Political Economy*, Garden City, NY, Doubleday, 399–424.

O'Donnell, G. (1973) *Modernization and Bureaucratic-authoritarianism: Studies in South American politics*, Berkeley, CA, Institute of International Studies.

OECD (2000) Development Assistance Committee data; available at: www.oecd.org

Ohmae, K. (1995) *The End of the Nation State: The rise of regional economics*, New York, NY, Free Press.

Olson, M. (1965) *The Logic of Collective Action*, Cambridge, MA, Harvard University Press.

Olson, M. (1982) *The Rise and Decline of Nations: Economic Growth, Stagflation and Social Rigidities*, New Haven, CT, Yale University Press.

Østerud, Ø. (1999) *Globaliseringen og nasjonalstaten*, Oslo, Ad Notam Gyldendal.

Ostrom, E. (1990) *Governing the Commons: The Evolution of Institutions for Collective Action*, Cambridge, Cambridge University Press.

Panitch, L. (1998) ' "The State in a Changing World": Social-democratizing global capitalism?', *Monthly Review*, 50, 5, 11–22.

Parsons, T. (1951) *The Social System*, New York, Free Press.

Parsons, T. and Shils, E. (eds) (1951) *Towards a General Theory of Action*, New York, Harper & Row.

Parsons, T. and Smelser, N. (1956) *Economy and Society*, London, Routledge & Kegan Paul.

Payne, J. L. (1989) *Why Nations Arm*, Oxford, Blackwell.

Peace Science Society (International) (1999) *Militarized Interstate Dispute* [data set: version 2.10]; available at: pss.ls.psu.edu/DATARES.HTM

Peacock, A. (1979) *The Economic Analysis of Government and Related Themes*, Oxford, Martin Robertson.

Perry, C. S. (1980) 'Political contestations in nations: 1960, 1963, 1967 and 1970, *Journal of Political and Military Sociology*, 8, 161–74.

Phillips, A. (1978) 'The concept of "development" ', *Review of African Political Economy*, 8, 7–20.

Portes, A. (1976) 'On the sociology of national development: theories and issues', *American Journal of Sociology*, 82, 55–85.

Pourgerami, A. (1988) 'The political economy of development: a cross-national causality test development-democracy-growth hypothesis', *Public Choice*, 58, 123–41.

Pourgerami, A. (1989) 'The political economy of development: an empirical examination of the wealth theory of democracy', (mimeo) Bakerfield, California State University, Dept of Economics.

Prakash, A. and Hark, J. A. (eds) (2000) *Globalization and Governance*, London, Routledge.

Pryor, F. L. (1968) *Public Expenditures in Communist and Capitalist Nations*, London, Allen & Unwin.

Pye, L. W. (1987) 'Political development', in Bogdanor, V. (ed.) *The Blackwell Encyclopedia of Political Institutions*, Oxford, Blackwell.

Pye, L. W. (1966) *Aspects of Political Development*, Boston, Little, Brown.

Ramade, F. (1995) *Eléments d'écologie: écologie appliquée*, Paris, Ediscience.

Rashid, S. (1998) *The Clash of Civilizations?: Asian responses*, Karachi, Oxford University Press.

Rawls, J. (1971) *A Theory of Justice*, Cambridge, MA, Harvard University Press.

Reynolds, L. G. (1985) *Economic Growth in the Third World, 1850–1980*, New Haven, CT, Yale University Press.

Ricketts, M. (1987) *The Economics of Business Enterprise*, Brighton, Harvester Wheatsheaf.

Riggs, F. W. (1964) *Administration in Developing Countries*, Boston, Houghton Mifflin.

Riggs, F. W. (1984) 'Development', in Sartori, G. (ed.) *Social Science Concepts*, Beverly Hills, CA, Sage, 125–203.

Robertson, R. (1992) *Globalization: Social theory and global culture*, London, Sage.

Rokkan, S. (1970) *Citizens, Elections, Parties: Approaches to the comparative study of the process of development*, Oslo, Universitetsforlaget.

Romer, D. (1996) *Advanced Macroeconomics*, Maidenhead, McGraw-Hill International Editions.

Romp, G. (1997) *Game Theory*, Oxford, Oxford University Press.

Rose, R. (1984) *Understanding Big Government*, London, Sage.

Rose, R. (1985) 'Getting by in three economies: the resources of the official, unofficial and domestic economies', in Lane, J.-E. (ed.) *State and Market*, London, Sage.

Rose, R. (1989) *Ordinary People in Public Policy*, London, Sage.

Rosen, H. S. (1988) *Public Finance*, Homewood, IL, Irwin.

Rueschemeyer, D., Stephens, E. H. and Stephens, J. I. (1992) *Capitalist Development and Democracy*, Cambridge, Polity Press.

Russett, B., Alker, H., Deutsch, K. W. and Lasswell, H. D. (1964) *World Handbook of Political and Social Indicators*, New Haven, CT, Yale University Press.

Rustow, D. A. (1970) 'Transitions to democracy: toward a dynamic model', *Comparative Politics*, 2, 337–63.

Rustow, D. A. and Ward, R. E. (1964) 'Introduction', in Ward, R. E. and Rustow, D. A. (eds) *Political Modernization in Japan and Turkey*, Princeton, NJ, Princeton University Press.

Rustow, W. W. (1991) *The Stages of Economic Growth*, Cambridge, Cambridge University Press.

Samuelson, P. (1983) *Foundations of Economic Analysis*, Cambridge, MA, Harvard University Press.

Sawyer, J. A. (1989) *Macroeconomic Theory*, Brighton, Harvester Wheatsheaf.

Schmidt, M. G. (1982) *Wohl fartsstaaliche politik und bürgerlichen und sozialdemokratischen Regierungen: ein internationaler Vergleich*, Frankfurt, Campus.

Schumpeter, J. (1944) *Capitalism, Socialism and Democracy*, London, Allen & Unwin.

Schumpeter, J. A. (1989) *Essays on Entrepreneurs, Innovations, Business Cycles and the Evolution of Capitalism*, New Brunswick, Transaction Publishers.

Scully, G. W. (1988) 'The institutional framework of economic development', *Journal of Political Economy*, 96, 652–62.

Scully, G. W. (1992) *Constitutional Environments and Economic Growth*, Princeton, NJ, Princeton University Press.

Segal, A. (1993) *Atlas of International Migration*, East Grinstead, UK, Hans Zell.

Sen, A. (1988) 'The concept of development', in Chenery, H. and Srinivasan, T. N. (eds) *Handbook of Development Economics*, Amsterdam, North-Holland.

Sen, A. (1990) 'More than 100 million women are missing', *New York Review of Books*, 37, No. 20, December 20, 61–6.

Sen, A. (1999) *Development as Freedom*, Oxford, Oxford University Press.

Sharpe, L. J. and Newton, K. (1984) *Does Politics Matter?*, Oxford, Clarendon Press.

Sherman, R. (1989) *The Regulation of Monopoly*, Cambridge, Cambridge University Press.

Sheridan K. (ed.) (1998) *Emerging Economic Systems in Asia*, St. Leonards, Australia, Allen & Unwin.

Sigelman, L. (1971) *Modernization and the Political System: A critique and preliminary empirical analysis*, Beverly Hills, CA, Sage.

Singleton, F. and Carter, B. (1982) *The Economy of Yugoslovia*, London, Croom Helm.

Sirowy, L. and Inkeles, A. (1990) 'The effects of democracy on economic growth and inequality: a review', *Studies in Comparative International Development*, 25, 126–57.

Sivard, R. L. (1980) *World Military and Social Expenditures 1980*, Leesburg, VA, World Priorities.

Sivard, R. L. (1983) *World Military and Social Expenditures 1983*, Washington, DC, World Priorities.

Smith, A. K. (1969) 'Socio-economic development and political democracy: a causal analysis', *Midwest Journal of Political Science*, 13, 95–125.

Södersten, B. (1965) *A Study of Economic Growth and International Trade*, Stockholm, Almqvist & Wicksell.

Spindler, Z. A. (1991) 'Liberty and development: a further empirical perspective', *Public Choice*, 69, 197–210.

Spulber, D. E. (1989) *Regulation and Markets*, Cambridge, MA, MIT Press.

Spulber, N. (1969) *The Soviet Economy: Structure, Principles, Problems*, New York, Norton.

Stiftung Entwicklung und Frieden (1995–1999) *Globale Trends: Fakten, Analysen, Prognosen*, Frankfurt-on-Main, Fischer Taschenbuch Verlag.

Stigler, G. (1966) *The Theory of Price*, New York, Macmillan.

Stigler, G. (1986) *The Essence of Stigler*. Edited by Leube, K. R. and Moore, T. G., Stanford, Hoover University Press.

Stigler, G. (1988) *Chicago Studies in Regulation*, Chicago, Chicago University Press.

Stiglitz, J. E. (1988) *Economics of the Public Sector*, New York, Norton.

Stiglitz, J. E. (1999) *Economics of the Public Sector*, New York, Norton. (3rd edition.)

Strange, S. (1996) *The Retreat of the State*, Cambridge, Cambridge University Press.

Strange, S. (1997) *Casino Capitalism*, Manchester, Manchester University Press.

Strange, S. (1998) *Mad Money*, Manchester, Manchester University Press.

Streeten, P. (1972) *The Frontiers of Development Studies*, London, Macmillan.

Sullivan, M. J. (1991) *Measuring Global Values: The Ranking of 162 Countries*, New York, Greenwood Pess.

Summers, R. and Heston, A. (1988) 'A new set of international comparisons of real product and price levels estimates for 130 countries, 1950–1985 (mark 4)', *Review of Income and Wealth*, 34, 1–25.

Summers, R. and Heston, A. (1991) 'The Penn World Table (mark 5): an expanded set of international comparisons, 1950–1988', *Quarterly Journal of Economics*, 56, May, 1–41.

Summers, R. and Heston, A. (1994) Penn World Tables, mark 5.6; available at nber.harvard.edu/pwt56.html (May 1996).

Sutton, F. X. (1963) 'Social theory and comparative politics', in Eckstein, H. and Apter, D. (eds) *Comparative Politics: A reader*, New York, Free Press, pp. 67–81.

Syrquin, M. (1988) 'Patterns of structural change', in Chenery, H. and Srinivasan, T. N. (eds) *Handbook of Development Economics*, Vol. I, Amsterdam, North Holland.

Tanzi, V. and Schuknecht, L. (2000) *Public Spending in the 20th Century: A global perspective*, Cambridge, Cambridge University Press.

Tarschys, D. (1975) 'The growth of public expenditures: nine modes of explanation', *Scandinavian Political Studies*, 10, 9–31.

Taylor, C. L. (1981) *Codebook to World Handbook of Political and Social Indicators*, Vol. I, Aggregate Data (3rd edn), West Berlin, IVG.

Taylor, C. L. and Hudson, M. (1972) *World Handbook of Political and Social Indicators* (2nd edn), New Haven, CT, Yale University Press.

Taylor, R. J. (1987) 'The poverty of international comparisons: some methodological lessons from world-system analysis', *Studies in Comparative International Development*, 22, 12–39.

The Economist (1997) 'Schools brief: One world?', 18 October.

The Economist Atlas (1989) London, Hutchinson.

Therborn, G. (2000) 'Globalizations: dimensions, historical waves, regional effects, normative governance', *International Sociology*, 15, 151–79.

Thirlwall, A. P. (1983) *Growth and Development: With special reference to developing economies*, London, Macmillan (4th edn, 1986).

Tietenberg, T. (2000) *Environmental and Natural Resource Economics*, Reading, MA, Addison-Wesley Longman.

Tilly, C. (ed.) (1975) *The Formation of Nation States in Western Europe*, Princeton, NJ, Princeton University Press.

Tinbergen, J. (1967) *Economic Policy: Principles and Design*, Amsterdam, North-Holland.

Todaro, M. P. (1985) *Economic Development in the Third World*, New York, Longman.

Toye, J. (1987) *Dilemmas of Development*, Oxford, Blackwell.

Transparency International (2000) 'Corruption perception index'; available at: www.transparency.org/documents/cpi/index.html; see also: www.gwdg.de/uwvw/

US Bureau of Census (2000) 'World population information'; available at: www.census.gov/ipc/www/world.html

US State Department (2000) '1999 country reports on human rights practices'; available at: http://www.state.gov

UNDP (1995) *Human Development Report 1995*, New York, NY, Oxford University Press.

UNDP (1999) *Human Development Report 1999*, New York, NY, Oxford University Press.

UNDP (2000) *Human Development Report 2000*, New York, NY, Oxford University Press.

UNHCR (various years) *The State of the World's Refugees*, Geneva, The Agency; also available at: www.unhcr.ch/statist/main.htm

Union of International Associations (UIA) (various years) *Yearbook of International Organizations*, Munich, Saur.

United Nations (1998) *World Population Prospects: The 1996 revision*, New York, NY, United Nations.

United Nations (2000) *Basic Facts about the United Nations*, New York, United Nations.

United Nations (various years) *Statistical Yearbook*, New York, NY, United Nations.

United Nations Conference on Trade and Development (UNCTAD) (various years) *World Investment Report*, Geneva, UNCTAD.

Vanhanen, T. (1990) *The Process of Democratization: A comparative study of 147 states, 1980–88*, New York, Crane Russak.

Varian, H. (1984) *Microeconomic Analysis*, New York, Norton.

Verma, S. P. and Sharma, S. K. (1984) *Development Administration*, New Delhi, Indian Institute of Public Administration.

Wade, R. (1990) *Governing the Market: Economic theory and the role of government in East Asian industrialization*, Princeton, NJ, Princeton University Press.

Wallensteen, P. and Sollenberg, M. (1995) 'After the cold war: emerging patterns of armed conflict 1989–94', *Journal of Peace Research*, 32, 345–60.

Wallensteen, P. and Sollenberg, M. (1999) 'Armed conflict, 1989–98', *Journal of Peace Research*, 36, 593–606.

Wallensteen, P. and Sollenberg, M. (2000) 'Armed conflict, 1989–99', *Journal of Peace Research*, 37, 635–49.

Wallerstein, I. (1974) *The Modern World-System: Capitalist agriculture and the origins of the European world-economy in the sixteenth century*, New York, Academic Press.

Wallerstein, I. (1979) *The Capitalist World-Economy*, Cambridge, Cambridge University Press.

Waters, M. (1995) *Globalization*, London, Routledge.

Webber, C. and Wildavsky, A. (1986) *A History of Taxation and Expenditure in the Western World*, New York, Simon & Schuster.

Weber, M. (1949) *The Methodology of the Social Sciences*, Glencoe, IL, Free Press.

Weber, M. (1978) *Economy and Society I-II*, Berkeley, CA, University of California Press.

Weber, M. (1995) *General Economic History*, Transaction Publishers, New Brunswick and London.

Weede, E. (1980) 'Beyond misspecification in sociological analysis of income inequality', *American Sociological Review*, 45, 497–501.

Weede, E. (1984) 'Political democracy' state strength and economic growth in LDCs: a cross-section analysis', *Review of International Studies*, 10, 297–312.

Weiss, L. (1998) *The Myth of the Powerless State: Governing the economy in a global era*, Cambridge, Polity.

Wiarda, H. J. (1983) 'Toward a non ethnocentric theory of development: alternative conceptions from the Third World', *Journal of Developing Areas*, 17, 433–52.

Wiener, J. (1999) *Globalization and the Harmonization of Laws*, London, Pinter.

Wildavsky, A. (1964, 1984) *The Politics of the Budgetary Process* (1st and 2nd edns), Boston, Little, Brown.

Wildavsky, A. (1973) 'If planning is everything, then maybe it is nothing', *Policy Sciences*, 4, 127–53.

Wildavsky, A. (1976; 2nd edn, 1986) *Budgeting: A comparative theory of the budgetary process* (2nd edn), New Brunswick, NJ, Transaction.

Wildavsky, A. (1984) *The Politics of the Budgetary Process* (2nd edn), Boston, Little, Brown.

Wildavsky, A. (1985) 'The logic of public sector growth', in Lane, J. E. (ed.) *State and Market*, London, Sage.

Wildavsky, A. (1988) *The New Politics of the Budgetary Process*, Boston, Scott, Foresman & Company.

Wilensky, H. (1975) *The Welfare State and Equality*, Berkeley, University of California Press.

Williamson, O. E. (1975) *Markets and Hierarchies: analysis and antitrust implications*, New York, Free Press.

Williamson, O. E. (1985) *The Economic Institutions of Capitalism*, New York, Free Press.

Williamson, O. E. (1986) *Economic Organization: Firms, market and policy control*, Brighton, Harvester Wheatsheaf.

Wolf, C. (1988) *Markets or Governments*, Cambridge, MA, MIT Press.

World Bank (WB) (1980) *World Tables 1980* (2nd edn), Baltimore, MD, Johns Hopkins University Press.

World Bank (WB) (1987) *World Development Report*, New York, Oxford University Press.

World Bank (WB) (1996) *World Bank Atlas 1996*, Washington, DC, World Bank.

World Bank (WB) (2000a) *World Development Indicators* (CD-ROM), Washington, DC, World Bank.

World Bank (WB) (2000b) *World Development Indicators 2000*, Washington, DC, World Bank.

World Bank (WB) (various years) *Global Development Finance*, Washington, DC, World Bank.

World Economic Survey (1999) New York, United Nations Publications.

World Tourism Organization (WTO) (1999) *Yearbook of Tourism Statistics*, Madrid, WTO.

Wright, D. M. (1947) *The Economics of Disturbance*, New York, Macmillan.

Yarbrough, B. Y. and Yarbrough, R. M. (1988) *The World Economy*, Chicago, Dryden Press.

Zaleski, E. (1980) *Stalinist Planning for Economic Growth*, London, Allen & Unwin.

Zlotnik, H. (1998) 'International migration 1965–96: An overview', *Population and Development Review*, 24, 429–68.

Zysman, J. (1983) *Governments, Markets and Finance*, Ithaca, NY, Cornell University Press.

Index